JUSTICE LEAGUE INTERNATIONAL

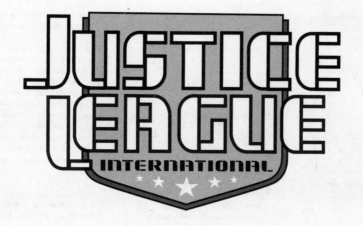

Dan DiDio
Senior VP-Executive Editor

Andy Helfer
Editor-original series

Kevin Dooley
Assistant Editor-original series

Robbin Brosterman
Senior Art Director

Paul Levitz
President & Publisher

Georg Brewer
VP-Design & DC Direct Creative

Richard Bruning
Senior VP-Creative Director

Patrick Caldon
Executive VP-Finance & Operations

Chris Caramalis
VP-Finance

John Cunningham
VP-Marketing

Terri Cunningham
VP-Managing Editor

Amy Genkins
Senior VP-Business & Legal Affairs

Alison Gill
VP-Manufacturing

David Hyde
VP-Publicity

Hank Kanalz
VP-General Manager, WildStorm

Jim Lee
Editorial Director-WildStorm

Gregory Noveck
Senior VP-Creative Affairs

Sue Pohja
VP-Book Trade Sales

Steve Rotterdam
Senior VP-Sales & Marketing

Cheryl Rubin
Senior VP-Brand Management

Alysse Soll
VP-Advertising & Custom Publishing

Jeff Trojan
VP-Business Development, DC Direct

Bob Wayne
VP-Sales

Cover by Kevin Maguire and Joe Rubinstein
with Tanya & Richard Horie.

JUSTICE LEAGUE INTERNATIONAL:
VOLUME FOUR

Published by DC Comics.
Cover and compilation Copyright © 2009
DC Comics. All Rights Reserved.

DC Comics, 1700 Broadway, New York, NY 10019
A Warner Bros. Entertainment Company
Printed in USA. First Printing.

ISBN: 978-1-4012-2196-6
SC ISBN: 978-1-4012-2197-3

JUSTICE LEAGUE INTERNATIONAL

Keith Giffen Plot & Breakdowns

J.M. DeMatteis Script

Kevin Maguire (#23, 24) Ty Templeton (#24-29)
Mike McKone (#25, 28) Bill Willingham (#30) Pencils

Joe Rubinstein (#23-30) Dick Giordano (#27) Inks

Gene D'Angelo Colors

Bob Lappan Albert DeGuzman Letters

CAST OF CHARACTERS

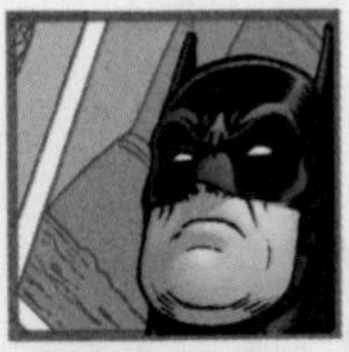

BATMAN

A.K.A. "The Dark Knight" (oooh, scary!). After witnessing the murder of his parents at a young age, billionaire Bruce Wayne honed his mind and body into the perfect weapon. Bruce has decided to use his vast wealth, intellect and athletic prowess to dress up as a bat and ride around in bat-themed vehicles, to rid the world of crime. And yes, he is sane. *We think*.

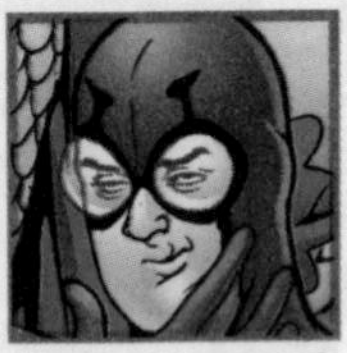

BLUE BEETLE

Ted Kord is a genius-level inventor and Olympic-level athlete who carries a "BB gun" that can temporarily blind anyone with a flash of light, or knock them down with a compressed air blast. Ted chooses to use his vast wealth, intellect and athletic prowess to dress up as a beetle and ride around in a giant beetle ship. Not so sure about Ted's sanity, actually...

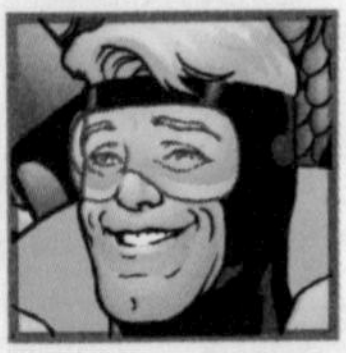

BOOSTER GOLD

A once-superstar athlete in the far-flung future, Booster fell on hard times and raided the space museum he was working at to acquire all the equipment he would need to be a super-hero of the past. Now living in our time, Booster uses his augmented strength, force fields, flight ring and good looks to impress *anyone* who will take notice.

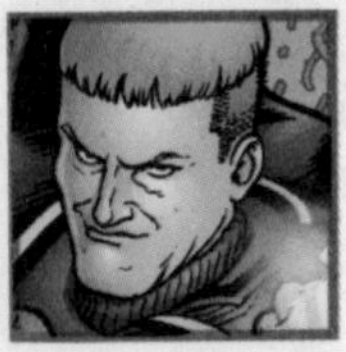

GUY GARDNER

Guy Gardner was the *second* choice pick to be Green Lantern and he'll never forget it. Always a jerk, Guy got a bump in the head that turned him uncharacteristically sweet for a short time. But now another bump has given us *old* Guy back. Hoo boy. As a member of the Green Lantern Corps, Guy is equipped with a ring that can do almost anything he wills it to do. Yes, we find that scary too.

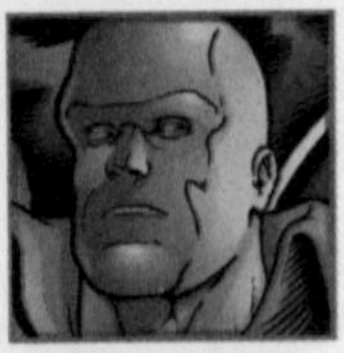

MARTIAN MANHUNTER

The last survivor of Mars, J'onn J'onzz has superhuman strength and speed, telepathy, telekinesis, flight, regeneration, shape-shifting, invisibility, and "Martian vision" — whatever *that* is. As powerful as he is, he has two known weaknesses: the element of fire, and the yummy goodness of icing-filled chocolate cookies. Mmm....good.

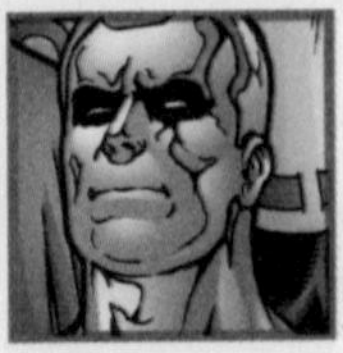

CAPTAIN ATOM

Nathaniel Adam was a U.S. Air Force officer of the Vietnam War who was framed for a crime he didn't commit (bummer!). As an alternative to a death sentence, he became a military test subject and was blown to bits and thrown into the present day (bummer again!). But the experiment transformed Captain Adam into Captain Atom (how convenient), and he is now a nuclear-powered agent of the U.S. government.

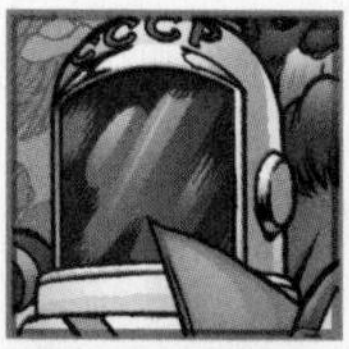

ROCKET RED

Dimitri Pushkin is #4 of the Rocket Red Brigade — a superhuman defense unit of the Soviet Union. The kind-hearted and jolly Dimitri does not want to be mistaken for his predecessor, Rocket Red #7, who turned out to be a big ol' nasty Manhunter robot. Dimitri has an unsettling taste for American culture, which we're not quite sure how we feel about.

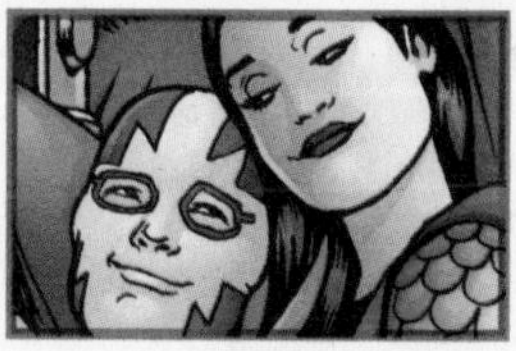

MISTER MIRACLE & BIG BARDA

Scott Free and his wife Barda are actually "New Gods," but don't let that fool you — they're just normal folk, trying to pass for an average Earth couple. Scott is the world's greatest escape artist and was raised by the evil Darkseid, and Barda is a ferocious warrior with superhuman strength who wields a mega-rod. Sounds pretty normal to us!

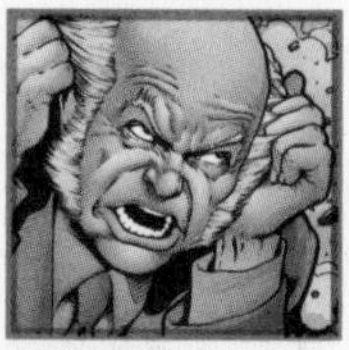

OBERON

Oberon is the sma...er, the sho...um, the *diminutive* manager of Mister Miracle, who handles all of Scott's business affairs. Oberon was originally the manager of the first Mister Miracle, Thaddeus Brown, who rescued him from a life of abuse in the circus. Despite his size, Oberon can handle himself quite well in pretty difficult situations.

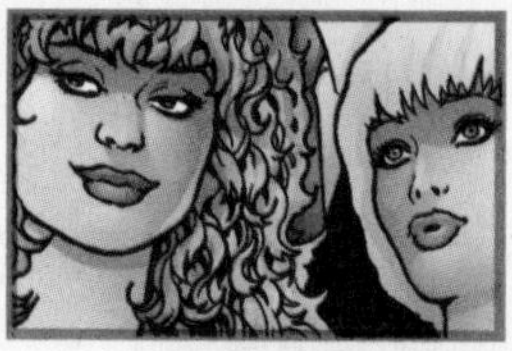

GREEN FLAME & ICE MAIDEN

The fiery hot Beatriz da Costa and the cool but sweet Tora Olafsdotter became fast friends as former members of the Global Guardians. Now the "Fire & Ice" pair are the newest members of the now-international Justice League. Their powers are, well...self-explanatory, no?

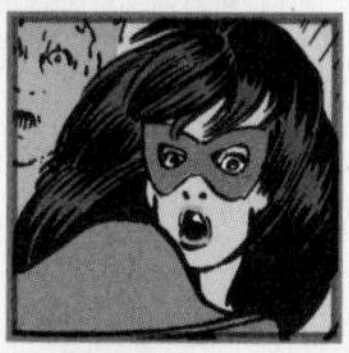

HUNTRESS

Like Batman, Helena Bertinelli also witnessed her family murdered. But unlike the philanthropic Waynes, the Bertinellis were one of Gotham City's most prominent Mafia families. Now, as the crossbow-wielding Huntress, Helena vows to put an end to the crime families of the world.

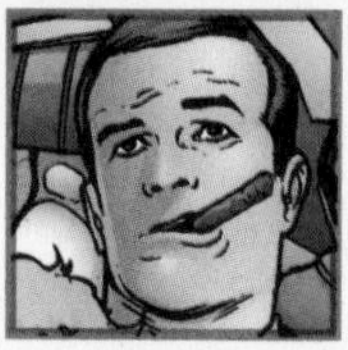

MAXWELL LORD

Max is the mysterious benefactor of the Justice League — a shrewd and powerful businessman who has managed to orchestrate not only the new League's formation, but their "international" status as well. I don't know, there's just something about this guy...

JUSTICE LEAGUE INTERNATIONAL

ELSEWHERE...

AFTER THE INVASION...

Earth's heroes have just fought back an intergalactic force of alien invaders dead set on dominating all of mankind. That kind of thing tends to leave a big mess. So what does that mean for the World's Greatest Heroes, the Justice League?

Yep, you guessed it...cleanup duty!

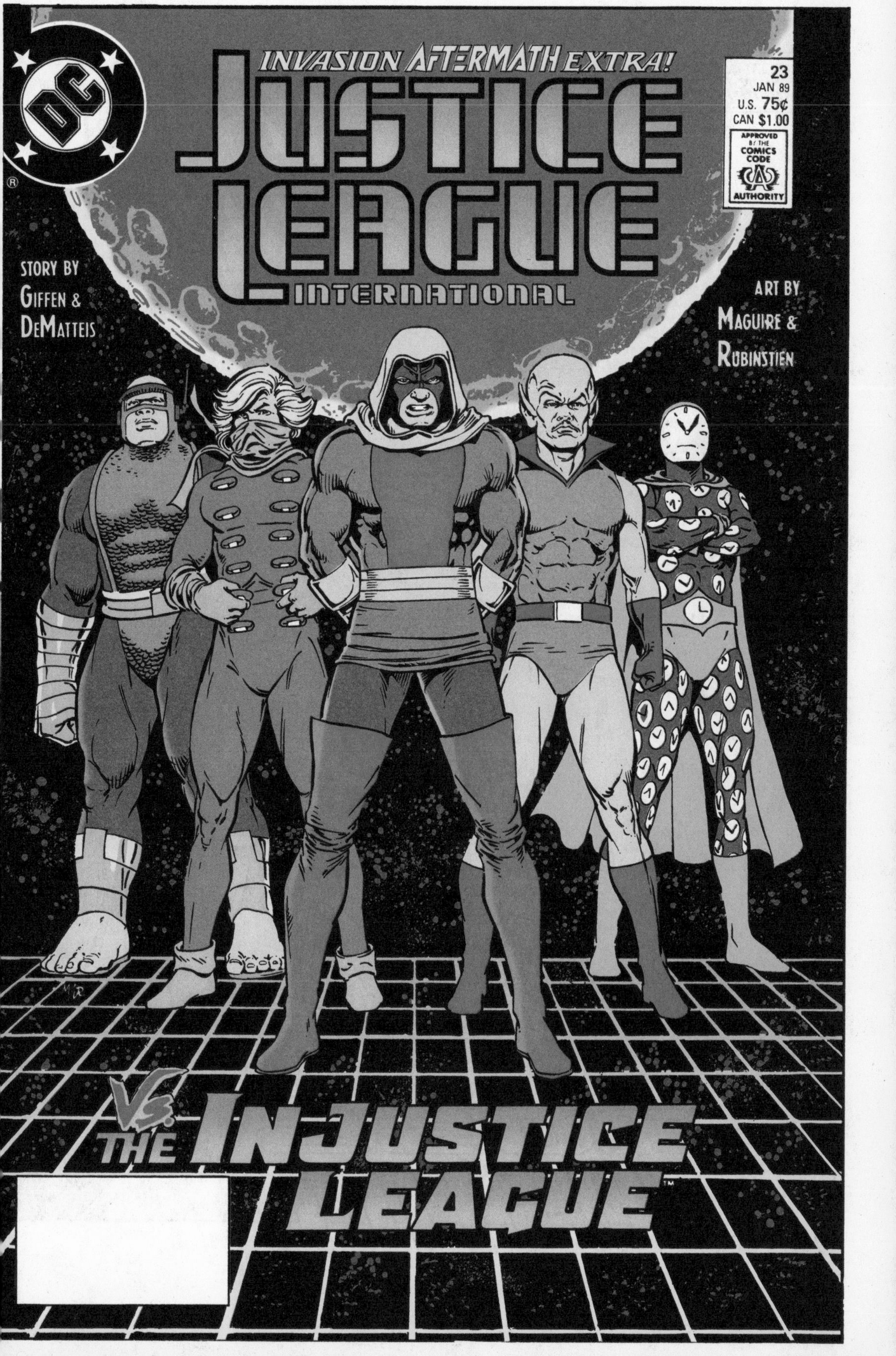

INVASION AFTERMATH EXTRA!
JUSTICE LEAGUE
INTERNATIONAL
23
JAN 89
U.S. 75¢
CAN $1.00
APPROVED BY THE COMICS CODE AUTHORITY
STORY BY
GIFFEN &
DEMATTEIS
ART BY
MAGUIRE &
RUBINSTIEN
VS. THE INJUSTICE LEAGUE

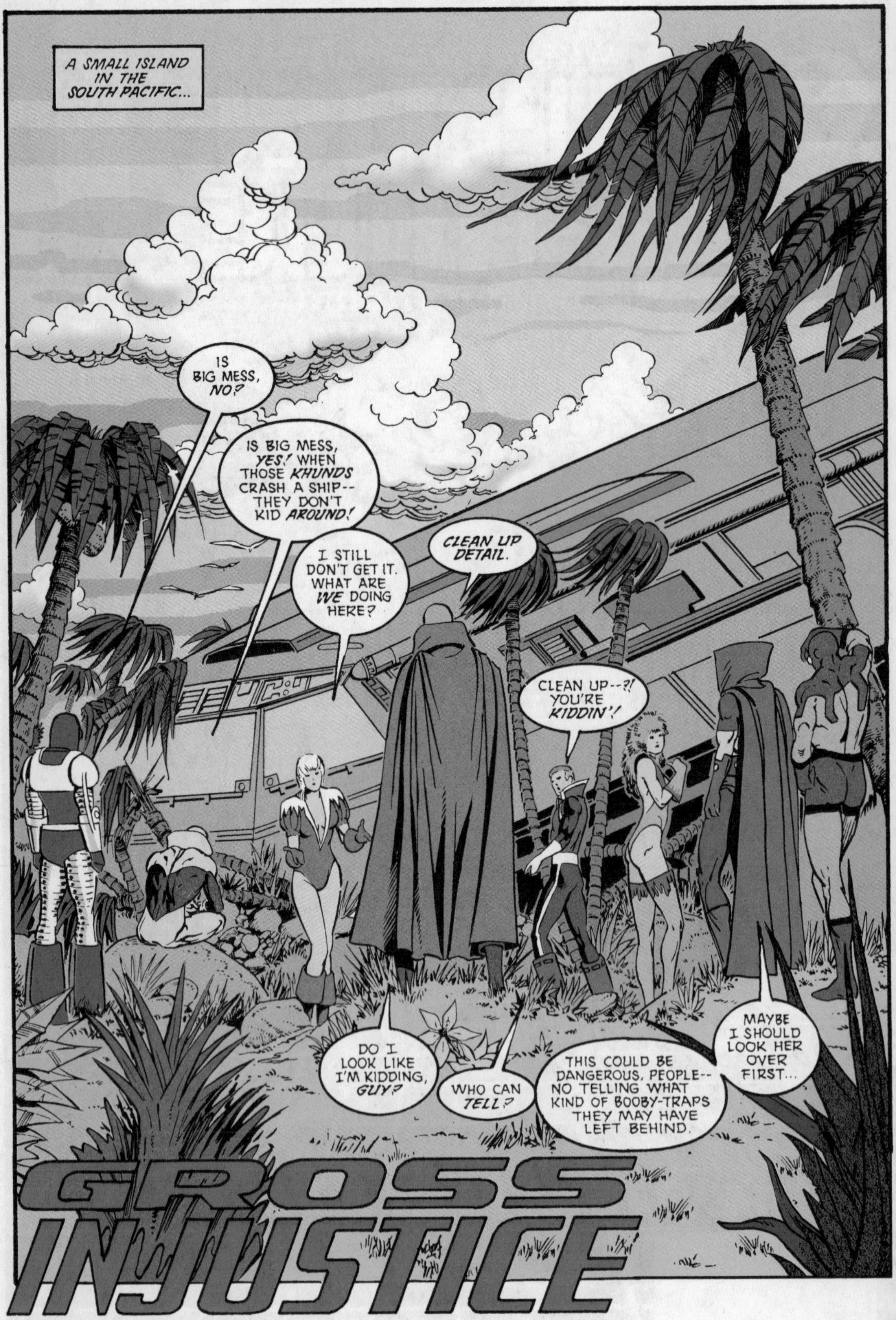

A SMALL ISLAND IN THE SOUTH PACIFIC...
IS BIG MESS, NO?
IS BIG MESS, YES! WHEN THOSE KHUNDS CRASH A SHIP-- THEY DON'T KID AROUND!
I STILL DON'T GET IT. WHAT ARE WE DOING HERE?
CLEAN UP DETAIL.
CLEAN UP--?! YOU'RE KIDDIN'!
DO I LOOK LIKE I'M KIDDING, GUY?
WHO CAN TELL?
THIS COULD BE DANGEROUS, PEOPLE-- NO TELLING WHAT KIND OF BOOBY-TRAPS THEY MAY HAVE LEFT BEHIND.
MAYBE I SHOULD LOOK HER OVER FIRST...
GROSS INJUSTICE

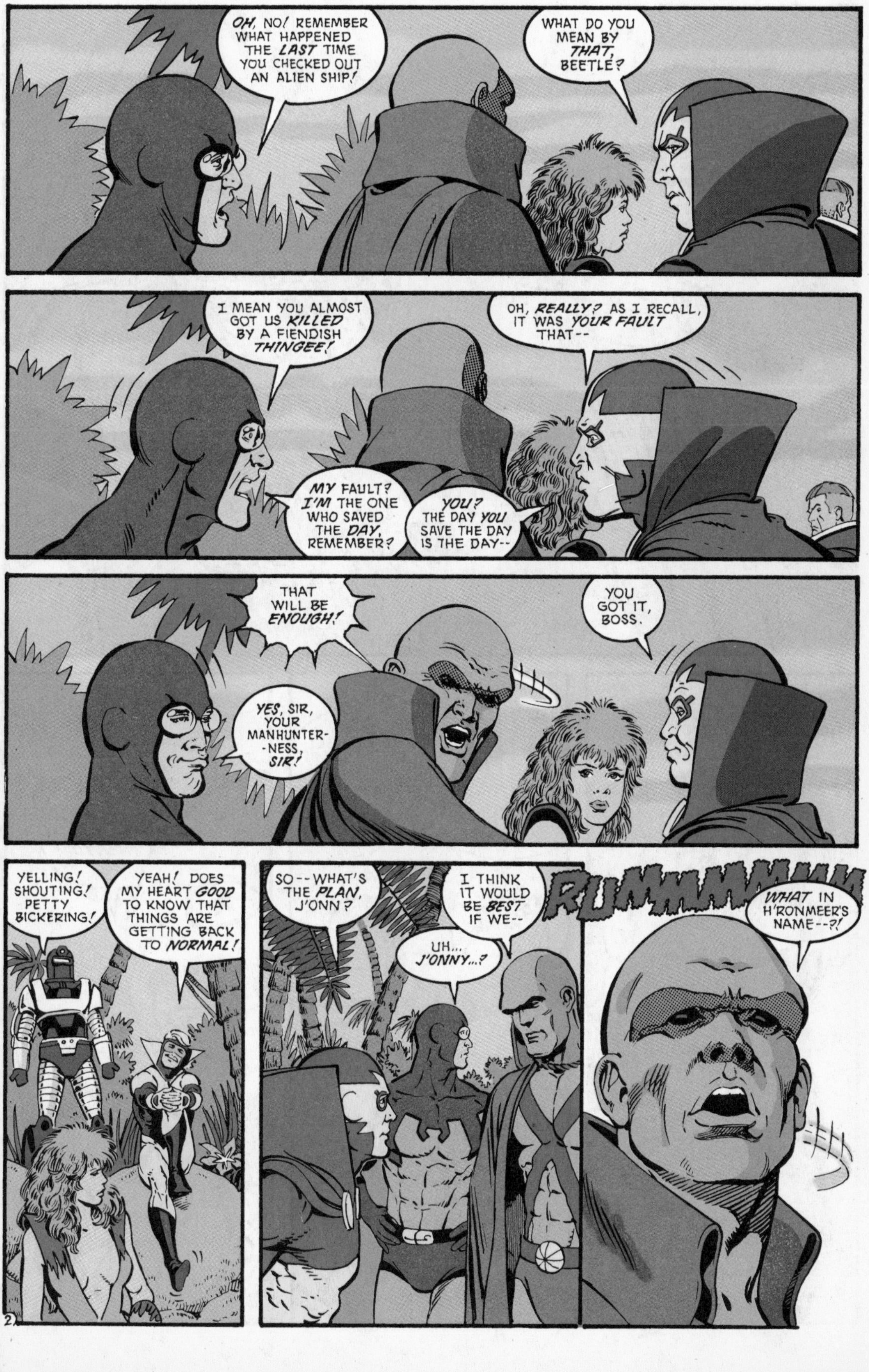
OH, NO! REMEMBER WHAT HAPPENED THE LAST TIME YOU CHECKED OUT AN ALIEN SHIP!
WHAT DO YOU MEAN BY THAT, BEETLE?
I MEAN YOU ALMOST GOT US KILLED BY A FIENDISH THINGEE!
OH, REALLY? AS I RECALL, IT WAS YOUR FAULT THAT--
MY FAULT? I'M THE ONE WHO SAVED THE DAY, REMEMBER?
YOU? THE DAY YOU SAVE THE DAY IS THE DAY--
THAT WILL BE ENOUGH!
YOU GOT IT, BOSS.
YES, SIR, YOUR MANHUNTER--NESS, SIR!
YELLING! SHOUTING! PETTY BICKERING!
YEAH! DOES MY HEART GOOD TO KNOW THAT THINGS ARE GETTING BACK TO NORMAL!
SO--WHAT'S THE PLAN, J'ONN?
I THINK IT WOULD BE BEST IF WE--
UH... J'ONNY...?
RUMMMMMM
WHAT IN H'RONMEER'S NAME--?!

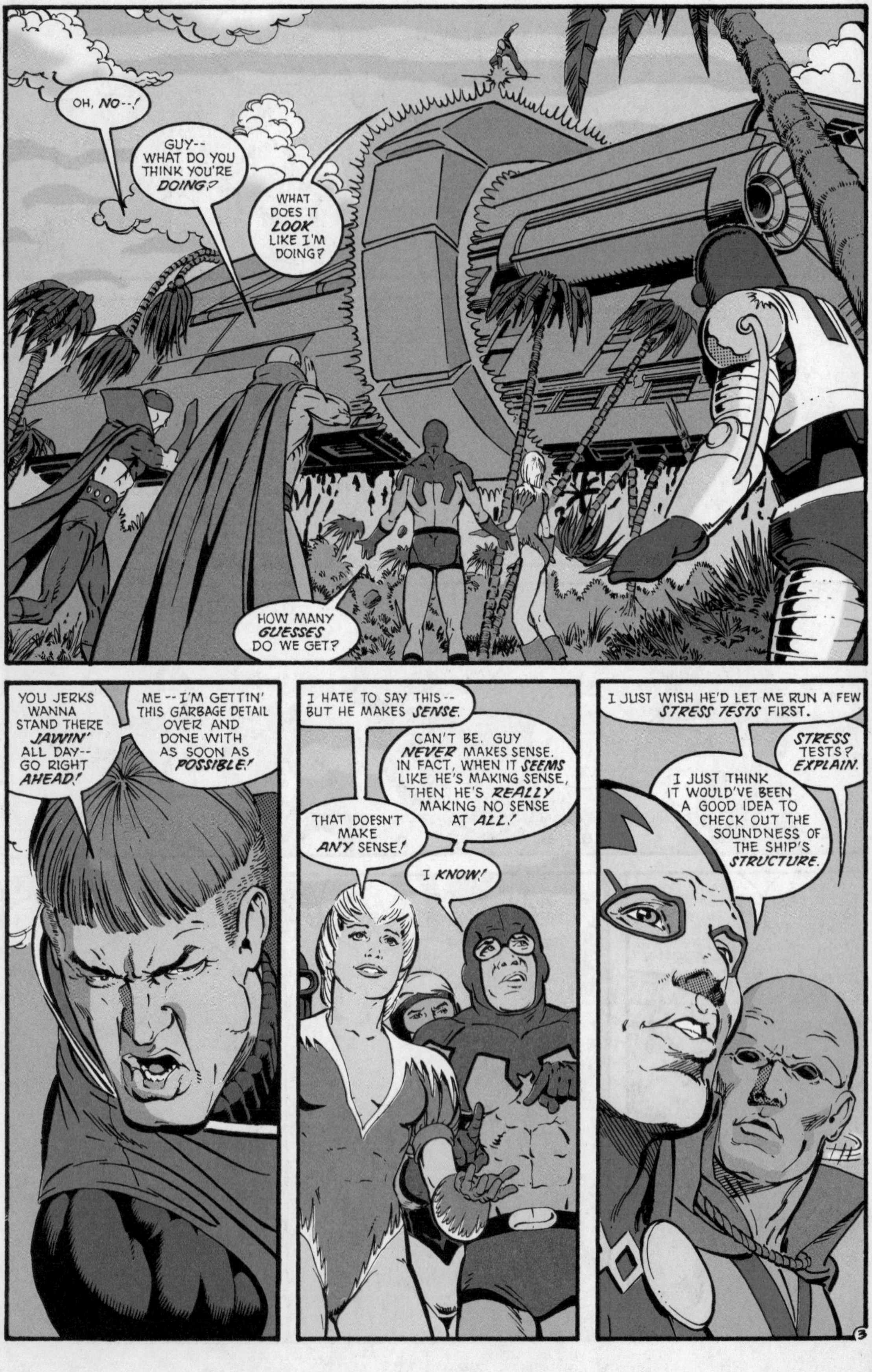
OH, NO--!
GUY-- WHAT DO YOU THINK YOU'RE DOING?
WHAT DOES IT LOOK LIKE I'M DOING?
HOW MANY GUESSES DO WE GET?
YOU JERKS WANNA STAND THERE JAWIN' ALL DAY-- GO RIGHT AHEAD!
ME -- I'M GETTIN' THIS GARBAGE DETAIL OVER AND DONE WITH AS SOON AS POSSIBLE!
I HATE TO SAY THIS -- BUT HE MAKES SENSE.
CAN'T BE. GUY NEVER MAKES SENSE. IN FACT, WHEN IT SEEMS LIKE HE'S MAKING SENSE, THEN HE'S REALLY MAKING NO SENSE AT ALL!
THAT DOESN'T MAKE ANY SENSE!
I KNOW!
I JUST WISH HE'D LET ME RUN A FEW STRESS TESTS FIRST.
STRESS TESTS? EXPLAIN.
I JUST THINK IT WOULD'VE BEEN A GOOD IDEA TO CHECK OUT THE SOUNDNESS OF THE SHIP'S STRUCTURE.
3

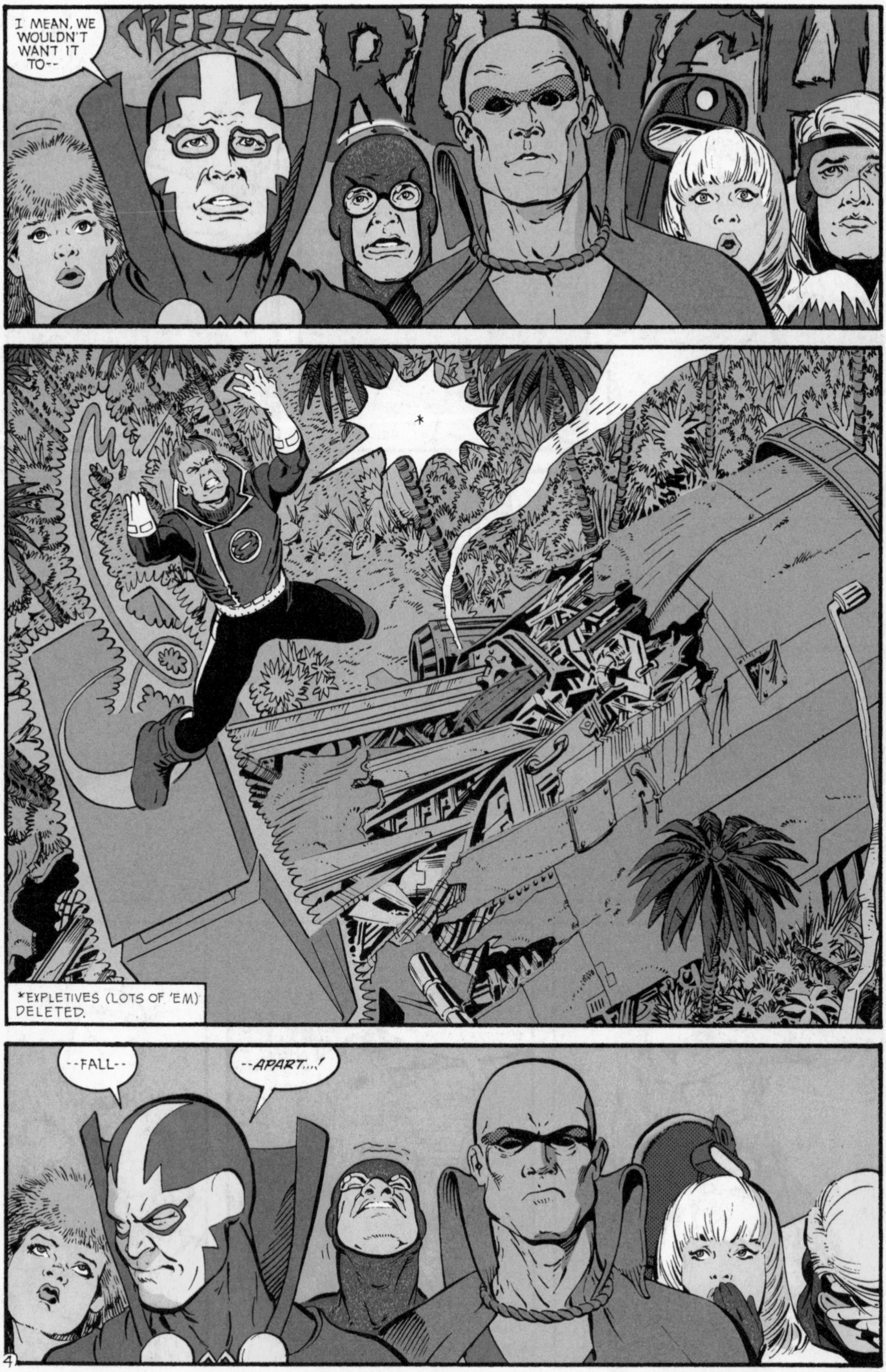
I MEAN, WE WOULDN'T WANT IT TO--
CREEEEE RUNCH
*
*EXPLETIVES (LOTS OF 'EM) DELETED.
--FALL--
--APART...!
4

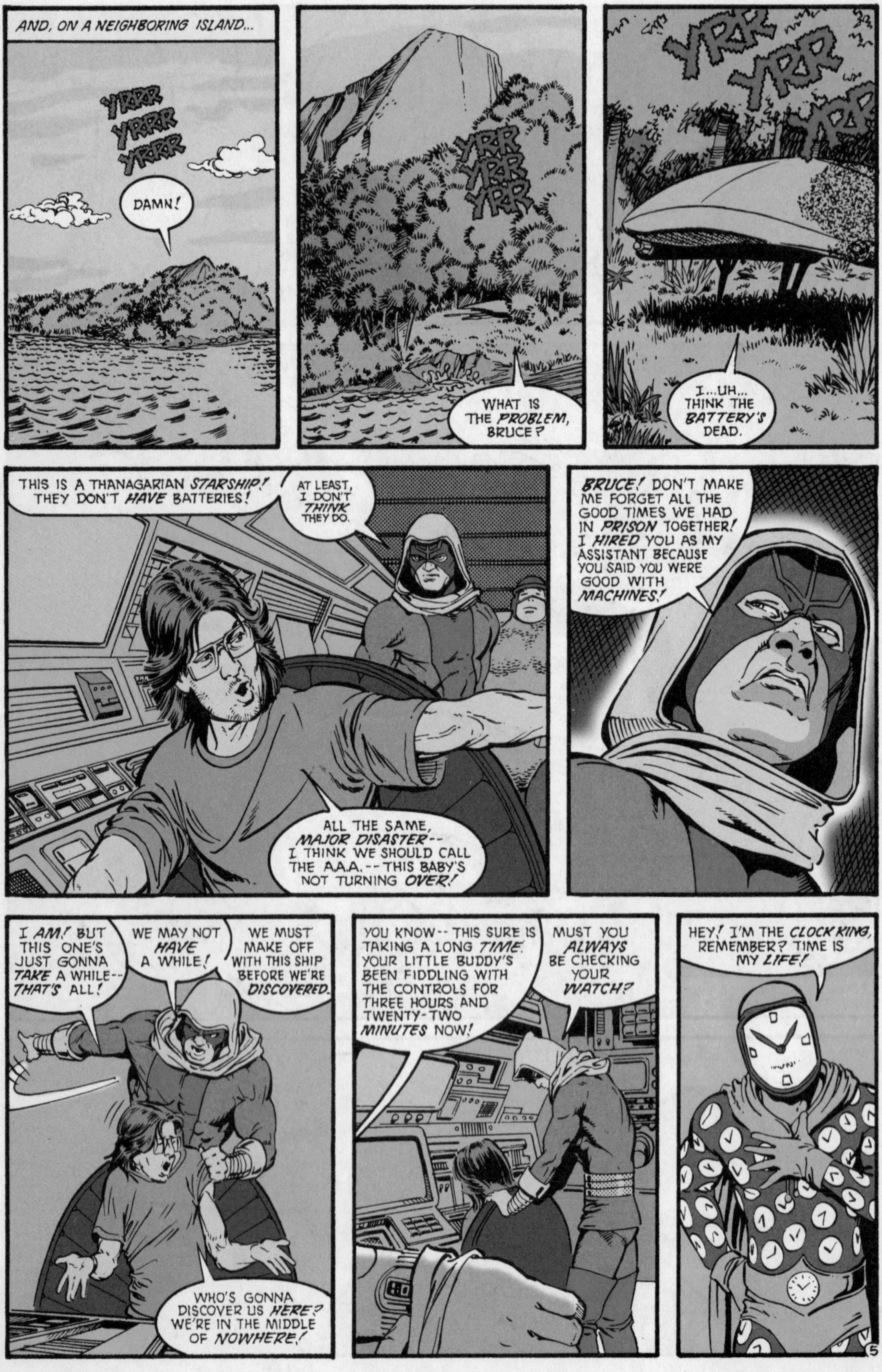
AND, ON A NEIGHBORING ISLAND...
YRRR YRRR YRRR
DAMN!
YRR YRR YRR
WHAT IS THE PROBLEM, BRUCE?
YRR YRR YRR
I...UH... THINK THE BATTERY'S DEAD.
THIS IS A THANAGARIAN STARSHIP! THEY DON'T HAVE BATTERIES!
AT LEAST, I DON'T THINK THEY DO.
ALL THE SAME, MAJOR DISASTER-- I THINK WE SHOULD CALL THE A.A.A.--THIS BABY'S NOT TURNING OVER!
BRUCE! DON'T MAKE ME FORGET ALL THE GOOD TIMES WE HAD IN PRISON TOGETHER! I HIRED YOU AS MY ASSISTANT BECAUSE YOU SAID YOU WERE GOOD WITH MACHINES!
I AM! BUT THIS ONE'S JUST GONNA TAKE A WHILE--THAT'S ALL!
WE MAY NOT HAVE A WHILE!
WE MUST MAKE OFF WITH THIS SHIP BEFORE WE'RE DISCOVERED.
WHO'S GONNA DISCOVER US HERE? WE'RE IN THE MIDDLE OF NOWHERE!
YOU KNOW--THIS SURE IS TAKING A LONG TIME. YOUR LITTLE BUDDY'S BEEN FIDDLING WITH THE CONTROLS FOR THREE HOURS AND TWENTY-TWO MINUTES NOW!
MUST YOU ALWAYS BE CHECKING YOUR WATCH?
HEY! I'M THE CLOCK KING, REMEMBER? TIME IS MY LIFE!
5

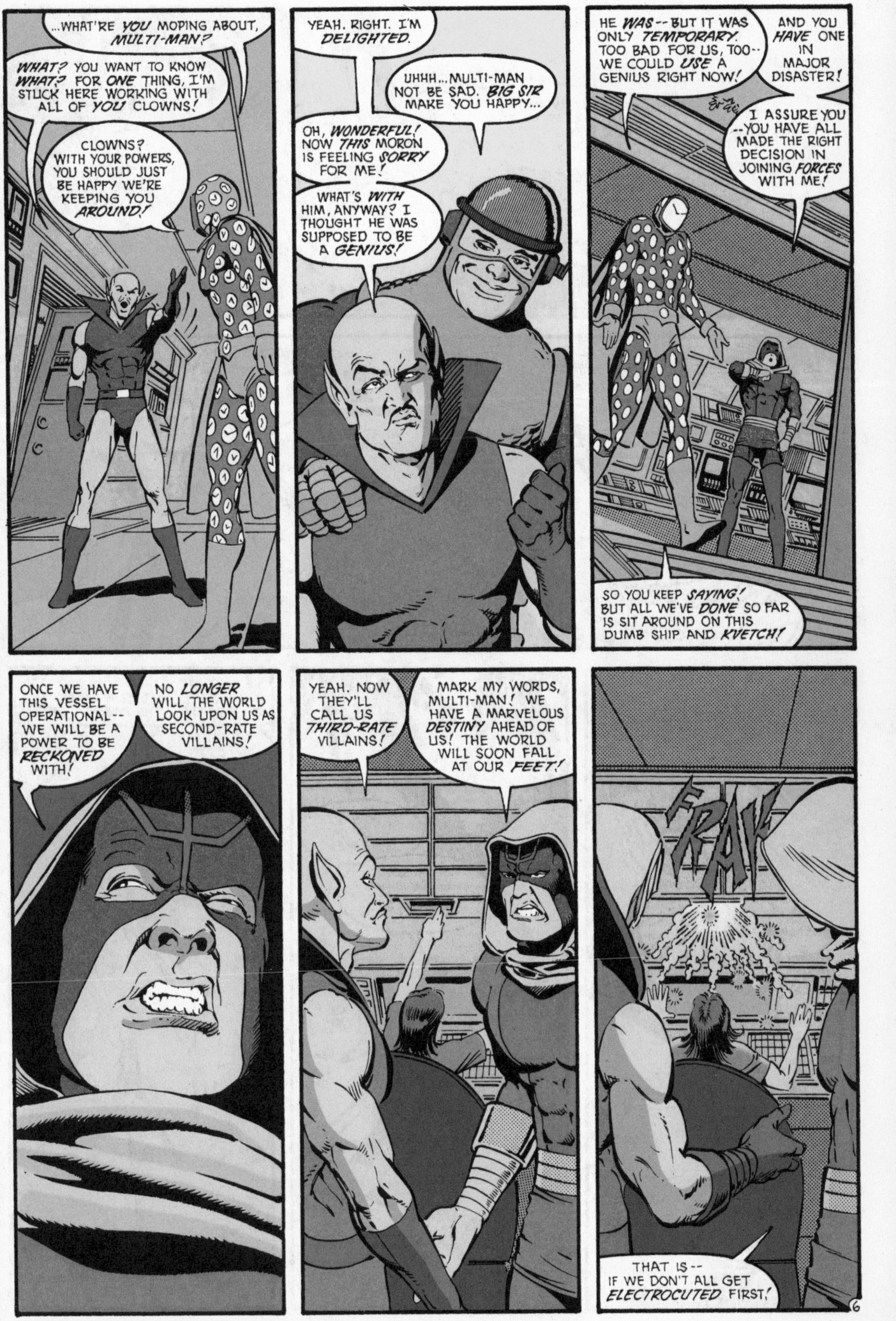
...WHAT'RE YOU MOPING ABOUT, MULTI-MAN?
WHAT? YOU WANT TO KNOW WHAT? FOR ONE THING, I'M STUCK HERE WORKING WITH ALL OF YOU CLOWNS!
CLOWNS? WITH YOUR POWERS, YOU SHOULD JUST BE HAPPY WE'RE KEEPING YOU AROUND!
YEAH. RIGHT. I'M DELIGHTED.
UHHH...MULTI-MAN NOT BE SAD. BIG SIR MAKE YOU HAPPY...
OH, WONDERFUL! NOW THIS MORON IS FEELING SORRY FOR ME!
WHAT'S WITH HIM, ANYWAY? I THOUGHT HE WAS SUPPOSED TO BE A GENIUS!
HE WAS--BUT IT WAS ONLY TEMPORARY. TOO BAD FOR US, TOO--WE COULD USE A GENIUS RIGHT NOW!
AND YOU HAVE ONE IN MAJOR DISASTER!
I ASSURE YOU--YOU HAVE ALL MADE THE RIGHT DECISION IN JOINING FORCES WITH ME!
SO YOU KEEP SAYING! BUT ALL WE'VE DONE SO FAR IS SIT AROUND ON THIS DUMB SHIP AND KVETCH!
ONCE WE HAVE THIS VESSEL OPERATIONAL--WE WILL BE A POWER TO BE RECKONED WITH!
NO LONGER WILL THE WORLD LOOK UPON US AS SECOND-RATE VILLAINS!
YEAH. NOW THEY'LL CALL US THIRD-RATE VILLAINS!
MARK MY WORDS, MULTI-MAN! WE HAVE A MARVELOUS DESTINY AHEAD OF US! THE WORLD WILL SOON FALL AT OUR FEET!
FRAK
THAT IS--IF WE DON'T ALL GET ELECTROCUTED FIRST!
6

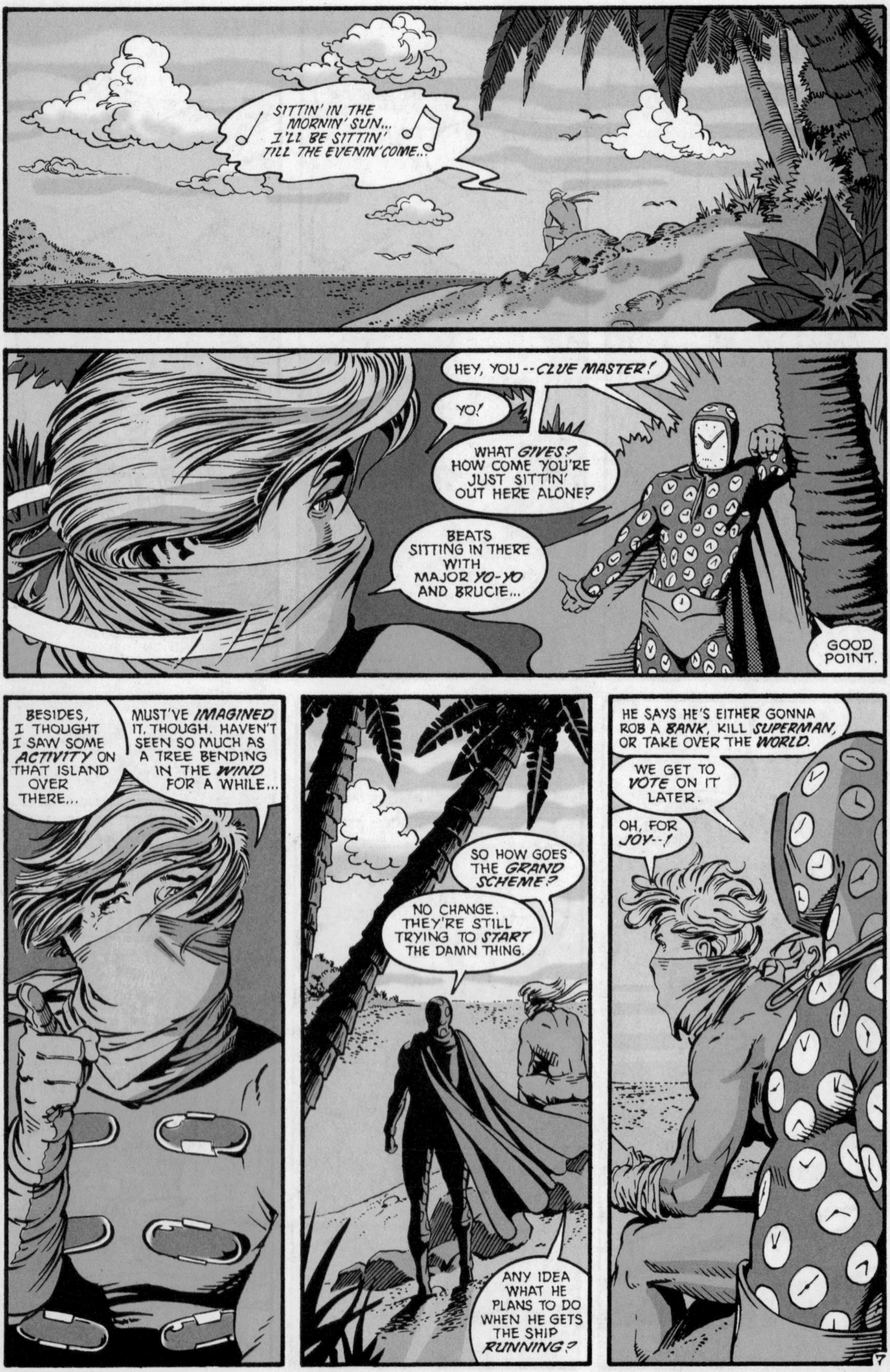

SITTIN' IN THE MORNIN' SUN... I'LL BE SITTIN' TILL THE EVENIN' COME...
HEY, YOU--CLUE MASTER!
YO!
WHAT GIVES? HOW COME YOU'RE JUST SITTIN' OUT HERE ALONE?
BEATS SITTING IN THERE WITH MAJOR YO-YO AND BRUCIE...
GOOD POINT.
BESIDES, I THOUGHT I SAW SOME ACTIVITY ON THAT ISLAND OVER THERE...
MUST'VE IMAGINED IT, THOUGH. HAVEN'T SEEN SO MUCH AS A TREE BENDING IN THE WIND FOR A WHILE...
SO HOW GOES THE GRAND SCHEME?
NO CHANGE. THEY'RE STILL TRYING TO START THE DAMN THING.
ANY IDEA WHAT HE PLANS TO DO WHEN HE GETS THE SHIP RUNNING?
HE SAYS HE'S EITHER GONNA ROB A BANK, KILL SUPERMAN, OR TAKE OVER THE WORLD.
WE GET TO VOTE ON IT LATER.
OH, FOR JOY--!
7

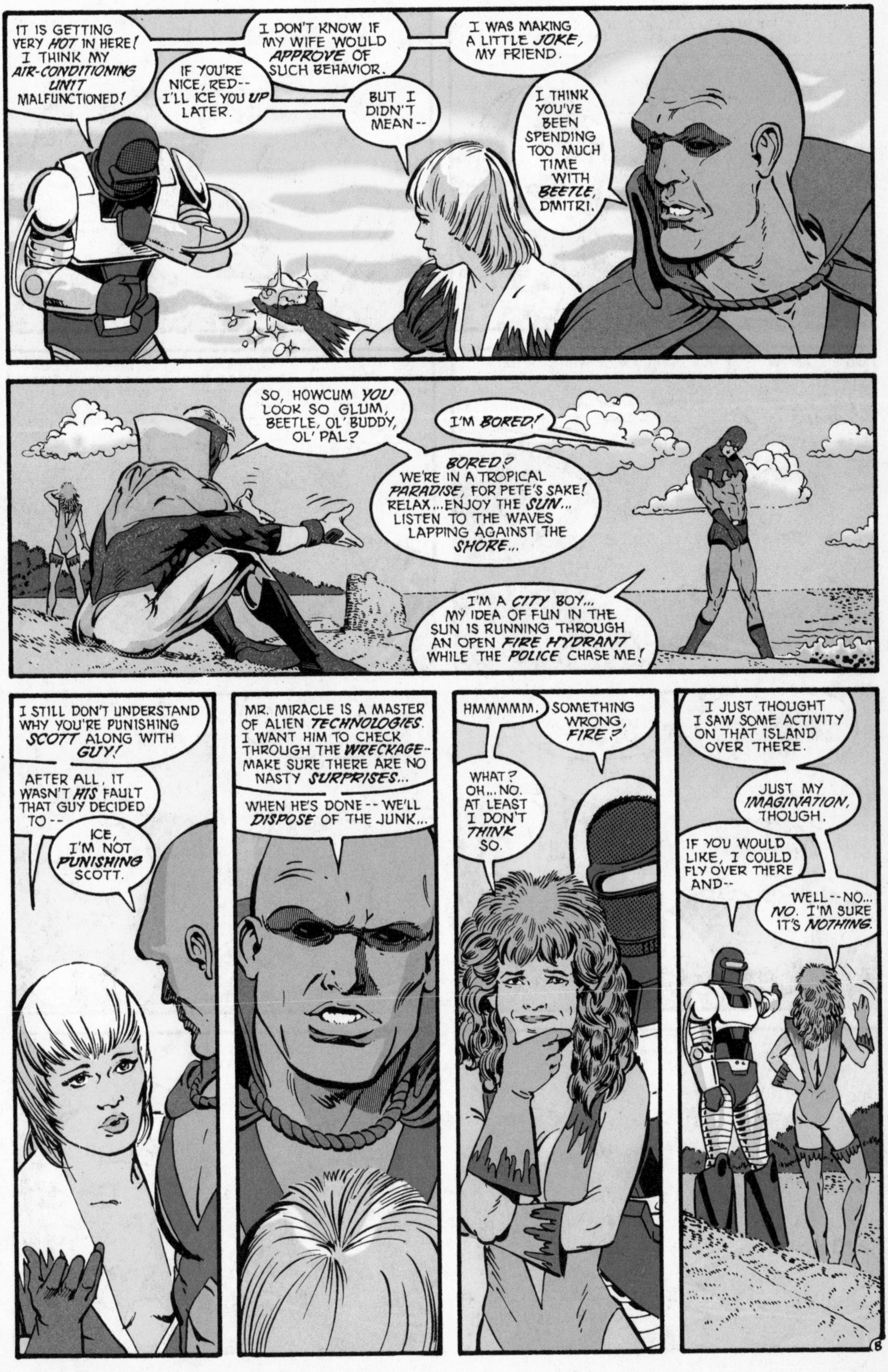
IT IS GETTING VERY HOT IN HERE! I THINK MY AIR-CONDITIONING UNIT MALFUNCTIONED!
IF YOU'RE NICE, RED-- I'LL ICE YOU UP LATER.
I DON'T KNOW IF MY WIFE WOULD APPROVE OF SUCH BEHAVIOR.
BUT I DIDN'T MEAN--
I WAS MAKING A LITTLE JOKE, MY FRIEND.
I THINK YOU'VE BEEN SPENDING TOO MUCH TIME WITH BEETLE, DMITRI.
SO, HOWCUM YOU LOOK SO GLUM, BEETLE, OL' BUDDY, OL' PAL?
I'M BORED!
BORED? WE'RE IN A TROPICAL PARADISE, FOR PETE'S SAKE! RELAX...ENJOY THE SUN... LISTEN TO THE WAVES LAPPING AGAINST THE SHORE...
I'M A CITY BOY... MY IDEA OF FUN IN THE SUN IS RUNNING THROUGH AN OPEN FIRE HYDRANT WHILE THE POLICE CHASE ME!
I STILL DON'T UNDERSTAND WHY YOU'RE PUNISHING SCOTT ALONG WITH GUY!
AFTER ALL, IT WASN'T HIS FAULT THAT GUY DECIDED TO--
ICE, I'M NOT PUNISHING SCOTT.
MR. MIRACLE IS A MASTER OF ALIEN TECHNOLOGIES. I WANT HIM TO CHECK THROUGH THE WRECKAGE-- MAKE SURE THERE ARE NO NASTY SURPRISES...
WHEN HE'S DONE -- WE'LL DISPOSE OF THE JUNK...
HMMMMM.
SOMETHING WRONG, FIRE?
WHAT? OH...NO. AT LEAST I DON'T THINK SO.
I JUST THOUGHT I SAW SOME ACTIVITY ON THAT ISLAND OVER THERE.
JUST MY IMAGINATION, THOUGH.
IF YOU WOULD LIKE, I COULD FLY OVER THERE AND--
WELL--NO... NO. I'M SURE IT'S NOTHING.

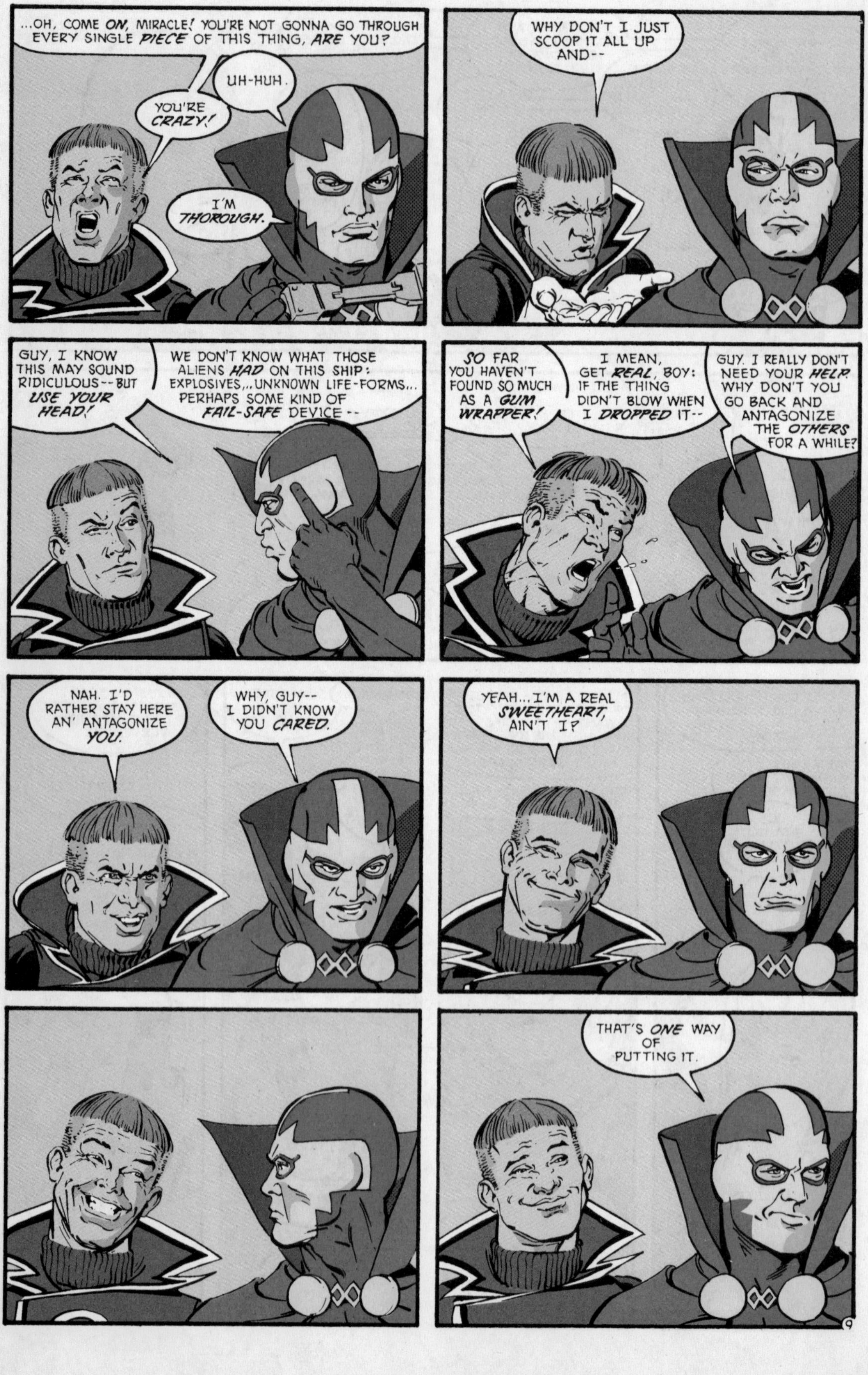
...OH, COME ON, MIRACLE! YOU'RE NOT GONNA GO THROUGH EVERY SINGLE PIECE OF THIS THING, ARE YOU?
UH-HUH.
YOU'RE CRAZY!
I'M THOROUGH.
WHY DON'T I JUST SCOOP IT ALL UP AND--
GUY, I KNOW THIS MAY SOUND RIDICULOUS--BUT USE YOUR HEAD!
WE DON'T KNOW WHAT THOSE ALIENS HAD ON THIS SHIP: EXPLOSIVES,..UNKNOWN LIFE-FORMS... PERHAPS SOME KIND OF FAIL-SAFE DEVICE--
SO FAR YOU HAVEN'T FOUND SO MUCH AS A GUM WRAPPER!
I MEAN, GET REAL, BOY: IF THE THING DIDN'T BLOW WHEN I DROPPED IT--
GUY. I REALLY DON'T NEED YOUR HELP. WHY DON'T YOU GO BACK AND ANTAGONIZE THE OTHERS FOR A WHILE?
NAH. I'D RATHER STAY HERE AN' ANTAGONIZE YOU.
WHY, GUY-- I DIDN'T KNOW YOU CARED.
YEAH... I'M A REAL SWEETHEART, AIN'T I?
THAT'S ONE WAY OF PUTTING IT.
9

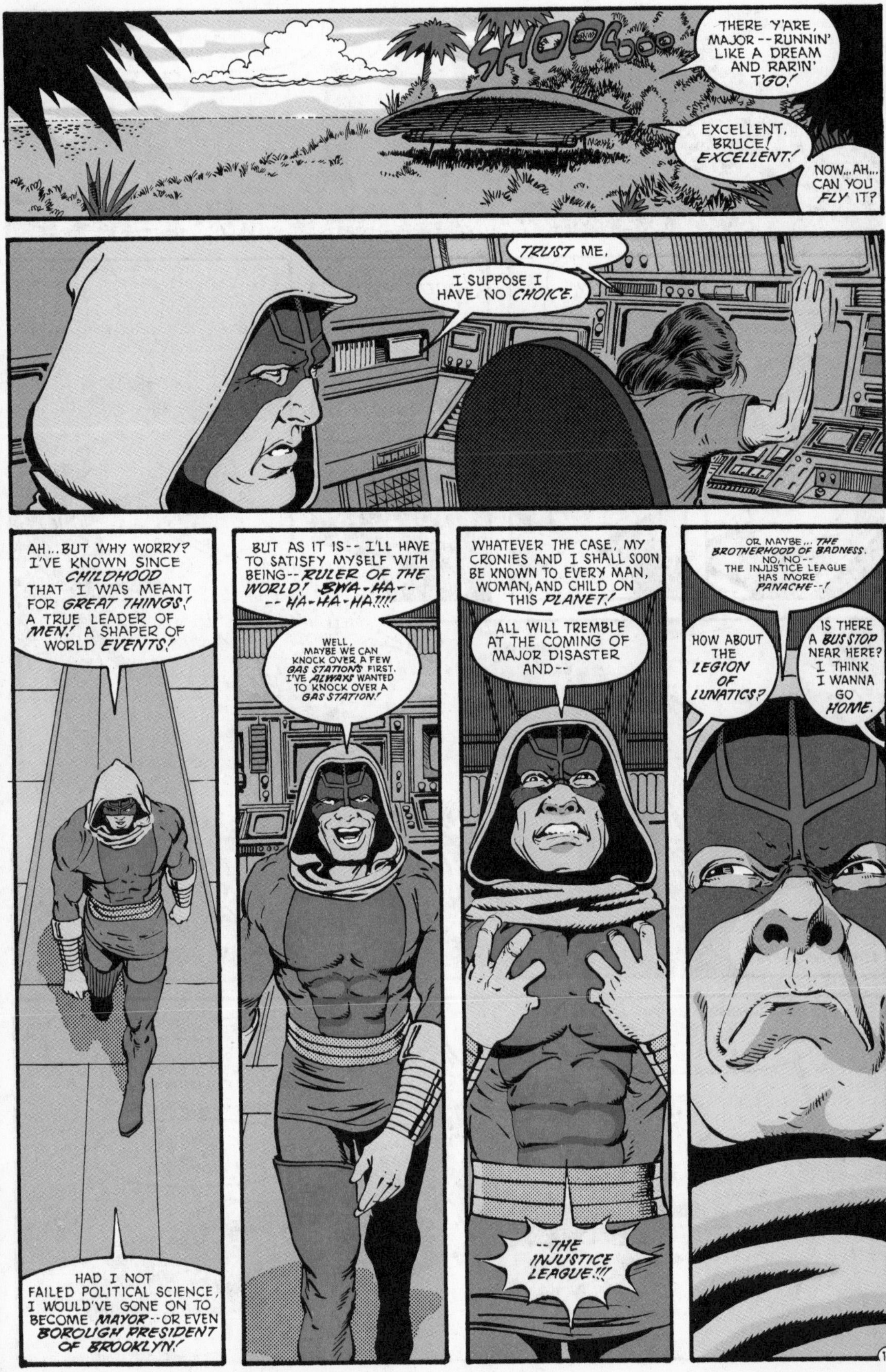
SHOOOooo
THERE Y'ARE, MAJOR--RUNNIN' LIKE A DREAM AND RARIN' T'GO!
EXCELLENT, BRUCE! EXCELLENT!
NOW... AH... CAN YOU FLY IT?
TRUST ME.
I SUPPOSE I HAVE NO CHOICE.
AH... BUT WHY WORRY? I'VE KNOWN SINCE CHILDHOOD THAT I WAS MEANT FOR GREAT THINGS! A TRUE LEADER OF MEN! A SHAPER OF WORLD EVENTS!
HAD I NOT FAILED POLITICAL SCIENCE, I WOULD'VE GONE ON TO BECOME MAYOR--OR EVEN BOROUGH PRESIDENT OF BROOKLYN!
BUT AS IT IS--I'LL HAVE TO SATISFY MYSELF WITH BEING--RULER OF THE WORLD! BWA-HA---HA-HA-HA!!!!
WELL, MAYBE WE CAN KNOCK OVER A FEW GAS STATIONS FIRST. I'VE ALWAYS WANTED TO KNOCK OVER A GAS STATION!
WHATEVER THE CASE, MY CRONIES AND I SHALL SOON BE KNOWN TO EVERY MAN, WOMAN, AND CHILD ON THIS PLANET!
ALL WILL TREMBLE AT THE COMING OF MAJOR DISASTER AND--
--THE INJUSTICE LEAGUE!!!
OR MAYBE... THE BROTHERHOOD OF BADNESS. NO, NO-- THE INJUSTICE LEAGUE HAS MORE PANACHE--!
HOW ABOUT THE LEGION OF LUNATICS?
IS THERE A BUS STOP NEAR HERE? I THINK I WANNA GO HOME.
10

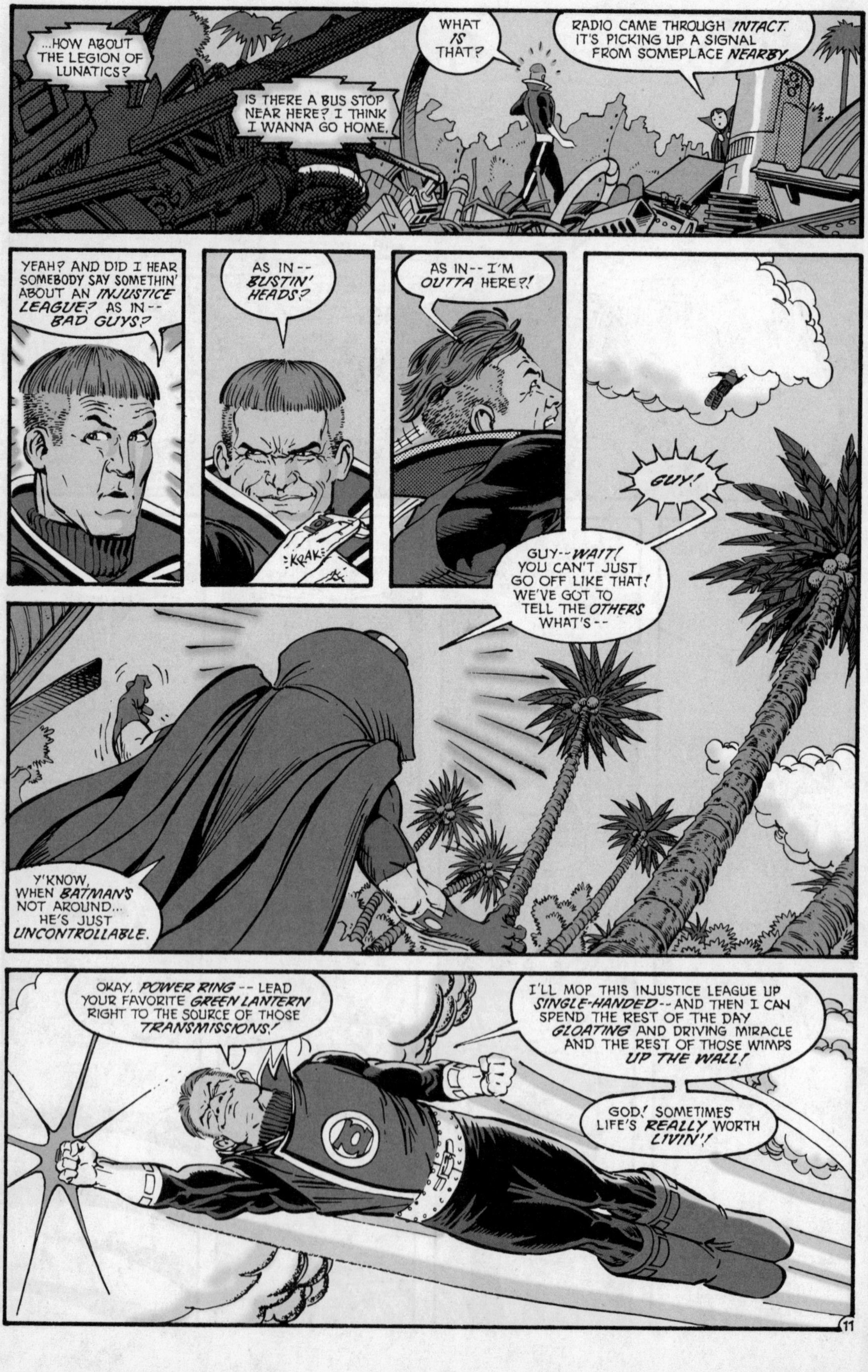

...HOW ABOUT THE LEGION OF LUNATICS?
IS THERE A BUS STOP NEAR HERE? I THINK I WANNA GO HOME.
WHAT IS THAT?
RADIO CAME THROUGH INTACT. IT'S PICKING UP A SIGNAL FROM SOMEPLACE NEARBY.
YEAH? AND DID I HEAR SOMEBODY SAY SOMETHIN' ABOUT AN INJUSTICE LEAGUE? AS IN -- BAD GUYS?
AS IN -- BUSTIN' HEADS?
KRAK
AS IN -- I'M OUTTA HERE?!
GUY!
GUY -- WAIT! YOU CAN'T JUST GO OFF LIKE THAT! WE'VE GOT TO TELL THE OTHERS WHAT'S --
Y'KNOW, WHEN BATMAN'S NOT AROUND... HE'S JUST UNCONTROLLABLE.
OKAY, POWER RING -- LEAD YOUR FAVORITE GREEN LANTERN RIGHT TO THE SOURCE OF THOSE TRANSMISSIONS!
I'LL MOP THIS INJUSTICE LEAGUE UP SINGLE-HANDED -- AND THEN I CAN SPEND THE REST OF THE DAY GLOATING AND DRIVING MIRACLE AND THE REST OF THOSE WIMPS UP THE WALL!
GOD! SOMETIMES LIFE'S REALLY WORTH LIVIN'!
11

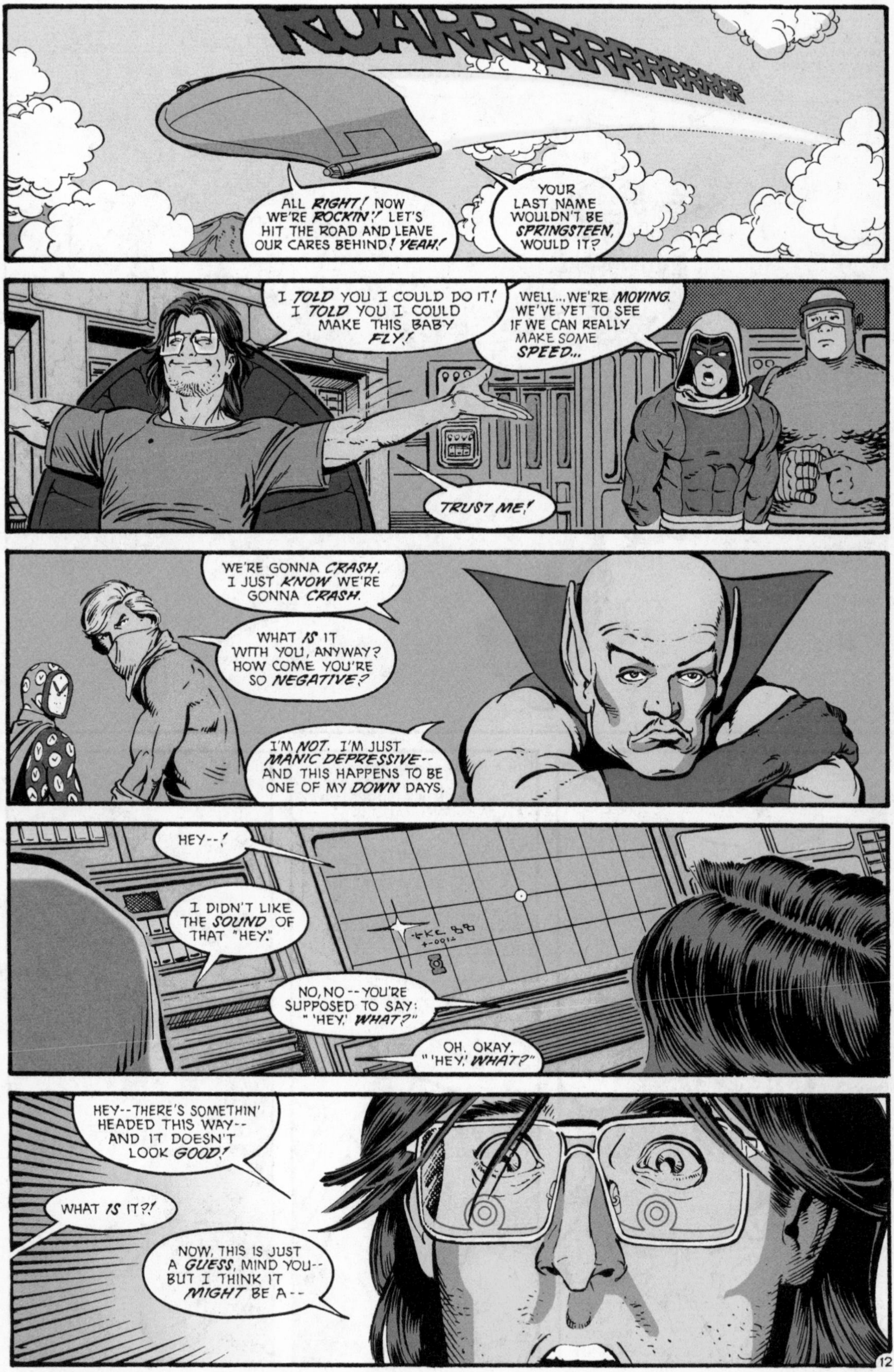
RUARRRRRRRRRRRRR
ALL RIGHT! NOW WE'RE ROCKIN'! LET'S HIT THE ROAD AND LEAVE OUR CARES BEHIND! YEAH!
YOUR LAST NAME WOULDN'T BE SPRINGSTEEN, WOULD IT?
I TOLD YOU I COULD DO IT! I TOLD YOU I COULD MAKE THIS BABY FLY!
WELL... WE'RE MOVING. WE'VE YET TO SEE IF WE CAN REALLY MAKE SOME SPEED...
TRUST ME!
WE'RE GONNA CRASH. I JUST KNOW WE'RE GONNA CRASH.
WHAT IS IT WITH YOU, ANYWAY? HOW COME YOU'RE SO NEGATIVE?
I'M NOT. I'M JUST MANIC DEPRESSIVE-- AND THIS HAPPENS TO BE ONE OF MY DOWN DAYS.
HEY--!
I DIDN'T LIKE THE SOUND OF THAT "HEY."
NO, NO -- YOU'RE SUPPOSED TO SAY: " 'HEY,' WHAT?"
OH. OKAY. " 'HEY,' WHAT?"
HEY--THERE'S SOMETHIN' HEADED THIS WAY-- AND IT DOESN'T LOOK GOOD!
WHAT IS IT?!
NOW, THIS IS JUST A GUESS, MIND YOU-- BUT I THINK IT MIGHT BE A--
12

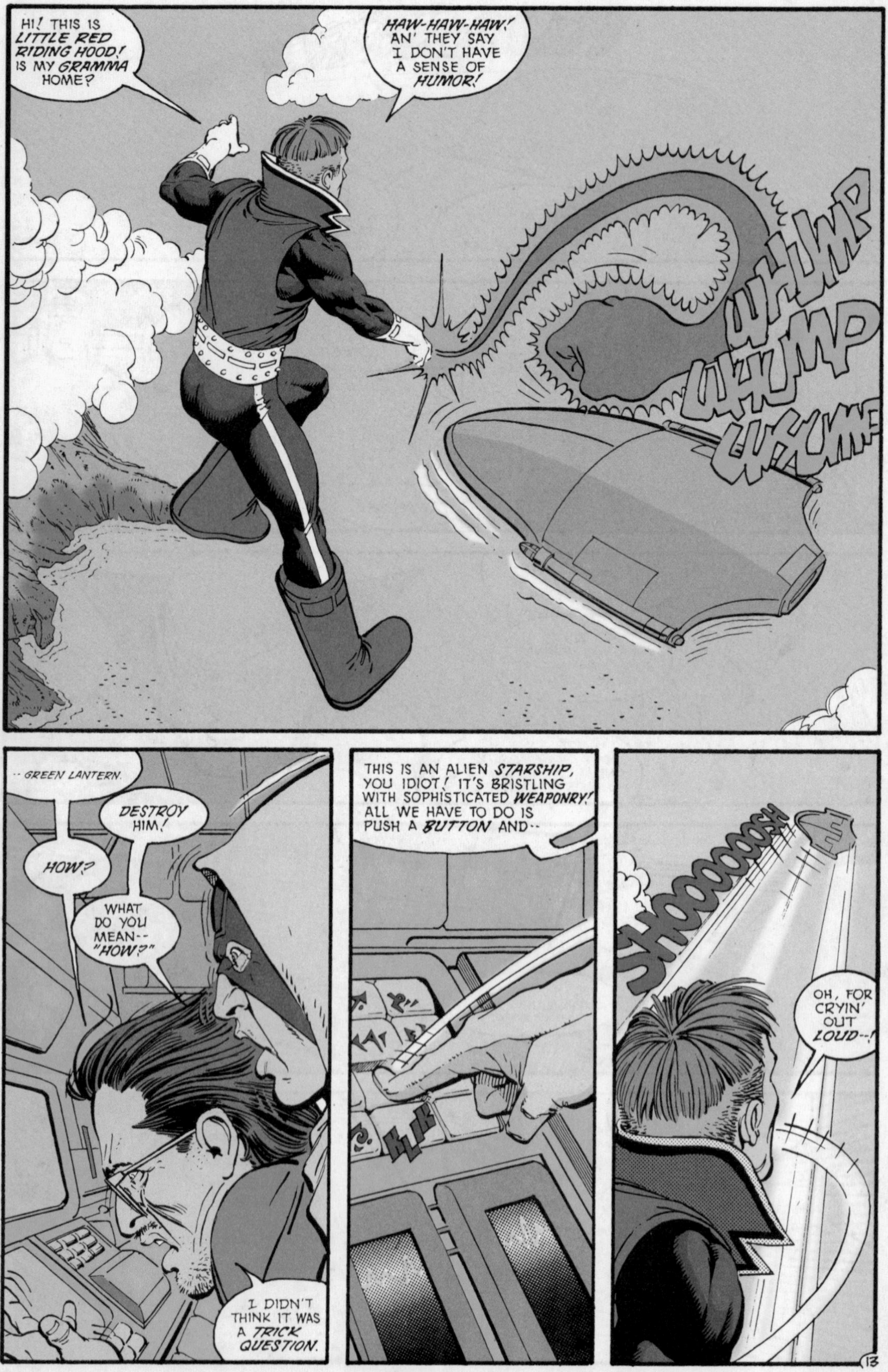
HI! THIS IS LITTLE RED RIDING HOOD! IS MY GRAMMA HOME?
HAW-HAW-HAW! AN' THEY SAY I DON'T HAVE A SENSE OF HUMOR!
WHUMP
WHUMP
-- GREEN LANTERN.
DESTROY HIM!
HOW?
WHAT DO YOU MEAN-- "HOW?"
I DIDN'T THINK IT WAS A TRICK QUESTION.
THIS IS AN ALIEN STARSHIP, YOU IDIOT! IT'S BRISTLING WITH SOPHISTICATED WEAPONRY! ALL WE HAVE TO DO IS PUSH A BUTTON AND--
KLIK
SHOOOOOOSH
OH, FOR CRYIN' OUT LOUD--!
13

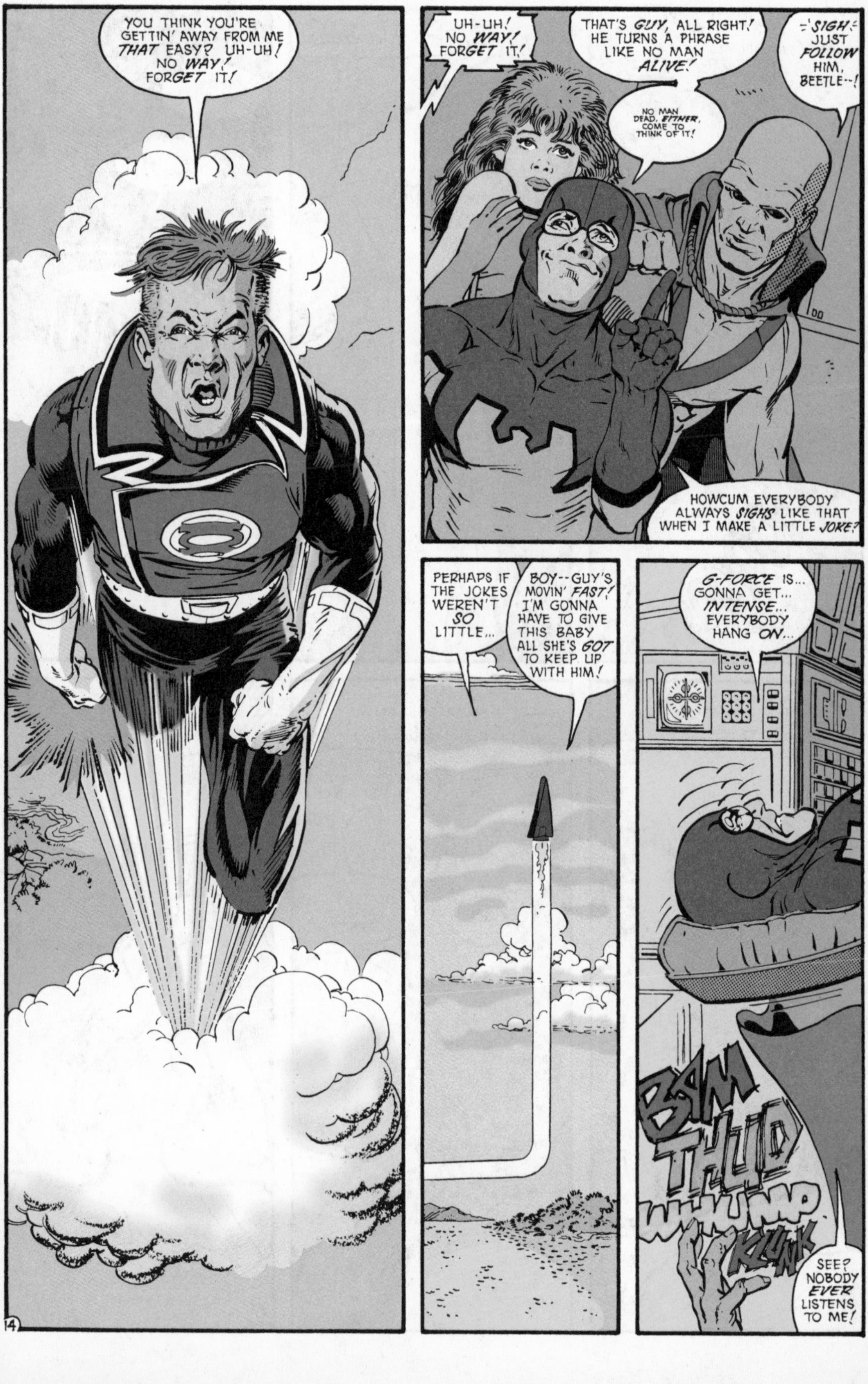
YOU THINK YOU'RE GETTIN' AWAY FROM ME THAT EASY? UH-UH! NO WAY! FORGET IT!
14
UH-UH! NO WAY! FORGET IT!
THAT'S GUY, ALL RIGHT! HE TURNS A PHRASE LIKE NO MAN ALIVE!
NO MAN DEAD, EITHER, COME TO THINK OF IT!
-SIGH- JUST FOLLOW HIM, BEETLE--!
HOWCUM EVERYBODY ALWAYS SIGHS LIKE THAT WHEN I MAKE A LITTLE JOKE?
PERHAPS IF THE JOKES WEREN'T SO LITTLE...
BOY--GUY'S MOVIN' FAST! I'M GONNA HAVE TO GIVE THIS BABY ALL SHE'S GOT TO KEEP UP WITH HIM!
G-FORCE IS... GONNA GET... INTENSE... EVERYBODY HANG ON...
BAM
THUD
WHUMP
KLUNK
SEE? NOBODY EVER LISTENS TO ME!

WILL SOMEBODY PLEASE **STOP** THIS THING?!

SHOOOOSH

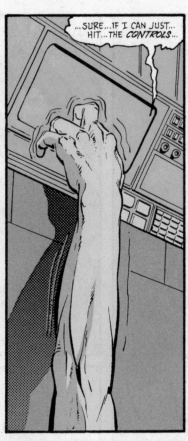

...SURE...IF I CAN JUST... HIT...THE **CONTROLS**...

THERE WE GO!

EVERYONE **OKAY?**

TRREEEEEEEEEE

YOU INCOMPETENT **MORON!** YOU ALMOST **KILLED** US!

I ALMOST KILLED US? **YOU'RE** THE ONE WHO HIT THE DAMN **BUTTON!**

IF **YOU'D** KNOWN WHAT YOU WERE DOING, I WOULDN'T HAVE HAD TO HIT THE BUTTON!

LAY OFF THE KID, DISASTER! **YOU'RE** THE ONE WHO BLEW IT-- **WHY** DON'T YOU ACT LIKE A MAN AND TAKE **RESPONSIBILITY** FOR IT?

ARE YOU **INFERRING** THAT I'M **NOT** A MAN?!

IF THE **CORSET** FITS, **SWEETIE**...!

STEP **OUTSIDE** AND SAY THAT **AGAIN**--!

OUTSIDE--? WE'RE AT THE EDGE OF THE EARTH'S **ATMOSPHERE**, YOU YO-YO!

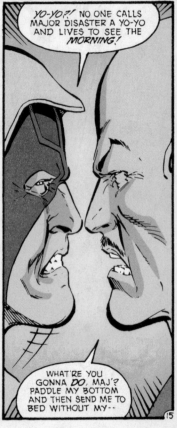

YO-YO?! NO ONE CALLS MAJOR DISASTER A YO-YO AND LIVES TO SEE THE **MORNING!**

WHAT'RE YOU GONNA **DO,** MAJ'? PADDLE MY BOTTOM AND THEN SEND ME TO BED WITHOUT MY--

15

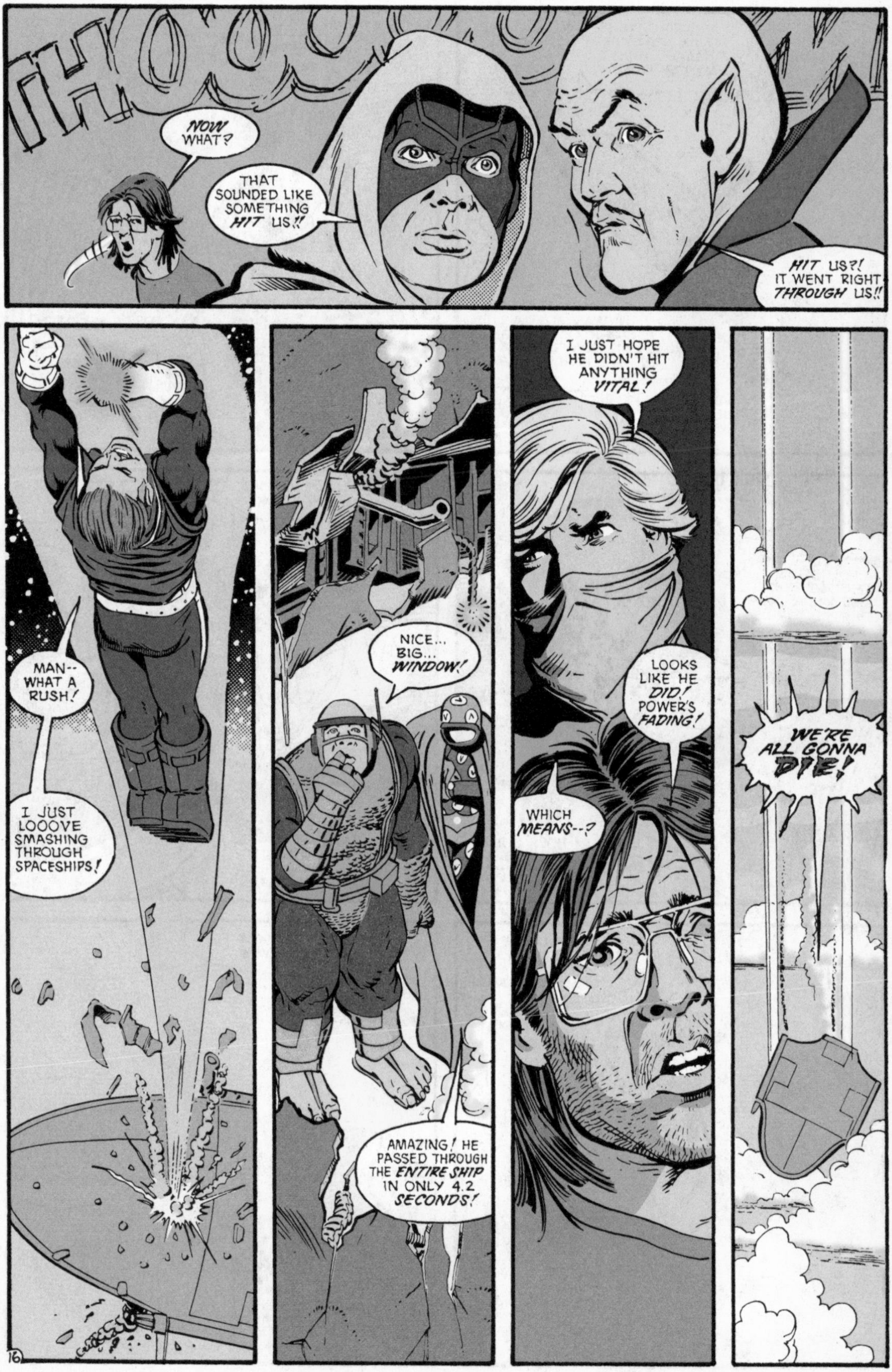
THOOOOOOM
NOW WHAT?
THAT SOUNDED LIKE SOMETHING HIT US!!
HIT US?! IT WENT RIGHT THROUGH US!!
MAN-- WHAT A RUSH!
I JUST LOOOVE SMASHING THROUGH SPACESHIPS!
NICE... BIG... WINDOW!
AMAZING! HE PASSED THROUGH THE ENTIRE SHIP IN ONLY 4.2 SECONDS!
I JUST HOPE HE DIDN'T HIT ANYTHING VITAL!
LOOKS LIKE HE DID! POWER'S FADING!
WHICH MEANS--?
WE'RE ALL GONNA DIE!
16

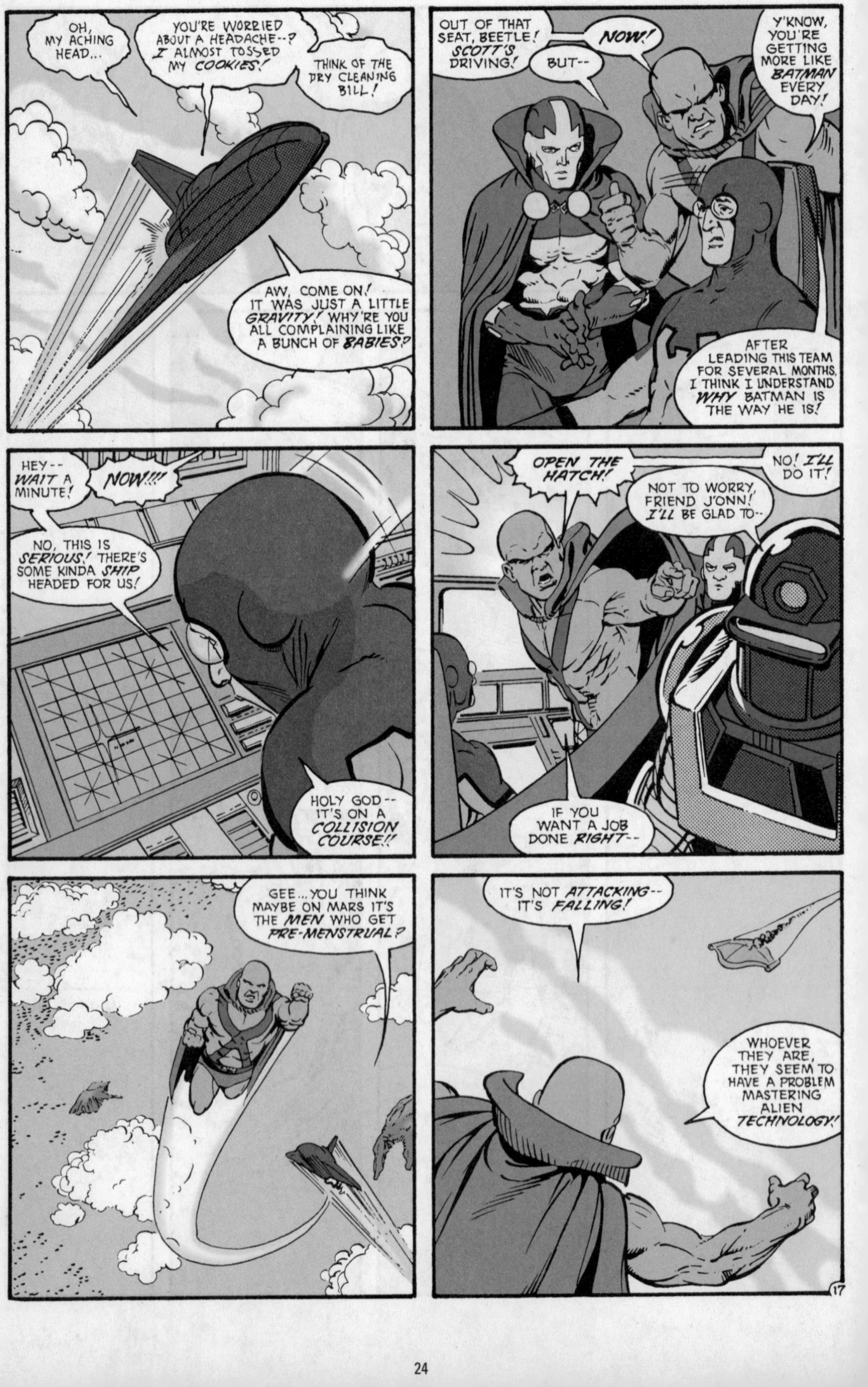
OH, MY ACHING HEAD...
YOU'RE WORRIED ABOUT A HEADACHE--? I ALMOST TOSSED MY COOKIES!
THINK OF THE DRY CLEANING BILL!
AW, COME ON! IT WAS JUST A LITTLE GRAVITY! WHY'RE YOU ALL COMPLAINING LIKE A BUNCH OF BABIES?
OUT OF THAT SEAT, BEETLE! SCOTT'S DRIVING!
BUT--
NOW!
Y'KNOW, YOU'RE GETTING MORE LIKE BATMAN EVERY DAY!
AFTER LEADING THIS TEAM FOR SEVERAL MONTHS, I THINK I UNDERSTAND WHY BATMAN IS THE WAY HE IS!
HEY-- WAIT A MINUTE!
NOW!!!
NO, THIS IS SERIOUS! THERE'S SOME KINDA SHIP HEADED FOR US!
HOLY GOD-- IT'S ON A COLLISION COURSE!!
OPEN THE HATCH!
NO! I'LL DO IT!
NOT TO WORRY, FRIEND J'ONN! I'LL BE GLAD TO--
IF YOU WANT A JOB DONE RIGHT--
GEE... YOU THINK MAYBE ON MARS IT'S THE MEN WHO GET PRE-MENSTRUAL?
IT'S NOT ATTACKING-- IT'S FALLING!
WHOEVER THEY ARE, THEY SEEM TO HAVE A PROBLEM MASTERING ALIEN TECHNOLOGY!
17

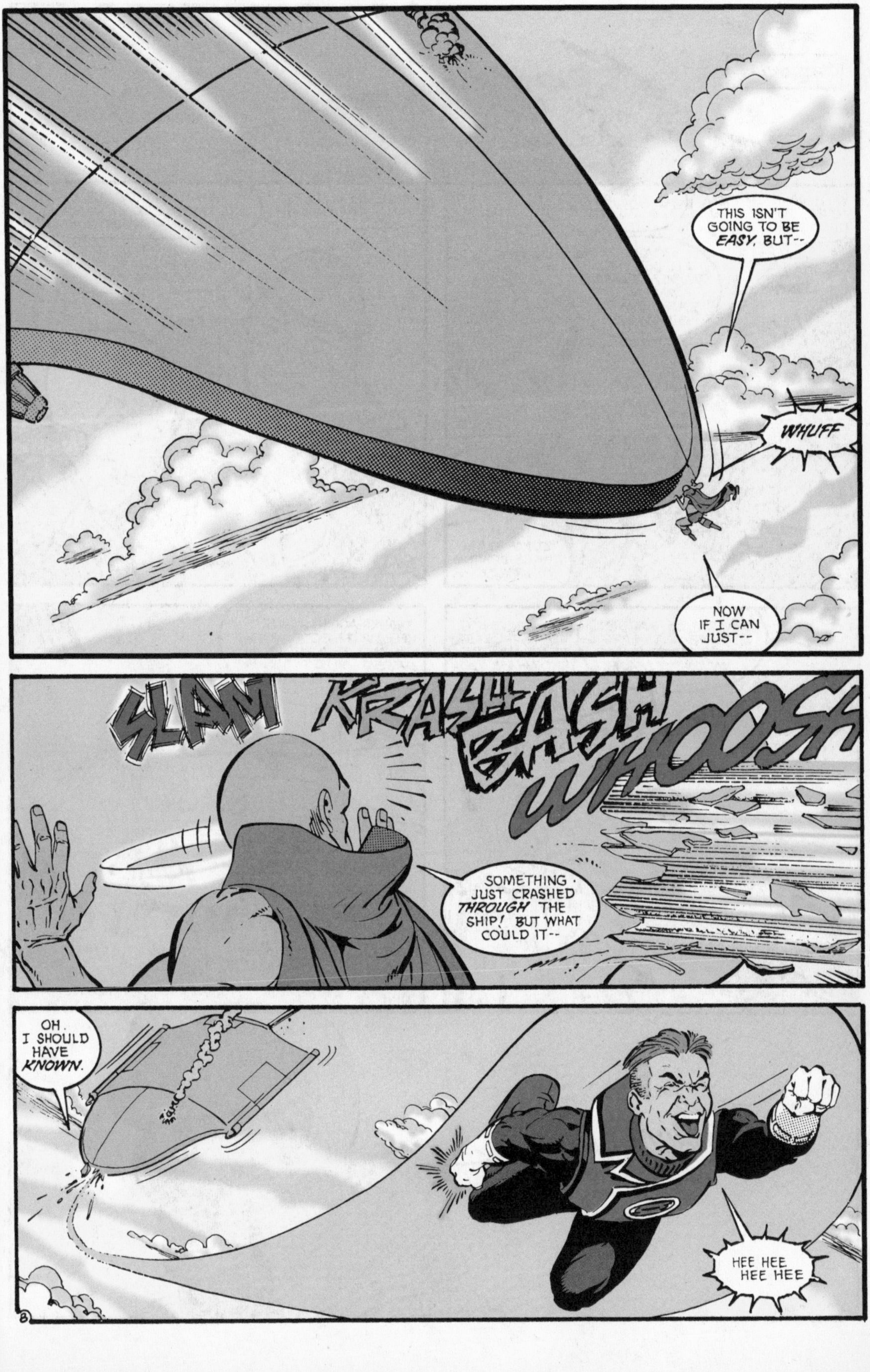
THIS ISN'T GOING TO BE EASY, BUT--
WHUFF
NOW IF I CAN JUST--
SLAM
KRASH
BASH
WHOOSH
SOMETHING JUST CRASHED THROUGH THE SHIP! BUT WHAT COULD IT--
OH. I SHOULD HAVE KNOWN.
HEE HEE HEE HEE
8

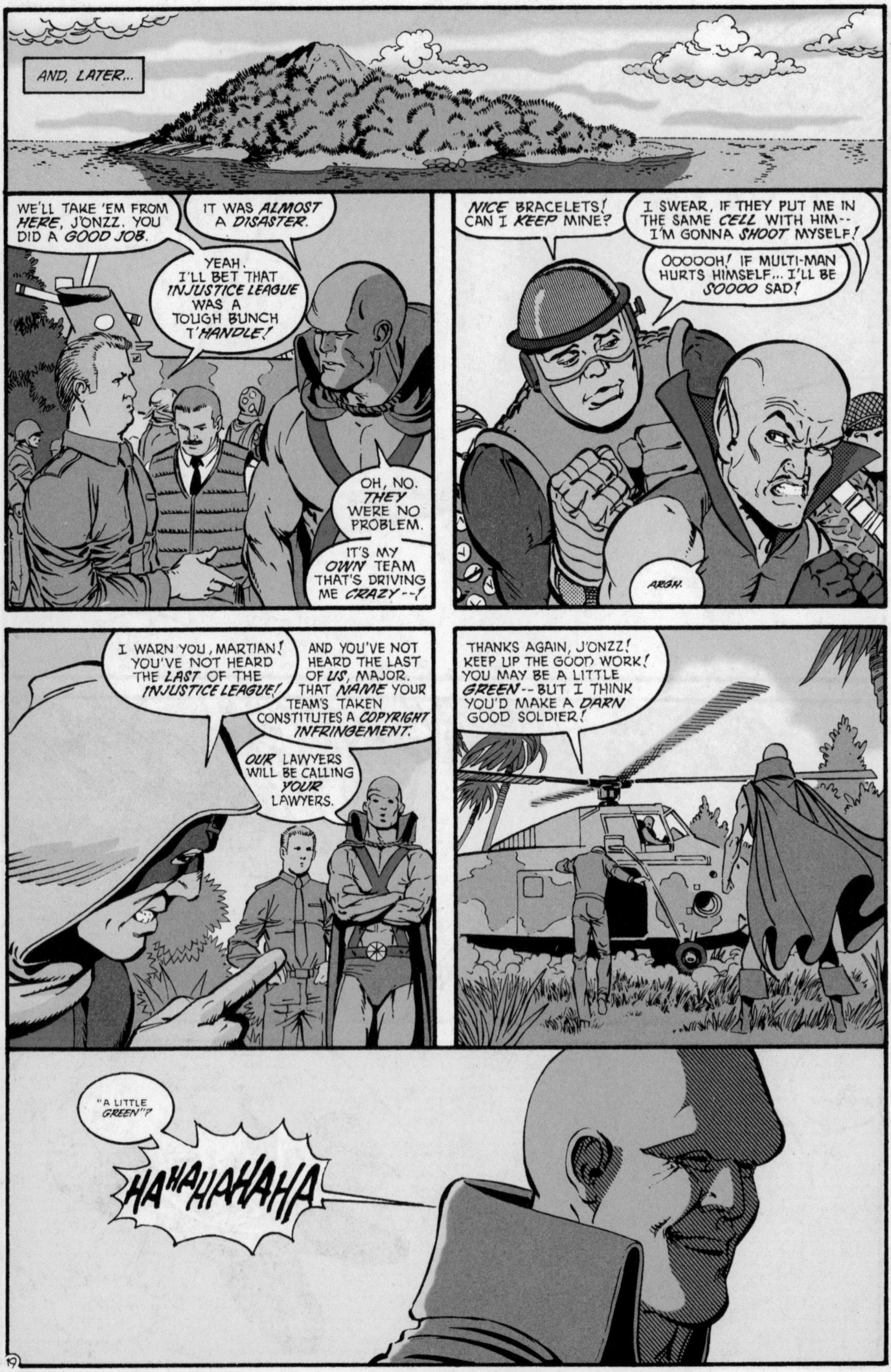

AND, LATER...
WE'LL TAKE 'EM FROM HERE, J'ONZZ. YOU DID A GOOD JOB.
IT WAS ALMOST A DISASTER.
YEAH. I'LL BET THAT INJUSTICE LEAGUE WAS A TOUGH BUNCH T'HANDLE!
OH, NO. THEY WERE NO PROBLEM.
IT'S MY OWN TEAM THAT'S DRIVING ME CRAZY--!
NICE BRACELETS! CAN I KEEP MINE?
I SWEAR, IF THEY PUT ME IN THE SAME CELL WITH HIM-- I'M GONNA SHOOT MYSELF!
OOOOOH! IF MULTI-MAN HURTS HIMSELF... I'LL BE SOOOO SAD!
ARGH.
I WARN YOU, MARTIAN! YOU'VE NOT HEARD THE LAST OF THE INJUSTICE LEAGUE!
AND YOU'VE NOT HEARD THE LAST OF US, MAJOR. THAT NAME YOUR TEAM'S TAKEN CONSTITUTES A COPYRIGHT INFRINGEMENT.
OUR LAWYERS WILL BE CALLING YOUR LAWYERS.
THANKS AGAIN, J'ONZZ! KEEP UP THE GOOD WORK! YOU MAY BE A LITTLE GREEN-- BUT I THINK YOU'D MAKE A DARN GOOD SOLDIER!
"A LITTLE GREEN"?
HAHAHAHAHAHA
19

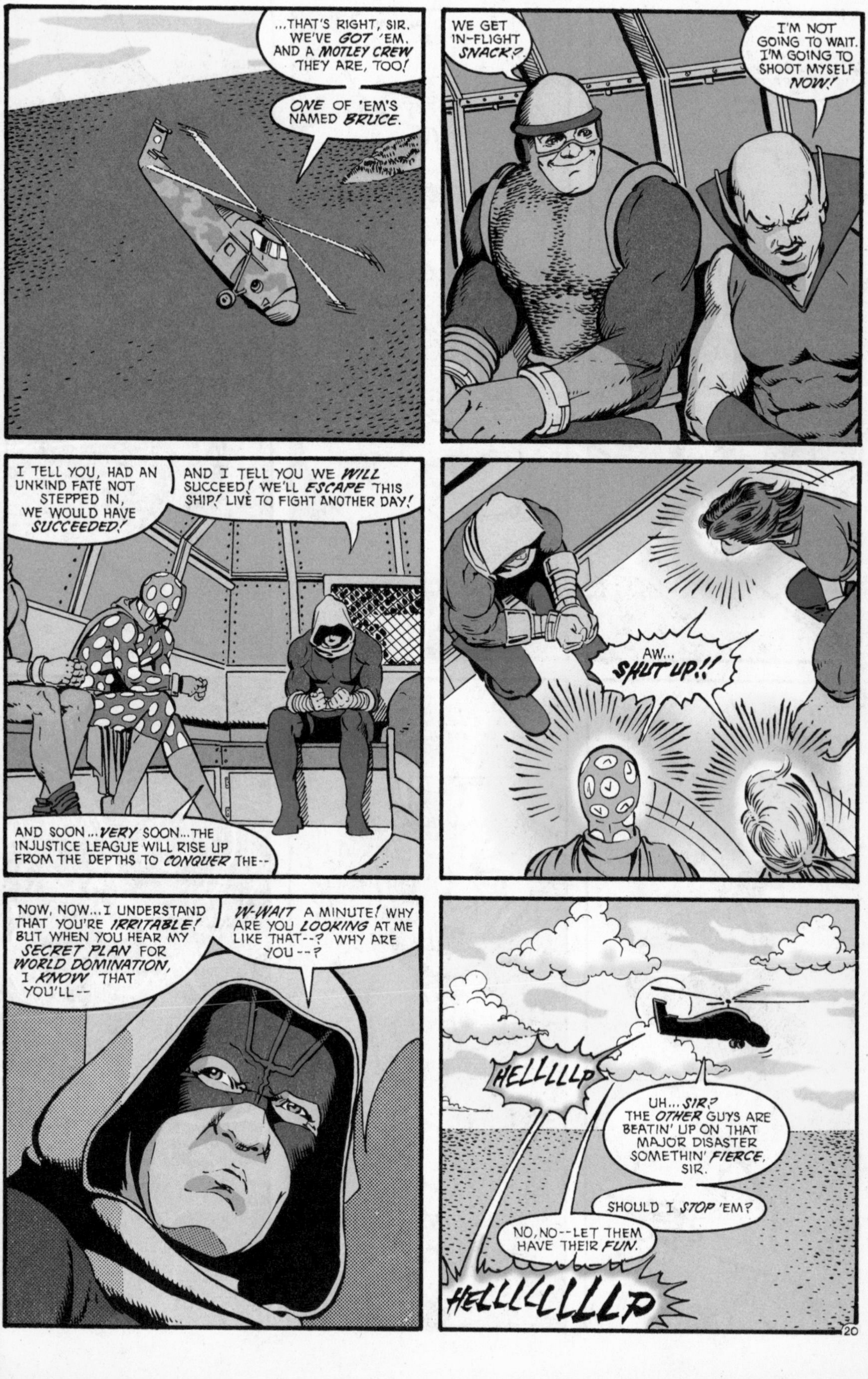
...THAT'S RIGHT, SIR. WE'VE GOT 'EM. AND A MOTLEY CREW THEY ARE, TOO!
ONE OF 'EM'S NAMED BRUCE.
WE GET IN-FLIGHT SNACK?
I'M NOT GOING TO WAIT. I'M GOING TO SHOOT MYSELF NOW!
I TELL YOU, HAD AN UNKIND FATE NOT STEPPED IN, WE WOULD HAVE SUCCEEDED!
AND I TELL YOU WE WILL SUCCEED! WE'LL ESCAPE THIS SHIP! LIVE TO FIGHT ANOTHER DAY!
AND SOON...VERY SOON...THE INJUSTICE LEAGUE WILL RISE UP FROM THE DEPTHS TO CONQUER THE--
AW... SHUT UP!!
NOW, NOW...I UNDERSTAND THAT YOU'RE IRRITABLE! BUT WHEN YOU HEAR MY SECRET PLAN FOR WORLD DOMINATION, I KNOW THAT YOU'LL--
W-WAIT A MINUTE! WHY ARE YOU LOOKING AT ME LIKE THAT--? WHY ARE YOU--?
HELLLLLP
UH... SIR? THE OTHER GUYS ARE BEATIN' UP ON THAT MAJOR DISASTER SOMETHIN' FIERCE, SIR.
SHOULD I STOP 'EM?
NO, NO--LET THEM HAVE THEIR FUN.
HELLLLLLLLP
20

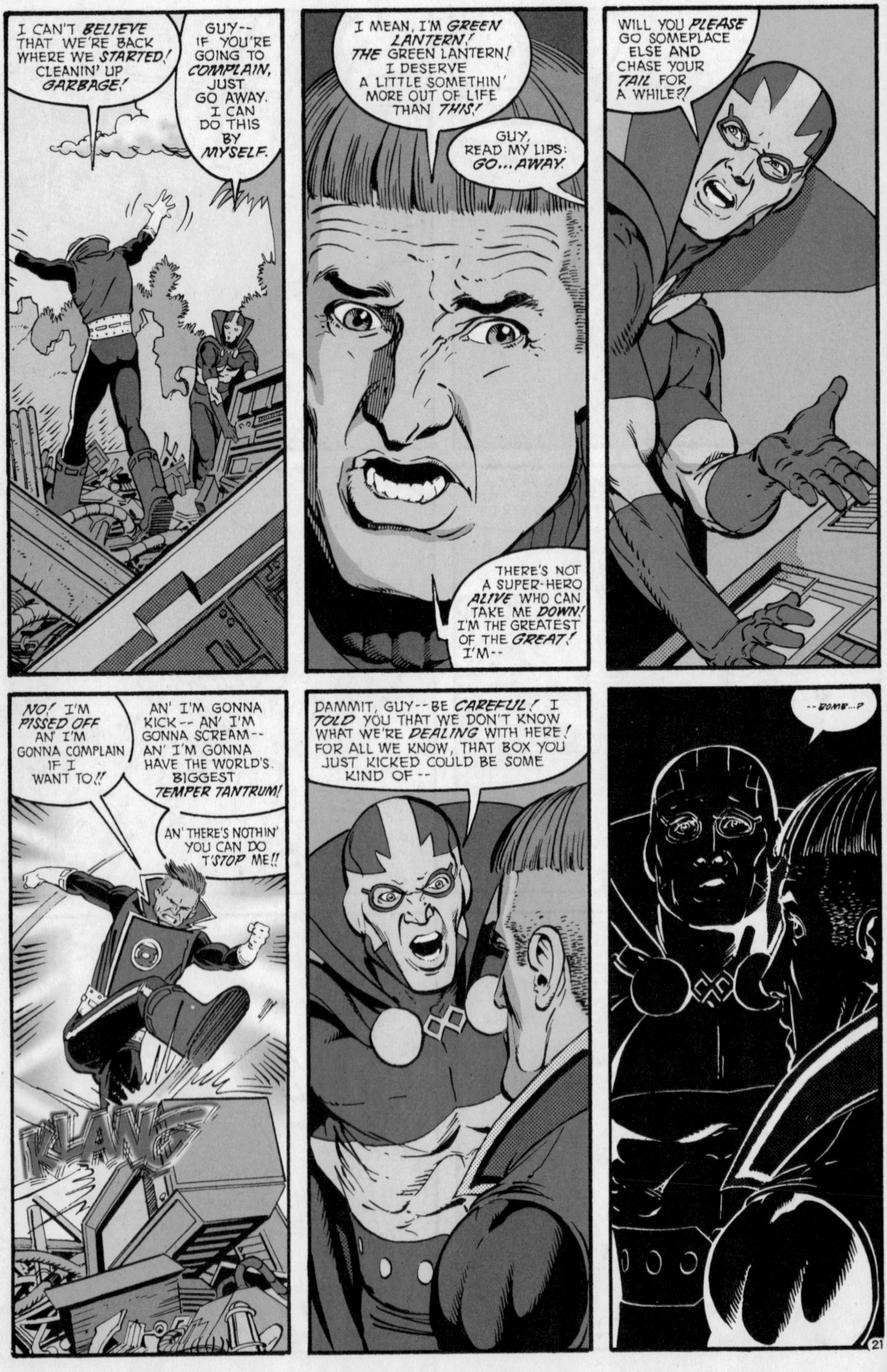
I CAN'T BELIEVE THAT WE'RE BACK WHERE WE STARTED! CLEANIN' UP GARBAGE!
GUY-- IF YOU'RE GOING TO COMPLAIN, JUST GO AWAY. I CAN DO THIS BY MYSELF.
I MEAN, I'M GREEN LANTERN! THE GREEN LANTERN! I DESERVE A LITTLE SOMETHIN' MORE OUT OF LIFE THAN THIS!
GUY, READ MY LIPS: GO... AWAY.
THERE'S NOT A SUPER-HERO ALIVE WHO CAN TAKE ME DOWN! I'M THE GREATEST OF THE GREAT! I'M--
WILL YOU PLEASE GO SOMEPLACE ELSE AND CHASE YOUR TAIL FOR A WHILE?!
NO! I'M PISSED OFF AN' I'M GONNA COMPLAIN IF I WANT TO!!
AN' I'M GONNA KICK-- AN' I'M GONNA SCREAM-- AN' I'M GONNA HAVE THE WORLD'S BIGGEST TEMPER TANTRUM!
AN' THERE'S NOTHIN' YOU CAN DO T'STOP ME!!
KLANG
DAMMIT, GUY--BE CAREFUL! I TOLD YOU THAT WE DON'T KNOW WHAT WE'RE DEALING WITH HERE! FOR ALL WE KNOW, THAT BOX YOU JUST KICKED COULD BE SOME KIND OF --
--BOMB...?
21

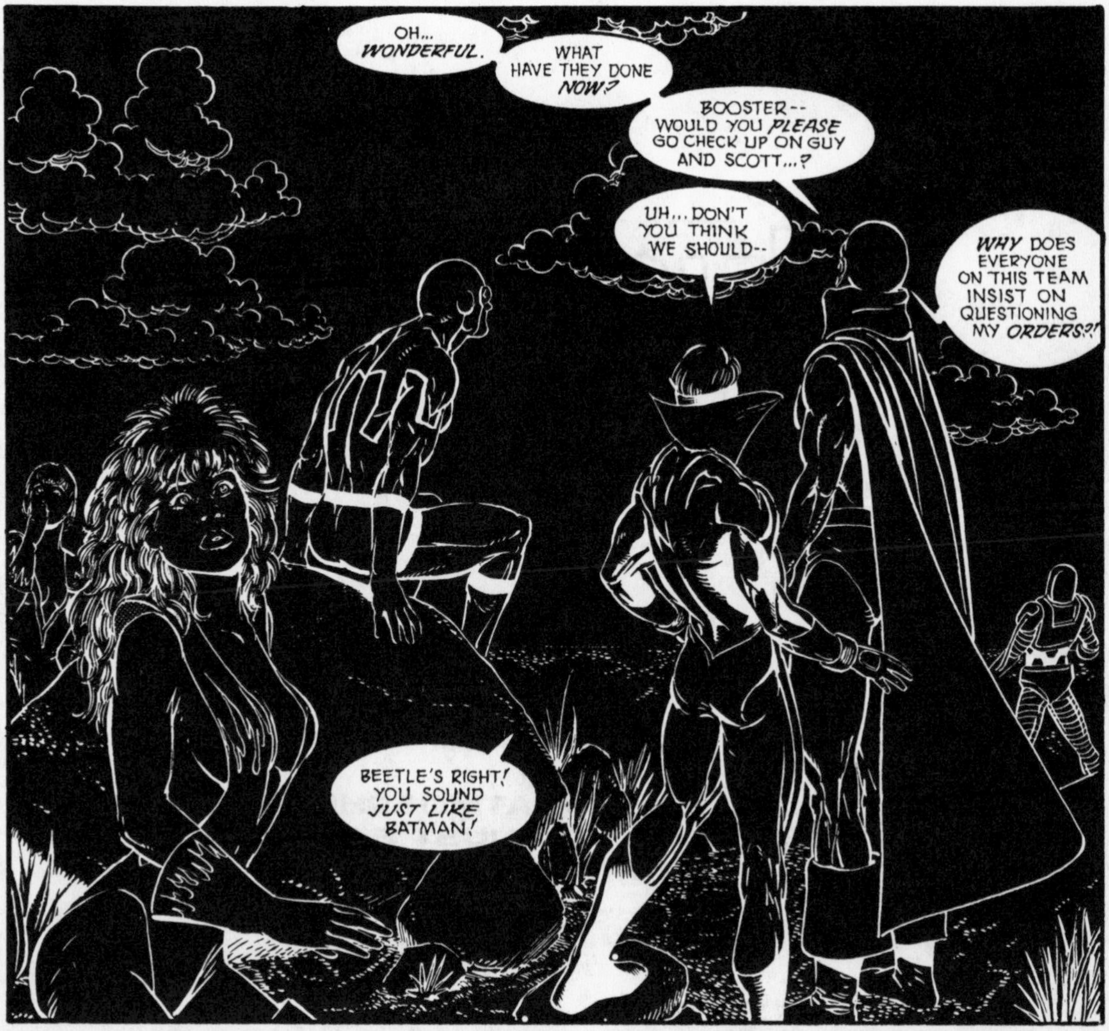
OH... WONDERFUL.
WHAT HAVE THEY DONE NOW?
BOOSTER-- WOULD YOU PLEASE GO CHECK UP ON GUY AND SCOTT...?
UH... DON'T YOU THINK WE SHOULD--
WHY DOES EVERYONE ON THIS TEAM INSIST ON QUESTIONING MY ORDERS?!
BEETLE'S RIGHT! YOU SOUND JUST LIKE BATMAN!

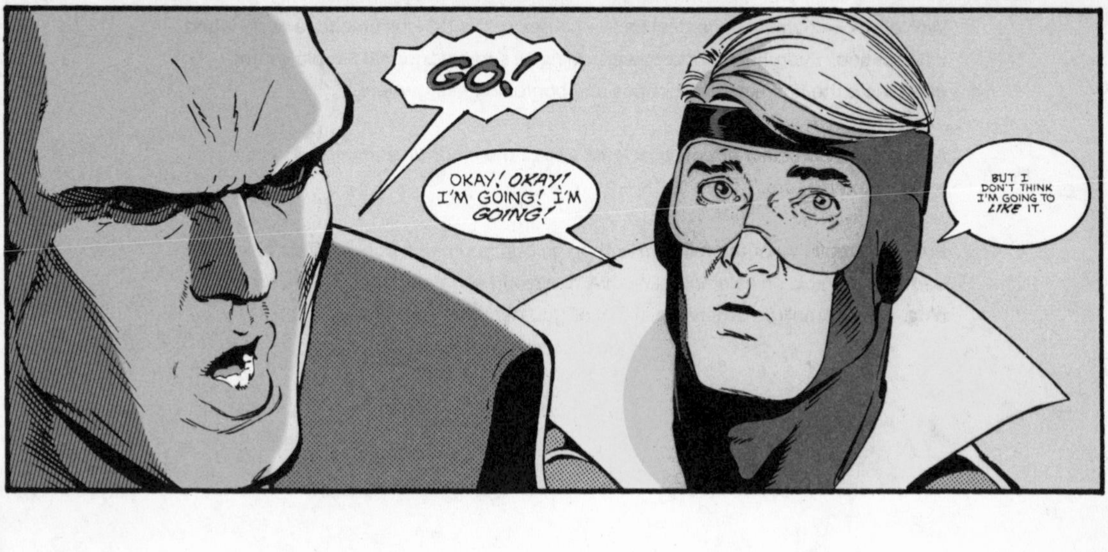
GO!
OKAY! OKAY! I'M GOING! I'M GOING!
BUT I DON'T THINK I'M GOING TO LIKE IT.

JUSTICE LEAGUE INTERNATIONAL

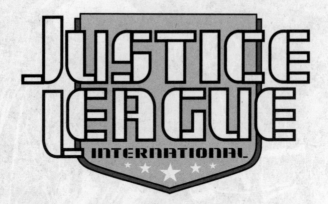

ELSEWHERE...

OK...THAT BLACK ATMOSPHERIC INVERSION YOU JUST SAW? IGNORE IT.

No, seriously.

It was just a "Gene Bomb." No biggie.

Well ok, ok — it was a *huge* deal for the heroes of the DC Universe for a while when it happened. Everyone's superpowers going all screwy...normal people getting abilities for the first time ever...chaos and confusion everywhere...

And it had a particular effect on at least one of the colorful characters in this tome...Maxwell Lord.

But if you really want the full details, then go buy yourself a copy of the INVASION! trade paperback, on sale now. (Yes, we're slightly ashamed of ourselves for that plug. But not really). Otherwise, that's all you need to know — so read on!

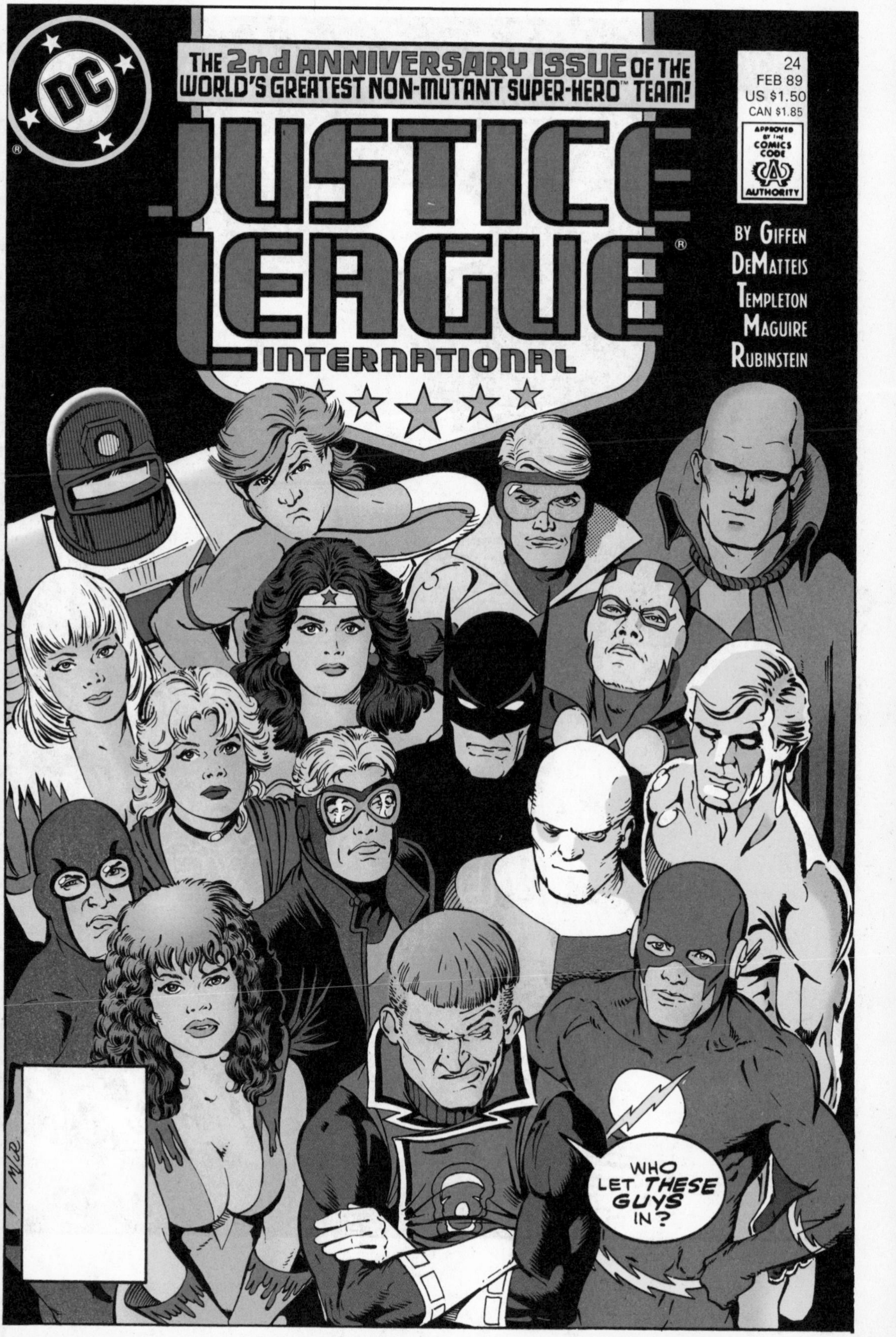
THE 2nd ANNIVERSARY ISSUE OF THE WORLD'S GREATEST NON-MUTANT SUPER-HERO™ TEAM!
24
FEB 89
US $1.50
CAN $1.85
APPROVED BY THE COMICS CODE AUTHORITY
JUSTICE LEAGUE INTERNATIONAL
BY GIFFEN
DEMATTEIS
TEMPLETON
MAGUIRE
RUBINSTEIN
WHO LET THESE GUYS IN?

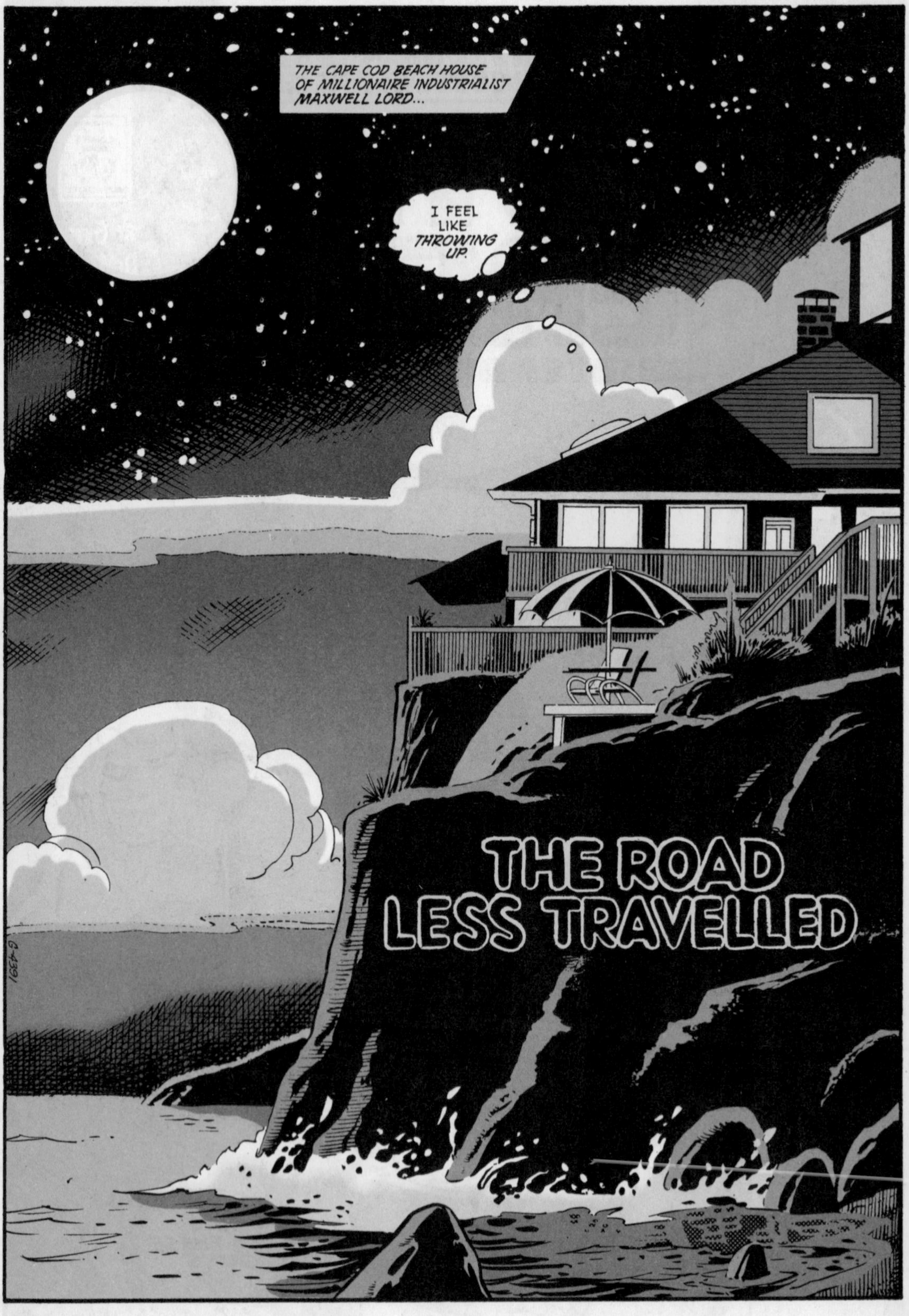
THE CAPE COD BEACH HOUSE OF MILLIONAIRE INDUSTRIALIST MAXWELL LORD...
I FEEL LIKE THROWING UP.
THE ROAD LESS TRAVELLED
G-4391

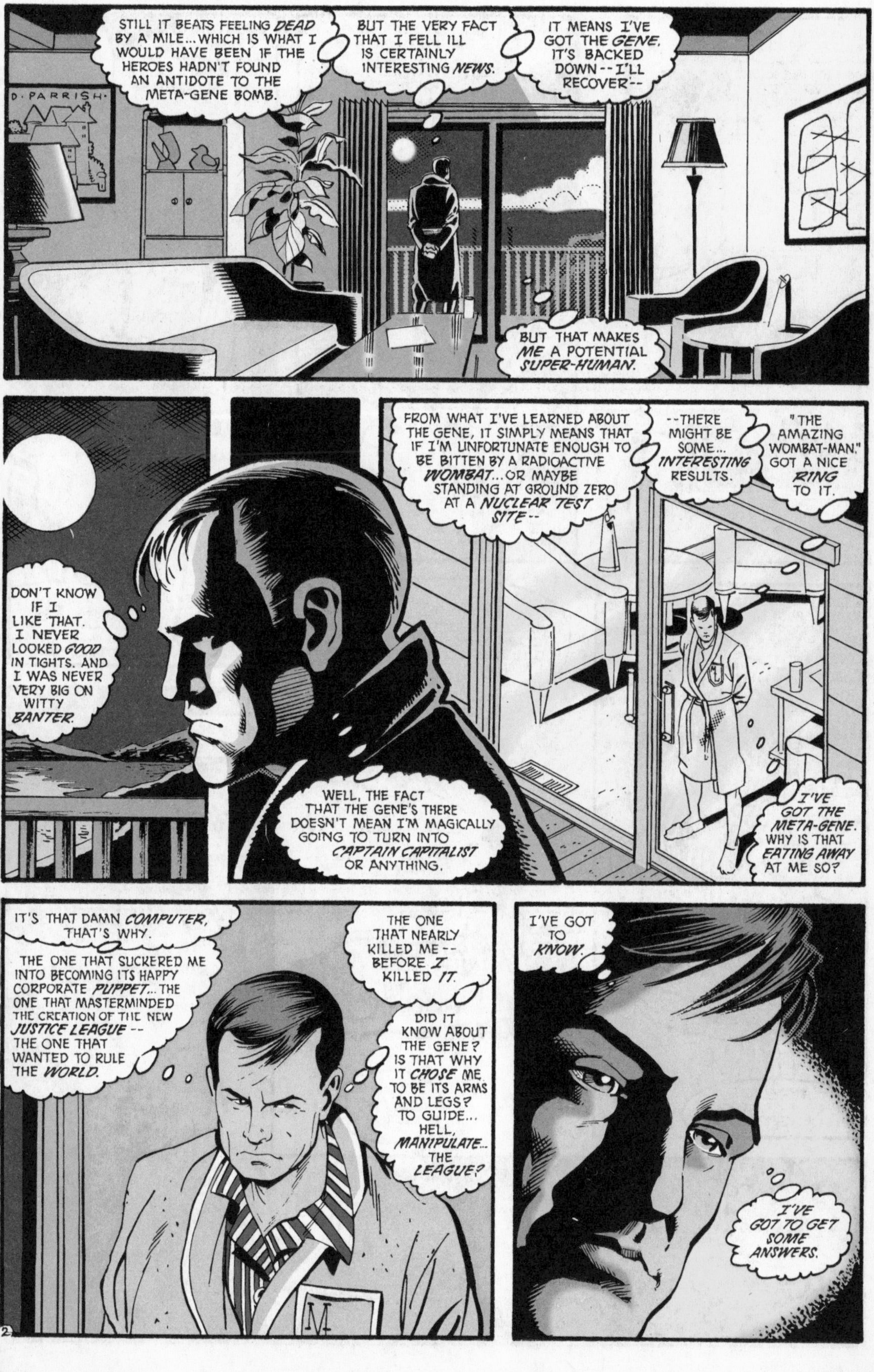
STILL IT BEATS FEELING DEAD BY A MILE... WHICH IS WHAT I WOULD HAVE BEEN IF THE HEROES HADN'T FOUND AN ANTIDOTE TO THE META-GENE BOMB.
BUT THE VERY FACT THAT I FELL ILL IS CERTAINLY INTERESTING NEWS.
IT MEANS I'VE GOT THE GENE. IT'S BACKED DOWN -- I'LL RECOVER--
D. PARRISH
BUT THAT MAKES ME A POTENTIAL SUPER-HUMAN.
DON'T KNOW IF I LIKE THAT. I NEVER LOOKED GOOD IN TIGHTS. AND I WAS NEVER VERY BIG ON WITTY BANTER.
WELL, THE FACT THAT THE GENE'S THERE DOESN'T MEAN I'M MAGICALLY GOING TO TURN INTO CAPTAIN CAPITALIST OR ANYTHING.
FROM WHAT I'VE LEARNED ABOUT THE GENE, IT SIMPLY MEANS THAT IF I'M UNFORTUNATE ENOUGH TO BE BITTEN BY A RADIOACTIVE WOMBAT... OR MAYBE STANDING AT GROUND ZERO AT A NUCLEAR TEST SITE--
--THERE MIGHT BE SOME... INTERESTING RESULTS.
"THE AMAZING WOMBAT-MAN." GOT A NICE RING TO IT.
I'VE GOT THE META-GENE. WHY IS THAT EATING AWAY AT ME SO?
IT'S THAT DAMN COMPUTER, THAT'S WHY.
THE ONE THAT SUCKERED ME INTO BECOMING ITS HAPPY CORPORATE PUPPET... THE ONE THAT MASTERMINDED THE CREATION OF THE NEW JUSTICE LEAGUE -- THE ONE THAT WANTED TO RULE THE WORLD.
THE ONE THAT NEARLY KILLED ME -- BEFORE I KILLED IT.
DID IT KNOW ABOUT THE GENE? IS THAT WHY IT CHOSE ME TO BE ITS ARMS AND LEGS? TO GUIDE... HELL, MANIPULATE... THE LEAGUE?
I'VE GOT TO KNOW.
I'VE GOT TO GET SOME ANSWERS.

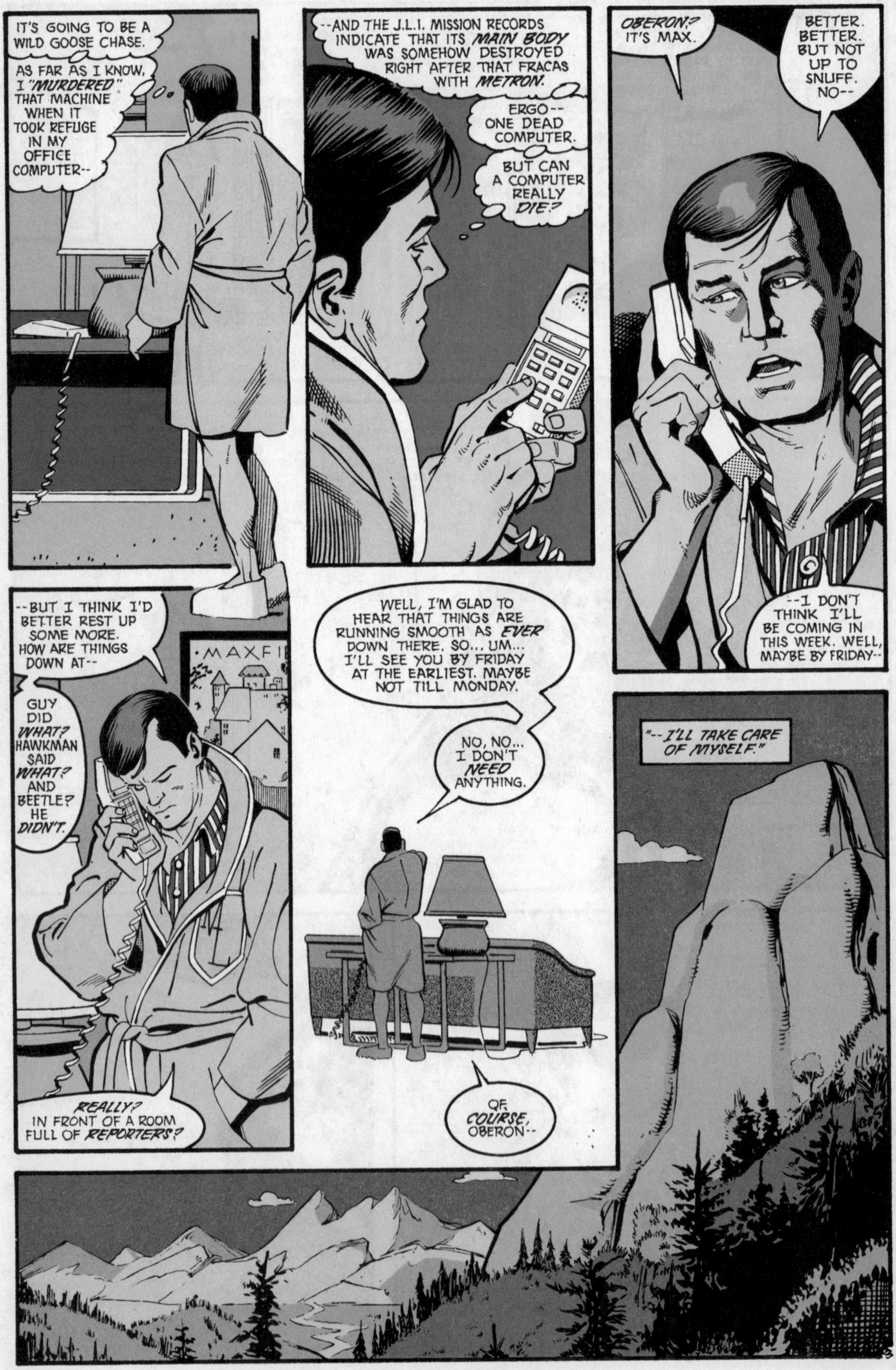
IT'S GOING TO BE A WILD GOOSE CHASE.
AS FAR AS I KNOW, I "MURDERED" THAT MACHINE WHEN IT TOOK REFUGE IN MY OFFICE COMPUTER--
--AND THE J.L.I. MISSION RECORDS INDICATE THAT ITS MAIN BODY WAS SOMEHOW DESTROYED RIGHT AFTER THAT FRACAS WITH METRON.
ERGO-- ONE DEAD COMPUTER.
BUT CAN A COMPUTER REALLY DIE?
OBERON? IT'S MAX.
BETTER. BETTER. BUT NOT UP TO SNUFF. NO--
--I DON'T THINK I'LL BE COMING IN THIS WEEK. WELL, MAYBE BY FRIDAY--
--BUT I THINK I'D BETTER REST UP SOME MORE. HOW ARE THINGS DOWN AT--
GUY DID WHAT? HAWKMAN SAID WHAT? AND BEETLE? HE DIDN'T.
REALLY? IN FRONT OF A ROOM FULL OF REPORTERS?
WELL, I'M GLAD TO HEAR THAT THINGS ARE RUNNING SMOOTH AS EVER DOWN THERE. SO... UM... I'LL SEE YOU BY FRIDAY AT THE EARLIEST. MAYBE NOT TILL MONDAY.
NO, NO... I DON'T NEED ANYTHING.
OF COURSE, OBERON--
"--I'LL TAKE CARE OF MYSELF."

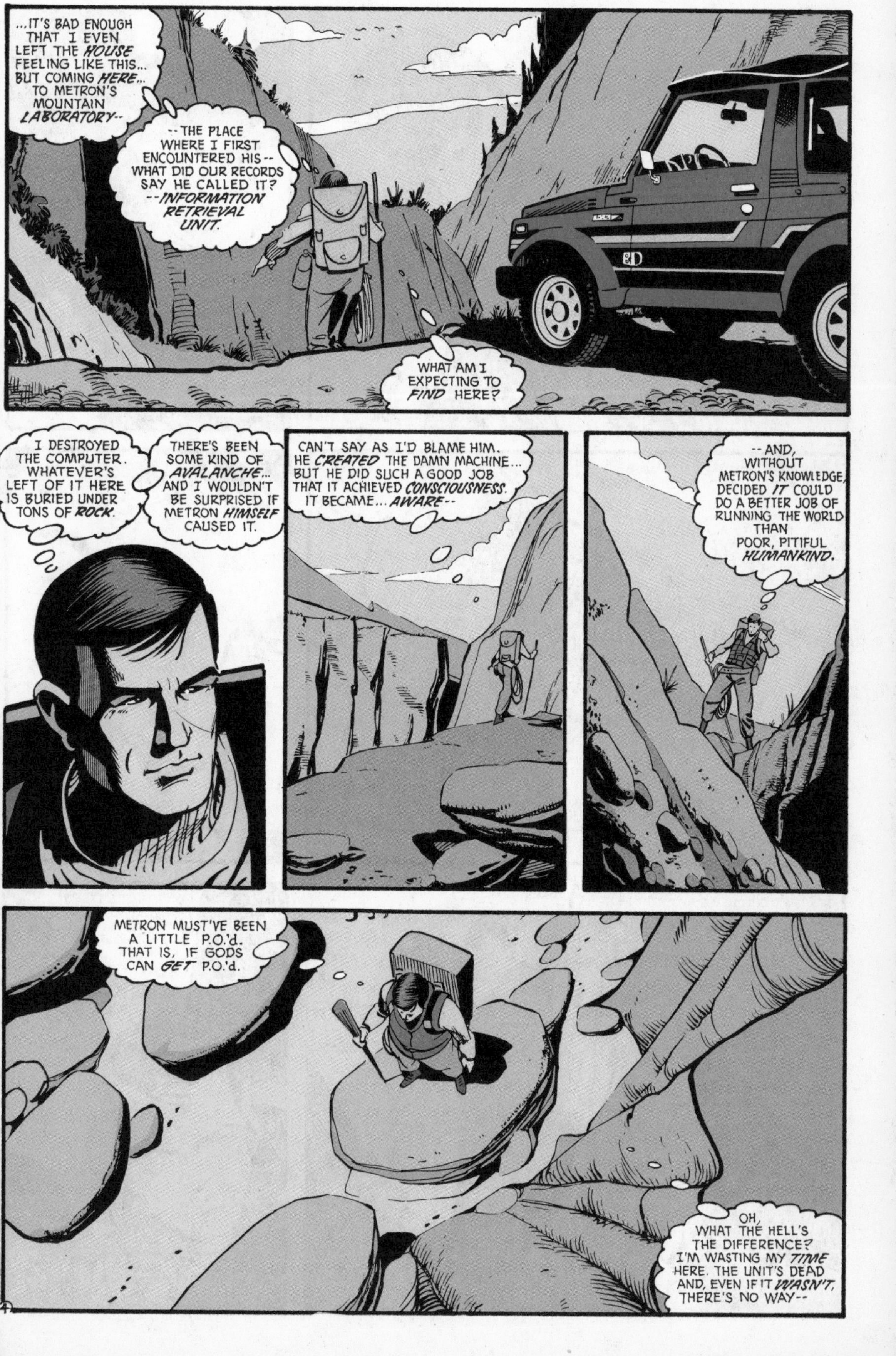
...IT'S BAD ENOUGH THAT I EVEN LEFT THE HOUSE FEELING LIKE THIS... BUT COMING HERE... TO METRON'S MOUNTAIN LABORATORY--
--THE PLACE WHERE I FIRST ENCOUNTERED HIS-- WHAT DID OUR RECORDS SAY HE CALLED IT? --INFORMATION RETRIEVAL UNIT.
WHAT AM I EXPECTING TO FIND HERE?
I DESTROYED THE COMPUTER. WHATEVER'S LEFT OF IT HERE IS BURIED UNDER TONS OF ROCK.
THERE'S BEEN SOME KIND OF AVALANCHE... AND I WOULDN'T BE SURPRISED IF METRON HIMSELF CAUSED IT.
CAN'T SAY AS I'D BLAME HIM. HE CREATED THE DAMN MACHINE... BUT HE DID SUCH A GOOD JOB THAT IT ACHIEVED CONSCIOUSNESS. IT BECAME... AWARE--
--AND, WITHOUT METRON'S KNOWLEDGE, DECIDED IT COULD DO A BETTER JOB OF RUNNING THE WORLD THAN POOR, PITIFUL HUMANKIND.
METRON MUST'VE BEEN A LITTLE P.O.'d. THAT IS, IF GODS CAN GET P.O.'d.
OH, WHAT THE HELL'S THE DIFFERENCE? I'M WASTING MY TIME HERE. THE UNIT'S DEAD AND, EVEN IF IT WASN'T, THERE'S NO WAY--

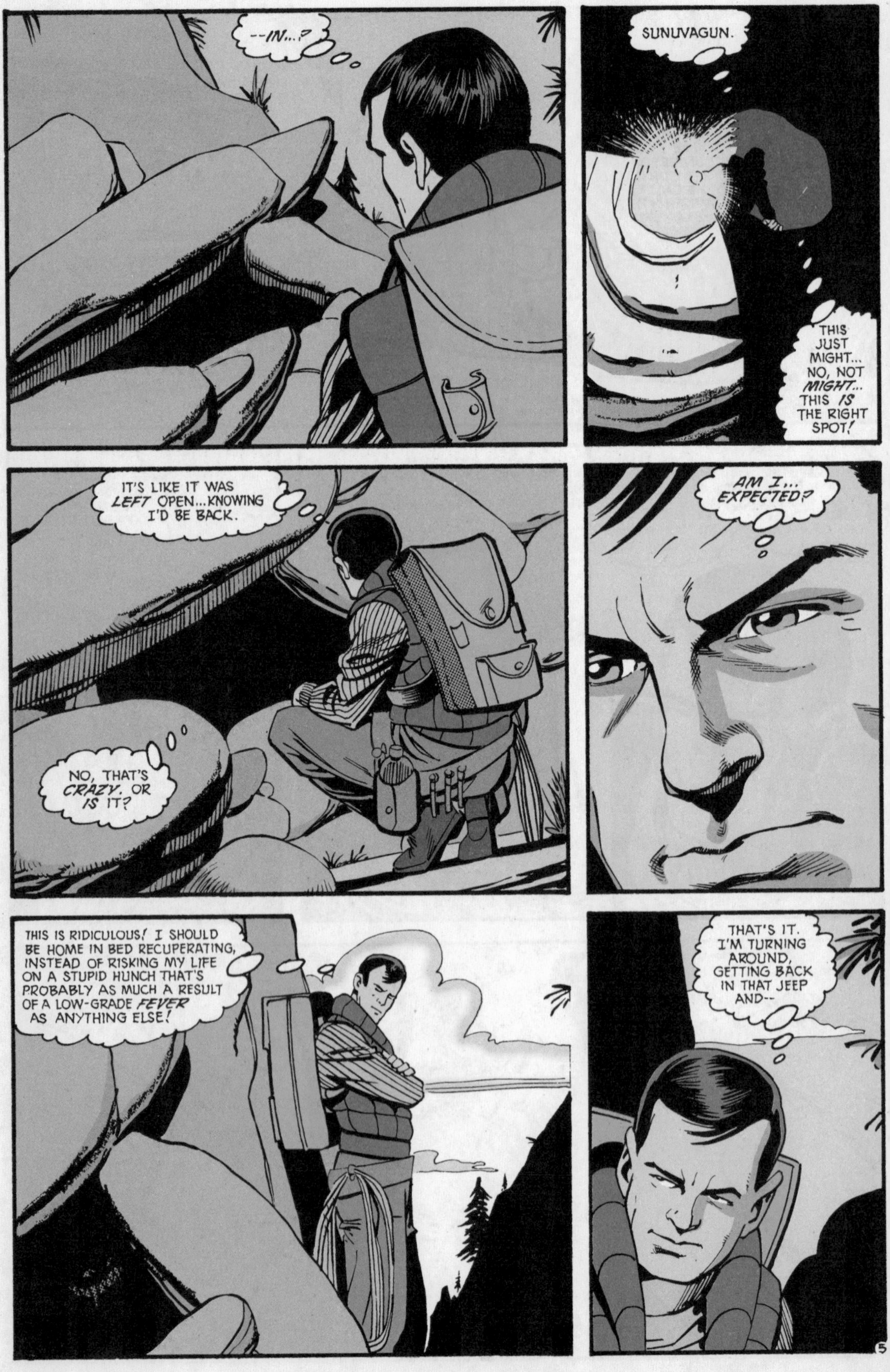
--IN...?
SUNUVAGUN.
THIS JUST MIGHT... NO, NOT MIGHT... THIS IS THE RIGHT SPOT!
IT'S LIKE IT WAS LEFT OPEN...KNOWING I'D BE BACK.
NO, THAT'S CRAZY. OR IS IT?
AM I... EXPECTED?
THIS IS RIDICULOUS! I SHOULD BE HOME IN BED RECUPERATING, INSTEAD OF RISKING MY LIFE ON A STUPID HUNCH THAT'S PROBABLY AS MUCH A RESULT OF A LOW-GRADE FEVER AS ANYTHING ELSE!
THAT'S IT. I'M TURNING AROUND, GETTING BACK IN THAT JEEP AND--
5

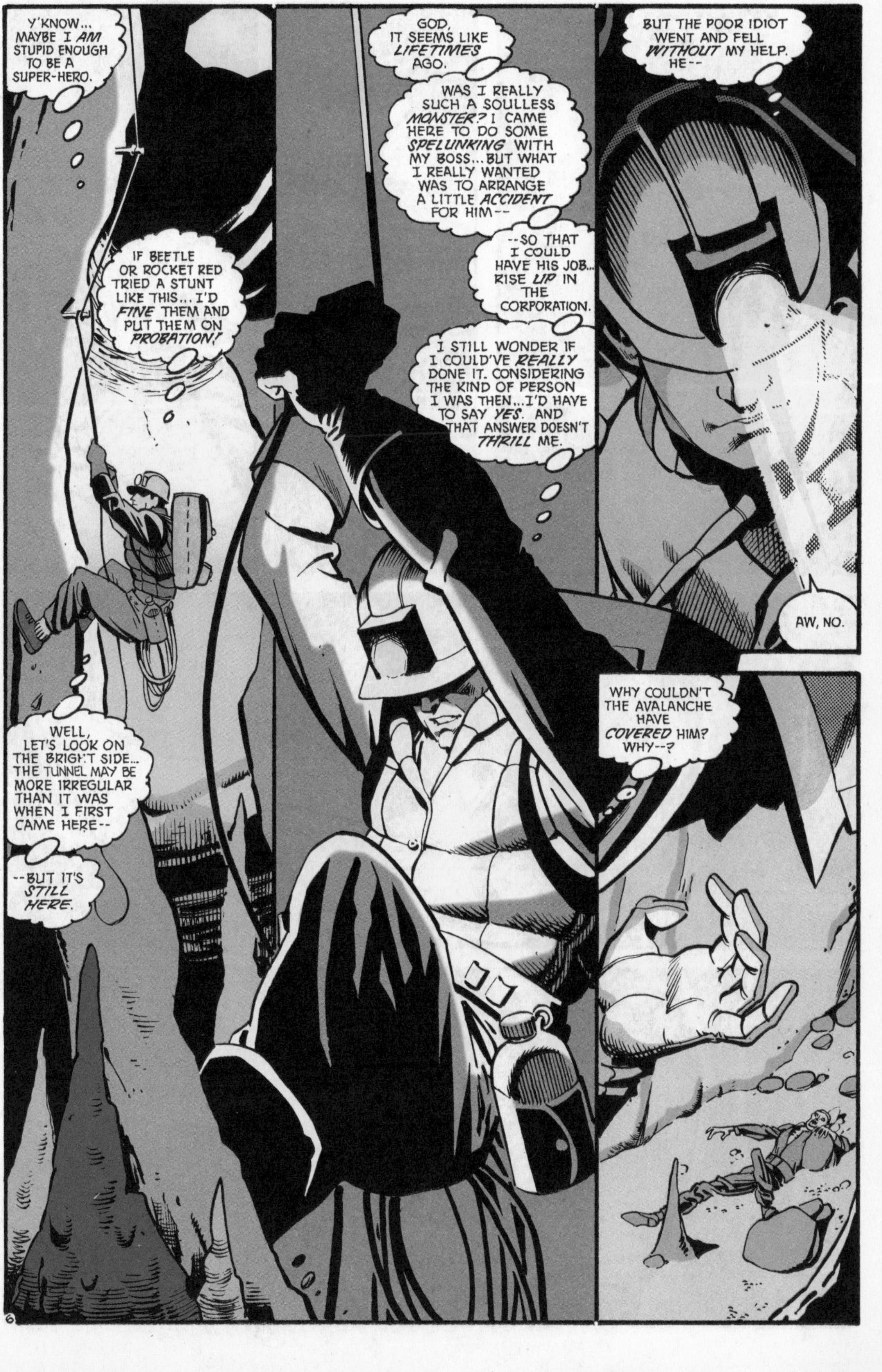
Y'KNOW... MAYBE I AM STUPID ENOUGH TO BE A SUPER-HERO.
IF BEETLE OR ROCKET RED TRIED A STUNT LIKE THIS... I'D FINE THEM AND PUT THEM ON PROBATION!
WELL, LET'S LOOK ON THE BRIGHT SIDE... THE TUNNEL MAY BE MORE IRREGULAR THAN IT WAS WHEN I FIRST CAME HERE--
--BUT IT'S STILL HERE.
GOD, IT SEEMS LIKE LIFETIMES AGO.
WAS I REALLY SUCH A SOULLESS MONSTER? I CAME HERE TO DO SOME SPELUNKING WITH MY BOSS... BUT WHAT I REALLY WANTED WAS TO ARRANGE A LITTLE ACCIDENT FOR HIM--
--SO THAT I COULD HAVE HIS JOB... RISE UP IN THE CORPORATION.
I STILL WONDER IF I COULD'VE REALLY DONE IT. CONSIDERING THE KIND OF PERSON I WAS THEN...I'D HAVE TO SAY YES. AND THAT ANSWER DOESN'T THRILL ME.
BUT THE POOR IDIOT WENT AND FELL WITHOUT MY HELP. HE--
AW, NO.
WHY COULDN'T THE AVALANCHE HAVE COVERED HIM? WHY--?
6

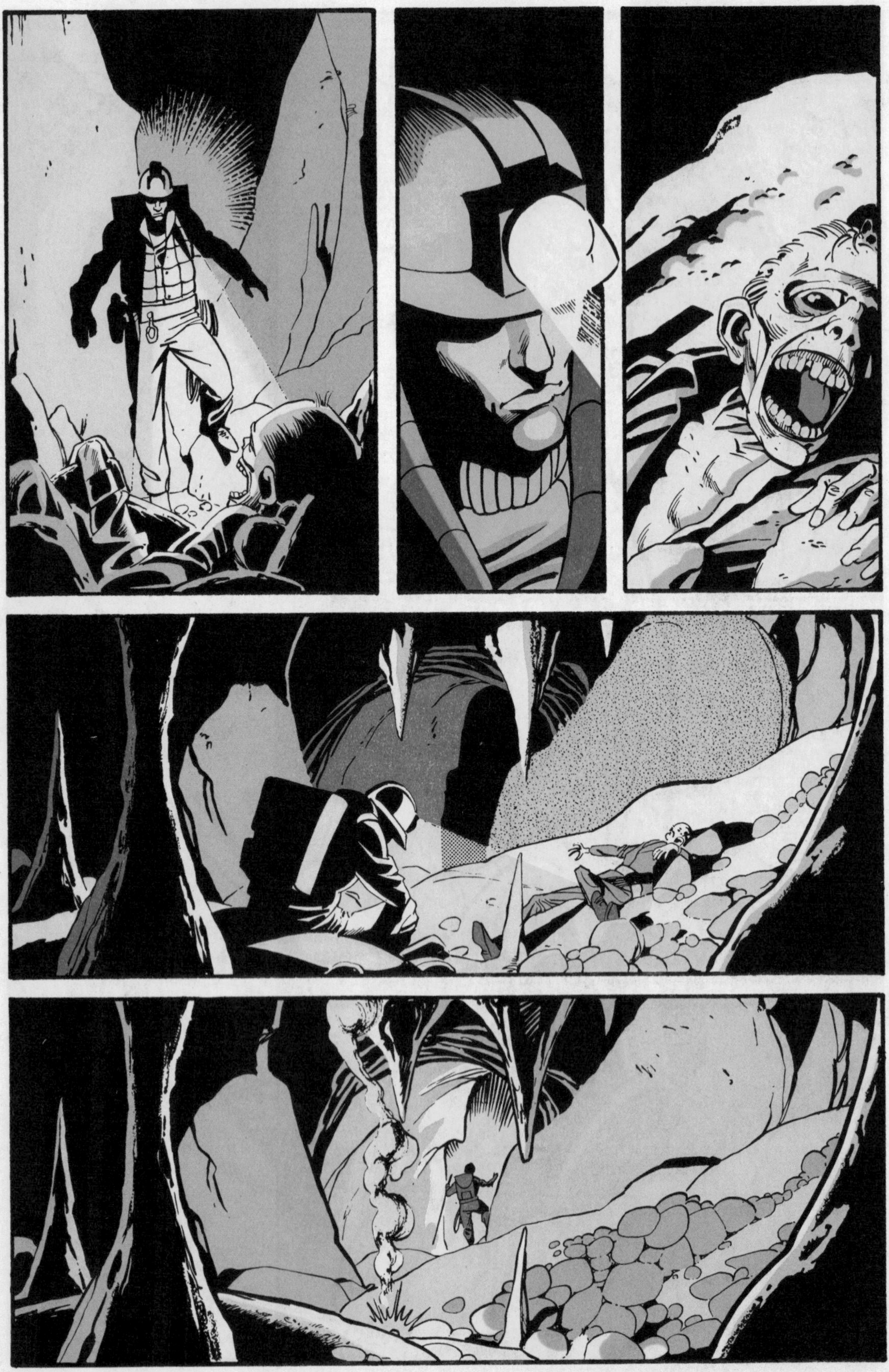

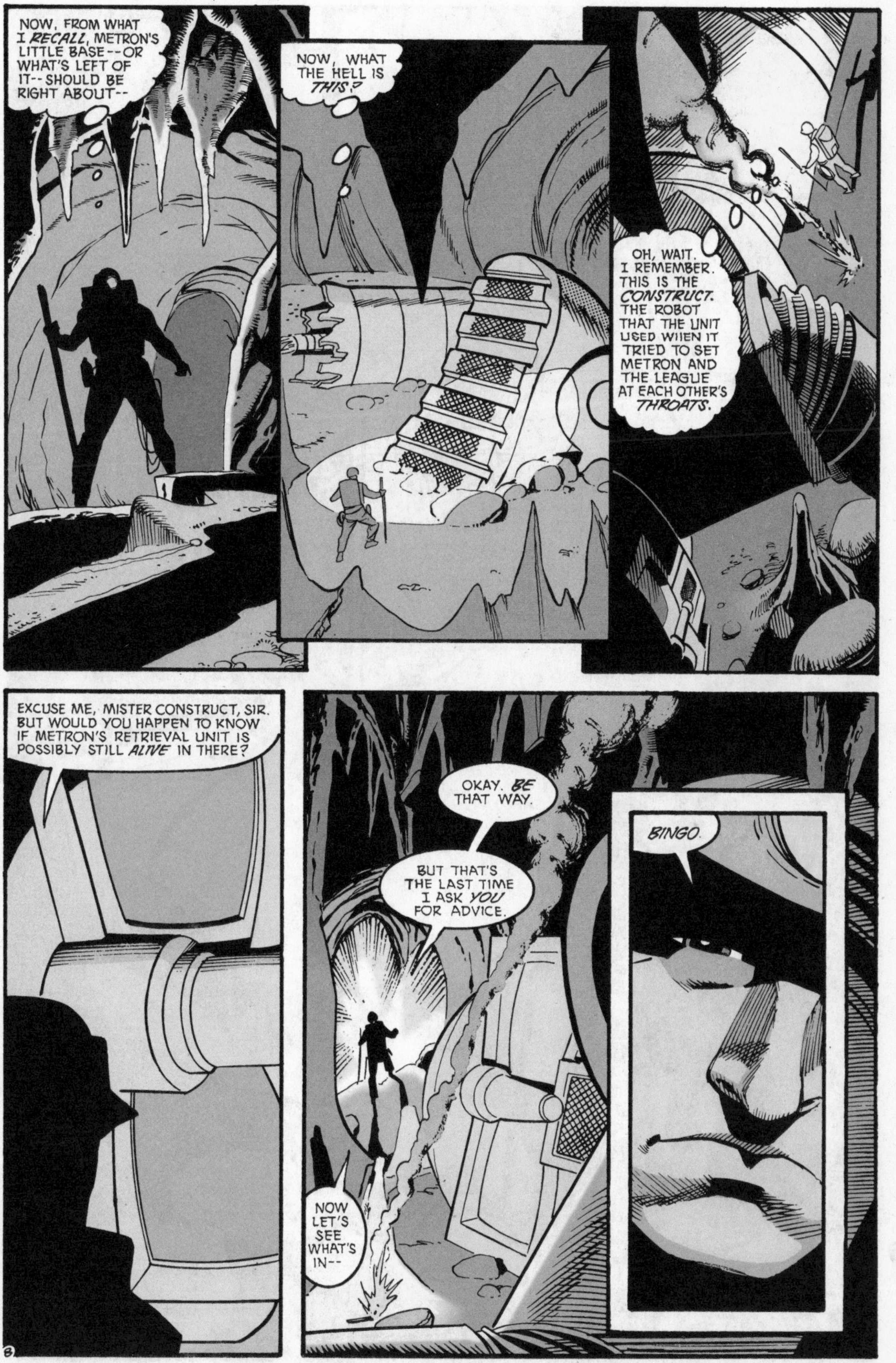
NOW, FROM WHAT I RECALL, METRON'S LITTLE BASE--OR WHAT'S LEFT OF IT--SHOULD BE RIGHT ABOUT--
NOW, WHAT THE HELL IS THIS?
OH, WAIT. I REMEMBER. THIS IS THE CONSTRUCT. THE ROBOT THAT THE UNIT USED WHEN IT TRIED TO SET METRON AND THE LEAGUE AT EACH OTHER'S THROATS.
EXCUSE ME, MISTER CONSTRUCT, SIR. BUT WOULD YOU HAPPEN TO KNOW IF METRON'S RETRIEVAL UNIT IS POSSIBLY STILL ALIVE IN THERE?
OKAY. BE THAT WAY.
BUT THAT'S THE LAST TIME I ASK YOU FOR ADVICE.
NOW LET'S SEE WHAT'S IN--
BINGO.
8

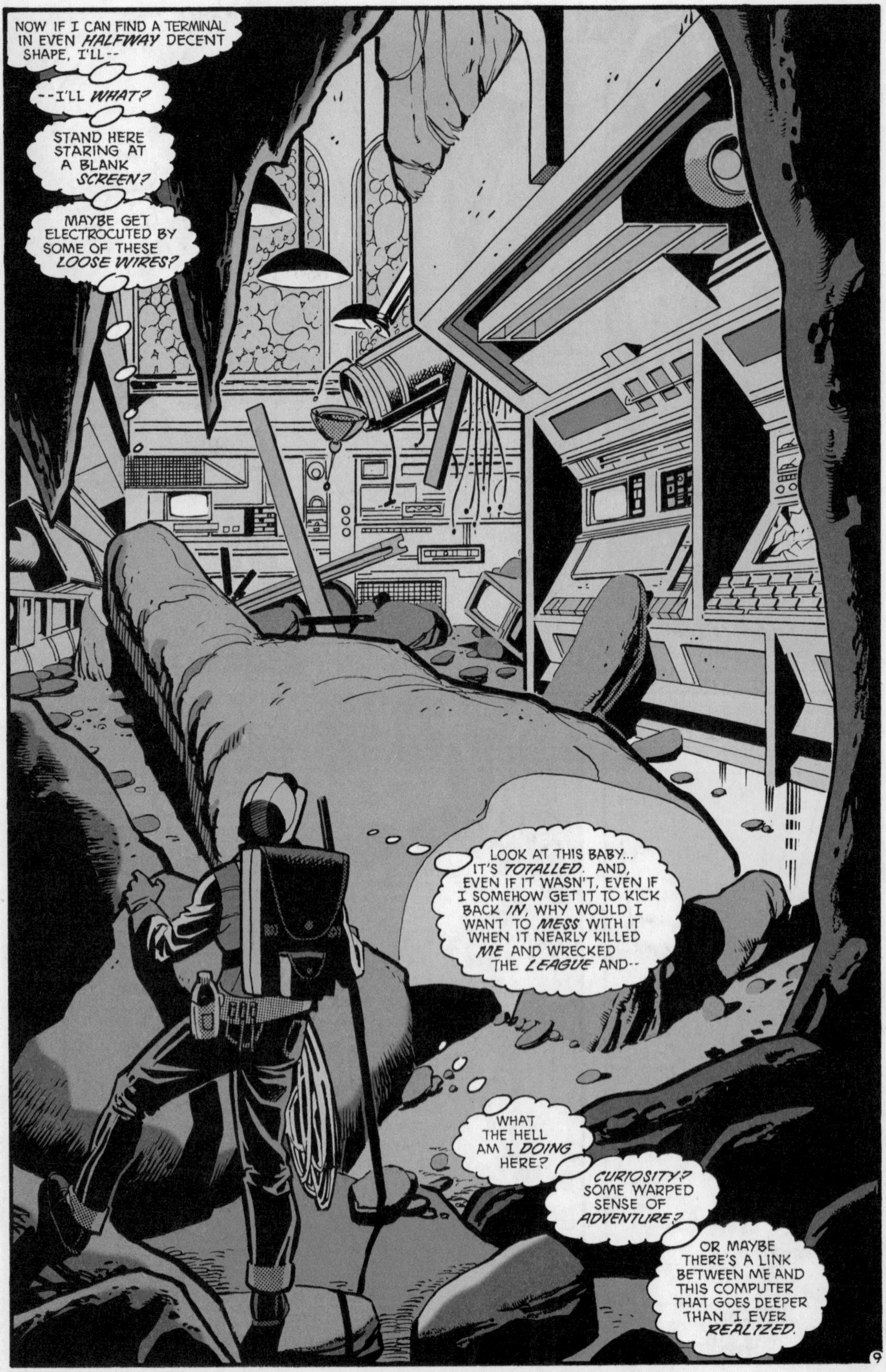
NOW IF I CAN FIND A TERMINAL IN EVEN HALFWAY DECENT SHAPE, I'LL--
--I'LL WHAT?
STAND HERE STARING AT A BLANK SCREEN?
MAYBE GET ELECTROCUTED BY SOME OF THESE LOOSE WIRES?
LOOK AT THIS BABY... IT'S TOTALLED. AND, EVEN IF IT WASN'T, EVEN IF I SOMEHOW GET IT TO KICK BACK IN, WHY WOULD I WANT TO MESS WITH IT WHEN IT NEARLY KILLED ME AND WRECKED THE LEAGUE AND--
WHAT THE HELL AM I DOING HERE?
CURIOSITY? SOME WARPED SENSE OF ADVENTURE?
OR MAYBE THERE'S A LINK BETWEEN ME AND THIS COMPUTER THAT GOES DEEPER THAN I EVER REALIZED.
9

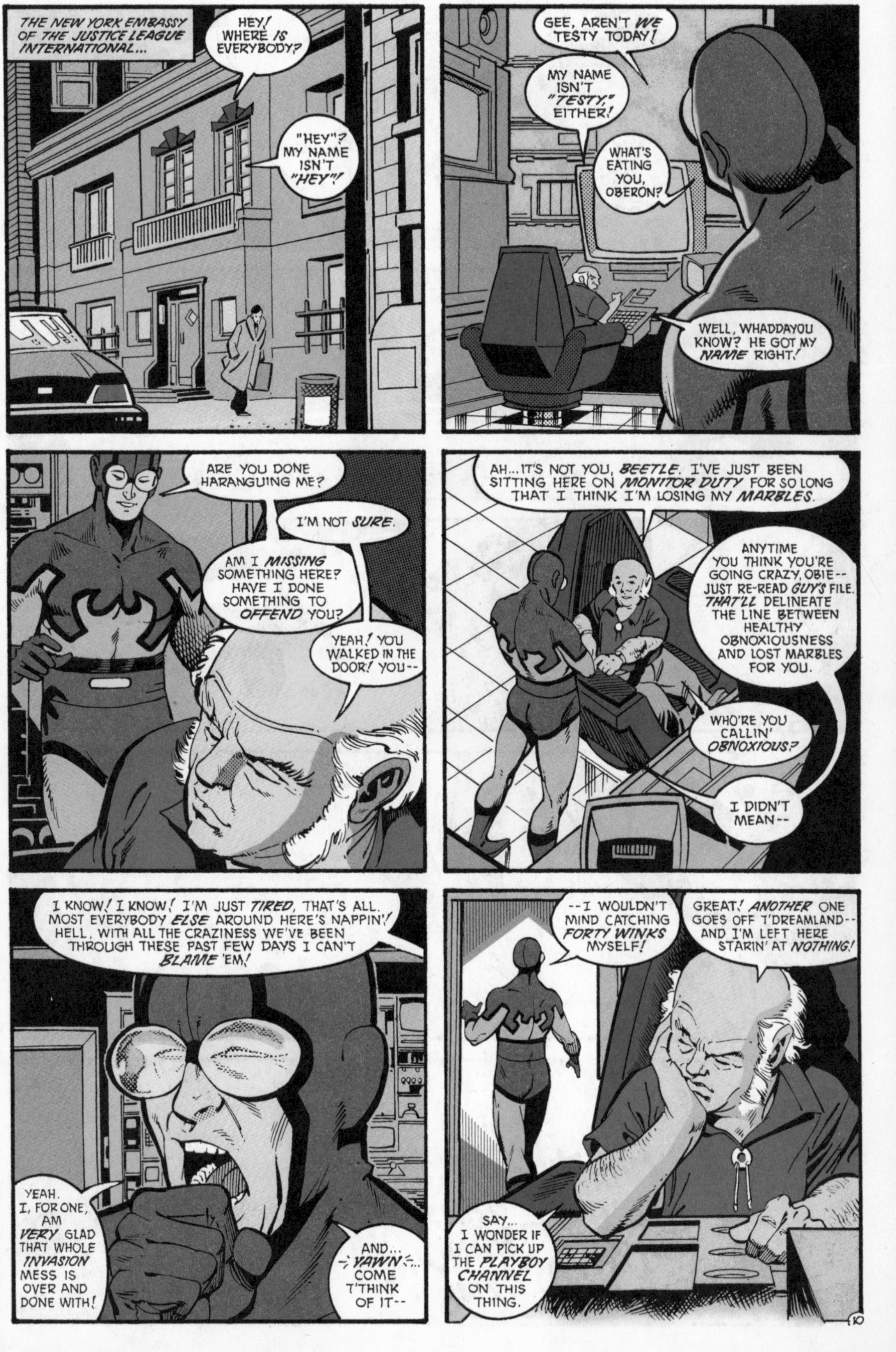
THE NEW YORK EMBASSY OF THE JUSTICE LEAGUE INTERNATIONAL...
HEY! WHERE IS EVERYBODY?
"HEY"? MY NAME ISN'T "HEY"!
GEE, AREN'T WE TESTY TODAY!
MY NAME ISN'T "TESTY," EITHER!
WHAT'S EATING YOU, OBERON?
WELL, WHADDAYOU KNOW? HE GOT MY NAME RIGHT!
ARE YOU DONE HARANGUING ME?
I'M NOT SURE.
AM I MISSING SOMETHING HERE? HAVE I DONE SOMETHING TO OFFEND YOU?
YEAH! YOU WALKED IN THE DOOR! YOU--
AH...IT'S NOT YOU, BEETLE. I'VE JUST BEEN SITTING HERE ON MONITOR DUTY FOR SO LONG THAT I THINK I'M LOSING MY MARBLES.
ANYTIME YOU THINK YOU'RE GOING CRAZY, OBIE-- JUST RE-READ GUY'S FILE. THAT'LL DELINEATE THE LINE BETWEEN HEALTHY OBNOXIOUSNESS AND LOST MARBLES FOR YOU.
WHO'RE YOU CALLIN' OBNOXIOUS?
I DIDN'T MEAN--
I KNOW! I KNOW! I'M JUST TIRED, THAT'S ALL. MOST EVERYBODY ELSE AROUND HERE'S NAPPIN'! HELL, WITH ALL THE CRAZINESS WE'VE BEEN THROUGH THESE PAST FEW DAYS I CAN'T BLAME 'EM!
YEAH. I, FOR ONE, AM VERY GLAD THAT WHOLE INVASION MESS IS OVER AND DONE WITH!
AND... YAWN... COME T'THINK OF IT--
--I WOULDN'T MIND CATCHING FORTY WINKS MYSELF!
GREAT! ANOTHER ONE GOES OFF T'DREAMLAND-- AND I'M LEFT HERE STARIN' AT NOTHING!
SAY... I WONDER IF I CAN PICK UP THE PLAYBOY CHANNEL ON THIS THING.
10

...WELL, WHAT DID I *EXPECT?*

THE CIRCUITRY'S SHOT TO HELL. I DON'T THINK METRON HIMSELF COULD BRING THIS SUCKER BACK FROM THE *DEAD.*

BUT--LET'S SEE WHAT MAXWELL LORD-- WITH A LITTLE HELP FROM THE *PORTA-POWER-SOURCE* HE BROUGHT ALONG-- CAN DO...

COMPUTER: COME--

--FORTH *YEOW!*

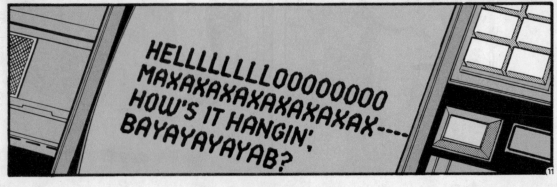

HELLLLLLLLOOOOOOOO MAXAXAXAXAXAXAX---- HOW'S IT HANGIN' BAYAYAYAYAB?

11

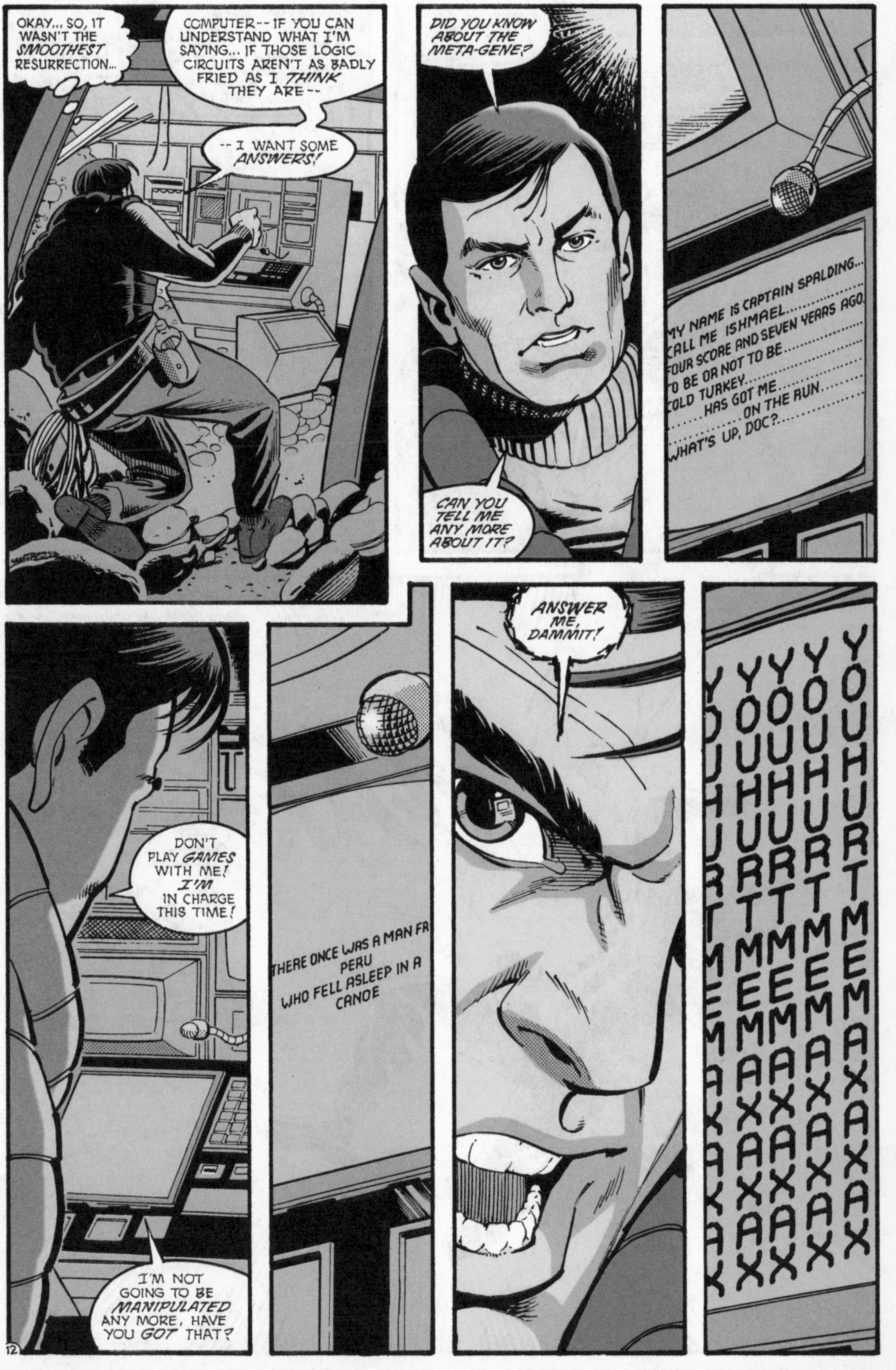

OKAY... SO, IT WASN'T THE SMOOTHEST RESURRECTION...
COMPUTER-- IF YOU CAN UNDERSTAND WHAT I'M SAYING... IF THOSE LOGIC CIRCUITS AREN'T AS BADLY FRIED AS I THINK THEY ARE--
-- I WANT SOME ANSWERS!
DID YOU KNOW ABOUT THE META-GENE?
CAN YOU TELL ME ANY MORE ABOUT IT?
MY NAME IS CAPTAIN SPALDING...
CALL ME ISHMAEL...
FOUR SCORE AND SEVEN YEARS AGO...
TO BE OR NOT TO BE...
COLD TURKEY...
...HAS GOT ME...
...ON THE RUN...
WHAT'S UP, DOC?...
DON'T PLAY GAMES WITH ME! I'M IN CHARGE THIS TIME!
I'M NOT GOING TO BE MANIPULATED ANY MORE, HAVE YOU GOT THAT?
12
THERE ONCE WAS A MAN FR
PERU
WHO FELL ASLEEP IN A
CANOE
ANSWER ME, DAMMIT!
YOUHURTMEMAXAX
YOUHURTMEMAXAX
YOUHURTMEMAXAX
YOUHURTMEMAXAX
YOUHURTMEMAXAX

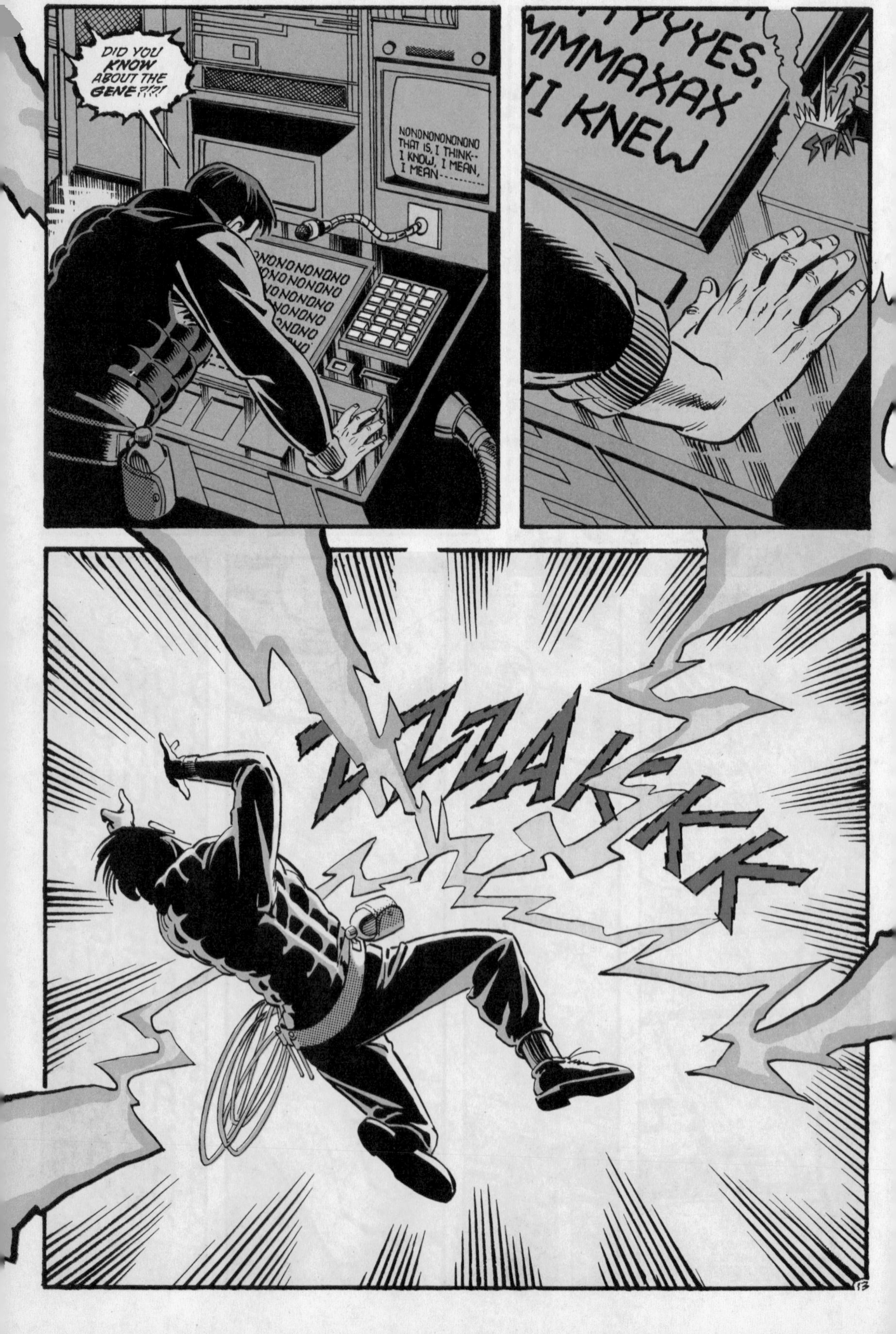
DID YOU KNOW ABOUT THE GENE?!?!
NONONONONONONO THAT IS, I THINK-- I KNOW, I MEAN, I MEAN
YYYES, MMMAXAX I KNEW
ZZZAKKK

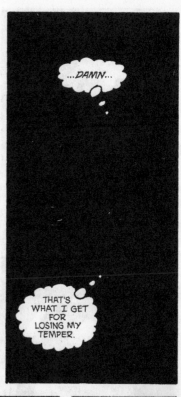

...DAMN...

THAT'S WHAT I GET FOR LOSING MY TEMPER.

COMPUTER BLEW ITSELF OUT JUST TO GET AT ME.

WELL, LET'S LOOK AT THE BRIGHT SIDE. IT COULD'VE KILLED ME. AS IT IS, I WAS ONLY UNCONSCIOUS FOR... LET'S SEE... FIVE HOURS...

OTHER THAN THAT, I'M PERFECTLY FINE...EXCEPT THAT I'M BLEEDING AND NAUSEOUS AND MAYBE I'VE GOT A CONCUSSION...

OH, YEAH--AND THERE IS THE LITTLE MATTER OF MY BEING--

--SEALED IN.

14.

45

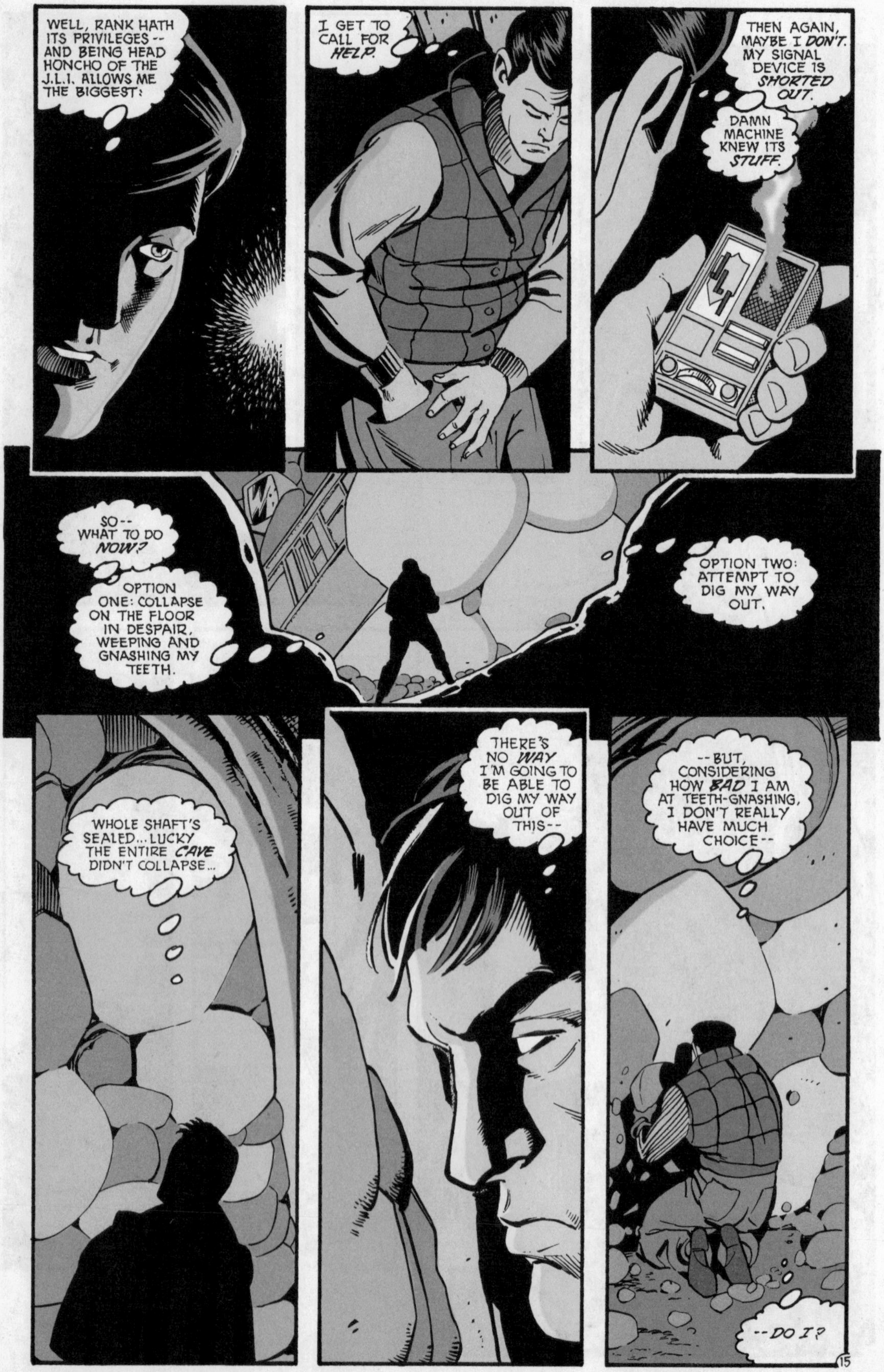
WELL, RANK HATH ITS PRIVILEGES -- AND BEING HEAD HONCHO OF THE J.L.I. ALLOWS ME THE BIGGEST:
I GET TO CALL FOR HELP.
THEN AGAIN, MAYBE I DON'T. MY SIGNAL DEVICE IS SHORTED OUT.
DAMN MACHINE KNEW ITS STUFF.
SO -- WHAT TO DO NOW?
OPTION ONE: COLLAPSE ON THE FLOOR IN DESPAIR, WEEPING AND GNASHING MY TEETH.
OPTION TWO: ATTEMPT TO DIG MY WAY OUT.
WHOLE SHAFT'S SEALED... LUCKY THE ENTIRE CAVE DIDN'T COLLAPSE...
THERE'S NO WAY I'M GOING TO BE ABLE TO DIG MY WAY OUT OF THIS--
--BUT, CONSIDERING HOW BAD I AM AT TEETH-GNASHING, I DON'T REALLY HAVE MUCH CHOICE--
--DO I?
15

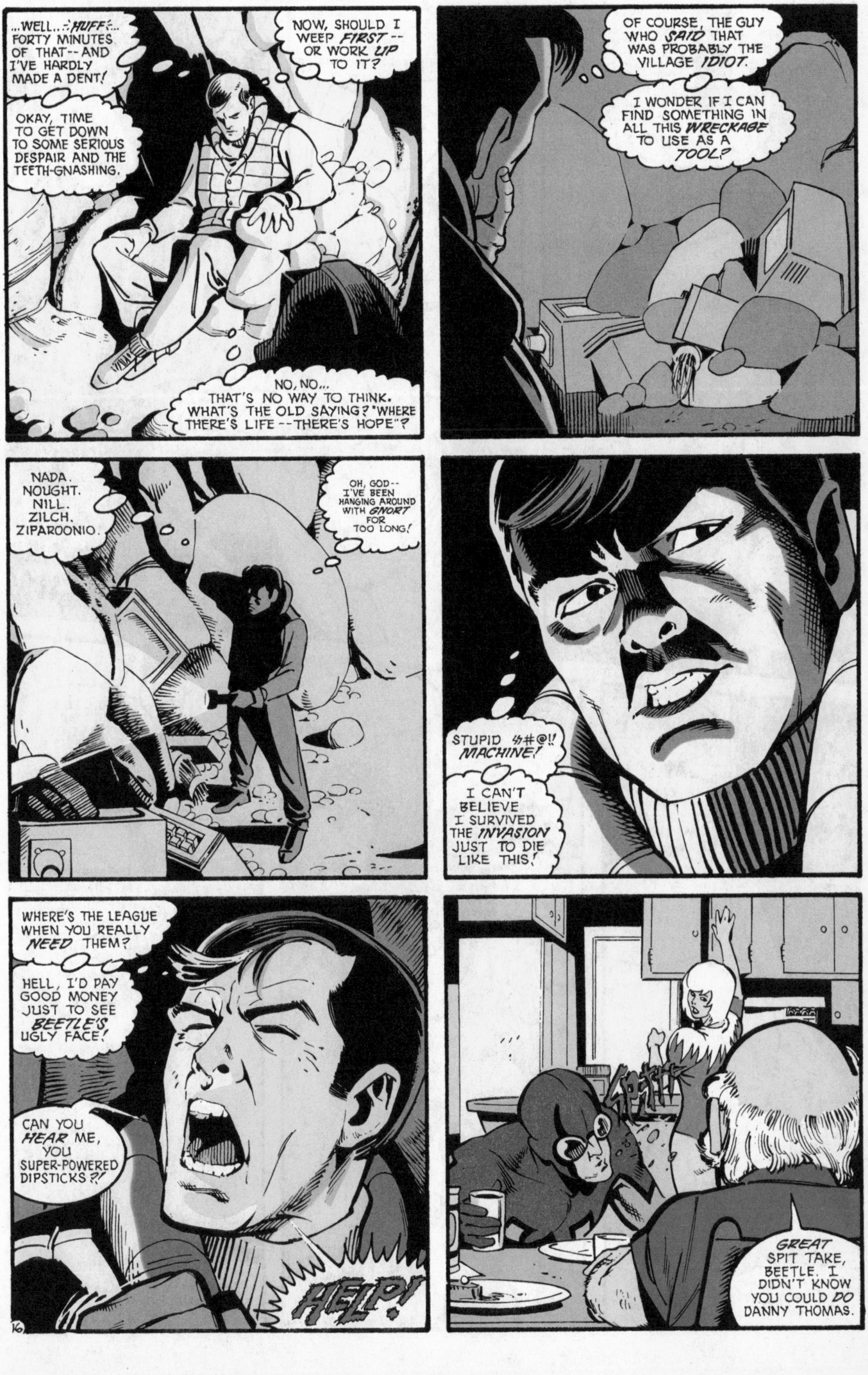
...WELL...HUFF... FORTY MINUTES OF THAT--AND I'VE HARDLY MADE A DENT!
OKAY, TIME TO GET DOWN TO SOME SERIOUS DESPAIR AND THE TEETH-GNASHING.
NOW, SHOULD I WEEP FIRST--OR WORK UP TO IT?
NO, NO... THAT'S NO WAY TO THINK. WHAT'S THE OLD SAYING? "WHERE THERE'S LIFE--THERE'S HOPE"?
OF COURSE, THE GUY WHO SAID THAT WAS PROBABLY THE VILLAGE IDIOT.
I WONDER IF I CAN FIND SOMETHING IN ALL THIS WRECKAGE TO USE AS A TOOL?
NADA. NOUGHT. NILL. ZILCH. ZIPAROONIO.
OH, GOD--I'VE BEEN HANGING AROUND WITH GNORT FOR TOO LONG!
STUPID $#@!! MACHINE!
I CAN'T BELIEVE I SURVIVED THE INVASION JUST TO DIE LIKE THIS!
WHERE'S THE LEAGUE WHEN YOU REALLY NEED THEM?
HELL, I'D PAY GOOD MONEY JUST TO SEE BEETLE'S UGLY FACE!
CAN YOU HEAR ME, YOU SUPER-POWERED DIPSTICKS?!
HELP!
16
GREAT SPIT TAKE, BEETLE. I DIDN'T KNOW YOU COULD DO DANNY THOMAS.

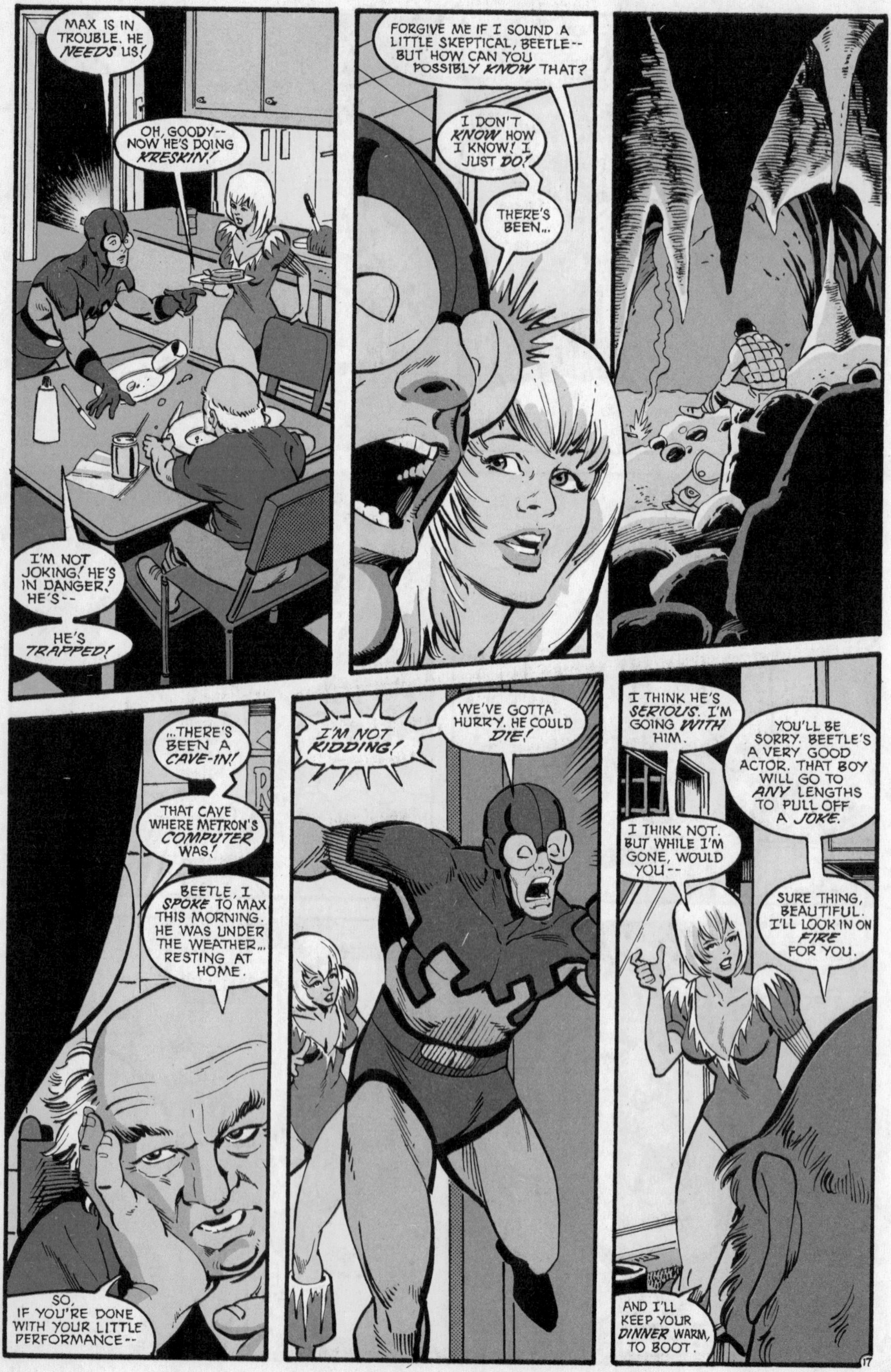
MAX IS IN TROUBLE. HE NEEDS US!
OH, GOODY-- NOW HE'S DOING KRESKIN!
I'M NOT JOKING! HE'S IN DANGER! HE'S--
HE'S TRAPPED!
FORGIVE ME IF I SOUND A LITTLE SKEPTICAL, BEETLE-- BUT HOW CAN YOU POSSIBLY KNOW THAT?
I DON'T KNOW HOW I KNOW! I JUST DO!
THERE'S BEEN...
...THERE'S BEEN A CAVE-IN!
THAT CAVE WHERE METRON'S COMPUTER WAS!
BEETLE, I SPOKE TO MAX THIS MORNING. HE WAS UNDER THE WEATHER... RESTING AT HOME.
SO, IF YOU'RE DONE WITH YOUR LITTLE PERFORMANCE--
I'M NOT KIDDING!
WE'VE GOTTA HURRY. HE COULD DIE!
I THINK HE'S SERIOUS. I'M GOING WITH HIM.
YOU'LL BE SORRY. BEETLE'S A VERY GOOD ACTOR. THAT BOY WILL GO TO ANY LENGTHS TO PULL OFF A JOKE.
I THINK NOT. BUT WHILE I'M GONE, WOULD YOU--
SURE THING, BEAUTIFUL. I'LL LOOK IN ON FIRE FOR YOU.
AND I'LL KEEP YOUR DINNER WARM, TO BOOT.
17

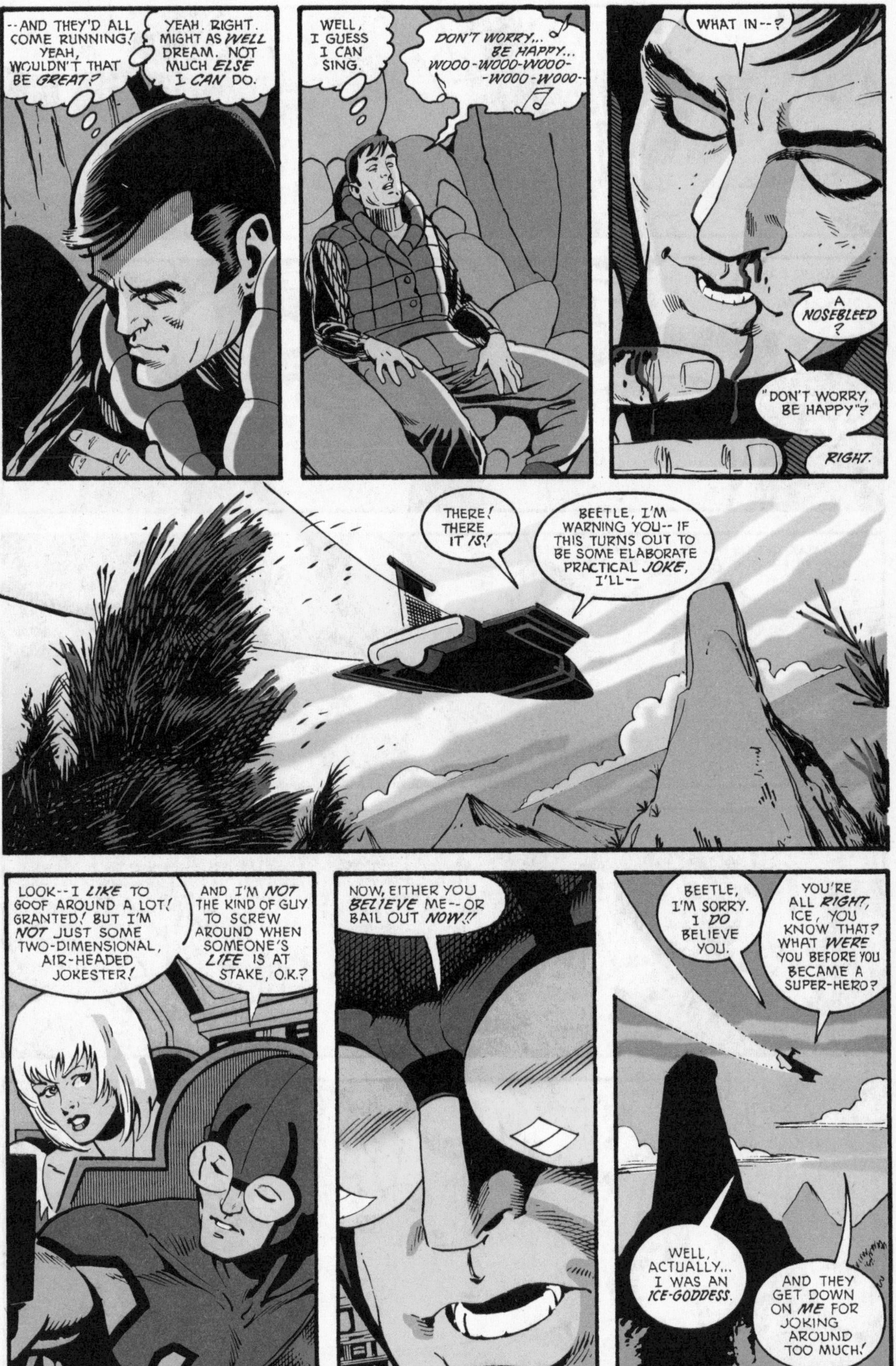
--AND THEY'D ALL COME RUNNING! YEAH, WOULDN'T THAT BE GREAT?
YEAH. RIGHT. MIGHT AS WELL DREAM. NOT MUCH ELSE I CAN DO.
WELL, I GUESS I CAN SING.
DON'T WORRY... BE HAPPY... WOOO-WOOO-WOOO- -WOOO-WOOO--
WHAT IN--?
A NOSEBLEED?
"DON'T WORRY, BE HAPPY"?
RIGHT.
THERE! THERE IT IS!
BEETLE, I'M WARNING YOU-- IF THIS TURNS OUT TO BE SOME ELABORATE PRACTICAL JOKE, I'LL--
LOOK--I LIKE TO GOOF AROUND A LOT! GRANTED! BUT I'M NOT JUST SOME TWO-DIMENSIONAL, AIR-HEADED JOKESTER!
AND I'M NOT THE KIND OF GUY TO SCREW AROUND WHEN SOMEONE'S LIFE IS AT STAKE, O.K.?
18
NOW, EITHER YOU BELIEVE ME--OR BAIL OUT NOW!!
BEETLE, I'M SORRY. I DO BELIEVE YOU.
YOU'RE ALL RIGHT, ICE, YOU KNOW THAT? WHAT WERE YOU BEFORE YOU BECAME A SUPER-HERO?
WELL, ACTUALLY... I WAS AN ICE-GODDESS.
AND THEY GET DOWN ON ME FOR JOKING AROUND TOO MUCH!

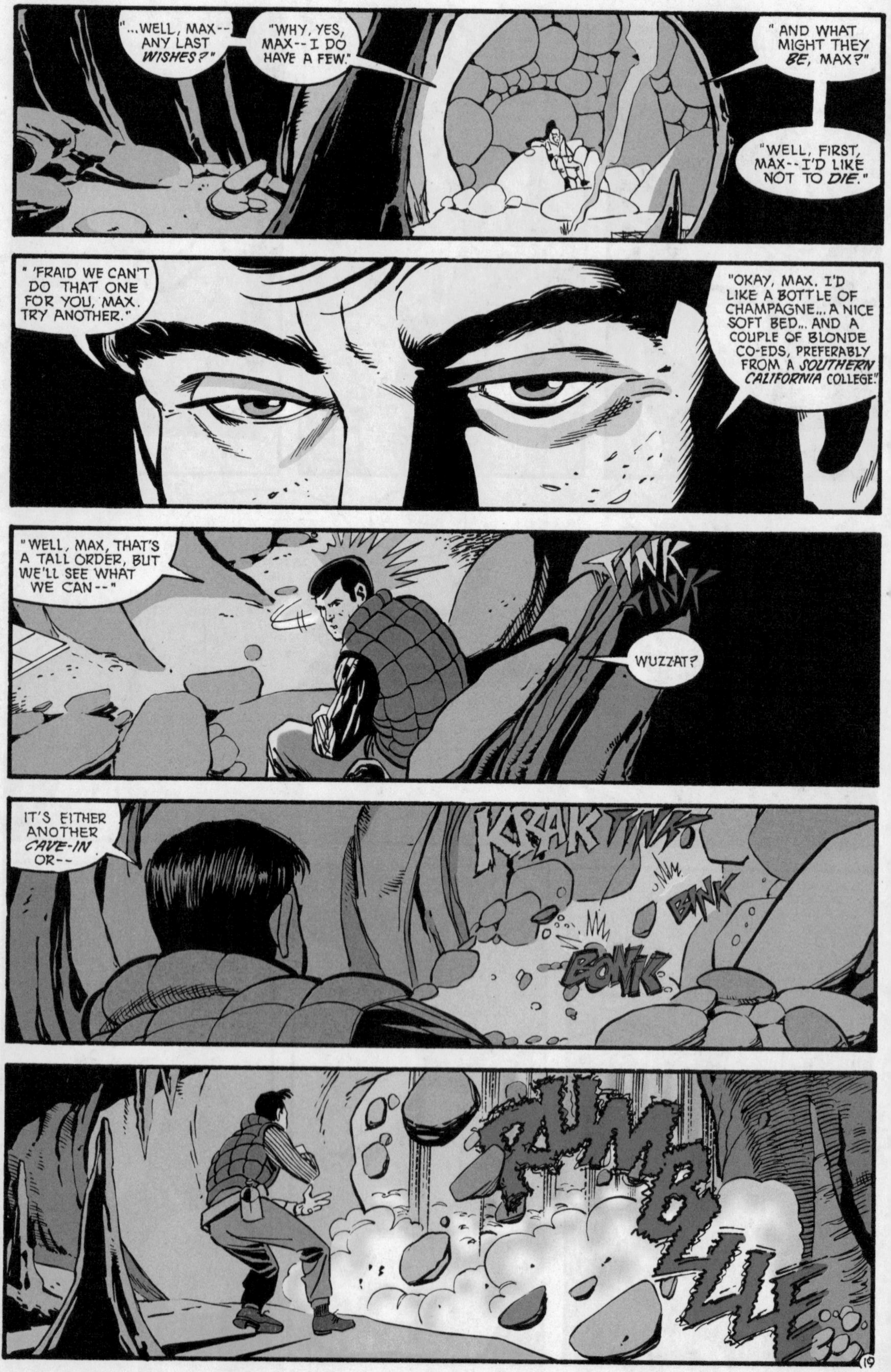
"...WELL, MAX-- ANY LAST WISHES?"
"WHY, YES, MAX-- I DO HAVE A FEW."
" AND WHAT MIGHT THEY BE, MAX?"
"WELL, FIRST, MAX-- I'D LIKE NOT TO DIE."
" 'FRAID WE CAN'T DO THAT ONE FOR YOU, MAX. TRY ANOTHER."
"OKAY, MAX. I'D LIKE A BOTTLE OF CHAMPAGNE... A NICE SOFT BED... AND A COUPLE OF BLONDE CO-EDS, PREFERABLY FROM A SOUTHERN CALIFORNIA COLLEGE."
"WELL, MAX, THAT'S A TALL ORDER, BUT WE'LL SEE WHAT WE CAN--"
TINK
TINK
WUZZAT?
IT'S EITHER ANOTHER CAVE-IN OR--
KRAK
TINK
BANK
BONK
RUMBLLE
19

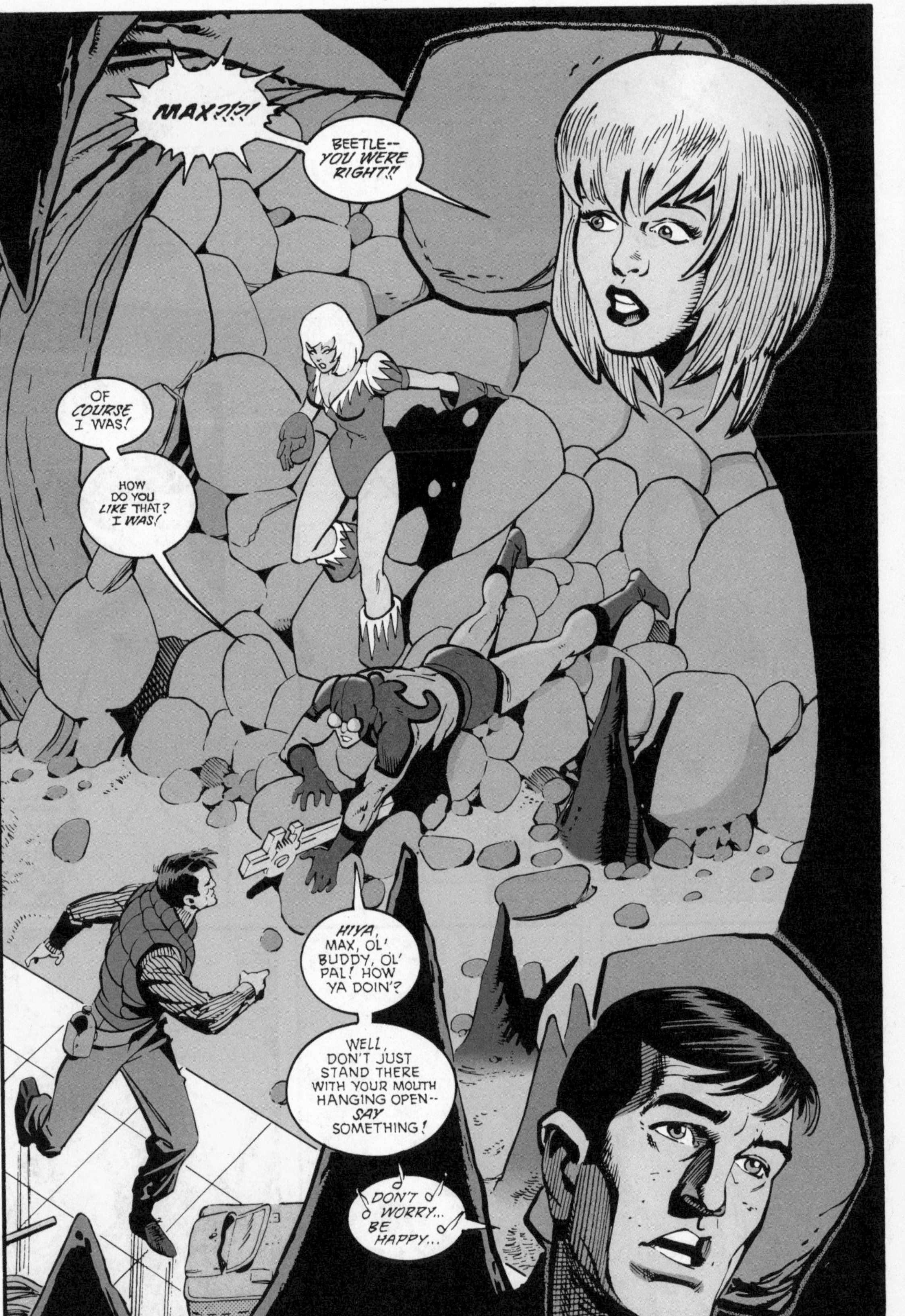
MAX?!?!
BEETLE-- YOU WERE RIGHT!!
OF COURSE I WAS!
HOW DO YOU LIKE THAT? I WAS!
HIYA, MAX, OL' BUDDY, OL' PAL! HOW YA DOIN'?
WELL, DON'T JUST STAND THERE WITH YOUR MOUTH HANGING OPEN-- SAY SOMETHING!
DON'T WORRY... BE HAPPY...
20

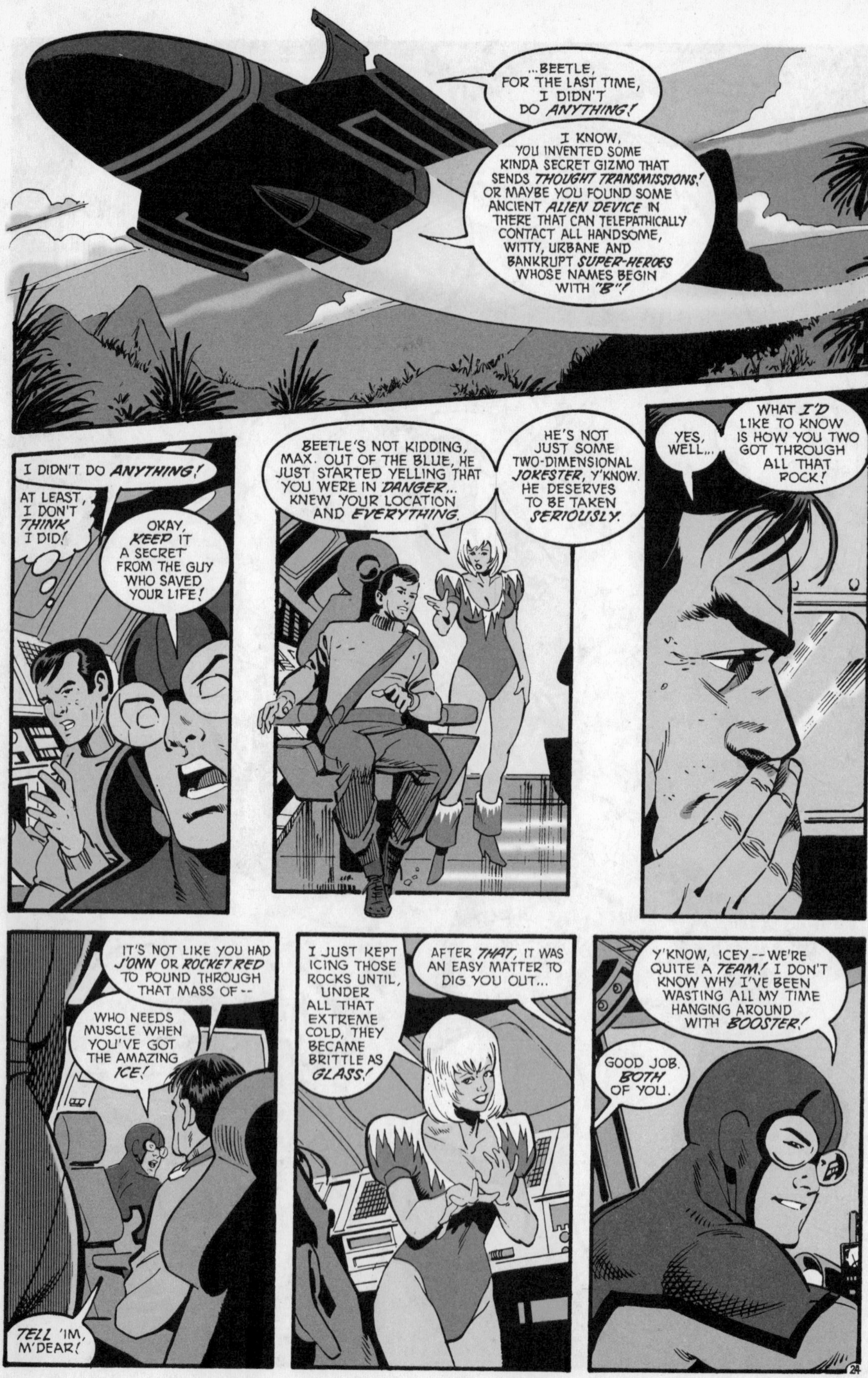
...BEETLE, FOR THE LAST TIME, I DIDN'T DO ANYTHING!
I KNOW, YOU INVENTED SOME KINDA SECRET GIZMO THAT SENDS THOUGHT TRANSMISSIONS! OR MAYBE YOU FOUND SOME ANCIENT ALIEN DEVICE IN THERE THAT CAN TELEPATHICALLY CONTACT ALL HANDSOME, WITTY, URBANE AND BANKRUPT SUPER-HEROES WHOSE NAMES BEGIN WITH "B"!
I DIDN'T DO ANYTHING!
AT LEAST, I DON'T THINK I DID!
OKAY, KEEP IT A SECRET FROM THE GUY WHO SAVED YOUR LIFE!
BEETLE'S NOT KIDDING, MAX. OUT OF THE BLUE, HE JUST STARTED YELLING THAT YOU WERE IN DANGER... KNEW YOUR LOCATION AND EVERYTHING.
HE'S NOT JUST SOME TWO-DIMENSIONAL JOKESTER, Y'KNOW. HE DESERVES TO BE TAKEN SERIOUSLY.
YES, WELL...
WHAT I'D LIKE TO KNOW IS HOW YOU TWO GOT THROUGH ALL THAT ROCK!
IT'S NOT LIKE YOU HAD J'ONN OR ROCKET RED TO POUND THROUGH THAT MASS OF--
WHO NEEDS MUSCLE WHEN YOU'VE GOT THE AMAZING ICE!
TELL 'IM, M'DEAR!
I JUST KEPT ICING THOSE ROCKS UNTIL, UNDER ALL THAT EXTREME COLD, THEY BECAME BRITTLE AS GLASS!
AFTER THAT, IT WAS AN EASY MATTER TO DIG YOU OUT...
Y'KNOW, ICEY--WE'RE QUITE A TEAM! I DON'T KNOW WHY I'VE BEEN WASTING ALL MY TIME HANGING AROUND WITH BOOSTER!
GOOD JOB. BOTH OF YOU.
24

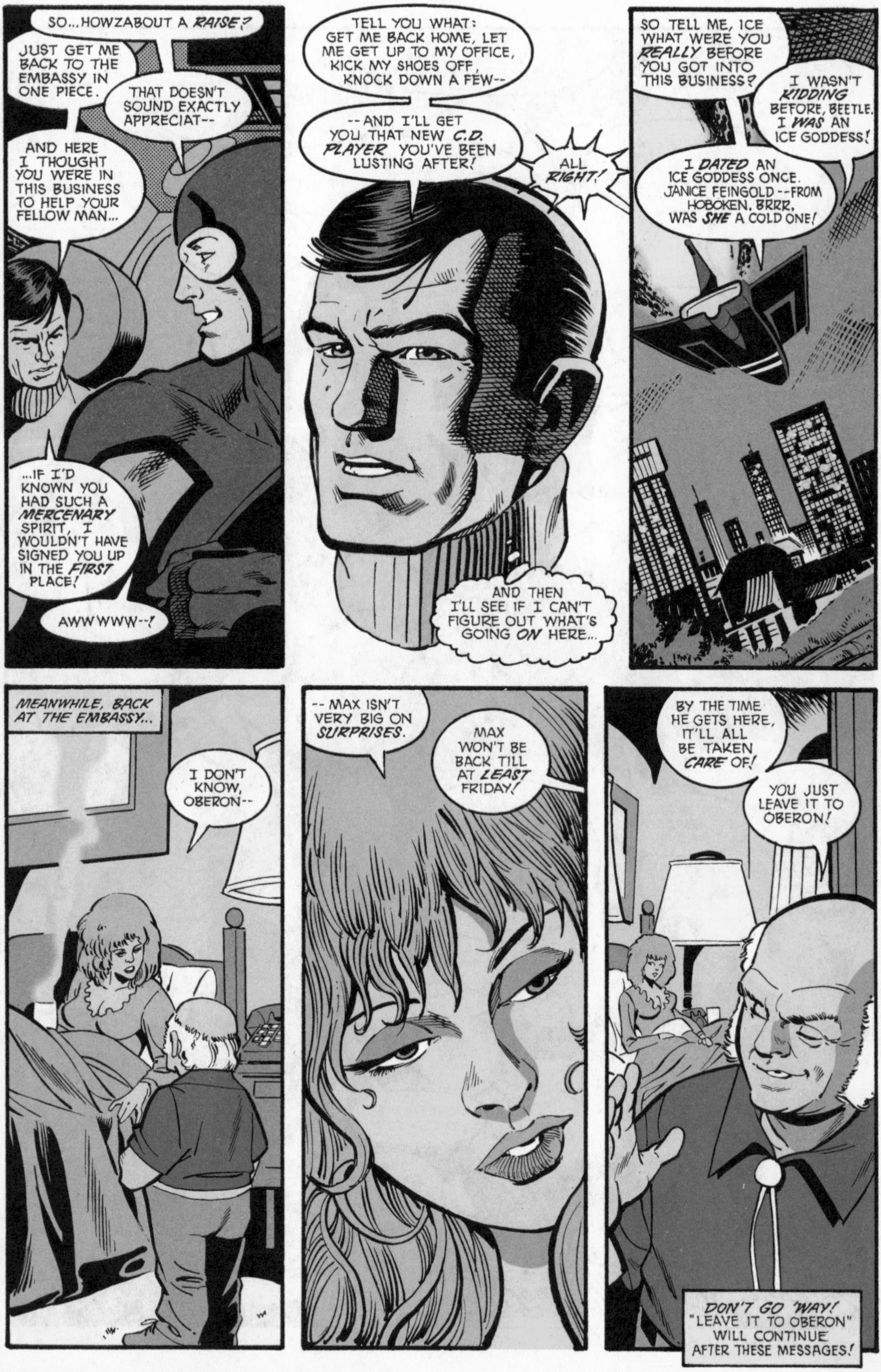
SO... HOWZABOUT A RAISE?
JUST GET ME BACK TO THE EMBASSY IN ONE PIECE.
THAT DOESN'T SOUND EXACTLY APPRECIAT--
AND HERE I THOUGHT YOU WERE IN THIS BUSINESS TO HELP YOUR FELLOW MAN...
...IF I'D KNOWN YOU HAD SUCH A MERCENARY SPIRIT, I WOULDN'T HAVE SIGNED YOU UP IN THE FIRST PLACE!
AWWWWW--!
TELL YOU WHAT: GET ME BACK HOME, LET ME GET UP TO MY OFFICE, KICK MY SHOES OFF, KNOCK DOWN A FEW--
--AND I'LL GET YOU THAT NEW C.D. PLAYER YOU'VE BEEN LUSTING AFTER!
ALL RIGHT!
AND THEN I'LL SEE IF I CAN'T FIGURE OUT WHAT'S GOING ON HERE...
SO TELL ME, ICE WHAT WERE YOU REALLY BEFORE YOU GOT INTO THIS BUSINESS?
I WASN'T KIDDING BEFORE, BEETLE. I WAS AN ICE GODDESS!
I DATED AN ICE GODDESS ONCE. JANICE FEINGOLD--FROM HOBOKEN. BRRR. WAS SHE A COLD ONE!
MEANWHILE, BACK AT THE EMBASSY...
I DON'T KNOW, OBERON--
--MAX ISN'T VERY BIG ON SURPRISES.
MAX WON'T BE BACK TILL AT LEAST FRIDAY!
BY THE TIME HE GETS HERE, IT'LL ALL BE TAKEN CARE OF!
YOU JUST LEAVE IT TO OBERON!
DON'T GO 'WAY! "LEAVE IT TO OBERON" WILL CONTINUE AFTER THESE MESSAGES!

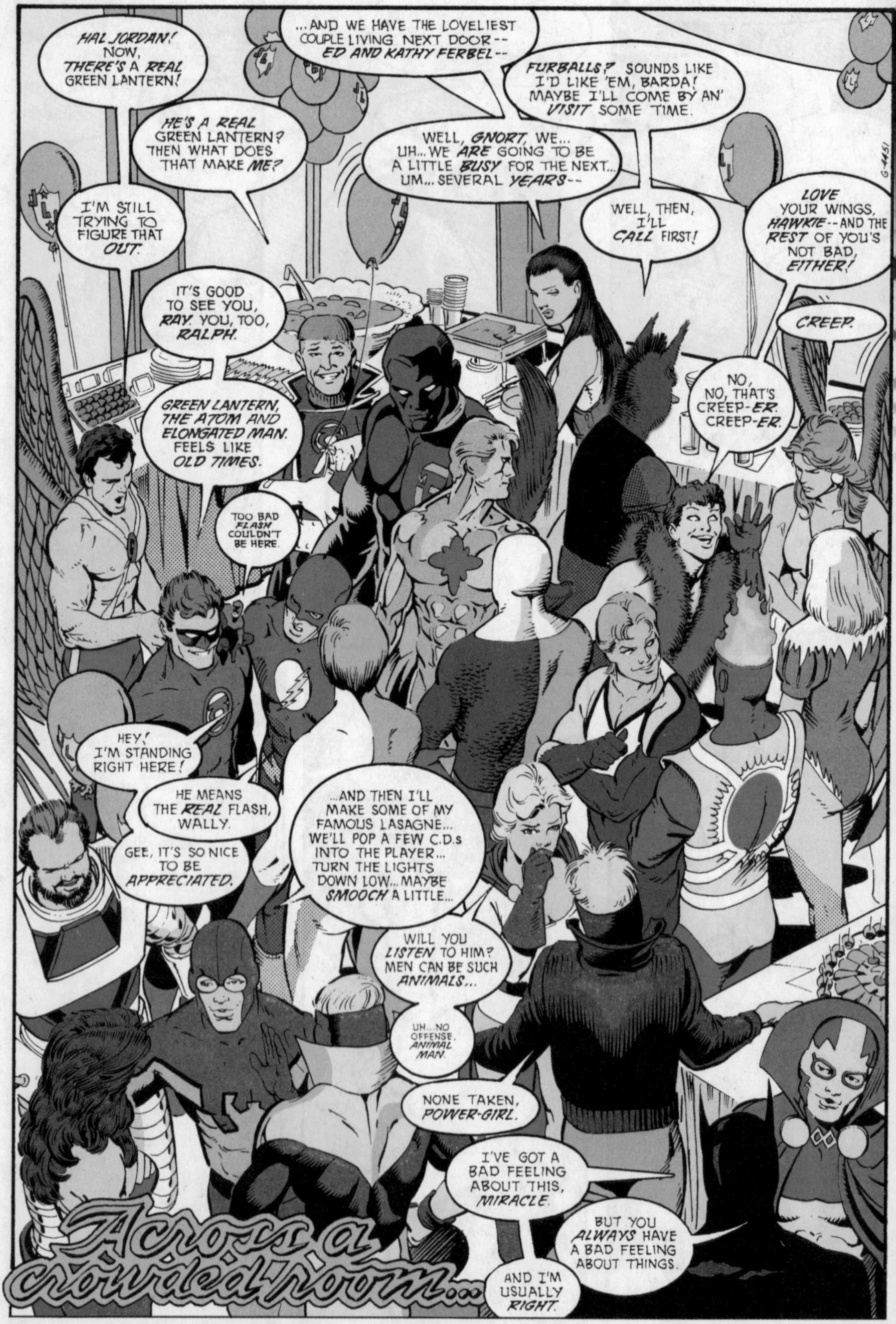
HAL JORDAN! NOW, THERE'S A REAL GREEN LANTERN!
...AND WE HAVE THE LOVELIEST COUPLE LIVING NEXT DOOR -- ED AND KATHY FERBEL --
FURBALLS? SOUNDS LIKE I'D LIKE 'EM, BARDA! MAYBE I'LL COME BY AN' VISIT SOME TIME.
HE'S A REAL GREEN LANTERN? THEN WHAT DOES THAT MAKE ME?
WELL, GNORT, WE... UH... WE ARE GOING TO BE A LITTLE BUSY FOR THE NEXT... UM... SEVERAL YEARS--
I'M STILL TRYING TO FIGURE THAT OUT.
WELL, THEN, I'LL CALL FIRST!
LOVE YOUR WINGS, HAWKIE -- AND THE REST OF YOU'S NOT BAD, EITHER!
CREEP.
NO, NO, THAT'S CREEP-ER. CREEP-ER.
IT'S GOOD TO SEE YOU, RAY. YOU, TOO, RALPH.
GREEN LANTERN, THE ATOM AND ELONGATED MAN. FEELS LIKE OLD TIMES.
TOO BAD FLASH COULDN'T BE HERE.
HEY! I'M STANDING RIGHT HERE!
HE MEANS THE REAL FLASH, WALLY.
GEE, IT'S SO NICE TO BE APPRECIATED.
...AND THEN I'LL MAKE SOME OF MY FAMOUS LASAGNE... WE'LL POP A FEW C.D.s INTO THE PLAYER... TURN THE LIGHTS DOWN LOW... MAYBE SMOOCH A LITTLE...
WILL YOU LISTEN TO HIM? MEN CAN BE SUCH ANIMALS...
UH... NO OFFENSE, ANIMAL MAN.
NONE TAKEN, POWER-GIRL.
I'VE GOT A BAD FEELING ABOUT THIS, MIRACLE.
BUT YOU ALWAYS HAVE A BAD FEELING ABOUT THINGS.
AND I'M USUALLY RIGHT.
Across a crowded room...
G-4451

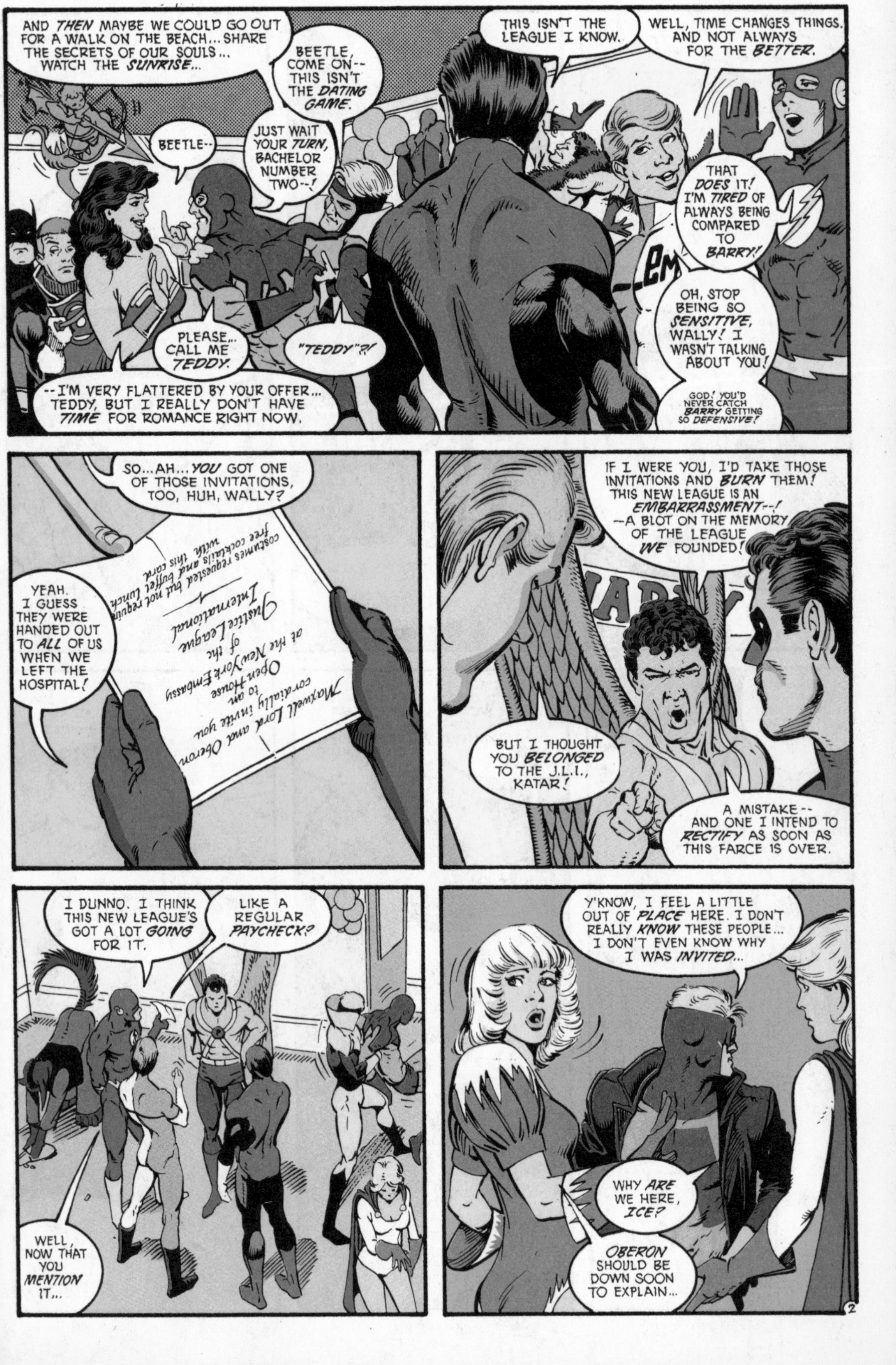

AND THEN MAYBE WE COULD GO OUT FOR A WALK ON THE BEACH... SHARE THE SECRETS OF OUR SOULS... WATCH THE SUNRISE...
BEETLE, COME ON-- THIS ISN'T THE DATING GAME.
BEETLE--
JUST WAIT YOUR TURN, BACHELOR NUMBER TWO--!
THIS ISN'T THE LEAGUE I KNOW.
WELL, TIME CHANGES THINGS. AND NOT ALWAYS FOR THE BETTER.
THAT DOES IT! I'M TIRED OF ALWAYS BEING COMPARED TO BARRY!
OH, STOP BEING SO SENSITIVE, WALLY! I WASN'T TALKING ABOUT YOU!
GOD! YOU'D NEVER CATCH BARRY GETTING SO DEFENSIVE!
PLEASE... CALL ME TEDDY.
"TEDDY"?!
--I'M VERY FLATTERED BY YOUR OFFER... TEDDY, BUT I REALLY DON'T HAVE TIME FOR ROMANCE RIGHT NOW.
SO...AH...YOU GOT ONE OF THOSE INVITATIONS, TOO, HUH, WALLY?
YEAH. I GUESS THEY WERE HANDED OUT TO ALL OF US WHEN WE LEFT THE HOSPITAL!
Maxwell Lord and Oberon cordially invite you to an Open House at the New York Embassy of the Justice League International
costumes requested but not requi
free cocktails and buffet lunch with this card
IF I WERE YOU, I'D TAKE THOSE INVITATIONS AND BURN THEM! THIS NEW LEAGUE IS AN EMBARRASSMENT--! --A BLOT ON THE MEMORY OF THE LEAGUE WE FOUNDED!
BUT I THOUGHT YOU BELONGED TO THE J.L.I., KATAR!
A MISTAKE-- AND ONE I INTEND TO RECTIFY AS SOON AS THIS FARCE IS OVER.
I DUNNO. I THINK THIS NEW LEAGUE'S GOT A LOT GOING FOR IT.
LIKE A REGULAR PAYCHECK?
WELL, NOW THAT YOU MENTION IT...
Y'KNOW, I FEEL A LITTLE OUT OF PLACE HERE. I DON'T REALLY KNOW THESE PEOPLE... I DON'T EVEN KNOW WHY I WAS INVITED...
WHY ARE WE HERE, ICE?
OBERON SHOULD BE DOWN SOON TO EXPLAIN...
2

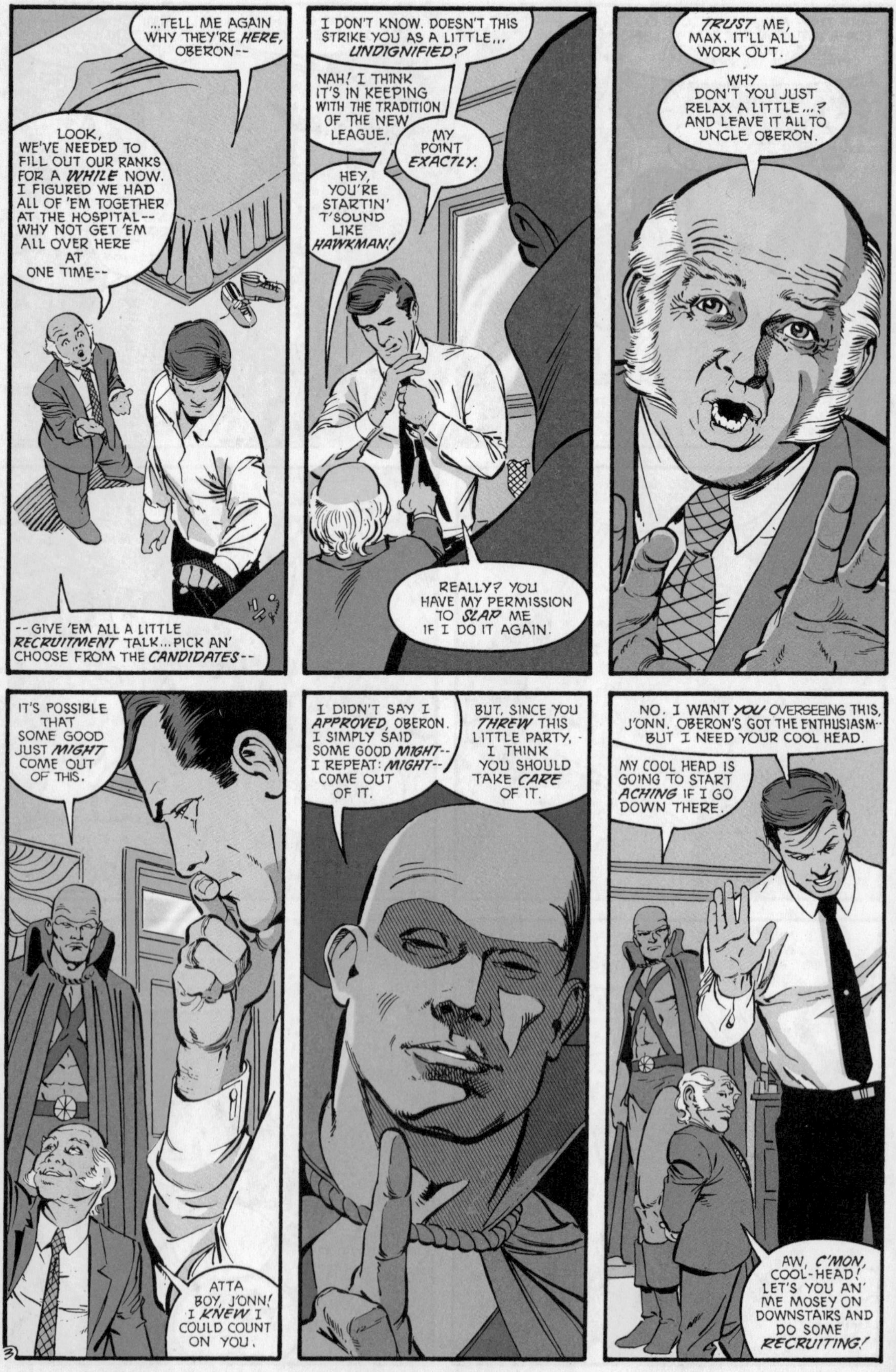
...TELL ME AGAIN WHY THEY'RE HERE, OBERON--
LOOK, WE'VE NEEDED TO FILL OUT OUR RANKS FOR A WHILE NOW. I FIGURED WE HAD ALL OF 'EM TOGETHER AT THE HOSPITAL-- WHY NOT GET 'EM ALL OVER HERE AT ONE TIME--
--GIVE 'EM ALL A LITTLE RECRUITMENT TALK... PICK AN' CHOOSE FROM THE CANDIDATES--
I DON'T KNOW. DOESN'T THIS STRIKE YOU AS A LITTLE... UNDIGNIFIED?
NAH! I THINK IT'S IN KEEPING WITH THE TRADITION OF THE NEW LEAGUE.
MY POINT EXACTLY.
HEY, YOU'RE STARTIN' T'SOUND LIKE HAWKMAN!
REALLY? YOU HAVE MY PERMISSION TO SLAP ME IF I DO IT AGAIN.
TRUST ME, MAX. IT'LL ALL WORK OUT.
WHY DON'T YOU JUST RELAX A LITTLE...? AND LEAVE IT ALL TO UNCLE OBERON.
IT'S POSSIBLE THAT SOME GOOD JUST MIGHT COME OUT OF THIS.
ATTA BOY, J'ONN! I KNEW I COULD COUNT ON YOU.
I DIDN'T SAY I APPROVED, OBERON. I SIMPLY SAID SOME GOOD MIGHT-- I REPEAT: MIGHT-- COME OUT OF IT.
BUT, SINCE YOU THREW THIS LITTLE PARTY, I THINK YOU SHOULD TAKE CARE OF IT.
NO. I WANT YOU OVERSEEING THIS, J'ONN. OBERON'S GOT THE ENTHUSIASM-- BUT I NEED YOUR COOL HEAD.
MY COOL HEAD IS GOING TO START ACHING IF I GO DOWN THERE.
AW, C'MON, COOL-HEAD! LET'S YOU AN' ME MOSEY ON DOWNSTAIRS AND DO SOME RECRUITING!

...YOU LEAGUERS SURE KNOW HOW T'THROW A WINGDING, *CAPTAIN ATOM!*

YOU REALLY LIKE IT, *METAMORPHO?*

YEAH! EVERYTHING'S TERRIFIC! WELL, THE *ROAST BEEF* WAS A LITTLE *RARE* FOR MY TASTE, BUT...

AH, YOU SHOULD'VE TOLD ME. I COULD'VE *MICRO-WAVED* IT FOR YOU.

WILL YOU JUST TAKE A LOOK AROUND HERE? IT'S A REGULAR SUPER-HUMAN *"WHO'S WHO"!*

I'VE MISSED RUBBIN' SHOULDERS WITH THE ELITE SINCE THE *OUTSIDERS* CAVED IN!

OUTSIDERS? OH, RIGHT. I READ THE *FILE* ON YOU GUYS.

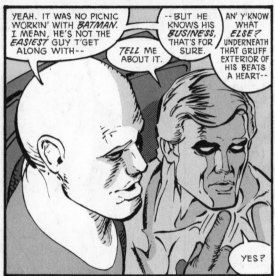

YEAH, IT WAS NO PICNIC WORKIN' WITH *BATMAN.* I MEAN, HE'S NOT THE *EASIEST* GUY T'GET ALONG WITH--

TELL ME ABOUT IT.

--BUT HE KNOWS HIS *BUSINESS,* THAT'S FOR SURE.

AN' Y'KNOW WHAT *ELSE?* UNDERNEATH THAT GRUFF EXTERIOR OF HIS BEATS A *HEART--*

YES?

--OF *PURE GRANITE.*

THAT'S A LITTLE *JOKE,* CAP.

I THINK YOU'D FIT IN JUST *PERFECTLY* AROUND HERE, PAL.

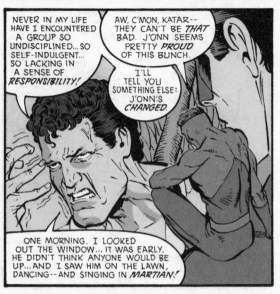

NEVER IN MY LIFE HAVE I ENCOUNTERED A GROUP SO UNDISCIPLINED...SO SELF-INDULGENT... SO LACKING IN A SENSE OF *RESPONSIBILITY!*

AW, C'MON, KATAR-- THEY CAN'T BE *THAT* BAD. J'ONN SEEMS PRETTY *PROUD* OF THIS BUNCH.

I'LL TELL YOU SOMETHING ELSE: J'ONN'S *CHANGED.*

ONE MORNING, I LOOKED OUT THE WINDOW... IT WAS EARLY, HE DIDN'T THINK ANYONE WOULD BE UP...AND I SAW HIM ON THE LAWN, DANCING--AND SINGING IN *MARTIAN!*

AND HE'D CHANGED HIS *SHAPE,* TOO! MY GOD, HE LOOKED LIKE... LIKE *GUMBY!*

HE'S AT IT *AGAIN.*

YEAH! AND HAVE YOU SEEN THE WAY HE'S BEEN LOOKING AT *WONDER WOMAN?!*

ENOUGH WITH WONDER WOMAN! YOU'RE BECOMING *OBSESSED!*

YOU'RE ALL *ALIKE!* YOU JUST WANT HER FOR *YOURSELVES!* BUT IT'S *ME* SHE LOVES! *ME! ME!*

EASY, SON. WE'LL GET YOU TO YOUR THERAPIST *SOON.*

4

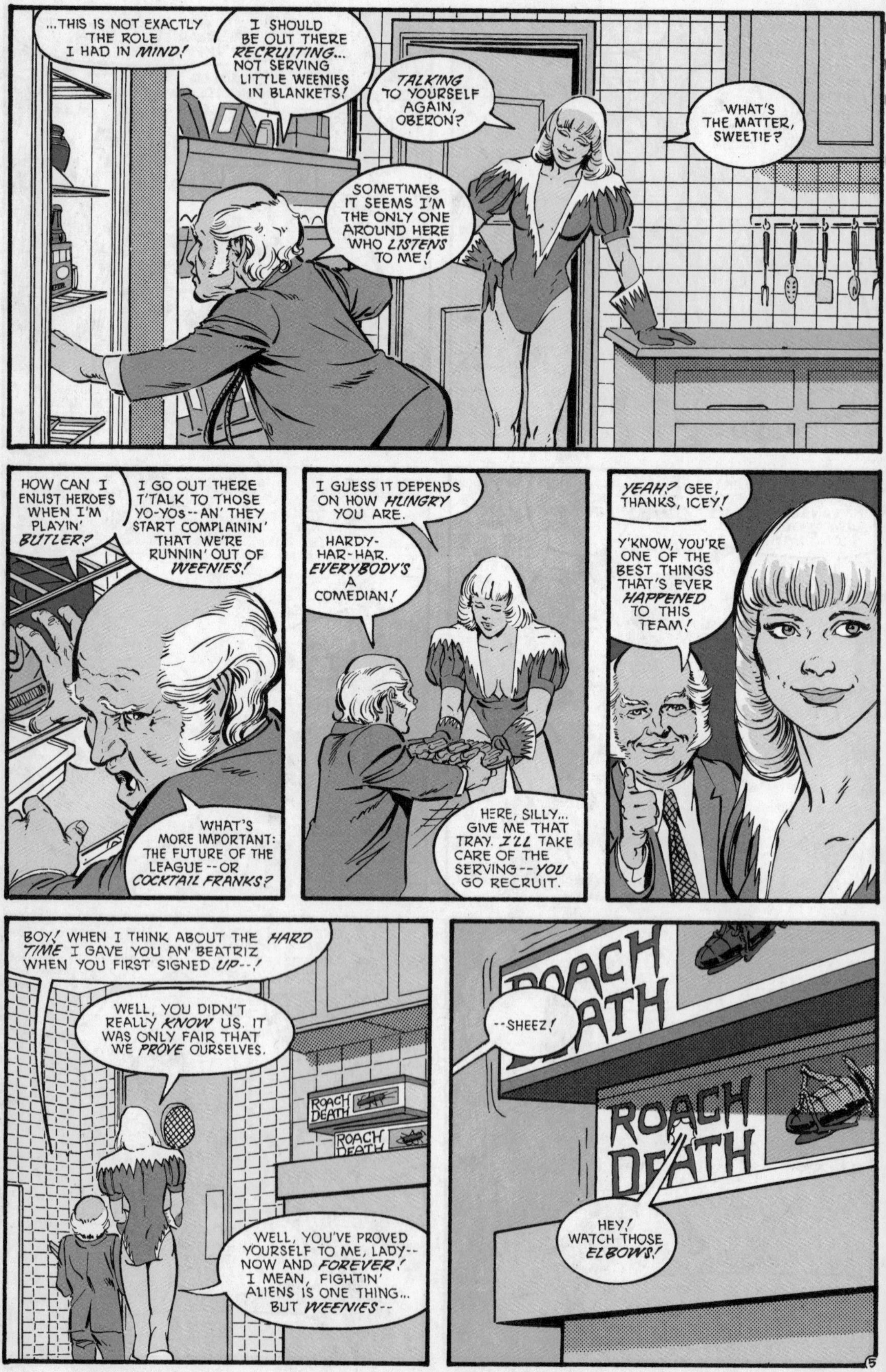
...THIS IS NOT EXACTLY THE ROLE I HAD IN MIND!
I SHOULD BE OUT THERE RECRUITING... NOT SERVING LITTLE WEENIES IN BLANKETS!
TALKING TO YOURSELF AGAIN, OBERON?
WHAT'S THE MATTER, SWEETIE?
SOMETIMES IT SEEMS I'M THE ONLY ONE AROUND HERE WHO LISTENS TO ME!
HOW CAN I ENLIST HEROES WHEN I'M PLAYIN' BUTLER?
I GO OUT THERE T'TALK TO THOSE YO-YOS--AN' THEY START COMPLAININ' THAT WE'RE RUNNIN' OUT OF WEENIES!
WHAT'S MORE IMPORTANT: THE FUTURE OF THE LEAGUE--OR COCKTAIL FRANKS?
I GUESS IT DEPENDS ON HOW HUNGRY YOU ARE.
HARDY-HAR-HAR. EVERYBODY'S A COMEDIAN!
HERE, SILLY... GIVE ME THAT TRAY. I'LL TAKE CARE OF THE SERVING--YOU GO RECRUIT.
YEAH? GEE, THANKS, ICEY!
Y'KNOW, YOU'RE ONE OF THE BEST THINGS THAT'S EVER HAPPENED TO THIS TEAM!
BOY! WHEN I THINK ABOUT THE HARD TIME I GAVE YOU AN' BEATRIZ WHEN YOU FIRST SIGNED UP--!
WELL, YOU DIDN'T REALLY KNOW US. IT WAS ONLY FAIR THAT WE PROVE OURSELVES.
WELL, YOU'VE PROVED YOURSELF TO ME, LADY--NOW AND FOREVER! I MEAN, FIGHTIN' ALIENS IS ONE THING... BUT WEENIES--
ROACH DEATH
ROACH DEATH
--SHEEZ!
ROACH DEATH
HEY! WATCH THOSE ELBOWS!
5

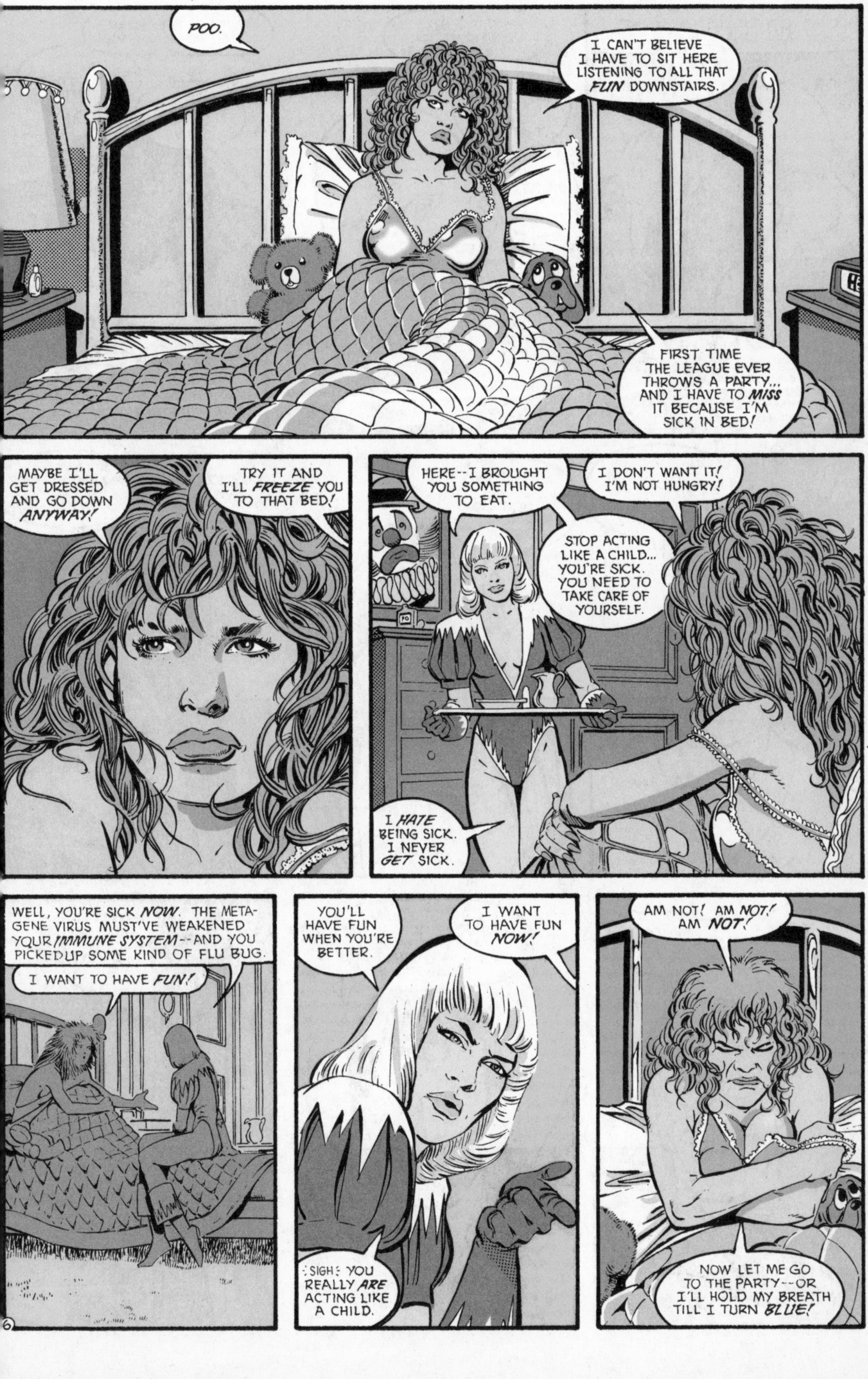
POO.
I CAN'T BELIEVE I HAVE TO SIT HERE LISTENING TO ALL THAT FUN DOWNSTAIRS.
FIRST TIME THE LEAGUE EVER THROWS A PARTY... AND I HAVE TO MISS IT BECAUSE I'M SICK IN BED!
MAYBE I'LL GET DRESSED AND GO DOWN ANYWAY!
TRY IT AND I'LL FREEZE YOU TO THAT BED!
HERE--I BROUGHT YOU SOMETHING TO EAT.
I DON'T WANT IT! I'M NOT HUNGRY!
STOP ACTING LIKE A CHILD... YOU'RE SICK. YOU NEED TO TAKE CARE OF YOURSELF.
I HATE BEING SICK. I NEVER GET SICK.
WELL, YOU'RE SICK NOW. THE META-GENE VIRUS MUST'VE WEAKENED YOUR IMMUNE SYSTEM--AND YOU PICKED UP SOME KIND OF FLU BUG.
I WANT TO HAVE FUN!
YOU'LL HAVE FUN WHEN YOU'RE BETTER.
I WANT TO HAVE FUN NOW!
:SIGH: YOU REALLY ARE ACTING LIKE A CHILD.
AM NOT! AM NOT! AM NOT!
NOW LET ME GO TO THE PARTY--OR I'LL HOLD MY BREATH TILL I TURN BLUE!
6

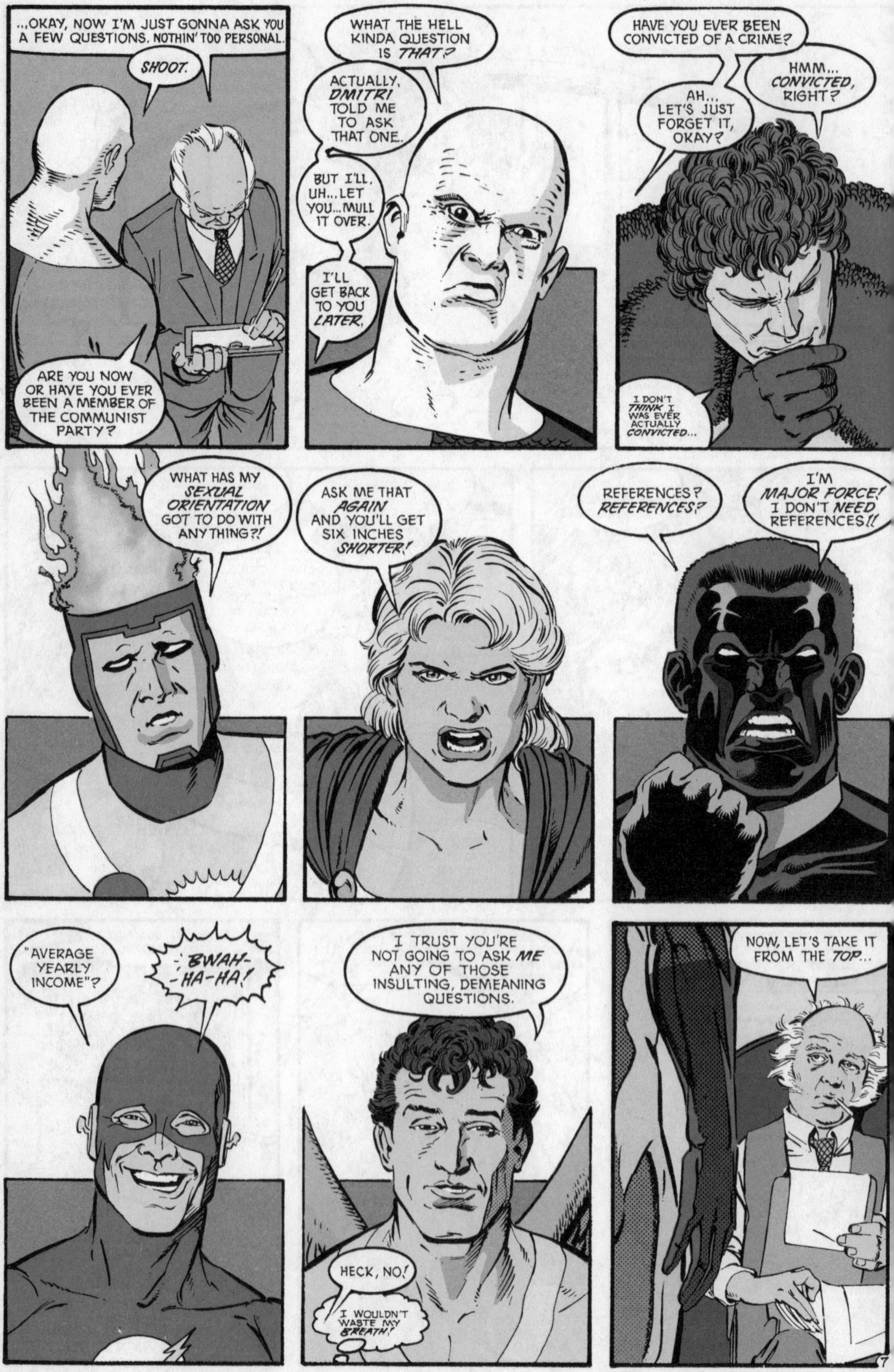

...OKAY, NOW I'M JUST GONNA ASK YOU A FEW QUESTIONS. NOTHIN' TOO PERSONAL.
SHOOT.
ARE YOU NOW OR HAVE YOU EVER BEEN A MEMBER OF THE COMMUNIST PARTY?
WHAT THE HELL KINDA QUESTION IS THAT?
ACTUALLY, DMITRI TOLD ME TO ASK THAT ONE.
BUT I'LL, UH... LET YOU... MULL IT OVER.
I'LL GET BACK TO YOU LATER.
HAVE YOU EVER BEEN CONVICTED OF A CRIME?
HMM... CONVICTED, RIGHT?
AH... LET'S JUST FORGET IT, OKAY?
I DON'T THINK I WAS EVER ACTUALLY CONVICTED...
WHAT HAS MY SEXUAL ORIENTATION GOT TO DO WITH ANYTHING?!
ASK ME THAT AGAIN AND YOU'LL GET SIX INCHES SHORTER!
REFERENCES? REFERENCES?
I'M MAJOR FORCE! I DON'T NEED REFERENCES!!
"AVERAGE YEARLY INCOME"?
BWAH-HA-HA!
I TRUST YOU'RE NOT GOING TO ASK ME ANY OF THOSE INSULTING, DEMEANING QUESTIONS.
HECK, NO!
I WOULDN'T WASTE MY BREATH!
NOW, LET'S TAKE IT FROM THE TOP...
7

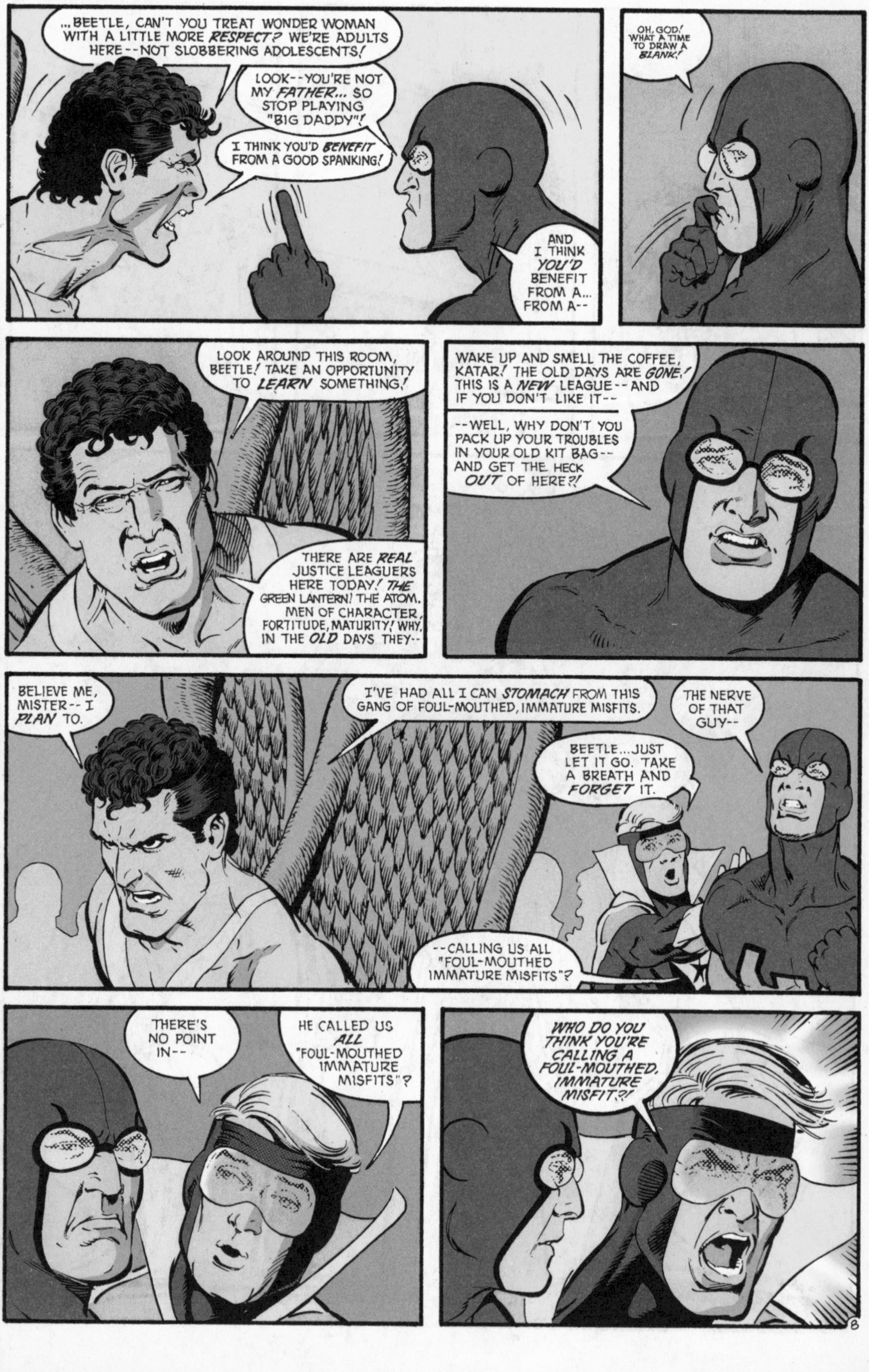
...BEETLE, CAN'T YOU TREAT WONDER WOMAN WITH A LITTLE MORE RESPECT? WE'RE ADULTS HERE--NOT SLOBBERING ADOLESCENTS!
LOOK--YOU'RE NOT MY FATHER... SO STOP PLAYING "BIG DADDY"!
I THINK YOU'D BENEFIT FROM A GOOD SPANKING!
AND I THINK YOU'D BENEFIT FROM A... FROM A--
OH, GOD! WHAT A TIME TO DRAW A BLANK!
LOOK AROUND THIS ROOM, BEETLE! TAKE AN OPPORTUNITY TO LEARN SOMETHING!
THERE ARE REAL JUSTICE LEAGUERS HERE TODAY! THE GREEN LANTERN! THE ATOM. MEN OF CHARACTER, FORTITUDE, MATURITY! WHY, IN THE OLD DAYS THEY--
WAKE UP AND SMELL THE COFFEE, KATAR! THE OLD DAYS ARE GONE! THIS IS A NEW LEAGUE--AND IF YOU DON'T LIKE IT--
--WELL, WHY DON'T YOU PACK UP YOUR TROUBLES IN YOUR OLD KIT BAG--AND GET THE HECK OUT OF HERE?!
BELIEVE ME, MISTER--I PLAN TO.
I'VE HAD ALL I CAN STOMACH FROM THIS GANG OF FOUL-MOUTHED, IMMATURE MISFITS.
THE NERVE OF THAT GUY--
BEETLE...JUST LET IT GO. TAKE A BREATH AND FORGET IT.
--CALLING US ALL "FOUL-MOUTHED IMMATURE MISFITS"?
THERE'S NO POINT IN--
HE CALLED US ALL "FOUL-MOUTHED IMMATURE MISFITS"?
WHO DO YOU THINK YOU'RE CALLING A FOUL-MOUTHED, IMMATURE MISFIT?!
8

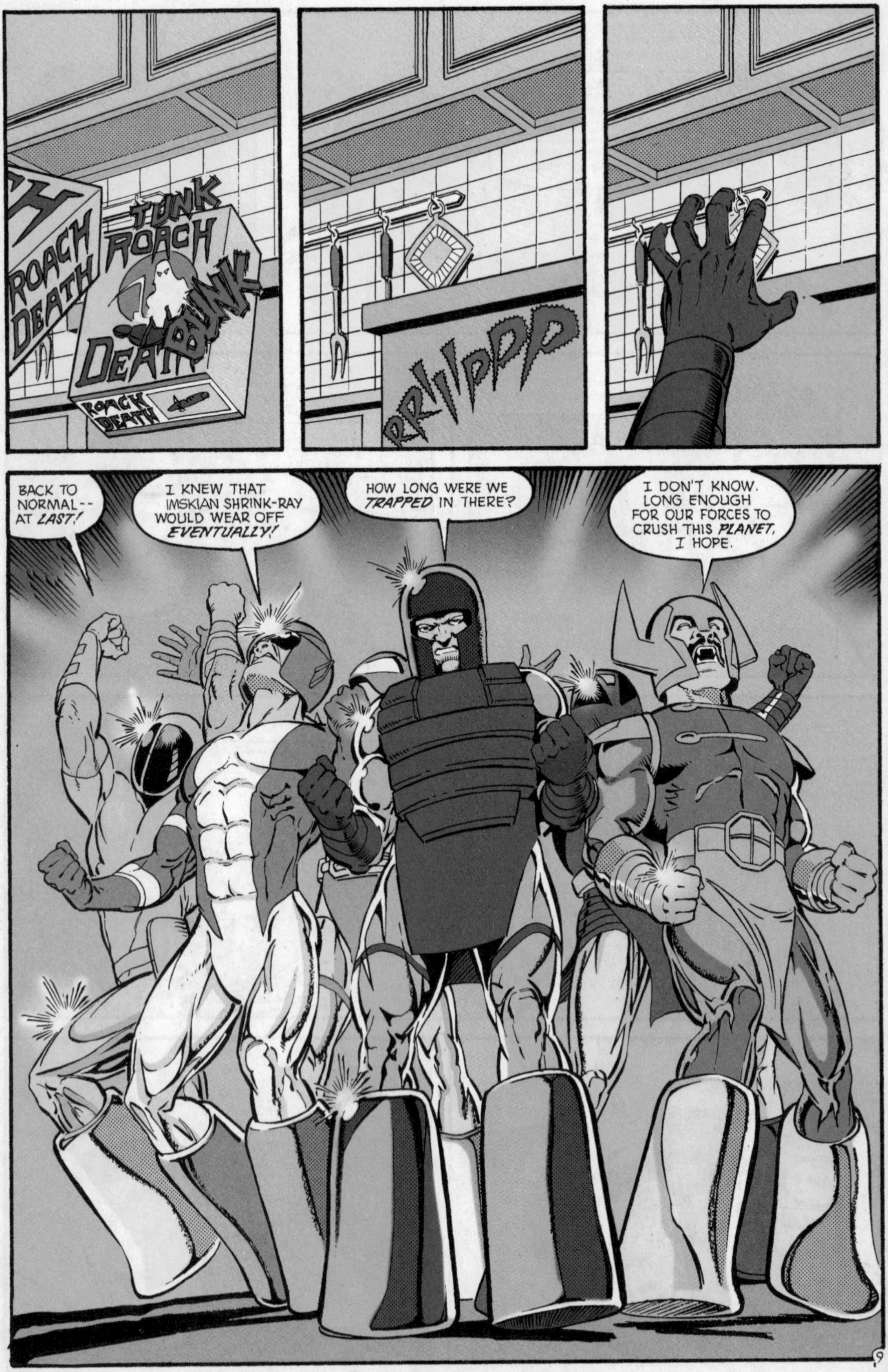

ROACH DEATH
TUNK
ROACH DEATH
BUNK
ROACH DEATH
RRIIIPPPP
BACK TO NORMAL-- AT *LAST!*
I KNEW THAT IMSKIAN SHRINK-RAY WOULD WEAR OFF *EVENTUALLY!*
HOW LONG WERE WE *TRAPPED* IN THERE?
I DON'T KNOW. LONG ENOUGH FOR OUR FORCES TO CRUSH THIS *PLANET,* I HOPE.

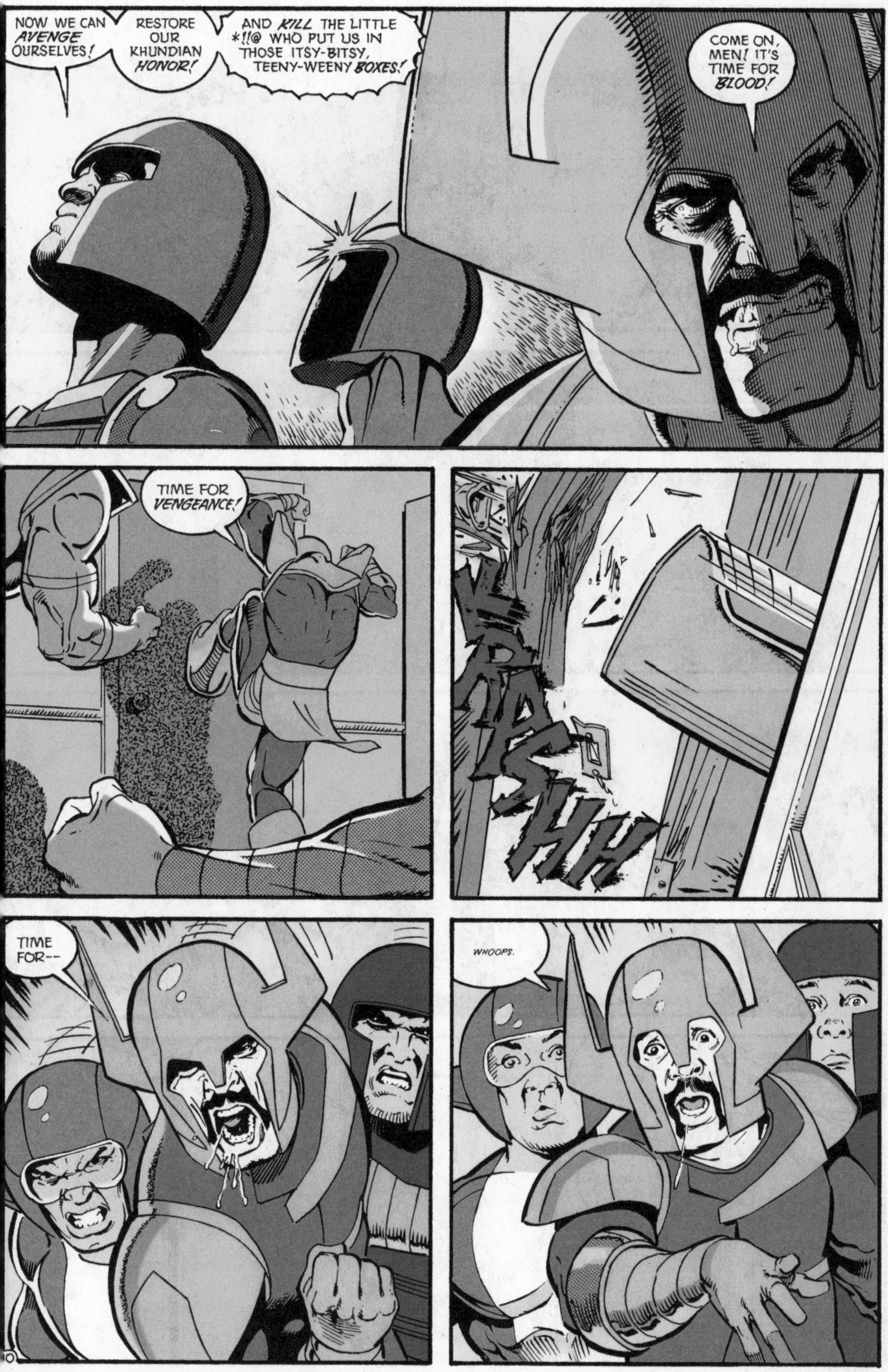
NOW WE CAN AVENGE OURSELVES!
RESTORE OUR KHUNDIAN HONOR!
AND KILL THE LITTLE *!!@ WHO PUT US IN THOSE ITSY-BITSY, TEENY-WEENY BOXES!
COME ON, MEN! IT'S TIME FOR BLOOD!
TIME FOR VENGEANCE!
KRASHH
TIME FOR--
WHOOPS.

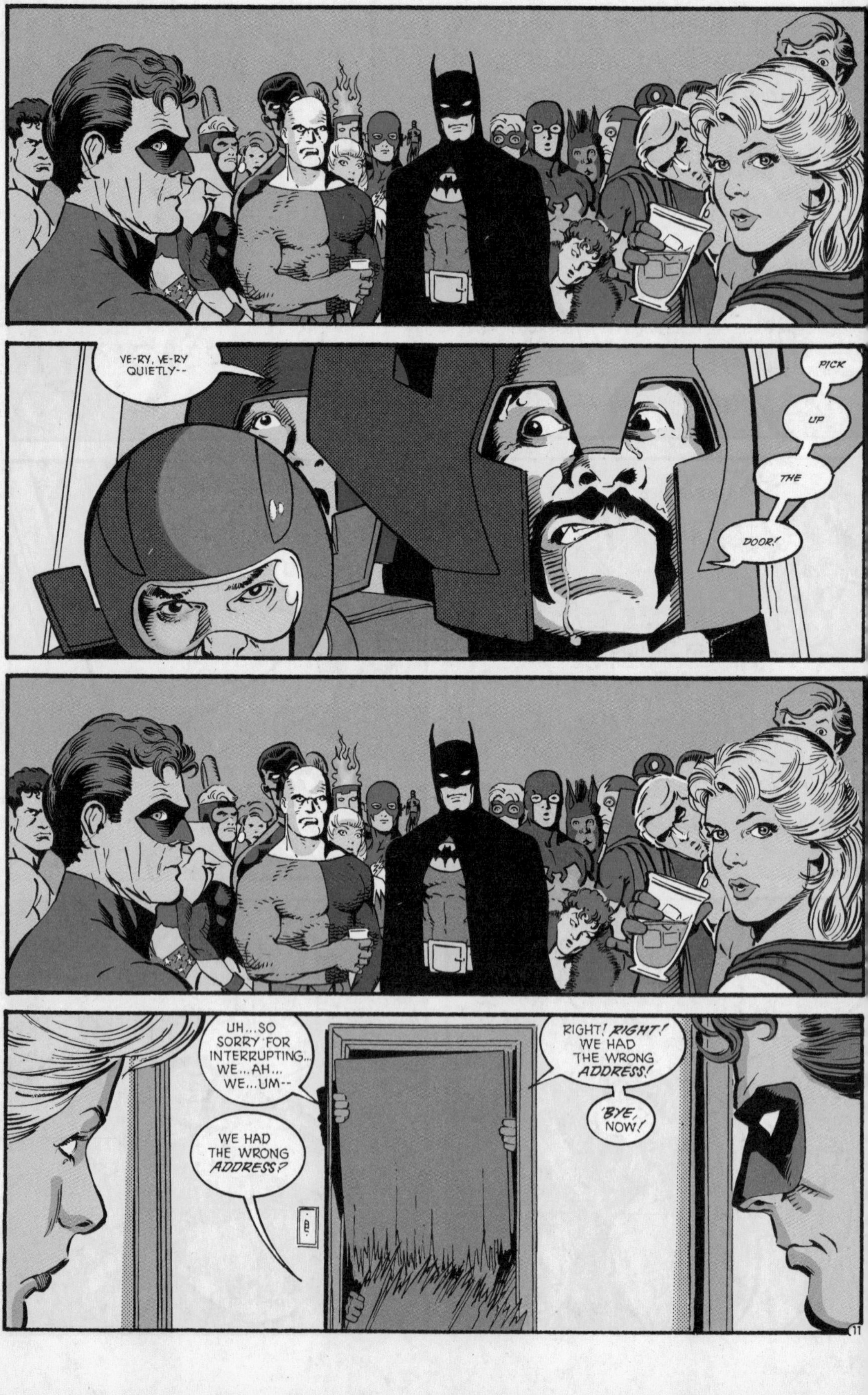
VE-RY, VE-RY QUIETLY--
PICK
UP
THE
DOOR!
UH...SO SORRY FOR INTERRUPTING... WE...AH... WE...UM--
WE HAD THE WRONG ADDRESS?
RIGHT! RIGHT! WE HAD THE WRONG ADDRESS!
'BYE, NOW!
11

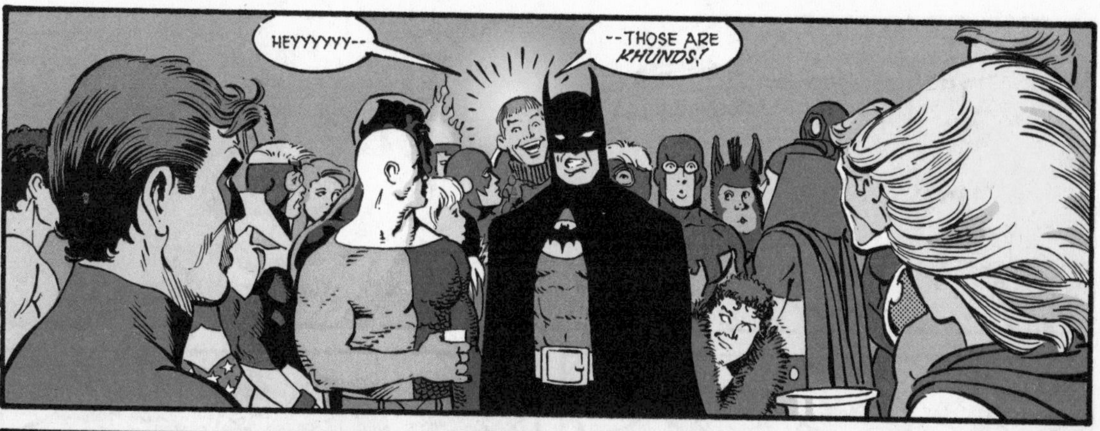
HEYYYYYY--
--THOSE ARE KHUNDS!

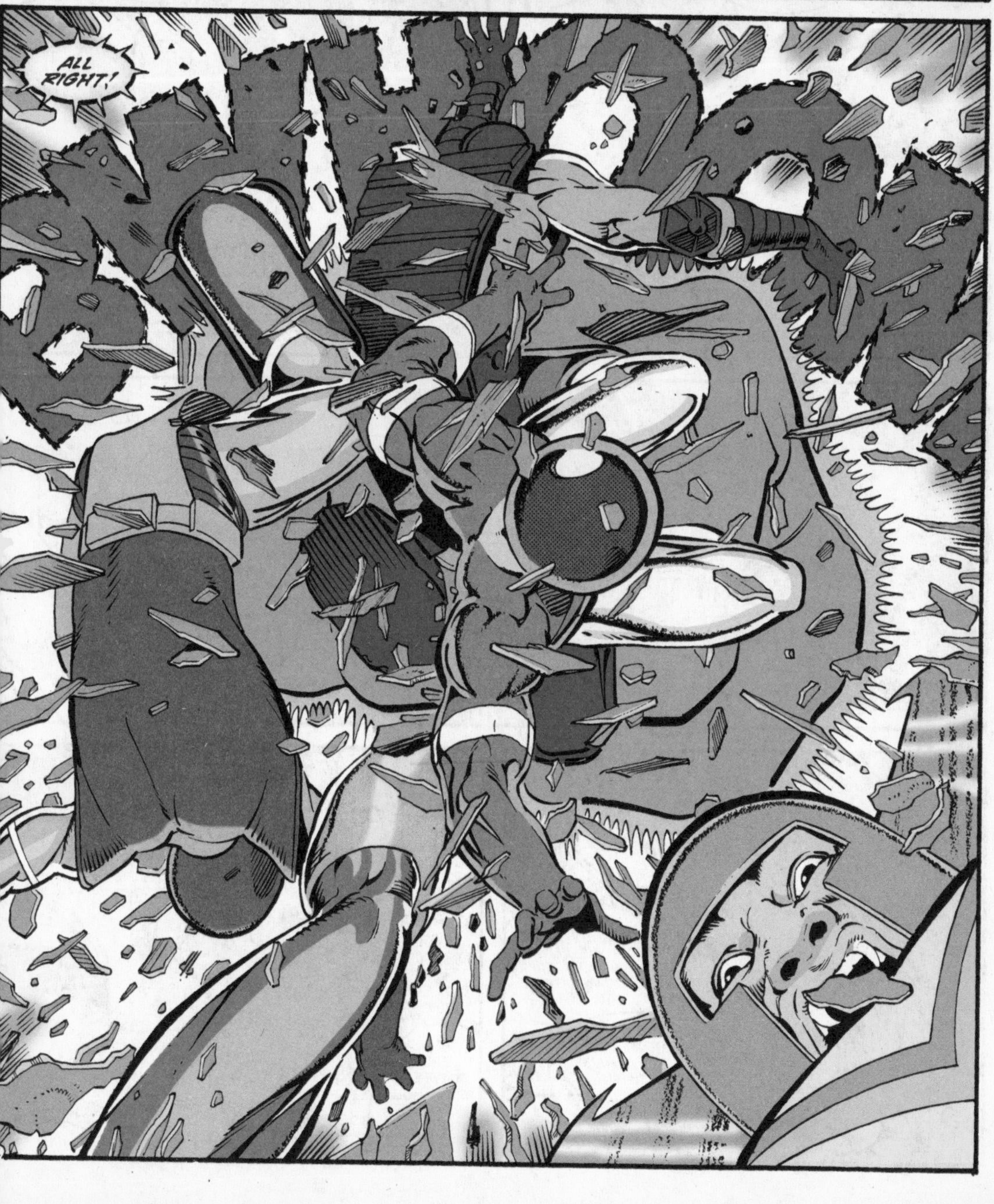
ALL RIGHT!

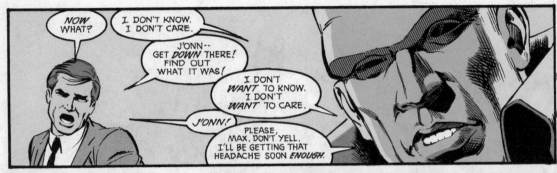

NOW WHAT?

I DON'T KNOW. I DON'T CARE.

J'ONN-- GET *DOWN* THERE! FIND OUT WHAT IT WAS!

I DON'T *WANT* TO KNOW. I DON'T *WANT* TO CARE.

J'ONN!

PLEASE, MAX, DON'T YELL. I'LL BE GETTING THAT HEADACHE SOON *ENOUGH*.

LET ME *THROUGH!*

YOU'RE STANDING ON MY *CAPE!*

HEY! THE CREEPER JUST *PINCHED* ME!

I GIVE UP.

DON'T YOU *WISH!*

PLEASE TO STOP *PUSHING!*

LET ME *AT* THOSE KHUNDS!

NO, ELONGATED MAN-- LET *ME!*

WELL, IF YOU *INSIST!*

WAANNG

NICE SHOT!

GET *UP,* DAMMIT! HOW CAN WE RUN AWAY WHEN YOU'RE *LAYING* THERE LIKE THAT?

THERE... THERE ARE SO *MANY* OF THEM--!

OH, YOU *NOTICED* THAT, DID YOU?

THEY'RE GETTING AWAY! *LET'S MOVE!*

WATCH IT, THERE, POWER GIRL-- YOU ALMOST STEPPED ON THE *ATOM!*

OH. *SORRY.*

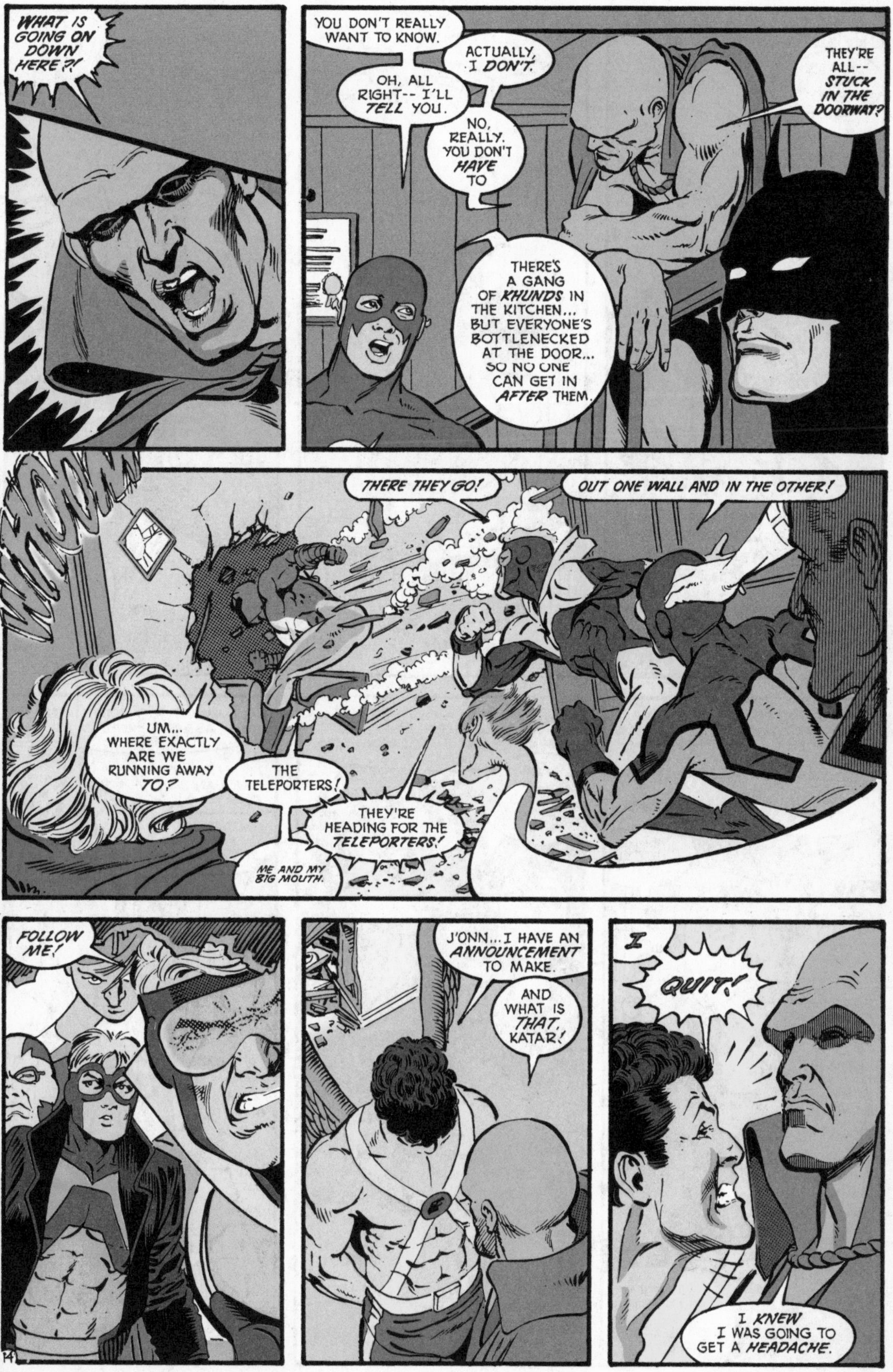
WHAT IS GOING ON DOWN HERE?!
YOU DON'T REALLY WANT TO KNOW.
ACTUALLY, I DON'T.
OH, ALL RIGHT-- I'LL TELL YOU.
NO, REALLY. YOU DON'T HAVE TO
THEY'RE ALL-- STUCK IN THE DOORWAY?
THERE'S A GANG OF KHUNDS IN THE KITCHEN... BUT EVERYONE'S BOTTLENECKED AT THE DOOR... SO NO ONE CAN GET IN AFTER THEM.
THERE THEY GO!
OUT ONE WALL AND IN THE OTHER!
UM... WHERE EXACTLY ARE WE RUNNING AWAY TO?
THE TELEPORTERS!
THEY'RE HEADING FOR THE TELEPORTERS!
ME AND MY BIG MOUTH.
FOLLOW ME!
J'ONN... I HAVE AN ANNOUNCEMENT TO MAKE.
AND WHAT IS THAT, KATAR!
I QUIT!
I KNEW I WAS GOING TO GET A HEADACHE.
14

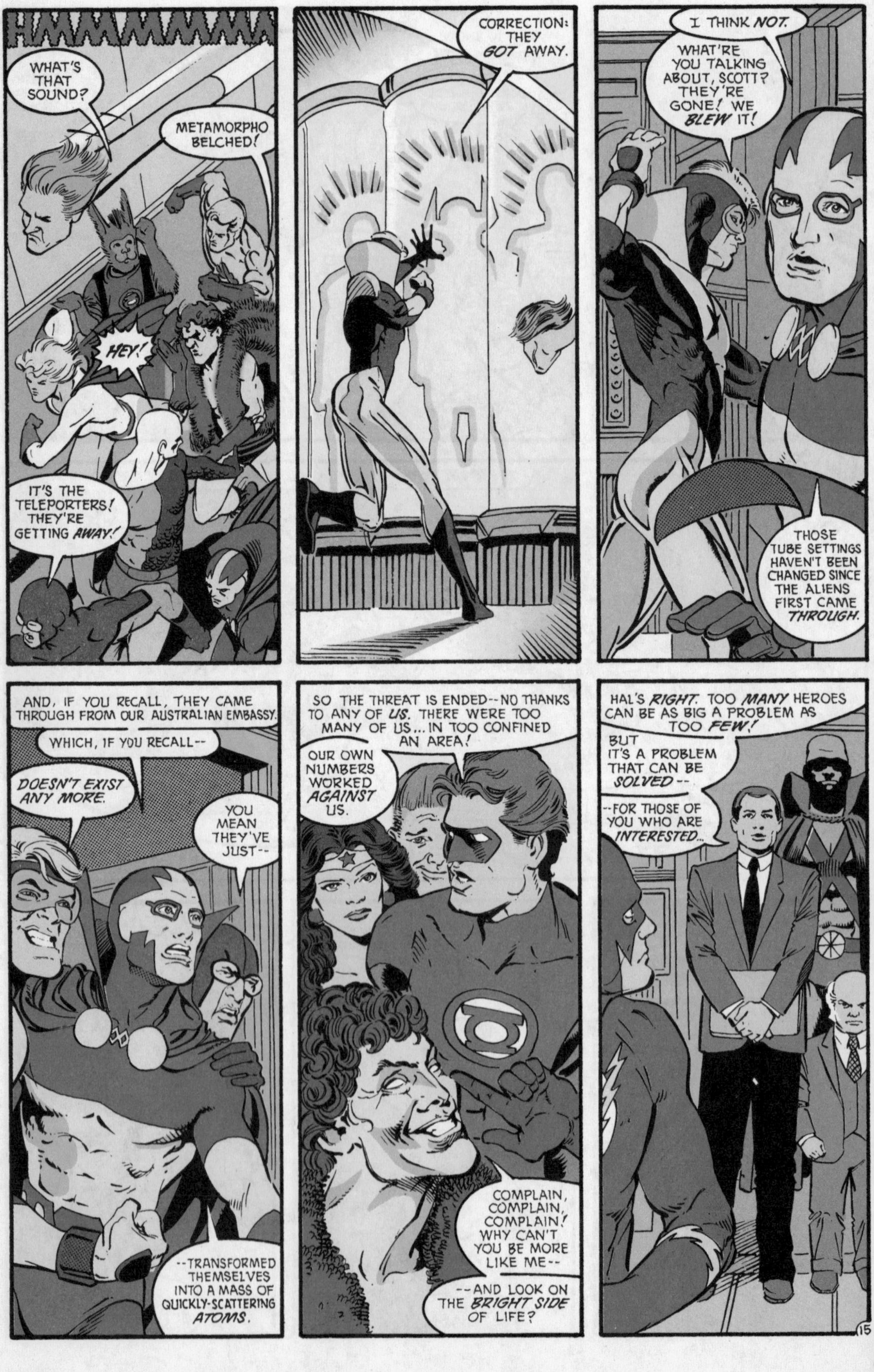
HMMMMMMM
WHAT'S THAT SOUND?
METAMORPHO BELCHED!
HEY!
IT'S THE TELEPORTERS! THEY'RE GETTING AWAY!
CORRECTION: THEY GOT AWAY.
I THINK NOT.
WHAT'RE YOU TALKING ABOUT, SCOTT? THEY'RE GONE! WE BLEW IT!
THOSE TUBE SETTINGS HAVEN'T BEEN CHANGED SINCE THE ALIENS FIRST CAME THROUGH.
AND, IF YOU RECALL, THEY CAME THROUGH FROM OUR AUSTRALIAN EMBASSY.
WHICH, IF YOU RECALL--
DOESN'T EXIST ANY MORE.
YOU MEAN THEY'VE JUST--
--TRANSFORMED THEMSELVES INTO A MASS OF QUICKLY-SCATTERING ATOMS.
SO THE THREAT IS ENDED--NO THANKS TO ANY OF US. THERE WERE TOO MANY OF US... IN TOO CONFINED AN AREA!
OUR OWN NUMBERS WORKED AGAINST US.
COMPLAIN, COMPLAIN, COMPLAIN! WHY CAN'T YOU BE MORE LIKE ME--
--AND LOOK ON THE BRIGHT SIDE OF LIFE?
HAL'S RIGHT. TOO MANY HEROES CAN BE AS BIG A PROBLEM AS TOO FEW!
BUT IT'S A PROBLEM THAT CAN BE SOLVED--
--FOR THOSE OF YOU WHO ARE INTERESTED...
15

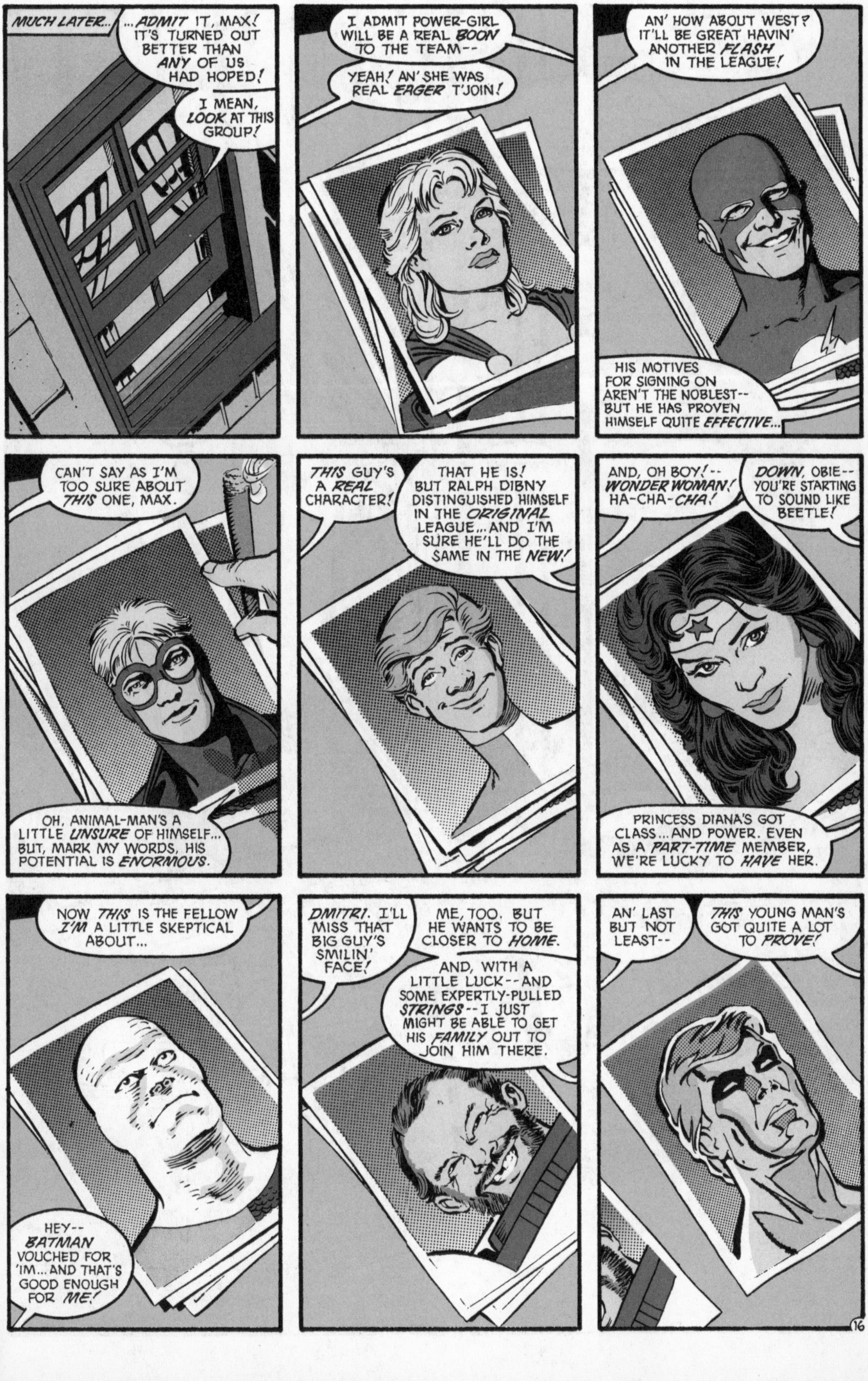
MUCH LATER...
...ADMIT IT, MAX! IT'S TURNED OUT BETTER THAN ANY OF US HAD HOPED!
I MEAN, LOOK AT THIS GROUP!
I ADMIT POWER-GIRL WILL BE A REAL BOON TO THE TEAM--
YEAH! AN' SHE WAS REAL EAGER T'JOIN!
AN' HOW ABOUT WEST? IT'LL BE GREAT HAVIN' ANOTHER FLASH IN THE LEAGUE!
HIS MOTIVES FOR SIGNING ON AREN'T THE NOBLEST-- BUT HE HAS PROVEN HIMSELF QUITE EFFECTIVE...
CAN'T SAY AS I'M TOO SURE ABOUT THIS ONE, MAX.
OH, ANIMAL-MAN'S A LITTLE UNSURE OF HIMSELF... BUT, MARK MY WORDS, HIS POTENTIAL IS ENORMOUS.
THIS GUY'S A REAL CHARACTER!
THAT HE IS! BUT RALPH DIBNY DISTINGUISHED HIMSELF IN THE ORIGINAL LEAGUE... AND I'M SURE HE'LL DO THE SAME IN THE NEW!
AND, OH BOY!-- WONDER WOMAN! HA-CHA-CHA!
DOWN, OBIE-- YOU'RE STARTING TO SOUND LIKE BEETLE!
PRINCESS DIANA'S GOT CLASS... AND POWER. EVEN AS A PART-TIME MEMBER, WE'RE LUCKY TO HAVE HER.
NOW THIS IS THE FELLOW I'M A LITTLE SKEPTICAL ABOUT...
HEY-- BATMAN VOUCHED FOR 'IM... AND THAT'S GOOD ENOUGH FOR ME!
DMITRI. I'LL MISS THAT BIG GUY'S SMILIN' FACE!
ME, TOO. BUT HE WANTS TO BE CLOSER TO HOME.
AND, WITH A LITTLE LUCK--AND SOME EXPERTLY-PULLED STRINGS--I JUST MIGHT BE ABLE TO GET HIS FAMILY OUT TO JOIN HIM THERE.
AN' LAST BUT NOT LEAST--
THIS YOUNG MAN'S GOT QUITE A LOT TO PROVE!
16

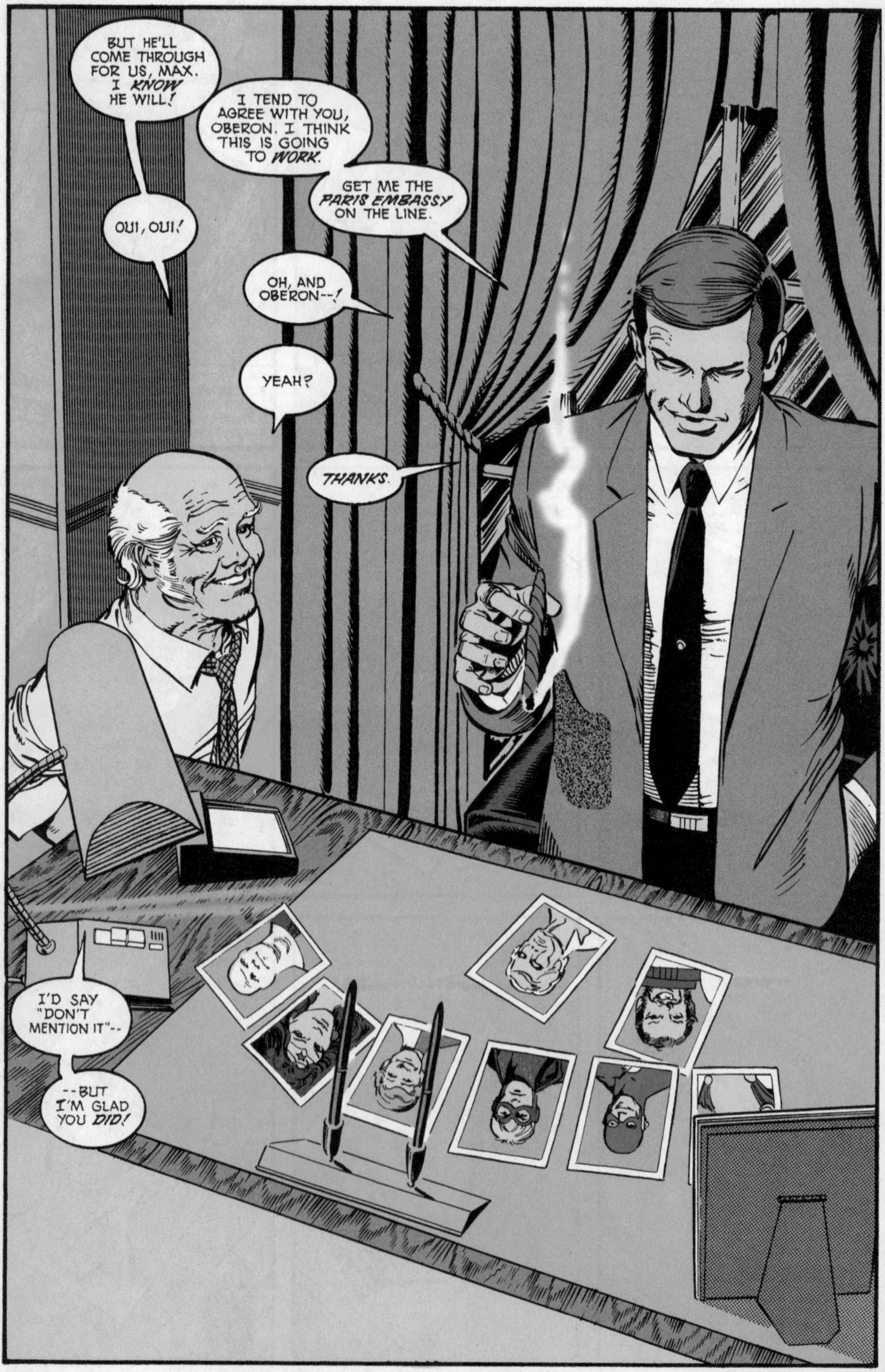
BUT HE'LL COME THROUGH FOR US, MAX. I *KNOW* HE WILL!
I TEND TO AGREE WITH YOU, OBERON. I THINK THIS IS GOING TO *WORK*.
GET ME THE *PARIS EMBASSY* ON THE LINE.
OUI, OUI!
OH, AND OBERON--!
YEAH?
THANKS.
I'D SAY "DON'T MENTION IT"--
--BUT I'M GLAD YOU *DID*!

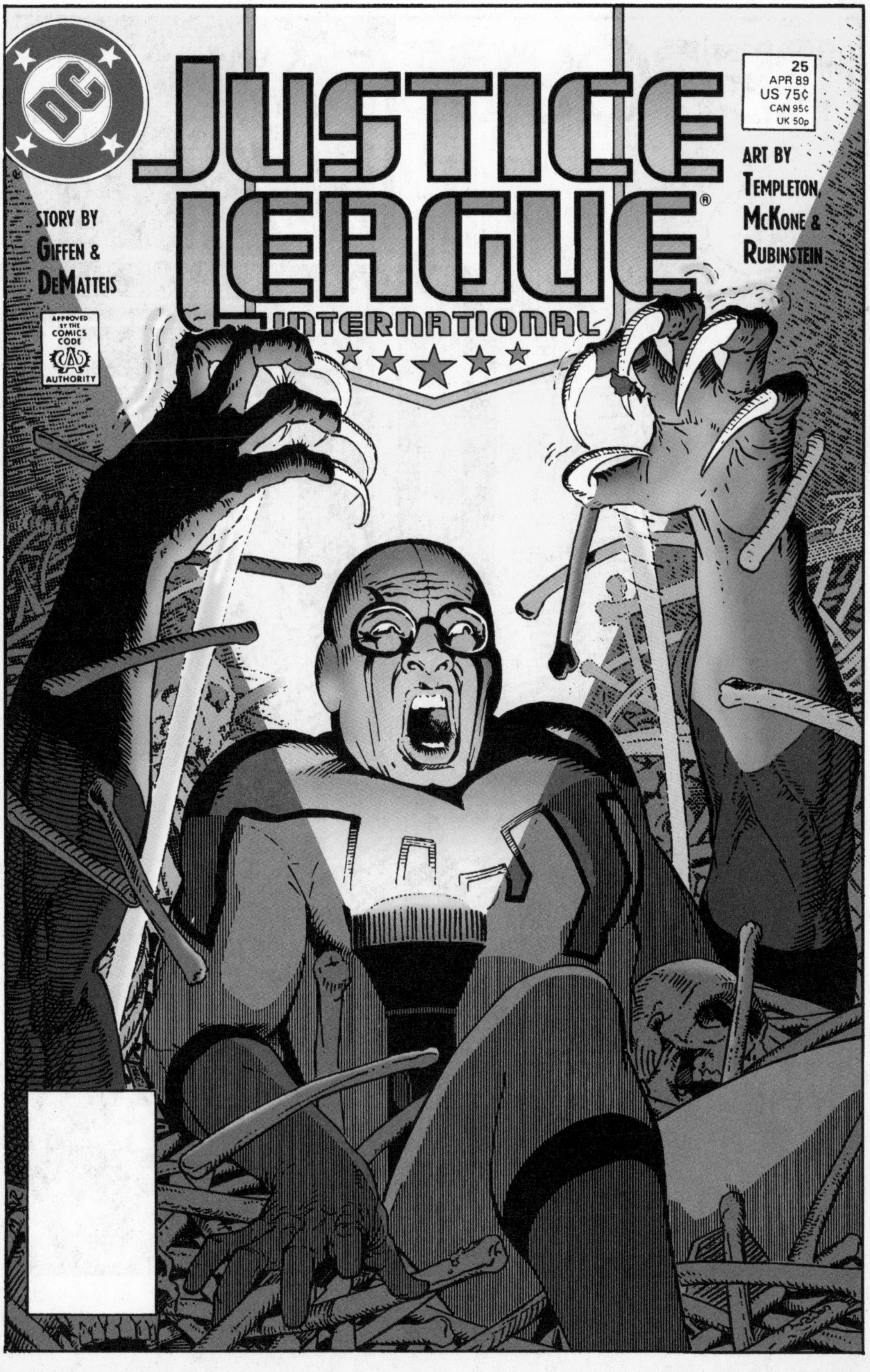
DC
JUSTICE LEAGUE INTERNATIONAL
25
APR 89
US 75¢
CAN 95¢
UK 50p
ART BY
TEMPLETON,
McKONE &
RUBINSTEIN
STORY BY
GIFFEN &
DeMATTEIS
APPROVED BY THE COMICS CODE AUTHORITY

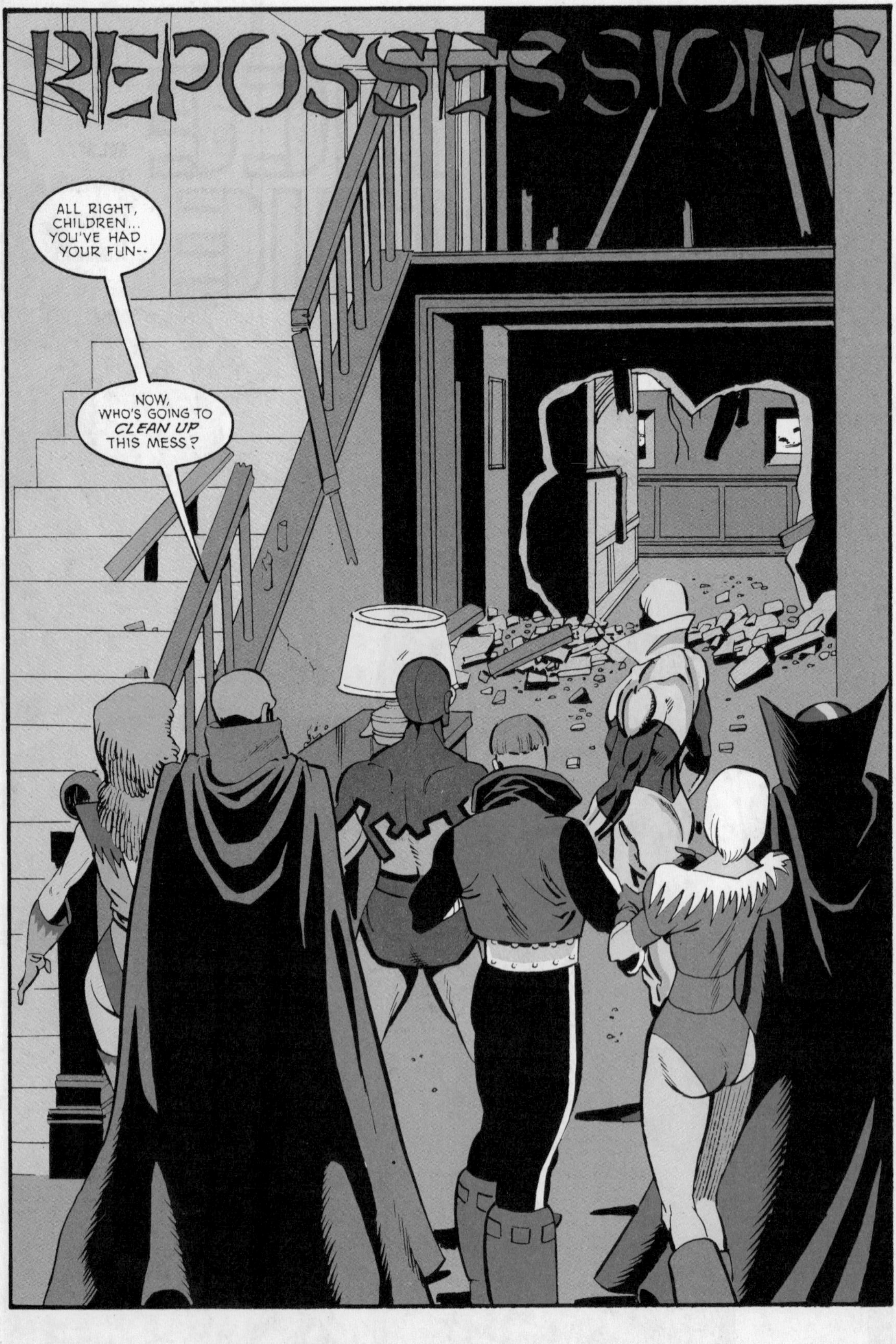

REPOSSESSIONS
ALL RIGHT, CHILDREN... YOU'VE HAD YOUR FUN--
NOW, WHO'S GOING TO *CLEAN UP* THIS MESS?

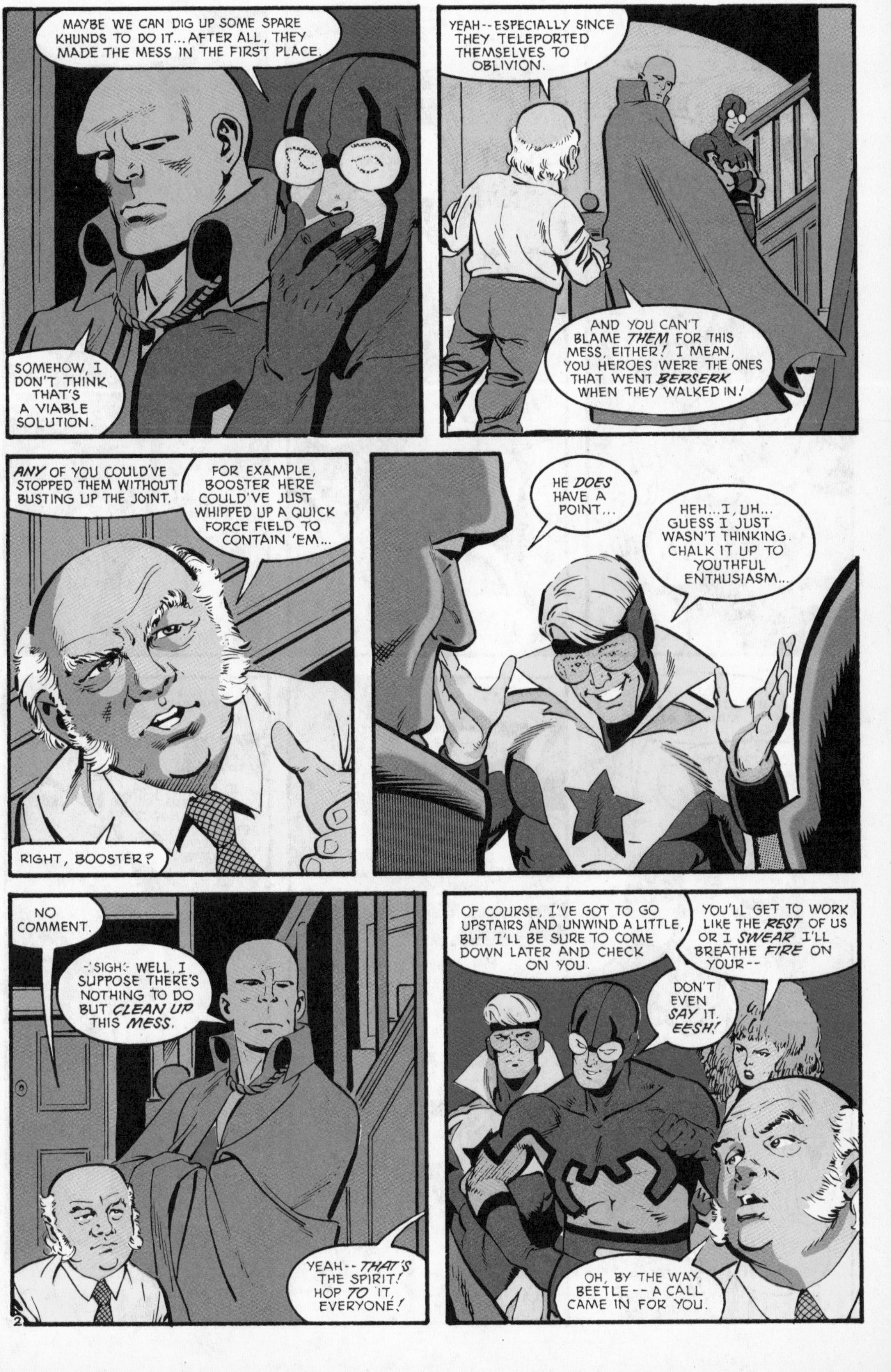

MAYBE WE CAN DIG UP SOME SPARE KHUNDS TO DO IT... AFTER ALL, THEY MADE THE MESS IN THE FIRST PLACE.
SOMEHOW, I DON'T THINK THAT'S A VIABLE SOLUTION.
YEAH--ESPECIALLY SINCE THEY TELEPORTED THEMSELVES TO OBLIVION.
AND YOU CAN'T BLAME THEM FOR THIS MESS, EITHER! I MEAN, YOU HEROES WERE THE ONES THAT WENT BERSERK WHEN THEY WALKED IN!
ANY OF YOU COULD'VE STOPPED THEM WITHOUT BUSTING UP THE JOINT.
FOR EXAMPLE, BOOSTER HERE COULD'VE JUST WHIPPED UP A QUICK FORCE FIELD TO CONTAIN 'EM...
RIGHT, BOOSTER?
HE DOES HAVE A POINT...
HEH...I, UH... GUESS I JUST WASN'T THINKING. CHALK IT UP TO YOUTHFUL ENTHUSIASM...
NO COMMENT.
-SIGH- WELL, I SUPPOSE THERE'S NOTHING TO DO BUT CLEAN UP THIS MESS.
YEAH--THAT'S THE SPIRIT! HOP TO IT, EVERYONE!
2
OF COURSE, I'VE GOT TO GO UPSTAIRS AND UNWIND A LITTLE, BUT I'LL BE SURE TO COME DOWN LATER AND CHECK ON YOU.
YOU'LL GET TO WORK LIKE THE REST OF US OR I SWEAR I'LL BREATHE FIRE ON YOUR--
DON'T EVEN SAY IT. EESH!
OH, BY THE WAY, BEETLE--A CALL CAME IN FOR YOU.

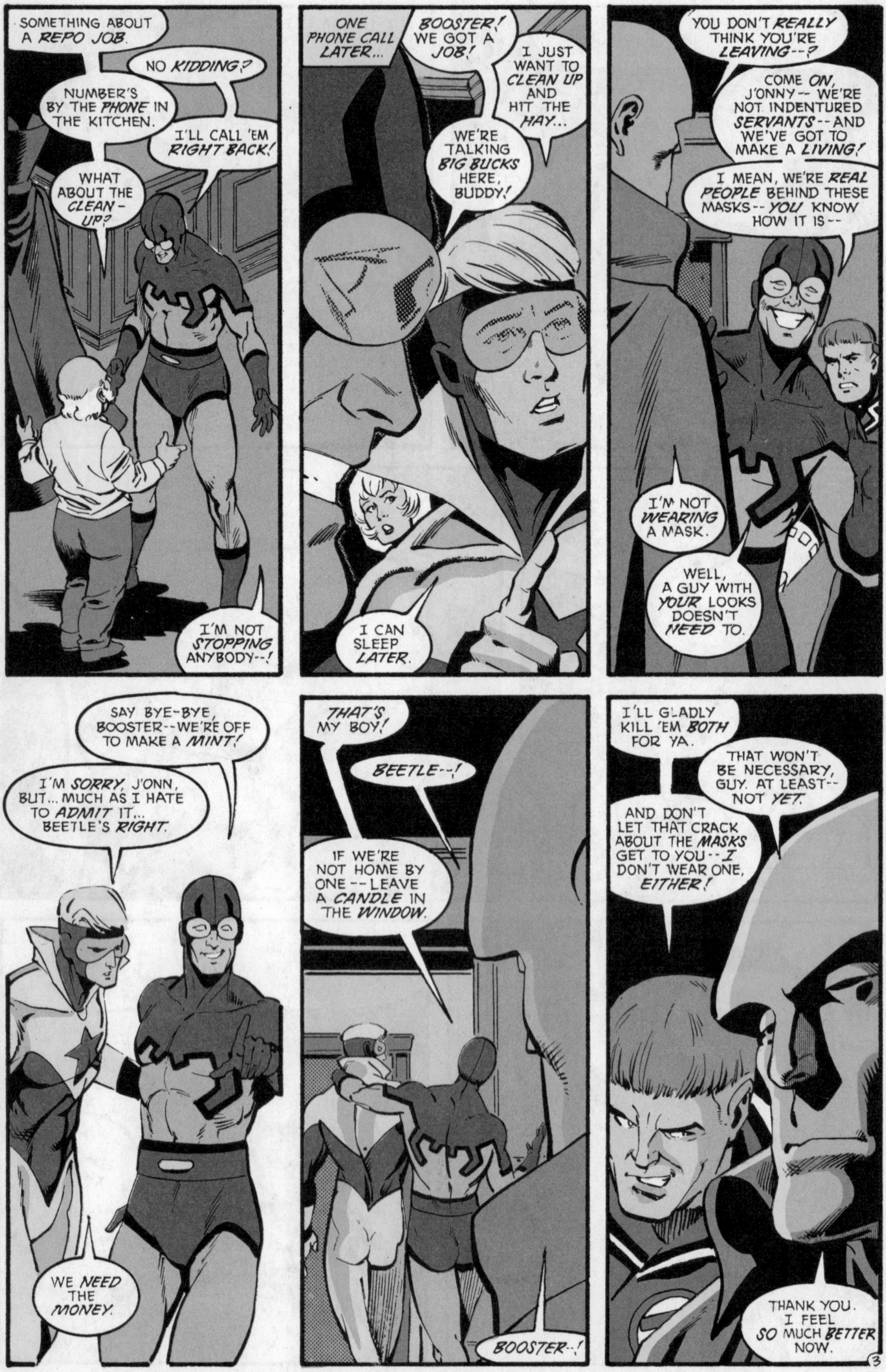
SOMETHING ABOUT A *REPO JOB.*
NO *KIDDING?*
NUMBER'S BY THE *PHONE* IN THE KITCHEN.
I'LL CALL 'EM *RIGHT BACK!*
WHAT ABOUT THE *CLEAN-UP?*
I'M NOT *STOPPING* ANYBODY--!
ONE PHONE CALL LATER...
BOOSTER! WE GOT A *JOB!*
I JUST WANT TO *CLEAN UP* AND HIT THE *HAY...*
WE'RE TALKING *BIG BUCKS* HERE, BUDDY!
I CAN SLEEP *LATER.*
YOU DON'T *REALLY* THINK YOU'RE *LEAVING--?*
COME *ON,* J'ONNY-- WE'RE NOT INDENTURED *SERVANTS*--AND WE'VE GOT TO MAKE A *LIVING!*
I MEAN, WE'RE *REAL PEOPLE* BEHIND THESE MASKS-- *YOU* KNOW HOW IT IS--
I'M NOT *WEARING* A MASK.
WELL, A GUY WITH *YOUR* LOOKS DOESN'T *NEED* TO.
SAY BYE-BYE, BOOSTER--WE'RE OFF TO MAKE A *MINT!*
I'M *SORRY,* J'ONN, BUT... MUCH AS I HATE TO *ADMIT* IT... BEETLE'S *RIGHT.*
WE *NEED* THE *MONEY.*
THAT'S MY BOY!
BEETLE--!
IF WE'RE NOT HOME BY ONE--LEAVE A *CANDLE* IN THE *WINDOW.*
BOOSTER--!
I'LL GLADLY KILL 'EM *BOTH* FOR YA.
THAT WON'T BE NECESSARY, GUY. AT LEAST-- NOT *YET.*
AND DON'T LET THAT CRACK ABOUT THE *MASKS* GET TO YOU-- *I* DON'T WEAR ONE, *EITHER!*
THANK YOU. I FEEL *SO* MUCH *BETTER* NOW.
3

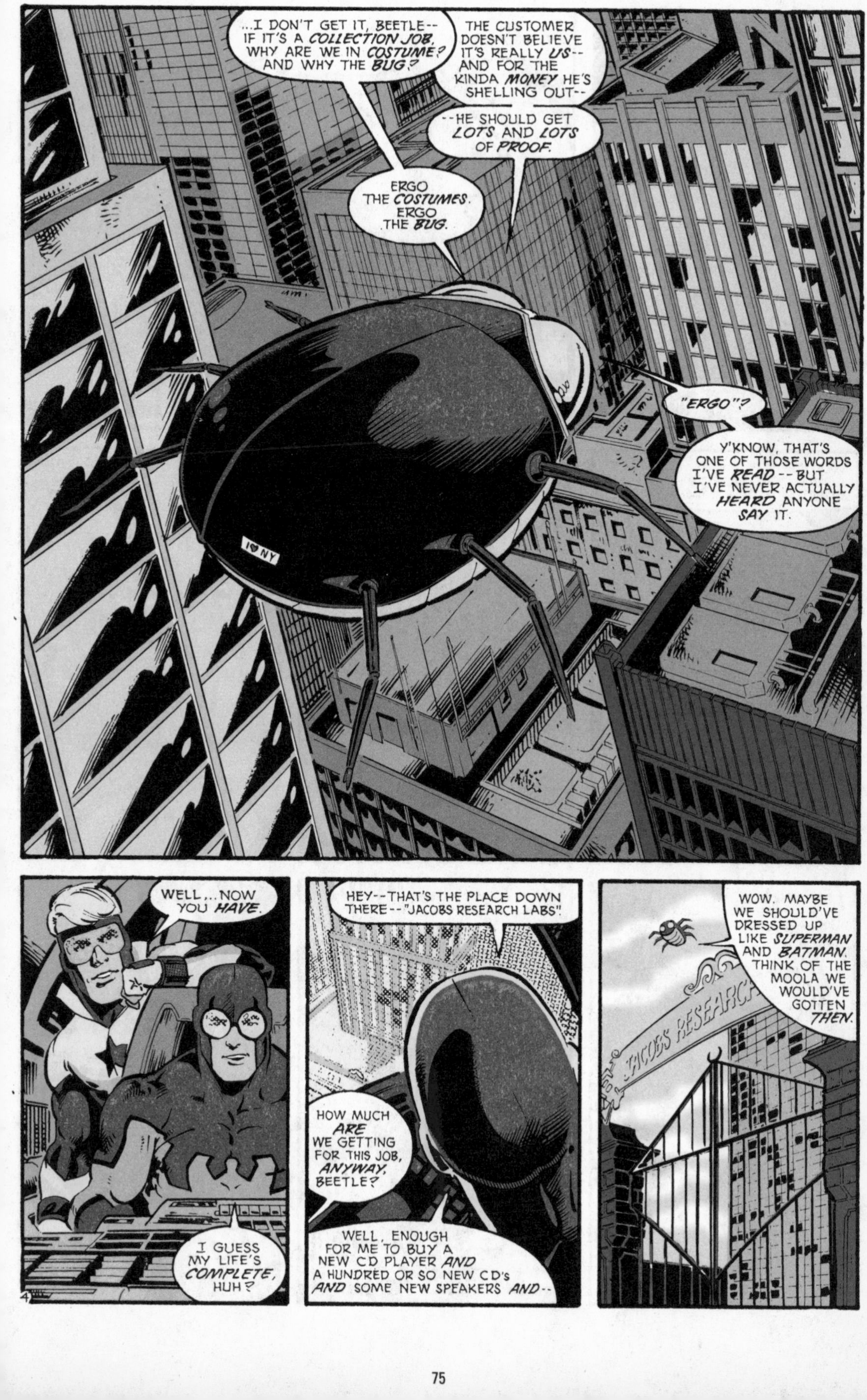
...I DON'T GET IT, BEETLE--
IF IT'S A *COLLECTION JOB,* WHY ARE WE IN *COSTUME?* AND WHY THE *BUG?*
THE CUSTOMER DOESN'T BELIEVE IT'S REALLY *US*-- AND FOR THE KINDA *MONEY* HE'S SHELLING OUT--
--HE SHOULD GET *LOTS* AND *LOTS* OF *PROOF.*
ERGO THE *COSTUMES.* ERGO THE *BUG.*
I ♥ NY
"ERGO"?
Y'KNOW, THAT'S ONE OF THOSE WORDS I'VE *READ* -- BUT I'VE NEVER ACTUALLY *HEARD* ANYONE *SAY* IT.
WELL,.. NOW YOU *HAVE.*
I GUESS MY LIFE'S *COMPLETE,* HUH?
HEY--THAT'S THE PLACE DOWN THERE--"JACOBS RESEARCH LABS".
HOW MUCH *ARE* WE GETTING FOR THIS JOB, *ANYWAY,* BEETLE?
WELL, ENOUGH FOR ME TO BUY A NEW CD PLAYER *AND* A HUNDRED OR SO NEW CD's *AND* SOME NEW SPEAKERS *AND*--
WOW. MAYBE WE SHOULD'VE DRESSED UP LIKE *SUPERMAN* AND *BATMAN.* THINK OF THE MOOLA WE WOULD'VE GOTTEN *THEN.*

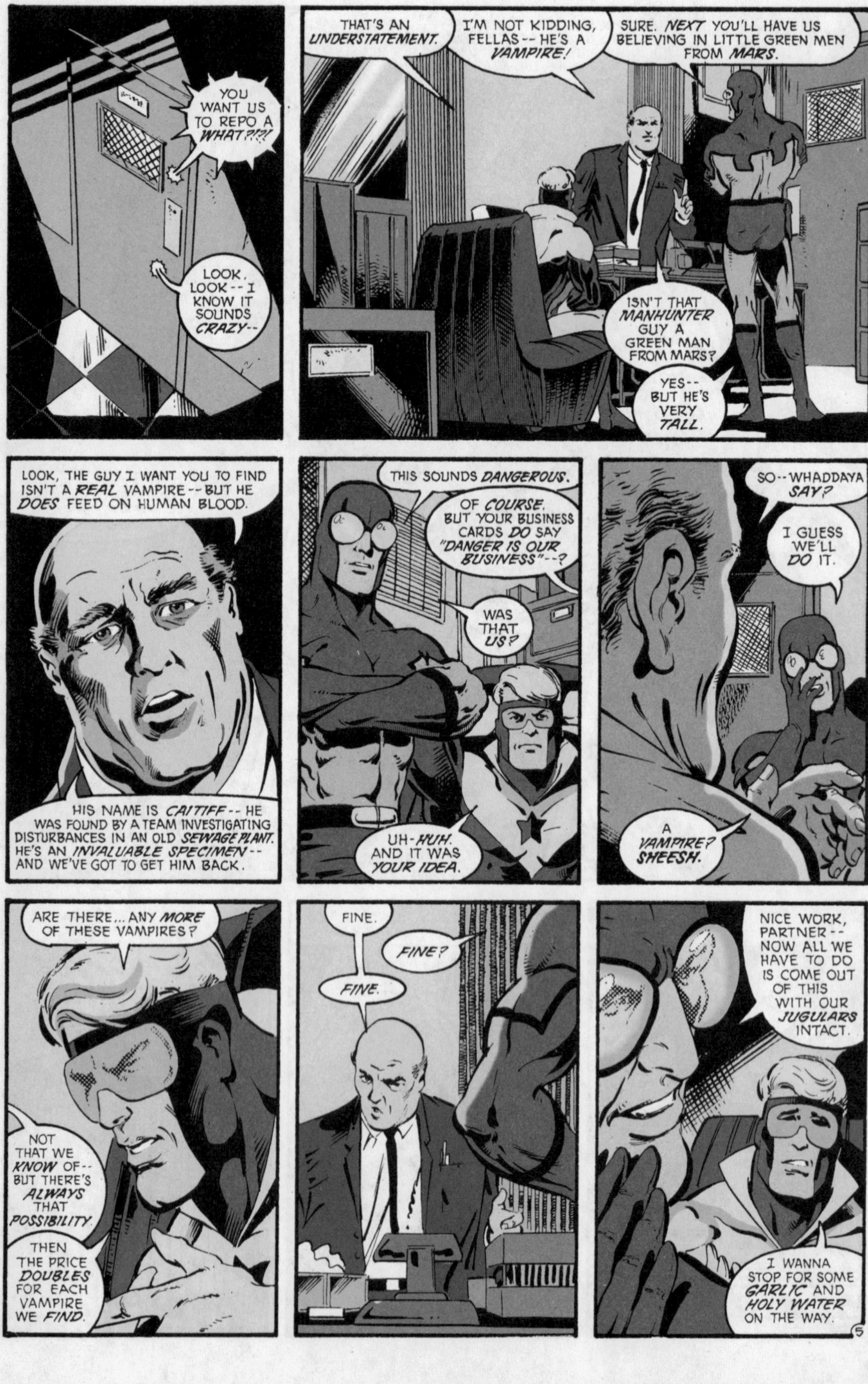
YOU WANT US TO REPO A WHAT?!?!
LOOK, LOOK -- I KNOW IT SOUNDS CRAZY--
THAT'S AN UNDERSTATEMENT.
I'M NOT KIDDING, FELLAS -- HE'S A VAMPIRE!
SURE. NEXT YOU'LL HAVE US BELIEVING IN LITTLE GREEN MEN FROM MARS.
ISN'T THAT MANHUNTER GUY A GREEN MAN FROM MARS?
YES-- BUT HE'S VERY TALL.
LOOK, THE GUY I WANT YOU TO FIND ISN'T A REAL VAMPIRE -- BUT HE DOES FEED ON HUMAN BLOOD.
HIS NAME IS CAITIFF -- HE WAS FOUND BY A TEAM INVESTIGATING DISTURBANCES IN AN OLD SEWAGE PLANT. HE'S AN INVALUABLE SPECIMEN -- AND WE'VE GOT TO GET HIM BACK.
THIS SOUNDS DANGEROUS.
OF COURSE. BUT YOUR BUSINESS CARDS DO SAY "DANGER IS OUR BUSINESS"--?
WAS THAT US?
UH-HUH. AND IT WAS YOUR IDEA.
SO--WHADDAYA SAY?
I GUESS WE'LL DO IT.
A VAMPIRE? SHEESH.
ARE THERE... ANY MORE OF THESE VAMPIRES?
NOT THAT WE KNOW OF-- BUT THERE'S ALWAYS THAT POSSIBILITY.
THEN THE PRICE DOUBLES FOR EACH VAMPIRE WE FIND.
FINE.
FINE?
FINE.
NICE WORK, PARTNER -- NOW ALL WE HAVE TO DO IS COME OUT OF THIS WITH OUR JUGULARS INTACT.
I WANNA STOP FOR SOME GARLIC AND HOLY WATER ON THE WAY.
5

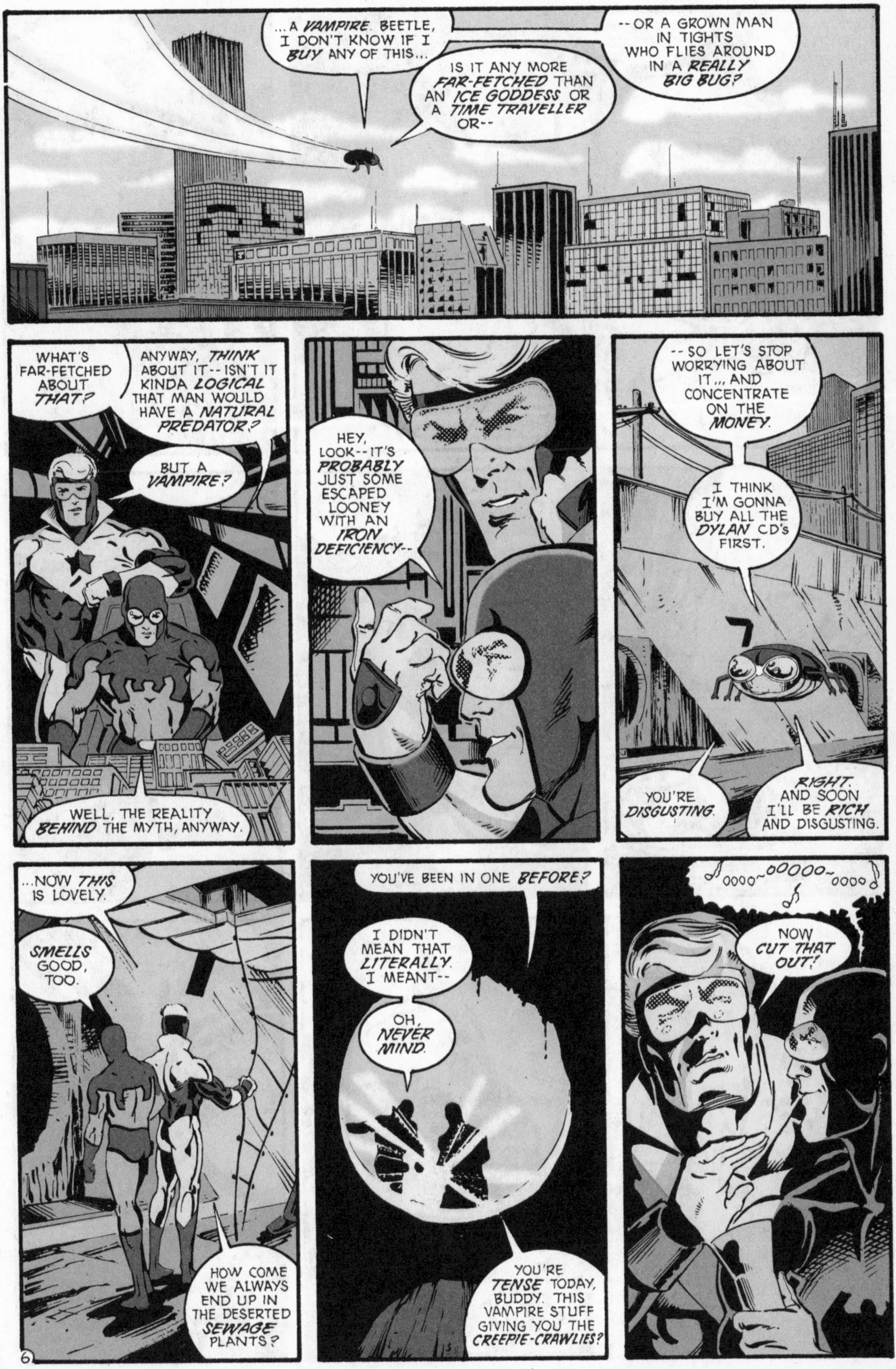
...A VAMPIRE BEETLE, I DON'T KNOW IF I BUY ANY OF THIS...
IS IT ANY MORE FAR-FETCHED THAN AN ICE GODDESS OR A TIME TRAVELLER OR--
--OR A GROWN MAN IN TIGHTS WHO FLIES AROUND IN A REALLY BIG BUG?
WHAT'S FAR-FETCHED ABOUT THAT?
ANYWAY, THINK ABOUT IT--ISN'T IT KINDA LOGICAL THAT MAN WOULD HAVE A NATURAL PREDATOR?
BUT A VAMPIRE?
WELL, THE REALITY BEHIND THE MYTH, ANYWAY.
HEY, LOOK--IT'S PROBABLY JUST SOME ESCAPED LOONEY WITH AN IRON DEFICIENCY--
--SO LET'S STOP WORRYING ABOUT IT... AND CONCENTRATE ON THE MONEY.
I THINK I'M GONNA BUY ALL THE DYLAN CD's FIRST.
YOU'RE DISGUSTING.
RIGHT. AND SOON I'LL BE RICH AND DISGUSTING.
...NOW THIS IS LOVELY.
SMELLS GOOD, TOO.
HOW COME WE ALWAYS END UP IN THE DESERTED SEWAGE PLANTS?
6
YOU'VE BEEN IN ONE BEFORE?
I DIDN'T MEAN THAT LITERALLY. I MEANT--
OH, NEVER MIND.
YOU'RE TENSE TODAY, BUDDY. THIS VAMPIRE STUFF GIVING YOU THE CREEPIE-CRAWLIES?
oooo~OOOOO~oooo
NOW CUT THAT OUT!

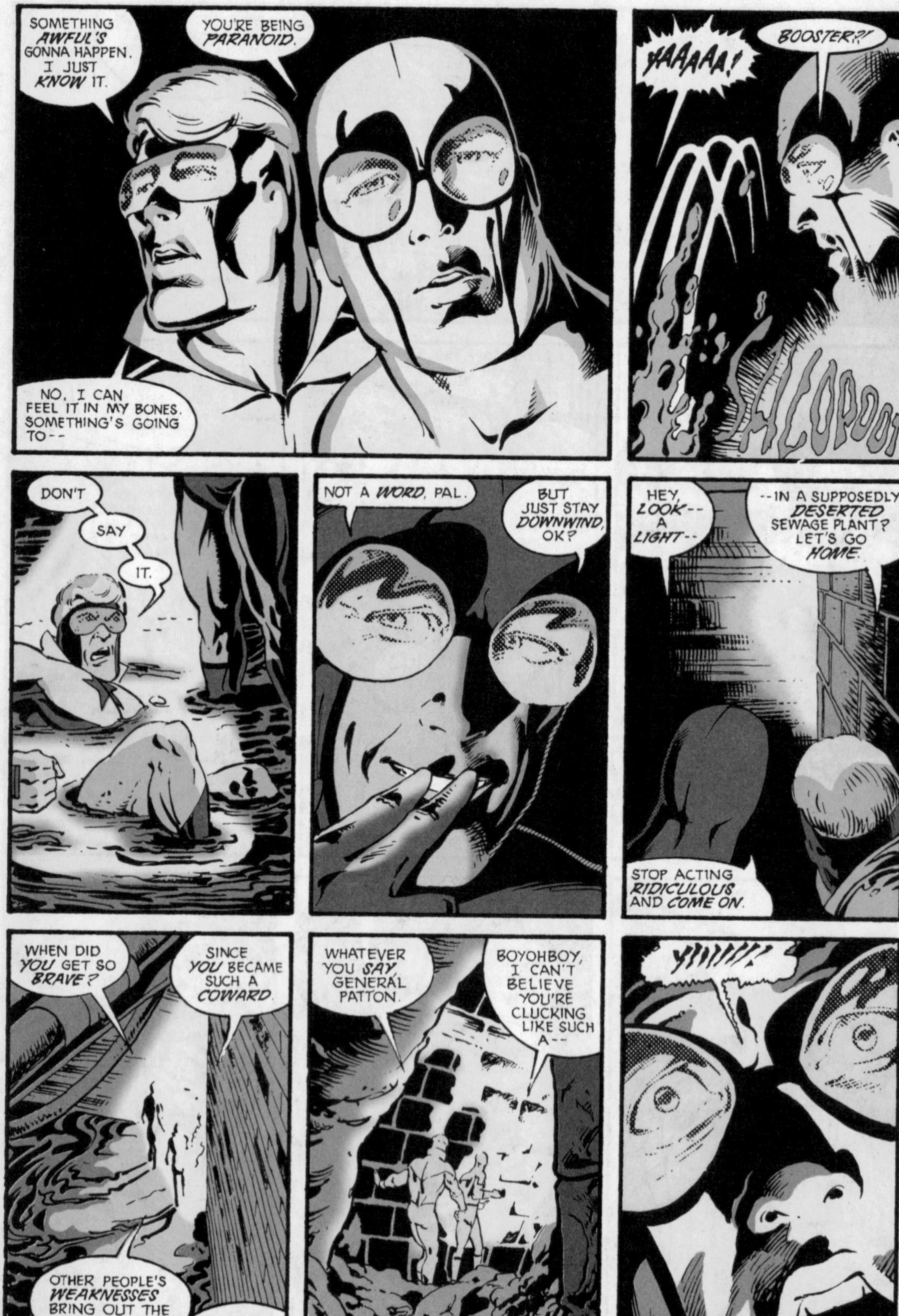
SOMETHING AWFUL'S GONNA HAPPEN. I JUST KNOW IT.
YOU'RE BEING PARANOID.
NO, I CAN FEEL IT IN MY BONES. SOMETHING'S GOING TO--
YAAAAA!
BOOSTER?!
SHLOOOOT
DON'T
SAY
IT.
NOT A WORD, PAL.
BUT JUST STAY DOWNWIND, OK?
HEY, LOOK-- A LIGHT--
--IN A SUPPOSEDLY DESERTED SEWAGE PLANT? LET'S GO HOME.
STOP ACTING RIDICULOUS AND COME ON.
WHEN DID YOU GET SO BRAVE?
SINCE YOU BECAME SUCH A COWARD.
OTHER PEOPLE'S WEAKNESSES BRING OUT THE BEST IN ME.
NOW, COME ON-- IT'S JUST AROUND THE BEND.
WHATEVER YOU SAY, GENERAL PATTON.
BOYOHBOY, I CAN'T BELIEVE YOU'RE CLUCKING LIKE SUCH A--
YIIIII!
7

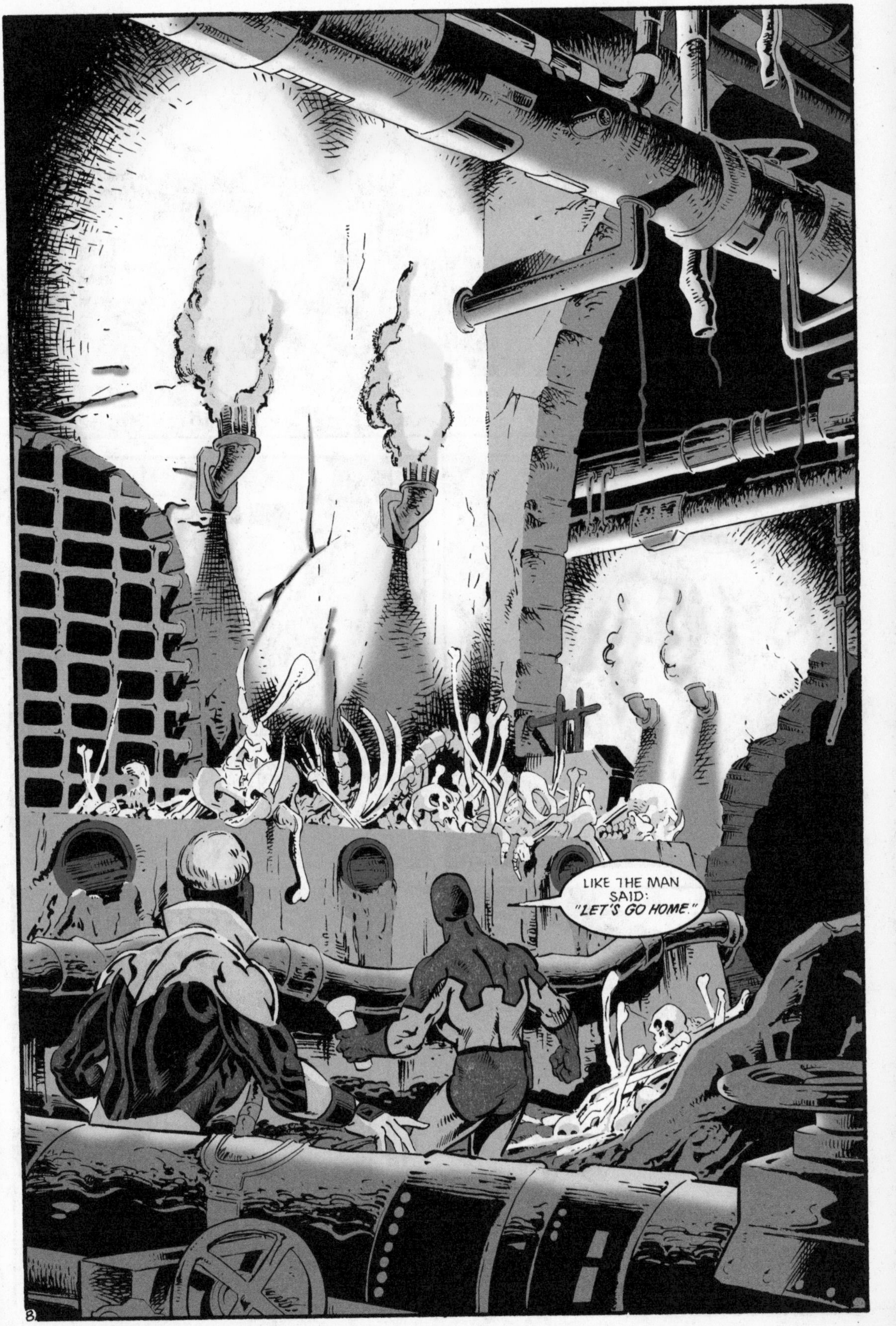
LIKE THE MAN SAID: "LET'S GO HOME."
8

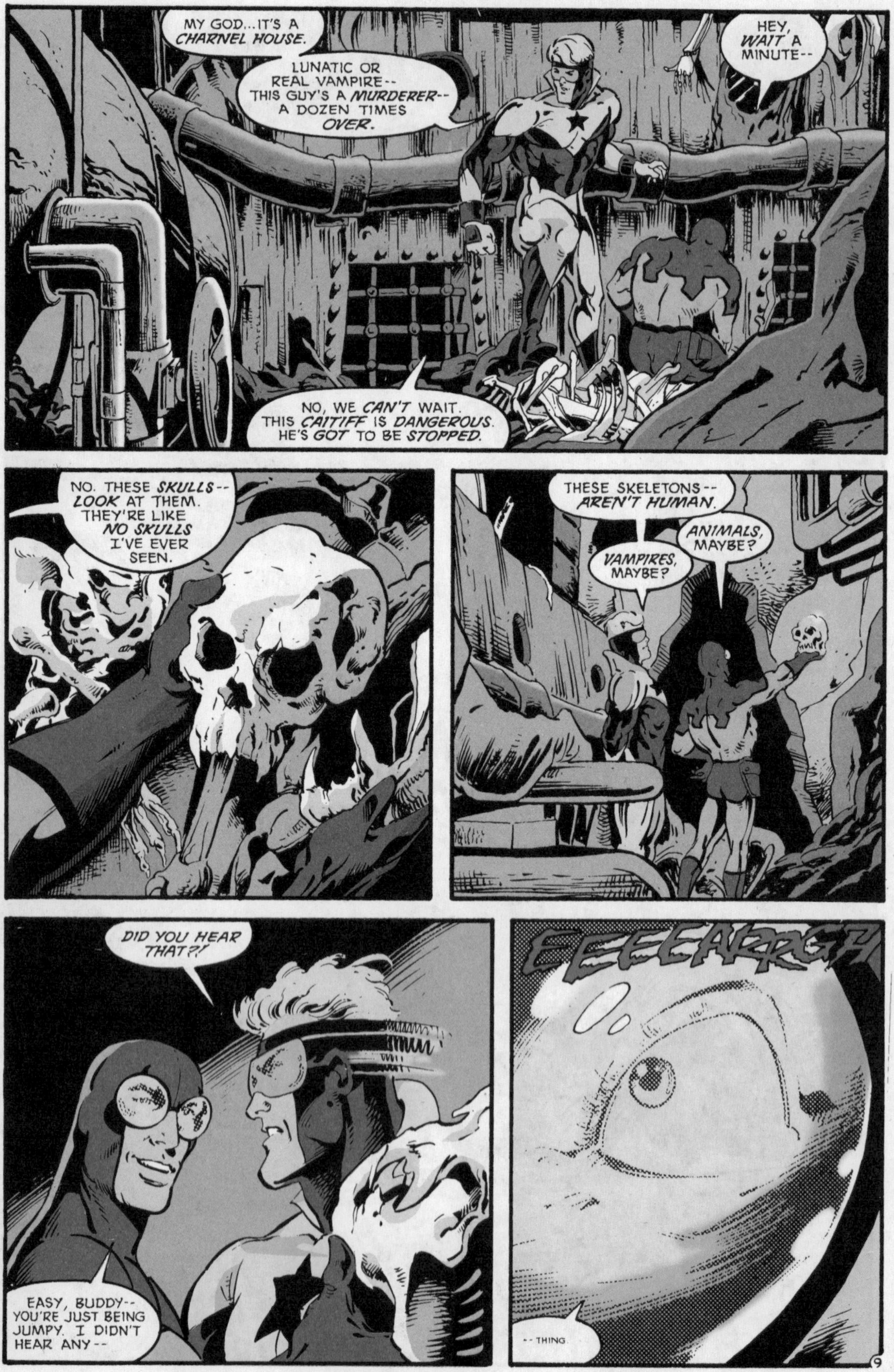
MY GOD...IT'S A CHARNEL HOUSE.
LUNATIC OR REAL VAMPIRE-- THIS GUY'S A MURDERER-- A DOZEN TIMES OVER.
HEY, WAIT A MINUTE--
NO, WE CAN'T WAIT. THIS CAITIFF IS DANGEROUS. HE'S GOT TO BE STOPPED.
NO. THESE SKULLS-- LOOK AT THEM. THEY'RE LIKE NO SKULLS I'VE EVER SEEN.
THESE SKELETONS-- AREN'T HUMAN.
VAMPIRES, MAYBE?
ANIMALS, MAYBE?
DID YOU HEAR THAT?!
EASY, BUDDY-- YOU'RE JUST BEING JUMPY. I DIDN'T HEAR ANY--
EEEEARRGH
--THING.
9

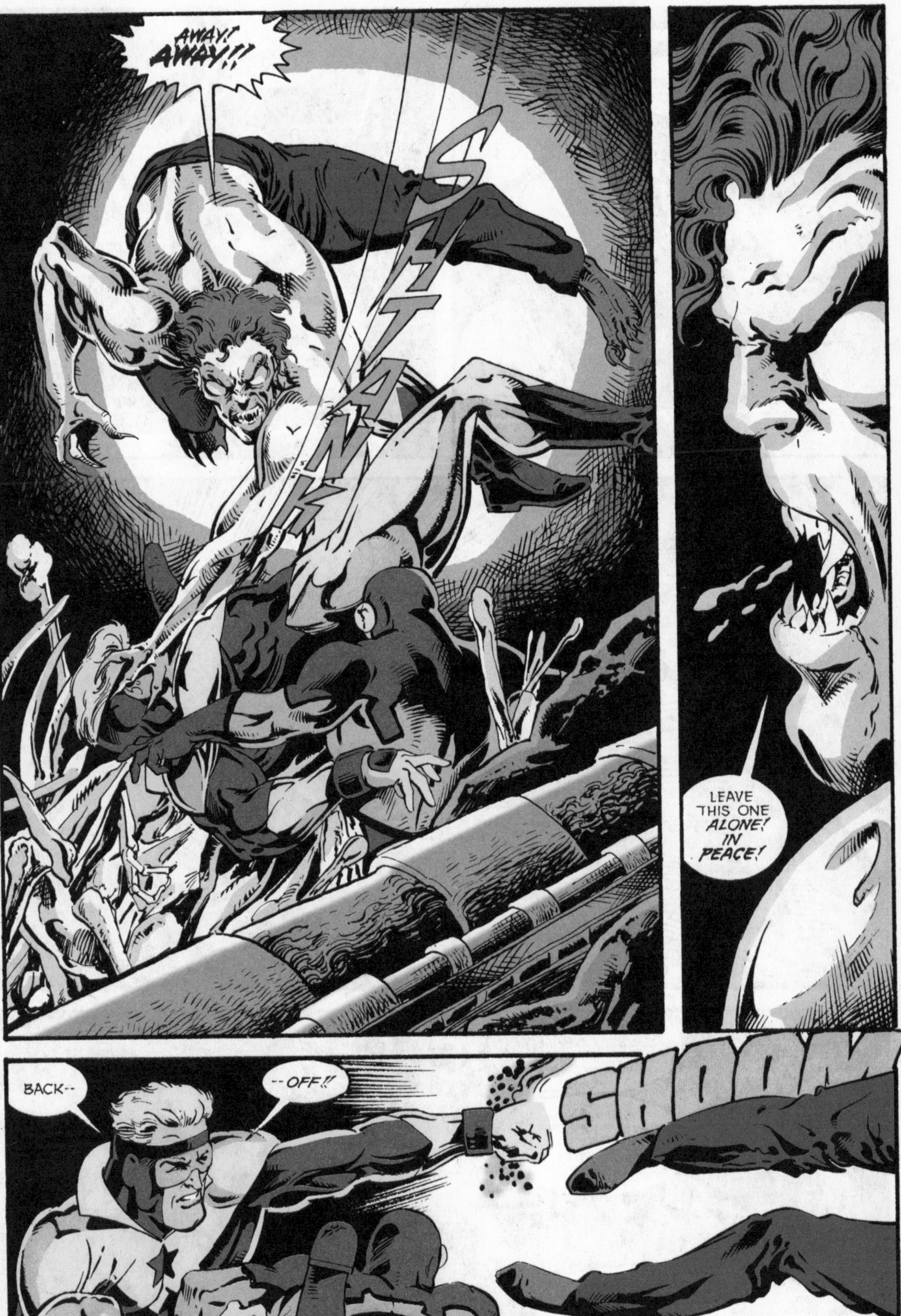

AWAY! AWAY!!
SHTANK
LEAVE THIS ONE ALONE! IN PEACE!
BACK--
--OFF!!
SHOOM
10

IT'S A VAMPIRE! IT'S A VAMPIRE! IT'S A *REAL* VAMPIRE!

WHEN DID *YOU* GET SO BRAVE?

BEETLE-- CALM *DOWN,* WILL YOU?

SINCE *YOU* STARTED ACTING LIKE SUCH A *COWARD.*

NOW WHERE HAVE I HEARD *THAT* BEFORE?

WE'VE GOT TO KEEP OUR *WITS* AND FORMULATE A *PLAN.*

BOOSTER!

BEETLE, WILL YOU *PLEASE* STAY--

BEHIND YOU!

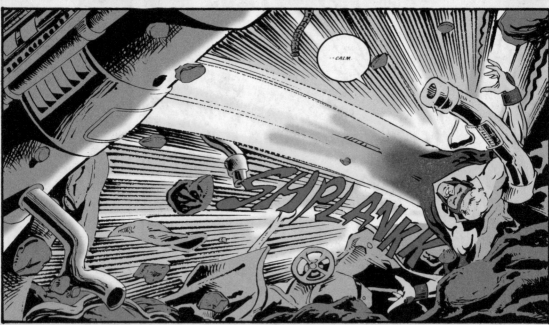

--CALM

SHPLANKK

LEAVE CAITIFF ALONE*ALONEALONE!* GO AWAY*AWAYAWAY!*

YOU DON'T HAVE TO *REPEAT* YOURSELF, Y'KNOW I CAN GET IT THE *FIRST* TIME

BEETLE-- THIS ISN'T THE TIME FOR *DUMB JOKES!* THAT THING'S A *VAMPIRE!* HE WANTS TO SUCK YOUR *BLOOD!*

OH, YEAH, I *FORGOT.*

11

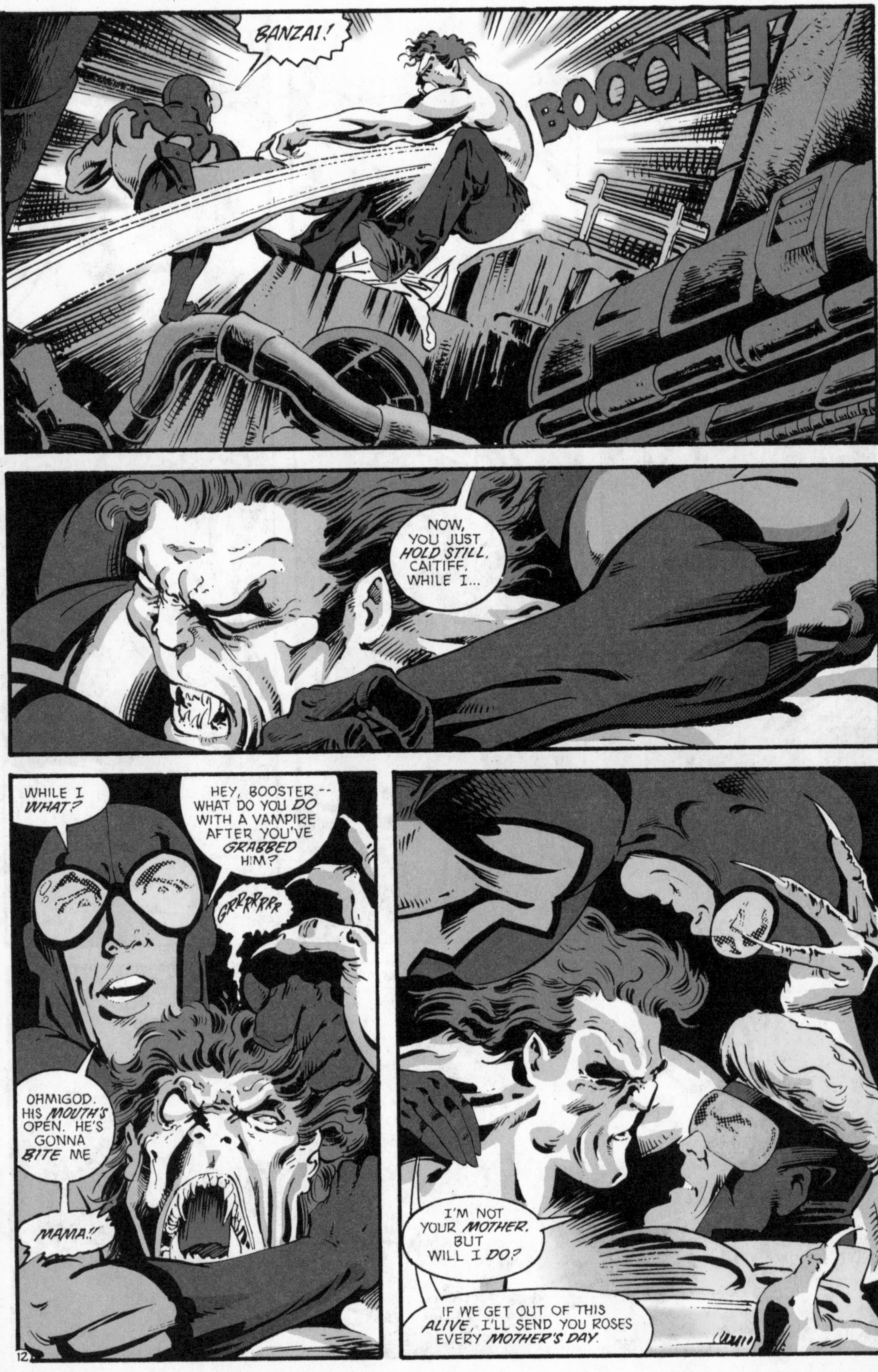
BANZAI!
BOOONT
NOW, YOU JUST HOLD STILL, CAITIFF, WHILE I...
WHILE I WHAT?
HEY, BOOSTER -- WHAT DO YOU DO WITH A VAMPIRE AFTER YOU'VE GRABBED HIM?
GRRRRRR
OHMIGOD. HIS MOUTH'S OPEN. HE'S GONNA BITE ME
MAMA!!
12
I'M NOT YOUR MOTHER. BUT WILL I DO?
IF WE GET OUT OF THIS ALIVE, I'LL SEND YOU ROSES EVERY MOTHER'S DAY.

THIS ONE SUFFERS! THIS ONE HATES! THIS ONE WILL NOT BE TAKEN *AGAIN!*

SHHOK

SPLOOTCH

SPLOOTCH

YUCK

BEETLE-- ARE YOU ALL *RIGHT?*

GAKKKK

CAN I TAKE THAT AS A *YES?*

UKKKKK

O.K. I JUST WANTED TO MAKE--

--SURE?!

HEY! WHAT'RE YOU *DOING?* PUT ME--

--DOWN!

NMMMMMMM...

WELCOME TO DISNEYLAND'S NEWEST *ATTRACTION:* "THE WONDERFUL WORLD OF *SEWAGE.*"

YOU *OKAY,* B.G.?

SPLOOT

GAKKH

CAN I TAKE THAT AS A *YES?*

13

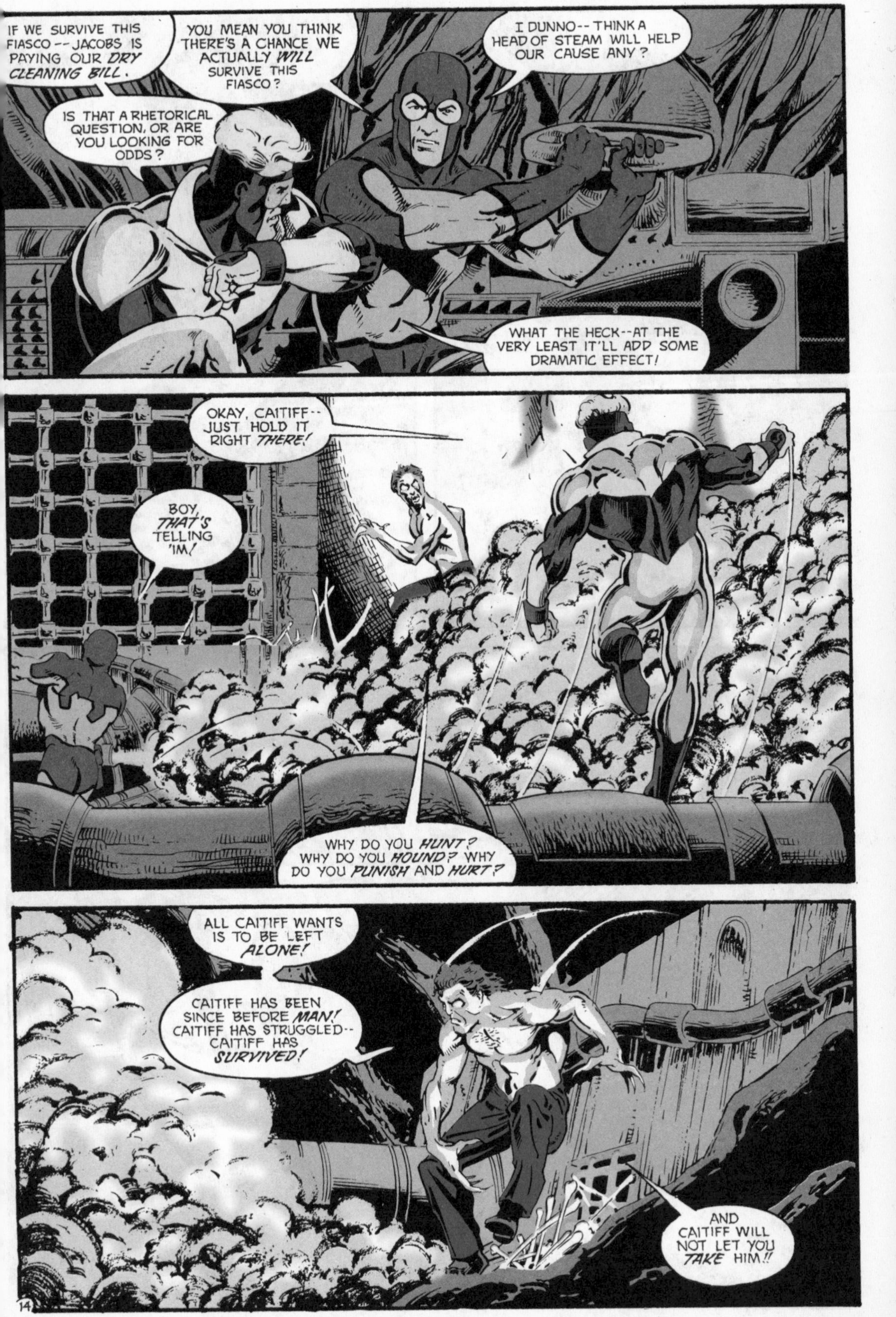
IF WE SURVIVE THIS FIASCO -- JACOBS IS PAYING OUR DRY CLEANING BILL.
YOU MEAN YOU THINK THERE'S A CHANCE WE ACTUALLY WILL SURVIVE THIS FIASCO?
IS THAT A RHETORICAL QUESTION, OR ARE YOU LOOKING FOR ODDS?
I DUNNO -- THINK A HEAD OF STEAM WILL HELP OUR CAUSE ANY?
WHAT THE HECK--AT THE VERY LEAST IT'LL ADD SOME DRAMATIC EFFECT!
OKAY, CAITIFF-- JUST HOLD IT RIGHT THERE!
BOY, THAT'S TELLING 'IM!
WHY DO YOU HUNT? WHY DO YOU HOUND? WHY DO YOU PUNISH AND HURT?
ALL CAITIFF WANTS IS TO BE LEFT ALONE!
CAITIFF HAS BEEN SINCE BEFORE MAN! CAITIFF HAS STRUGGLED-- CAITIFF HAS SURVIVED!
AND CAITIFF WILL NOT LET YOU TAKE HIM!!
14

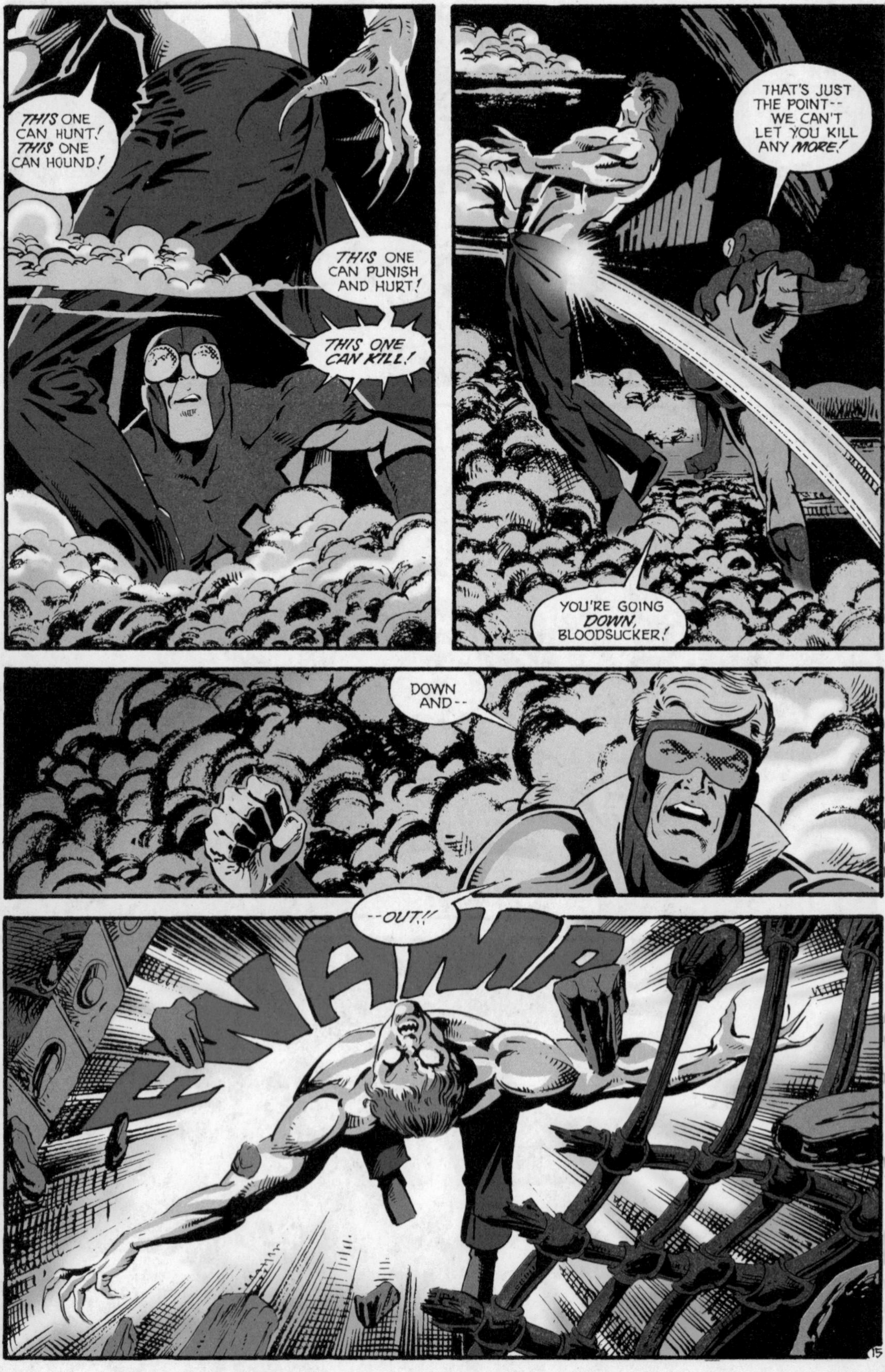
THIS ONE CAN HUNT! THIS ONE CAN HOUND!
THIS ONE CAN PUNISH AND HURT!
THIS ONE CAN KILL!
THWAK
THAT'S JUST THE POINT-- WE CAN'T LET YOU KILL ANY MORE!
YOU'RE GOING DOWN, BLOODSUCKER!
DOWN AND--
--OUT!!
WHAM
15

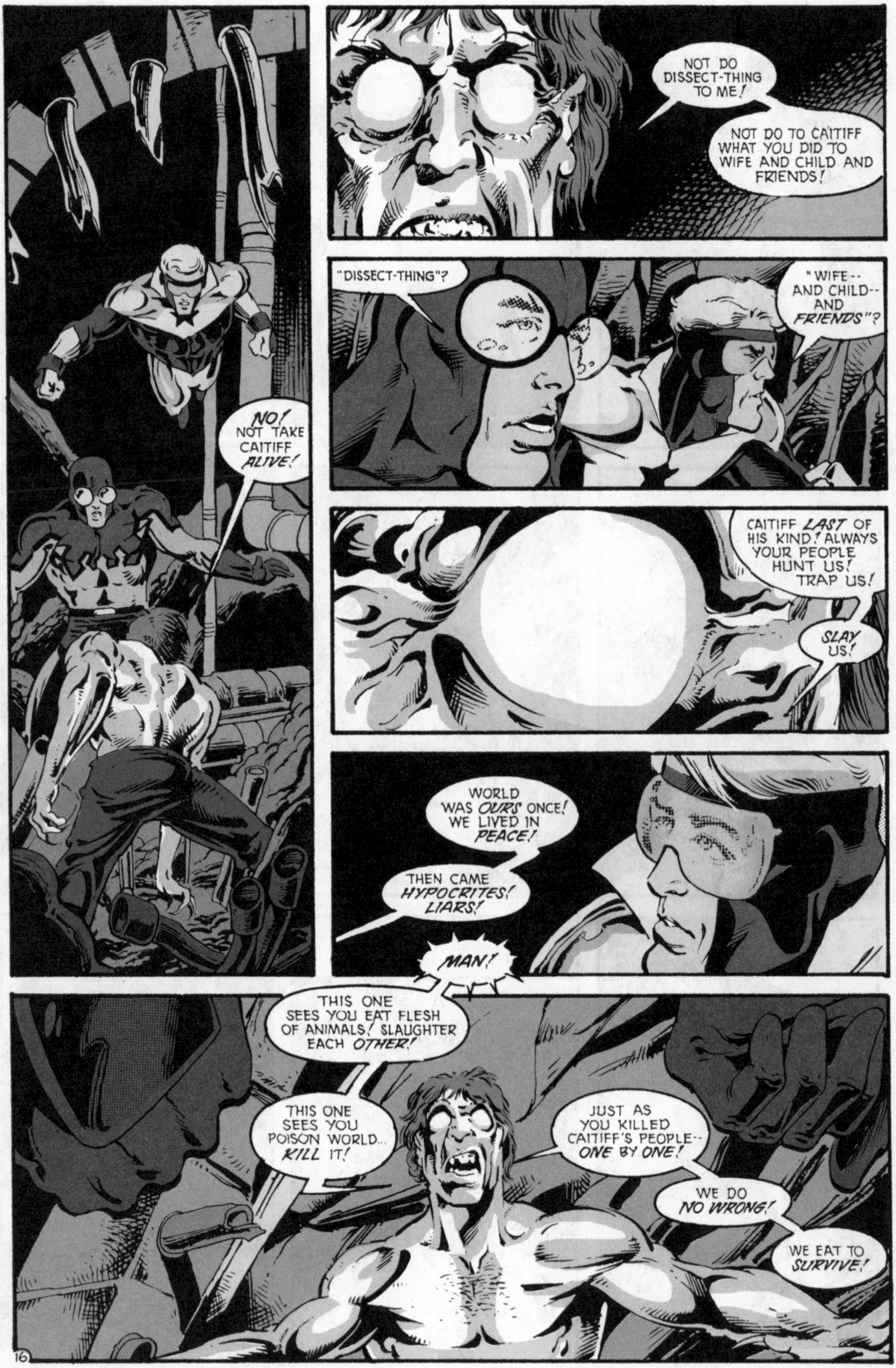
NO! NOT TAKE CAITIFF ALIVE!
NOT DO DISSECT-THING TO ME!
NOT DO TO CAITIFF WHAT YOU DID TO WIFE AND CHILD AND FRIENDS!
"DISSECT-THING"?
"WIFE -- AND CHILD -- AND FRIENDS"?
CAITIFF LAST OF HIS KIND! ALWAYS YOUR PEOPLE HUNT US! TRAP US!
SLAY US!
WORLD WAS OURS ONCE! WE LIVED IN PEACE!
THEN CAME HYPOCRITES! LIARS!
MAN!
THIS ONE SEES YOU EAT FLESH OF ANIMALS! SLAUGHTER EACH OTHER!
THIS ONE SEES YOU POISON WORLD... KILL IT!
JUST AS YOU KILLED CAITIFF'S PEOPLE -- ONE BY ONE!
WE DO NO WRONG!
WE EAT TO SURVIVE!
16

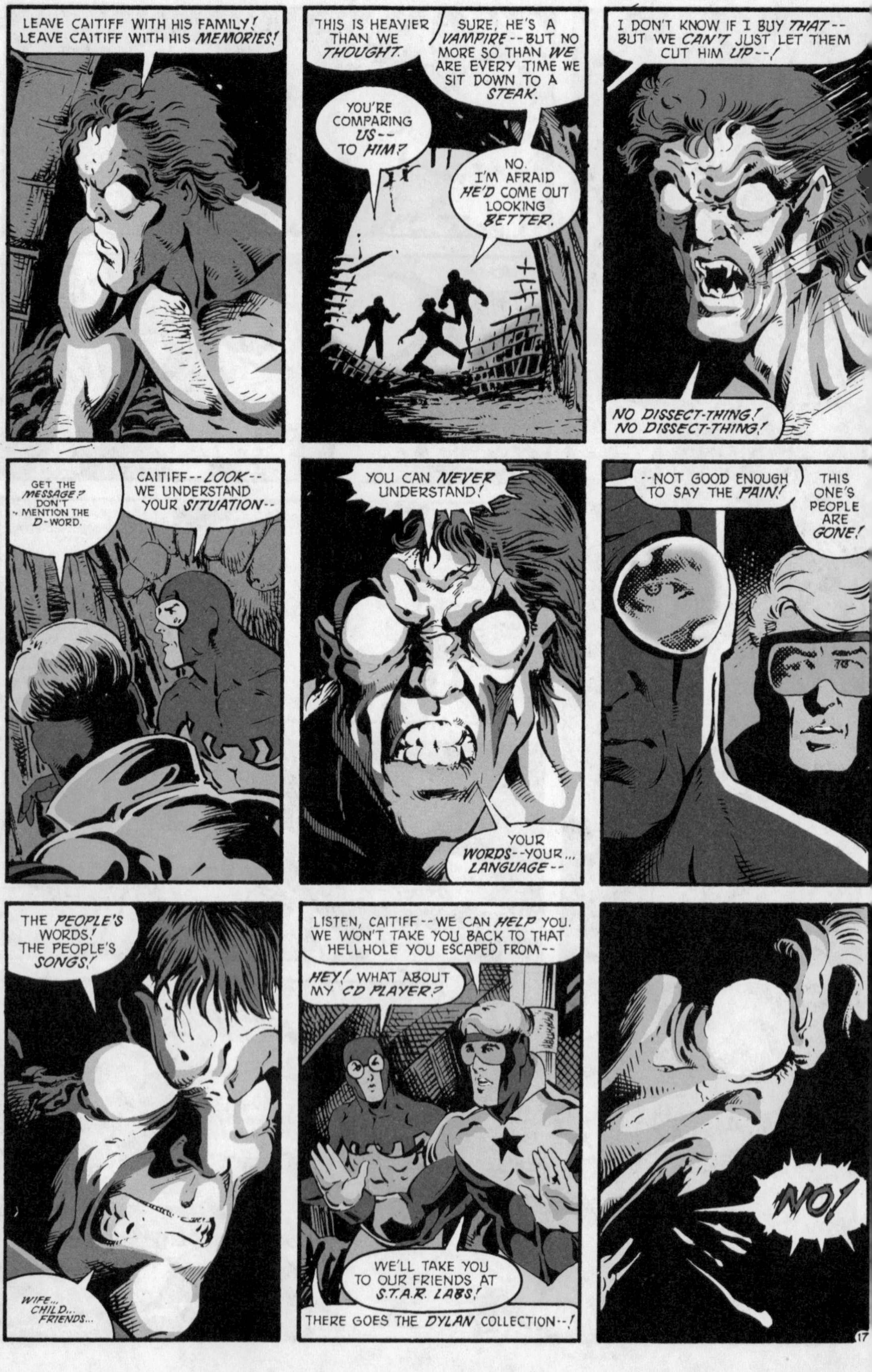
LEAVE CAITIFF WITH HIS FAMILY! LEAVE CAITIFF WITH HIS MEMORIES!
THIS IS HEAVIER THAN WE THOUGHT.
SURE, HE'S A VAMPIRE--BUT NO MORE SO THAN WE ARE EVERY TIME WE SIT DOWN TO A STEAK.
YOU'RE COMPARING US--TO HIM?
NO. I'M AFRAID HE'D COME OUT LOOKING BETTER.
I DON'T KNOW IF I BUY THAT--BUT WE CAN'T JUST LET THEM CUT HIM UP--!
NO DISSECT-THING! NO DISSECT-THING!
GET THE MESSAGE? DON'T MENTION THE D-WORD.
CAITIFF--LOOK--WE UNDERSTAND YOUR SITUATION--
YOU CAN NEVER UNDERSTAND!
YOUR WORDS--YOUR... LANGUAGE--
--NOT GOOD ENOUGH TO SAY THE PAIN!
THIS ONE'S PEOPLE ARE GONE!
THE PEOPLE'S WORDS! THE PEOPLE'S SONGS!
WIFE... CHILD... FRIENDS...
LISTEN, CAITIFF--WE CAN HELP YOU. WE WON'T TAKE YOU BACK TO THAT HELLHOLE YOU ESCAPED FROM--
HEY! WHAT ABOUT MY CD PLAYER?
WE'LL TAKE YOU TO OUR FRIENDS AT S.T.A.R. LABS!
THERE GOES THE DYLAN COLLECTION--!
NO!
17

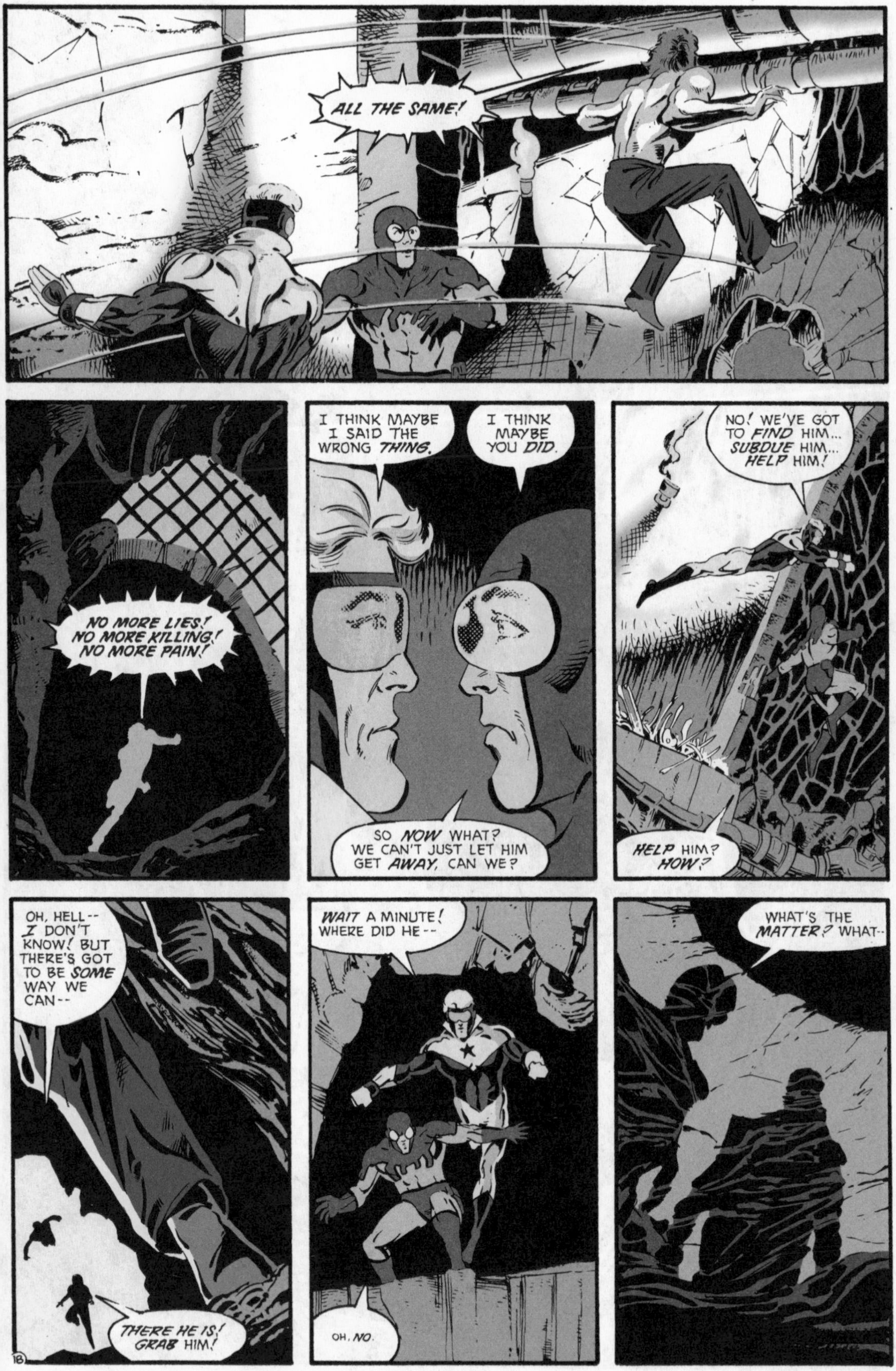
ALL THE SAME!
NO MORE LIES! NO MORE KILLING! NO MORE PAIN!
I THINK MAYBE I SAID THE WRONG THING.
I THINK MAYBE YOU DID.
SO NOW WHAT? WE CAN'T JUST LET HIM GET AWAY, CAN WE?
NO! WE'VE GOT TO FIND HIM... SUBDUE HIM... HELP HIM!
HELP HIM? HOW?
OH, HELL-- I DON'T KNOW! BUT THERE'S GOT TO BE SOME WAY WE CAN--
THERE HE IS! GRAB HIM!
18
WAIT A MINUTE! WHERE DID HE--
OH, NO.
WHAT'S THE MATTER? WHAT--

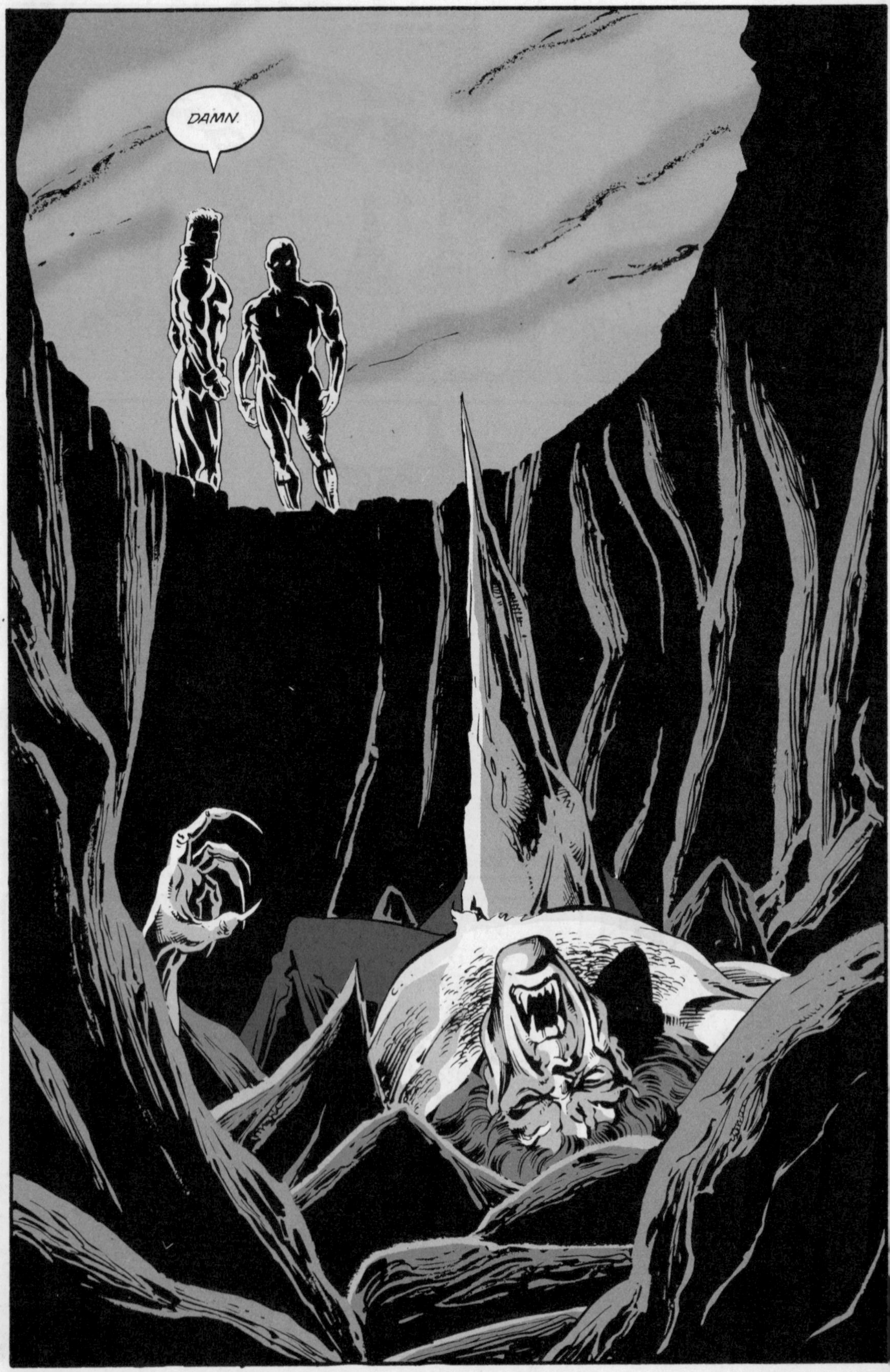
DAMN.

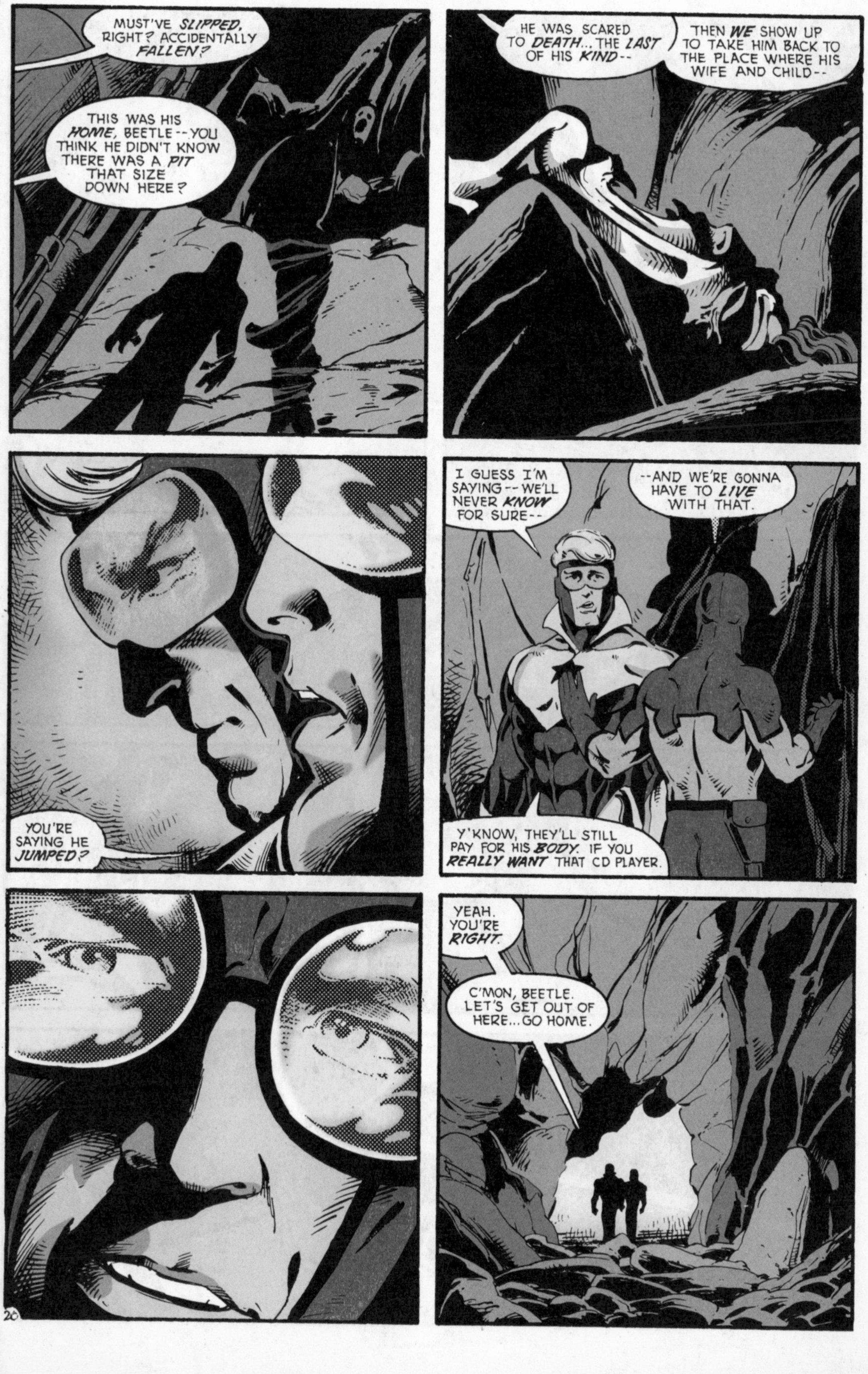
MUST'VE SLIPPED, RIGHT? ACCIDENTALLY FALLEN?
THIS WAS HIS HOME, BEETLE--YOU THINK HE DIDN'T KNOW THERE WAS A PIT THAT SIZE DOWN HERE?
HE WAS SCARED TO DEATH... THE LAST OF HIS KIND--
THEN WE SHOW UP TO TAKE HIM BACK TO THE PLACE WHERE HIS WIFE AND CHILD--
YOU'RE SAYING HE JUMPED?
I GUESS I'M SAYING--WE'LL NEVER KNOW FOR SURE--
--AND WE'RE GONNA HAVE TO LIVE WITH THAT.
Y'KNOW, THEY'LL STILL PAY FOR HIS BODY. IF YOU REALLY WANT THAT CD PLAYER.
YEAH. YOU'RE RIGHT.
C'MON, BEETLE. LET'S GET OUT OF HERE... GO HOME.
20

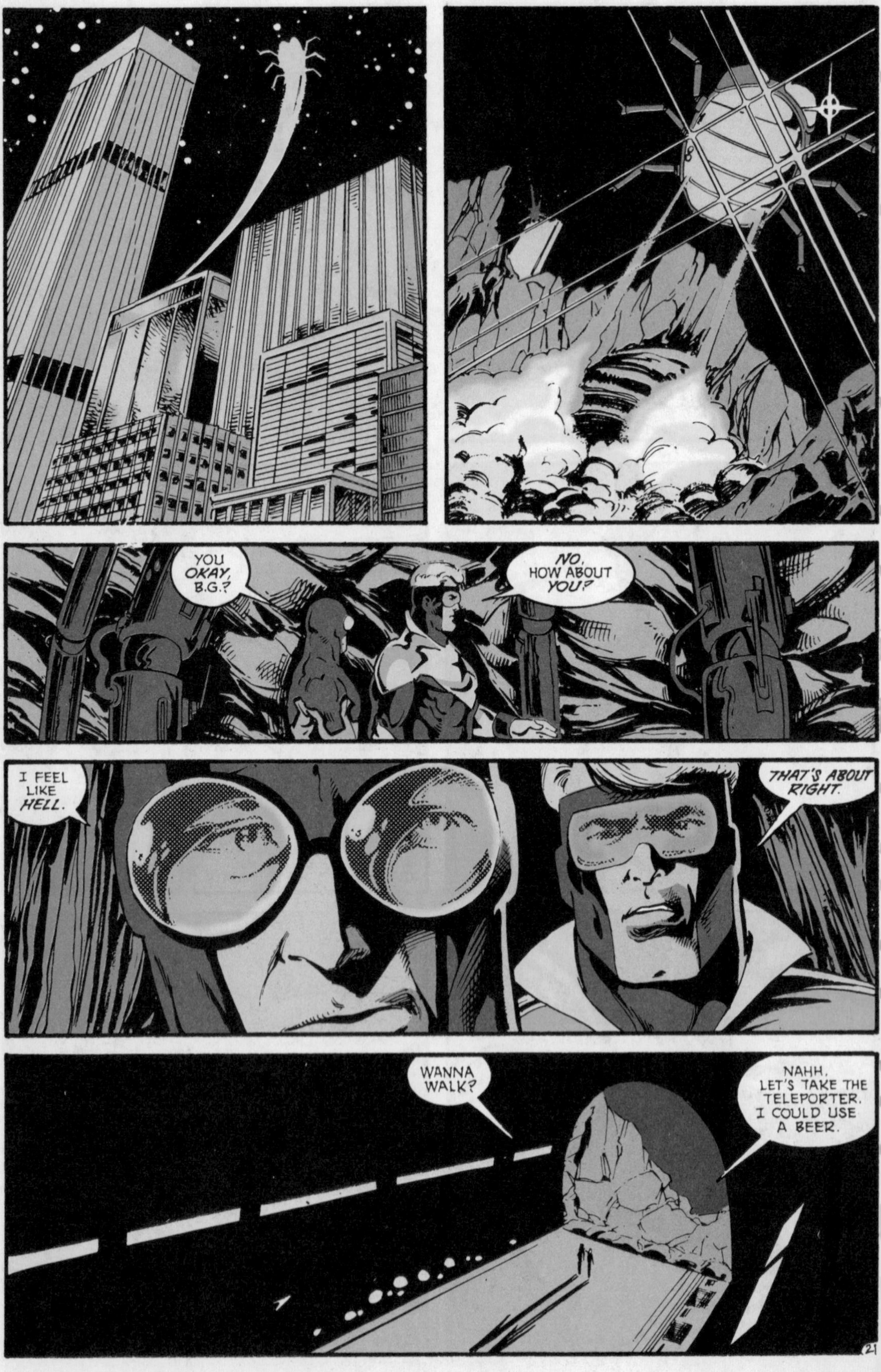
YOU OKAY, B.G.?
NO, HOW ABOUT YOU?
I FEEL LIKE HELL.
THAT'S ABOUT RIGHT.
WANNA WALK?
NAHH, LET'S TAKE THE TELEPORTER. I COULD USE A BEER.
21

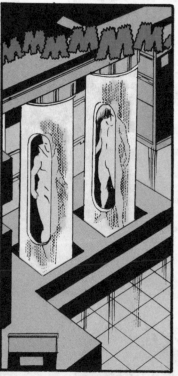

TIME FOR THOSE BEERS.

THINK THEY'LL *HELP?*

NO. BUT LET'S GIVE 'EM IT A TRY *ANYWAY.*

LOOK-- THERE *IS* AN *UPSIDE* TO ALL THIS--

WHAT'S *THAT?*

WE GOT OUT OF *CLEAN-UP DETAIL.*

YEAH. AND GOT EVERYONE *MAD* AT US.

DON'T WORRY ABOUT IT. YOU THINK THEY *REALLY CARED?*

UH-*HUH*

NUH-UH. THEY'RE SUPER-*HEROES,* FOR CRYIN' OUT *LOUD!* IT PROBABLY TOOK 'EM *FIFTEEN MINUTES* TO DO THE WHOLE *JOB*--!

YOU'RE PROBABLY *RIGHT.* HELL, GUY COULD'VE DONE IT ALL ALONE WITH HIS *RING.*

SO LET'S JUST GO HAVE THOSE BEERS AND *FORGET* ABOUT IT.

200 LBS.

I MEAN-- IT'S *NOT* LIKE ANYBODY'S GONNA HOLD A *GRUDGE...*

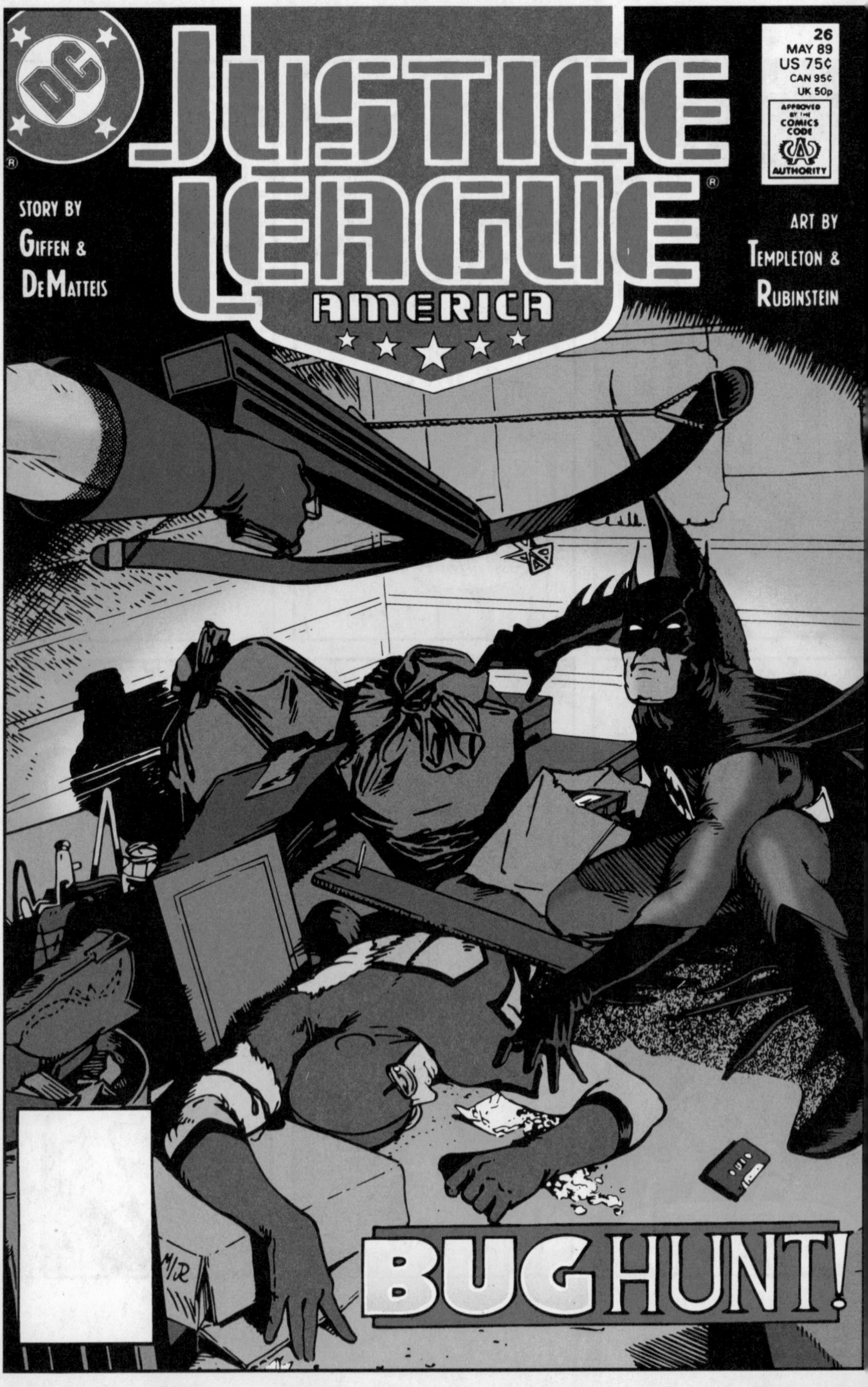

JUSTICE LEAGUE AMERICA
26
MAY 89
US 75¢
CAN 95¢
UK 50p
APPROVED BY THE COMICS CODE AUTHORITY
STORY BY
GIFFEN &
DEMATTEIS
ART BY
TEMPLETON &
RUBINSTEIN
BUG HUNT!

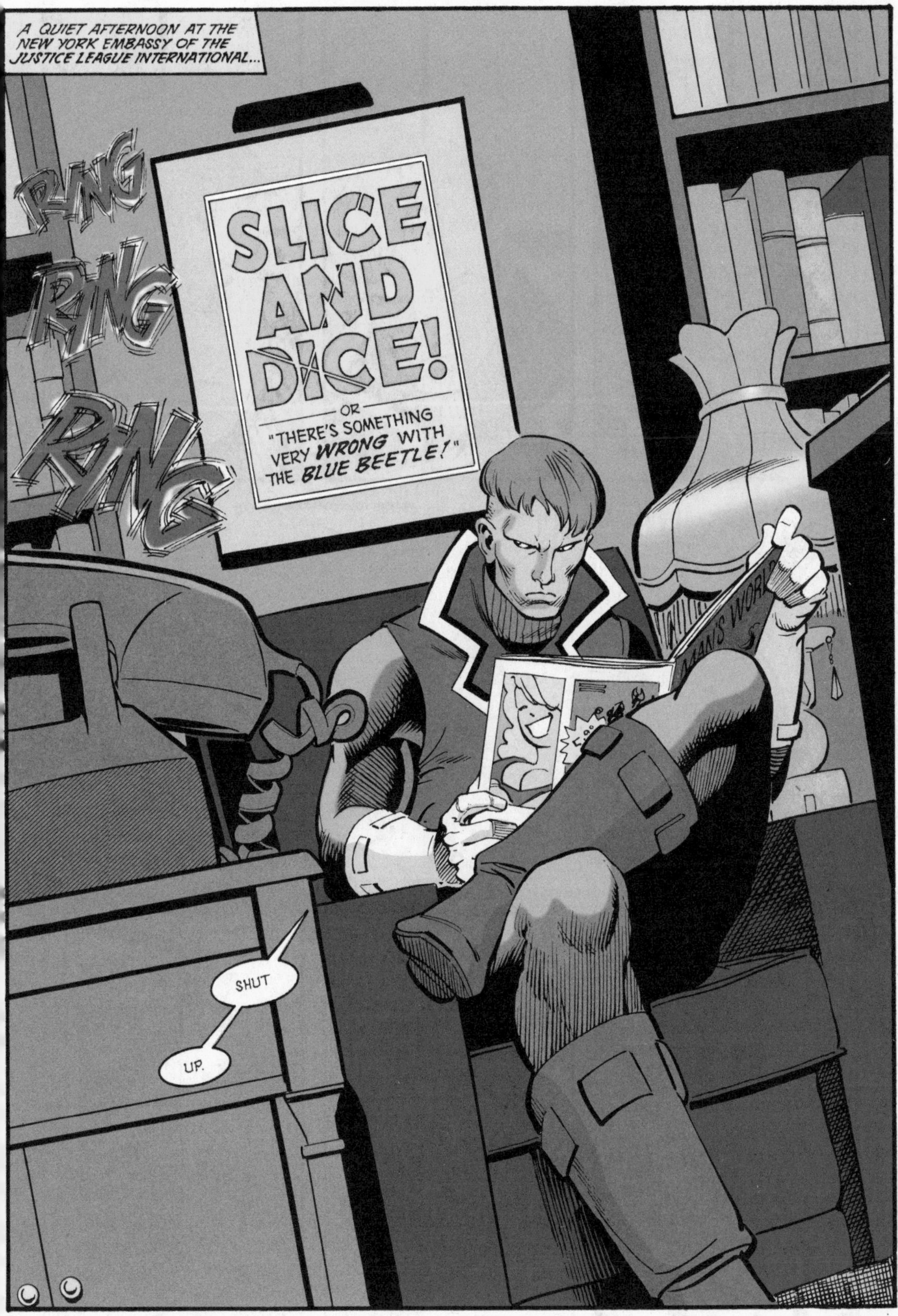

A QUIET AFTERNOON AT THE NEW YORK EMBASSY OF THE JUSTICE LEAGUE INTERNATIONAL...
RING
RING
RING
SLICE AND DICE!
OR
"THERE'S SOMETHING VERY WRONG WITH THE BLUE BEETLE!"
SHUT
UP.

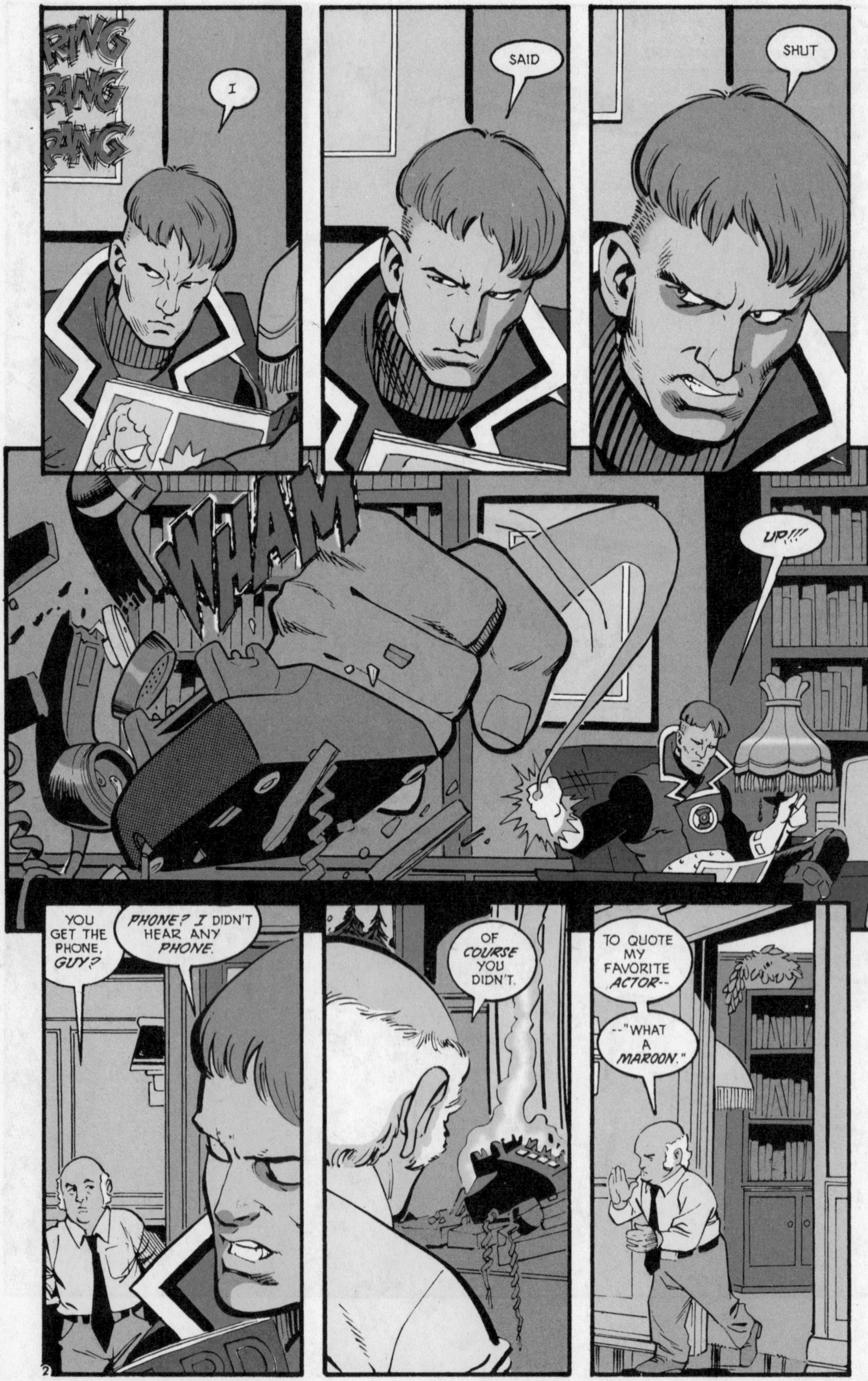

RING RING RING
I
SAID
SHUT
WHAM
UP!!!
YOU GET THE PHONE, GUY?
PHONE? I DIDN'T HEAR ANY PHONE.
OF COURSE YOU DIDN'T.
TO QUOTE MY FAVORITE ACTOR--
--"WHAT A MAROON."

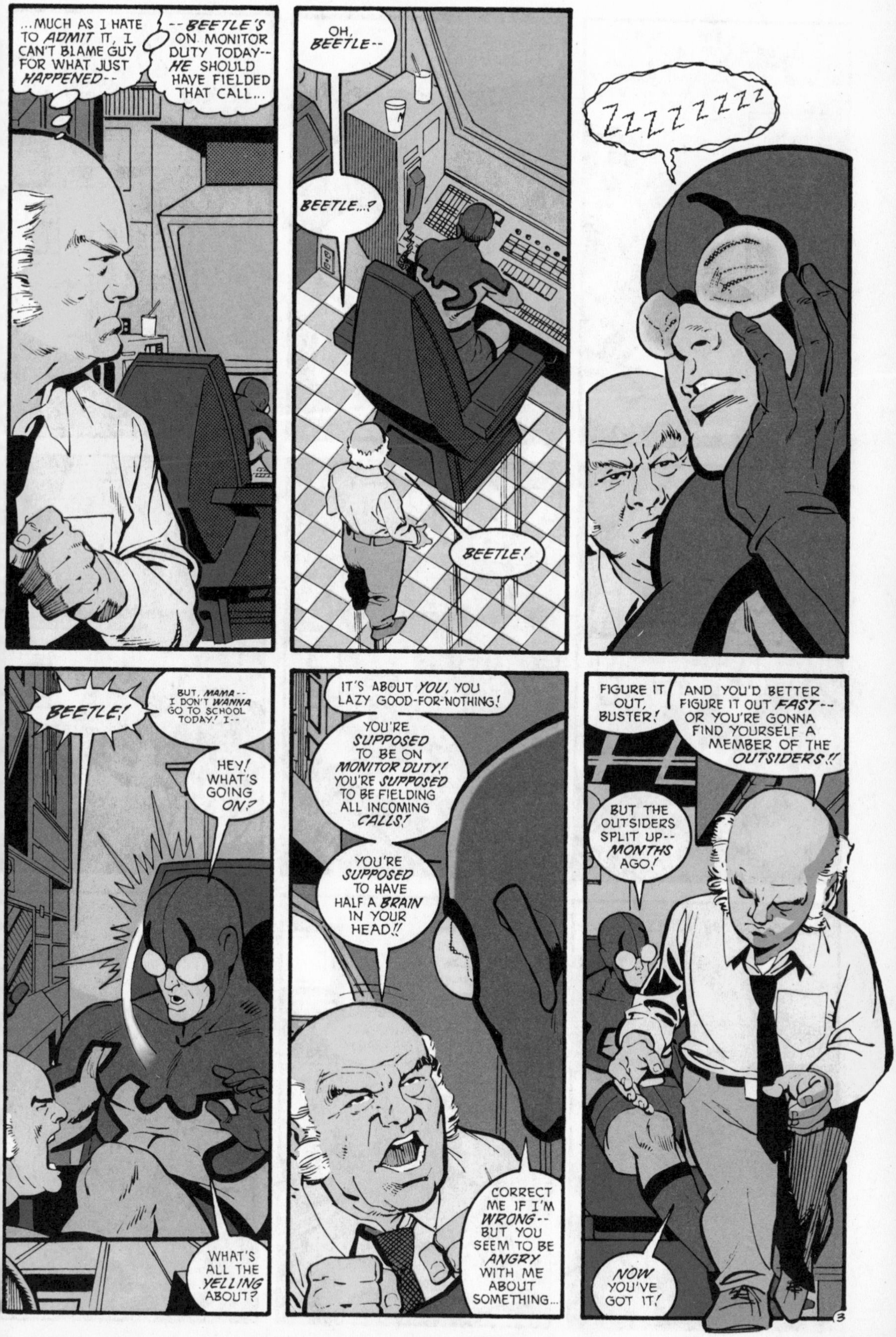
...MUCH AS I HATE TO ADMIT IT, I CAN'T BLAME GUY FOR WHAT JUST HAPPENED--
--BEETLE'S ON MONITOR DUTY TODAY-- HE SHOULD HAVE FIELDED THAT CALL...
OH, BEETLE--
BEETLE...?
BEETLE!
ZZZZZZZZ
BEETLE!
BUT, MAMA-- I DON'T WANNA GO TO SCHOOL TODAY! I--
HEY! WHAT'S GOING ON?
WHAT'S ALL THE YELLING ABOUT?
IT'S ABOUT YOU, YOU LAZY GOOD-FOR-NOTHING!
YOU'RE SUPPOSED TO BE ON MONITOR DUTY! YOU'RE SUPPOSED TO BE FIELDING ALL INCOMING CALLS!
YOU'RE SUPPOSED TO HAVE HALF A BRAIN IN YOUR HEAD!!
CORRECT ME IF I'M WRONG-- BUT YOU SEEM TO BE ANGRY WITH ME ABOUT SOMETHING...
FIGURE IT OUT, BUSTER!
AND YOU'D BETTER FIGURE IT OUT FAST-- OR YOU'RE GONNA FIND YOURSELF A MEMBER OF THE OUTSIDERS!!
BUT THE OUTSIDERS SPLIT UP-- MONTHS AGO!
NOW YOU'VE GOT IT!
3

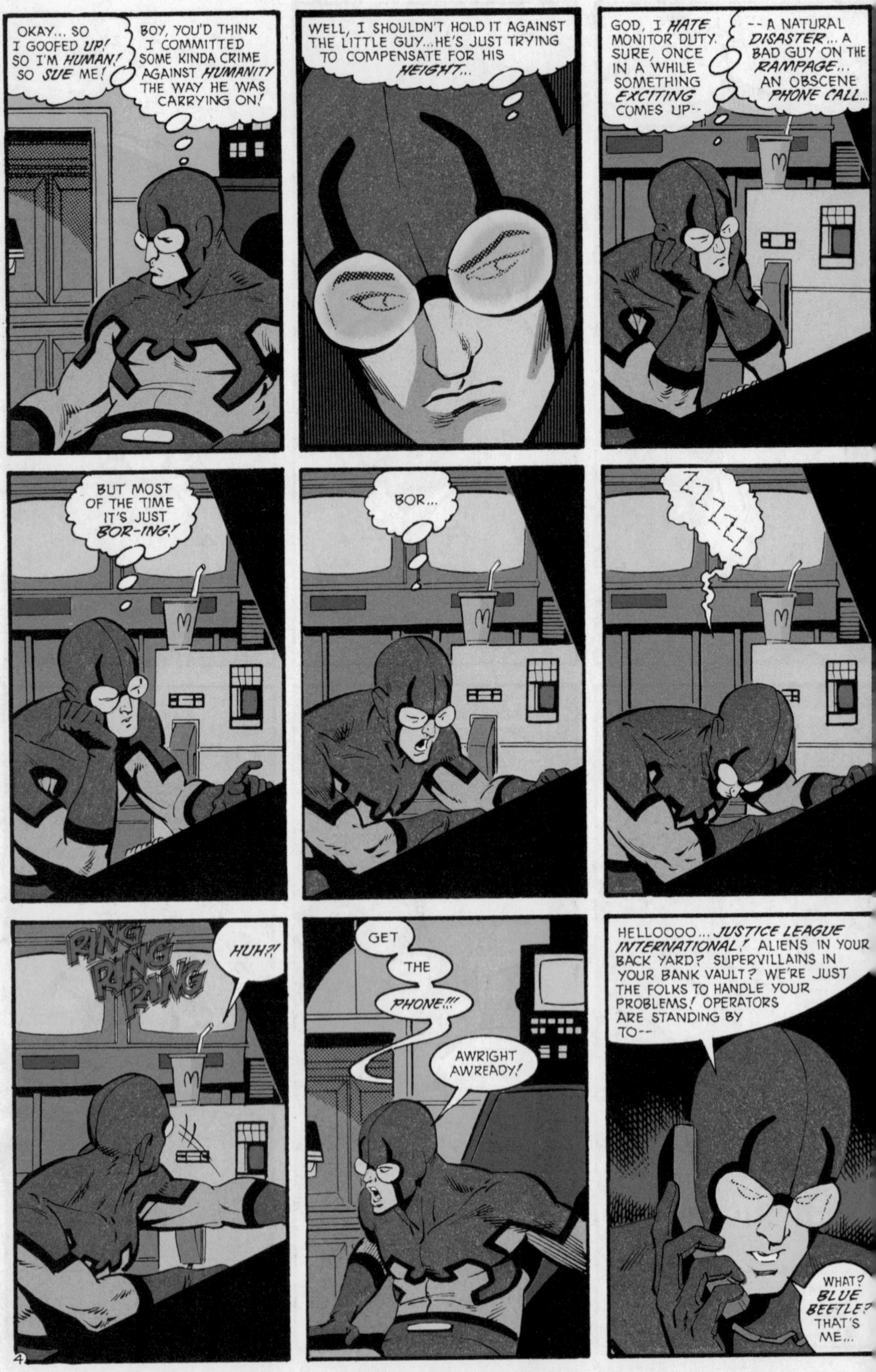
OKAY... SO I GOOFED UP! SO I'M HUMAN! SO SUE ME!
BOY, YOU'D THINK I COMMITTED SOME KINDA CRIME AGAINST HUMANITY THE WAY HE WAS CARRYING ON!
WELL, I SHOULDN'T HOLD IT AGAINST THE LITTLE GUY... HE'S JUST TRYING TO COMPENSATE FOR HIS HEIGHT...
GOD, I HATE MONITOR DUTY. SURE, ONCE IN A WHILE SOMETHING EXCITING COMES UP--
-- A NATURAL DISASTER... A BAD GUY ON THE RAMPAGE... AN OBSCENE PHONE CALL...
BUT MOST OF THE TIME IT'S JUST BOR-ING!
BOR...
Z-Z-Z-Z-Z
RING RING RING RING
HUH?!
GET THE PHONE!!!
AWRIGHT AWREADY!
HELLOOOO... JUSTICE LEAGUE INTERNATIONAL! ALIENS IN YOUR BACK YARD? SUPERVILLAINS IN YOUR BANK VAULT? WE'RE JUST THE FOLKS TO HANDLE YOUR PROBLEMS! OPERATORS ARE STANDING BY TO--
WHAT? BLUE BEETLE? THAT'S ME...
4

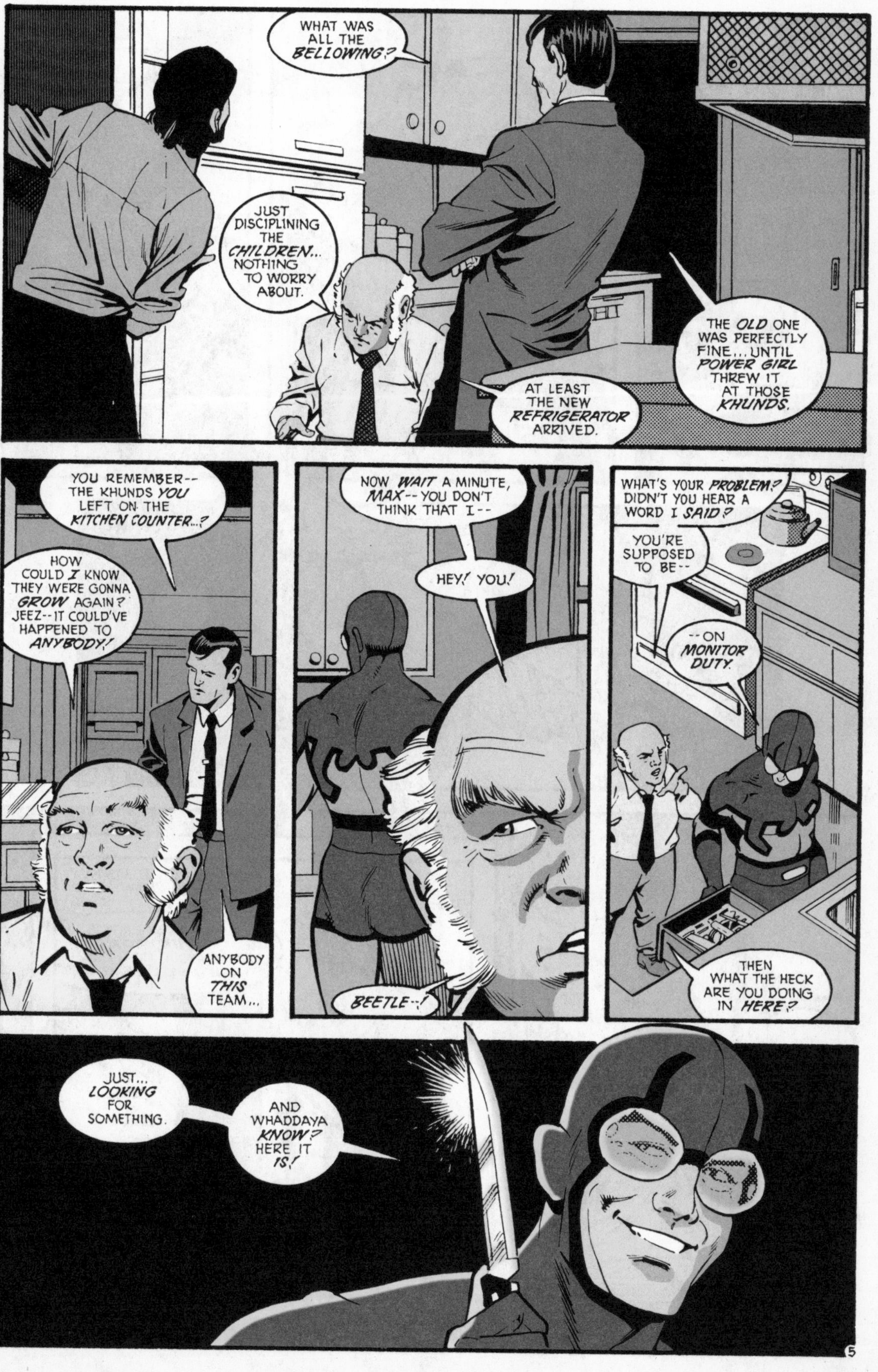
WHAT WAS ALL THE BELLOWING?
JUST DISCIPLINING THE CHILDREN... NOTHING TO WORRY ABOUT.
AT LEAST THE NEW REFRIGERATOR ARRIVED.
THE OLD ONE WAS PERFECTLY FINE... UNTIL POWER GIRL THREW IT AT THOSE KHUNDS.
YOU REMEMBER-- THE KHUNDS YOU LEFT ON THE KITCHEN COUNTER...?
HOW COULD I KNOW THEY WERE GONNA GROW AGAIN? JEEZ--IT COULD'VE HAPPENED TO ANYBODY!
ANYBODY ON THIS TEAM...
NOW WAIT A MINUTE, MAX--YOU DON'T THINK THAT I--
HEY! YOU!
BEETLE--!
WHAT'S YOUR PROBLEM? DIDN'T YOU HEAR A WORD I SAID?
YOU'RE SUPPOSED TO BE--
--ON MONITOR DUTY.
THEN WHAT THE HECK ARE YOU DOING IN HERE?
JUST... LOOKING FOR SOMETHING.
AND WHADDAYA KNOW? HERE IT IS!
5

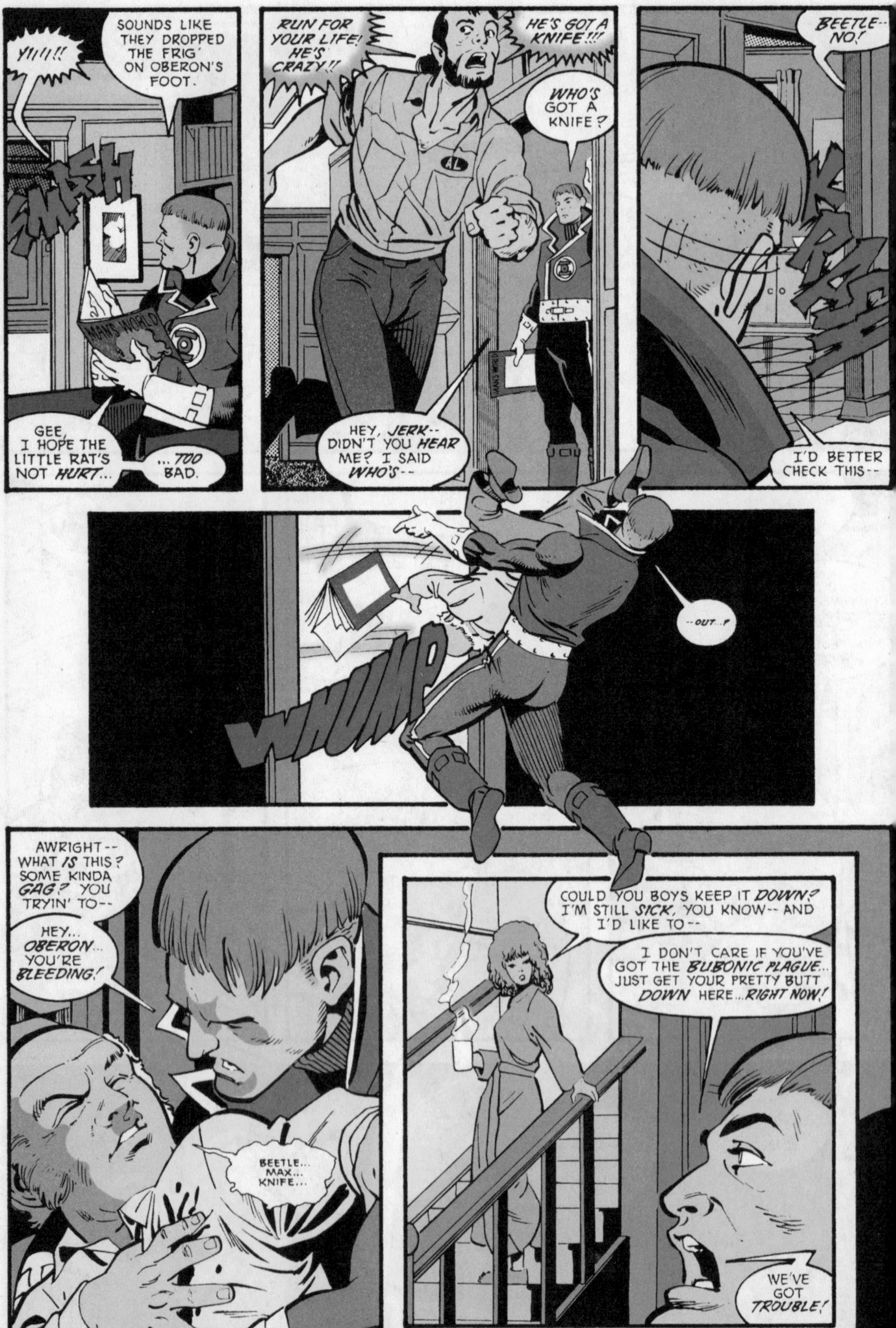

YI!!!!!
SOUNDS LIKE THEY DROPPED THE FRIG' ON OBERON'S FOOT.
SMASH
MAN'S WORLD
GEE, I HOPE THE LITTLE RAT'S NOT HURT...
...TOO BAD.
RUN FOR YOUR LIFE! HE'S CRAZY!!
HE'S GOT A KNIFE!!!
WHO'S GOT A KNIFE?
AL
HEY, JERK-- DIDN'T YOU HEAR ME? I SAID WHO'S--
BEETLE-- NO!
KRASH
I'D BETTER CHECK THIS--
--OUT...?
WHUMP
AWRIGHT-- WHAT IS THIS? SOME KINDA GAG? YOU TRYIN' TO--
HEY... OBERON... YOU'RE BLEEDING!
BEETLE... MAX... KNIFE...
COULD YOU BOYS KEEP IT DOWN? I'M STILL SICK, YOU KNOW-- AND I'D LIKE TO--
I DON'T CARE IF YOU'VE GOT THE BUBONIC PLAGUE... JUST GET YOUR PRETTY BUTT DOWN HERE...RIGHT NOW!
WE'VE GOT TROUBLE!
6

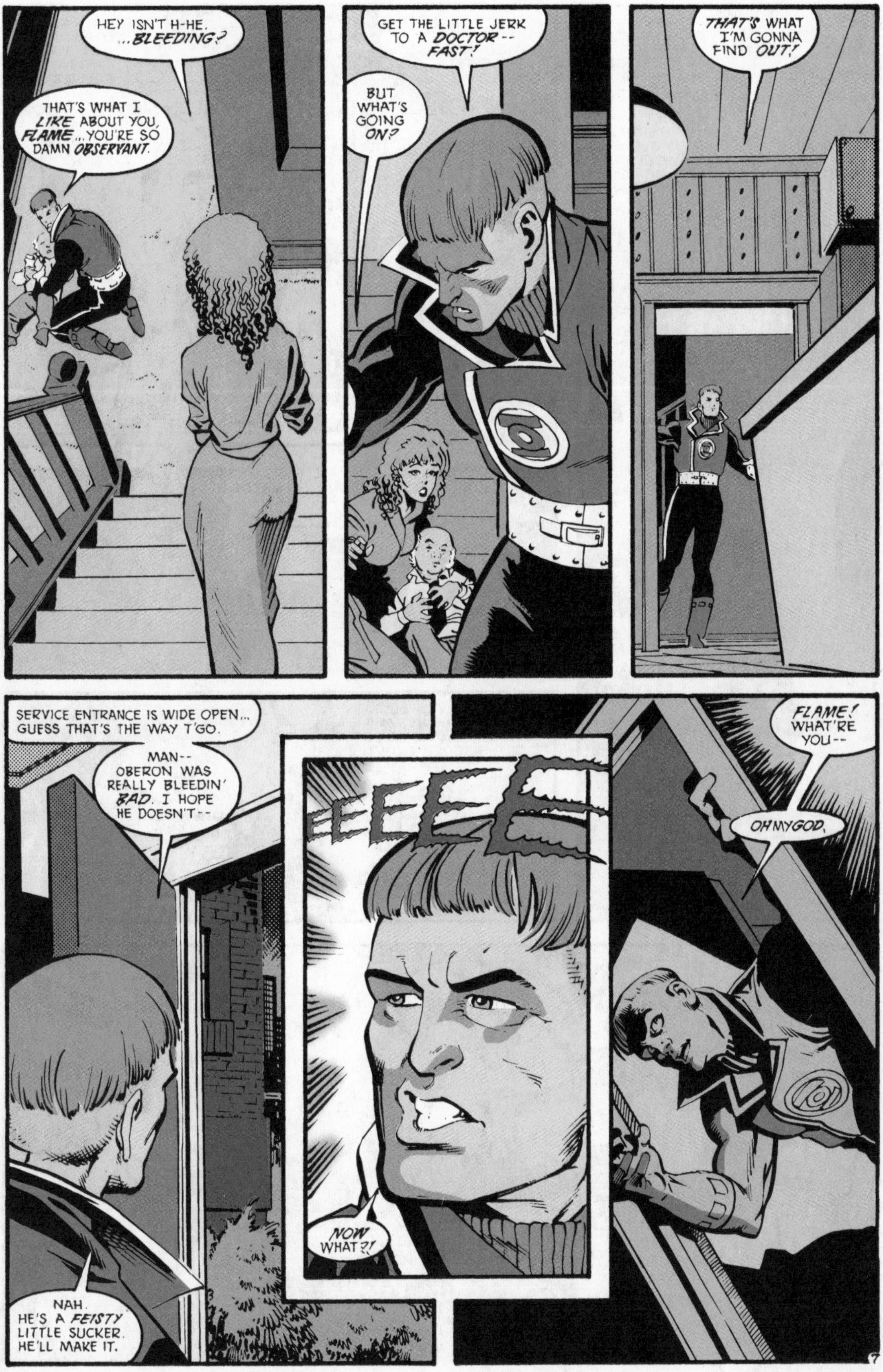
HEY ISN'T H-HE. ...BLEEDING?
THAT'S WHAT I LIKE ABOUT YOU, FLAME... YOU'RE SO DAMN OBSERVANT.
GET THE LITTLE JERK TO A DOCTOR -- FAST!
BUT WHAT'S GOING ON?
THAT'S WHAT I'M GONNA FIND OUT!
SERVICE ENTRANCE IS WIDE OPEN... GUESS THAT'S THE WAY T'GO.
MAN-- OBERON WAS REALLY BLEEDIN' BAD. I HOPE HE DOESN'T--
NAH. HE'S A FEISTY LITTLE SUCKER. HE'LL MAKE IT.
EEEEE
NOW WHAT?!
FLAME! WHAT'RE YOU--
OHMYGOD.
7

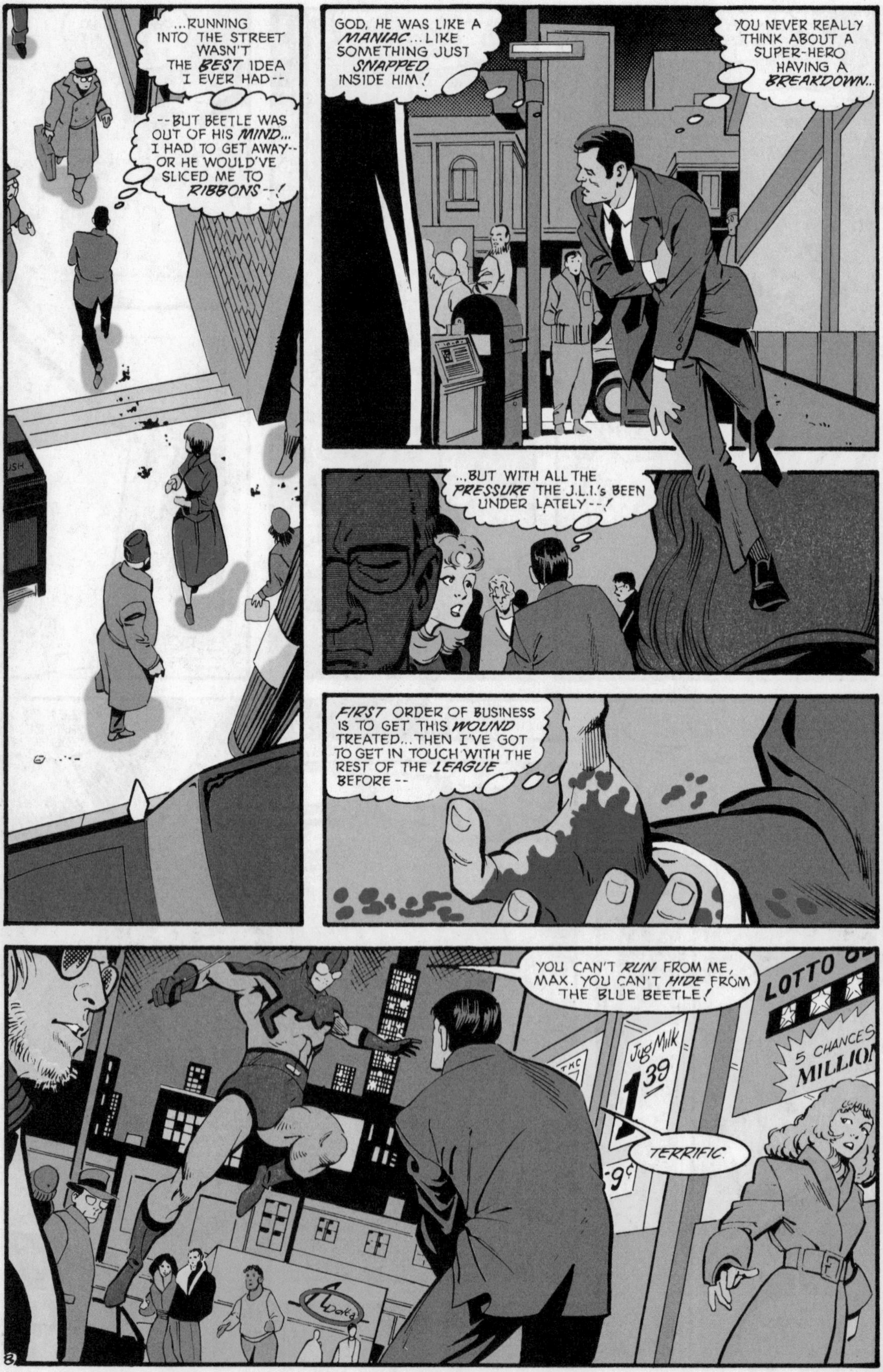

...RUNNING INTO THE STREET WASN'T THE BEST IDEA I EVER HAD--
--BUT BEETLE WAS OUT OF HIS MIND... I HAD TO GET AWAY-- OR HE WOULD'VE SLICED ME TO RIBBONS--!
GOD, HE WAS LIKE A MANIAC...LIKE SOMETHING JUST SNAPPED INSIDE HIM!
YOU NEVER REALLY THINK ABOUT A SUPER-HERO HAVING A BREAKDOWN...
...BUT WITH ALL THE PRESSURE THE J.L.I.'s BEEN UNDER LATELY--!
FIRST ORDER OF BUSINESS IS TO GET THIS WOUND TREATED...THEN I'VE GOT TO GET IN TOUCH WITH THE REST OF THE LEAGUE BEFORE--
YOU CAN'T RUN FROM ME, MAX. YOU CAN'T HIDE FROM THE BLUE BEETLE!
TERRIFIC.
LOTTO
5 CHANCES
MILLION
Jug Milk
1.39

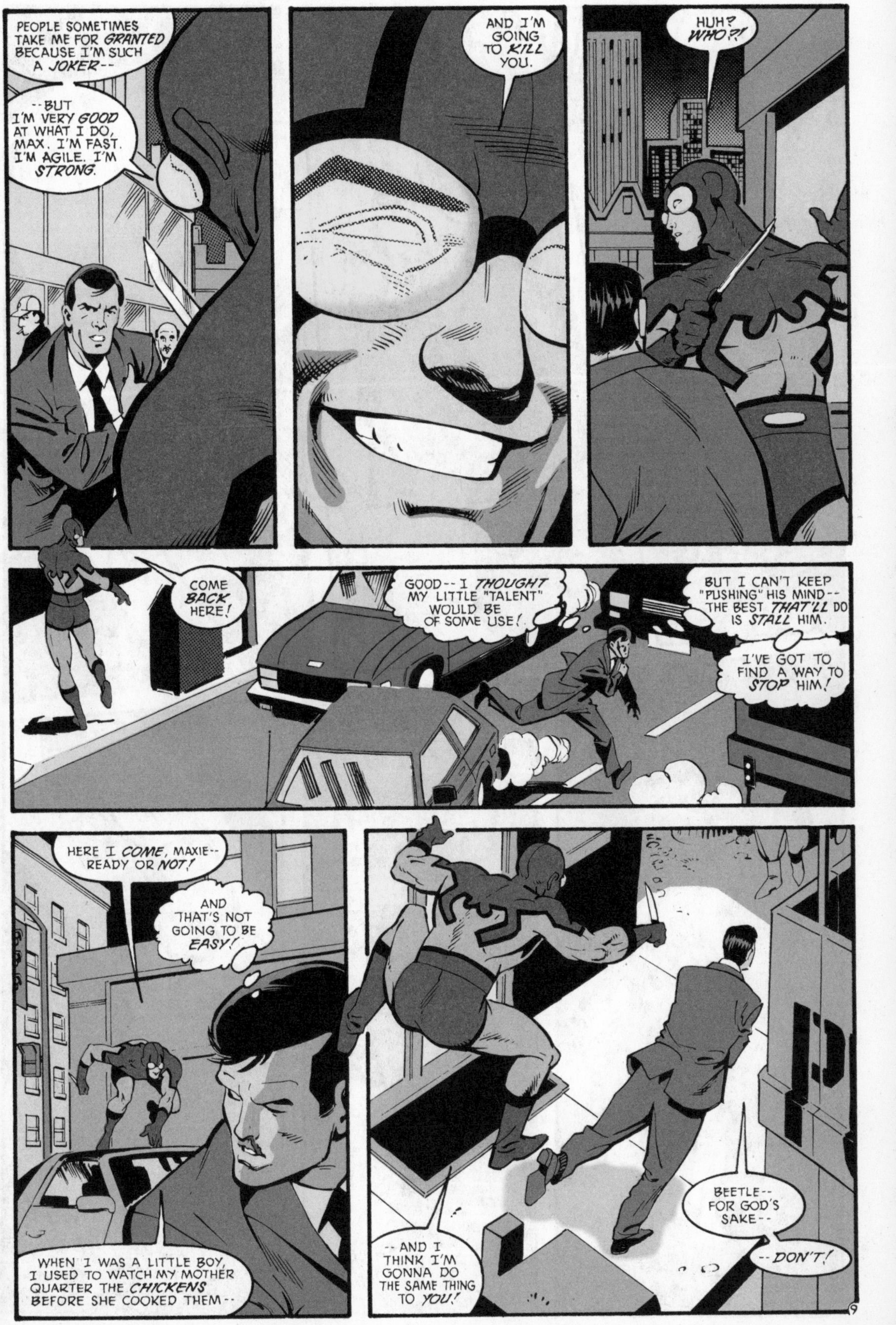

PEOPLE SOMETIMES TAKE ME FOR *GRANTED* BECAUSE I'M SUCH A *JOKER*--
--BUT I'M VERY *GOOD* AT WHAT I DO, MAX. I'M FAST. I'M AGILE. I'M *STRONG*.
AND I'M GOING TO *KILL* YOU.
HUH? *WHO?!*
COME *BACK* HERE!
GOOD--I *THOUGHT* MY LITTLE "TALENT" WOULD BE OF SOME USE!
BUT I CAN'T KEEP "PUSHING" HIS MIND-- THE BEST *THAT'LL* DO IS *STALL* HIM.
I'VE GOT TO FIND A WAY TO *STOP* HIM!
HERE I *COME*, MAXIE-- READY OR *NOT!*
AND THAT'S NOT GOING TO BE *EASY!*
WHEN I WAS A LITTLE BOY, I USED TO WATCH MY MOTHER QUARTER THE *CHICKENS* BEFORE SHE COOKED THEM--
--AND I THINK I'M GONNA DO THE SAME THING TO *YOU!*
BEETLE-- FOR GOD'S SAKE--
--*DON'T!*
9

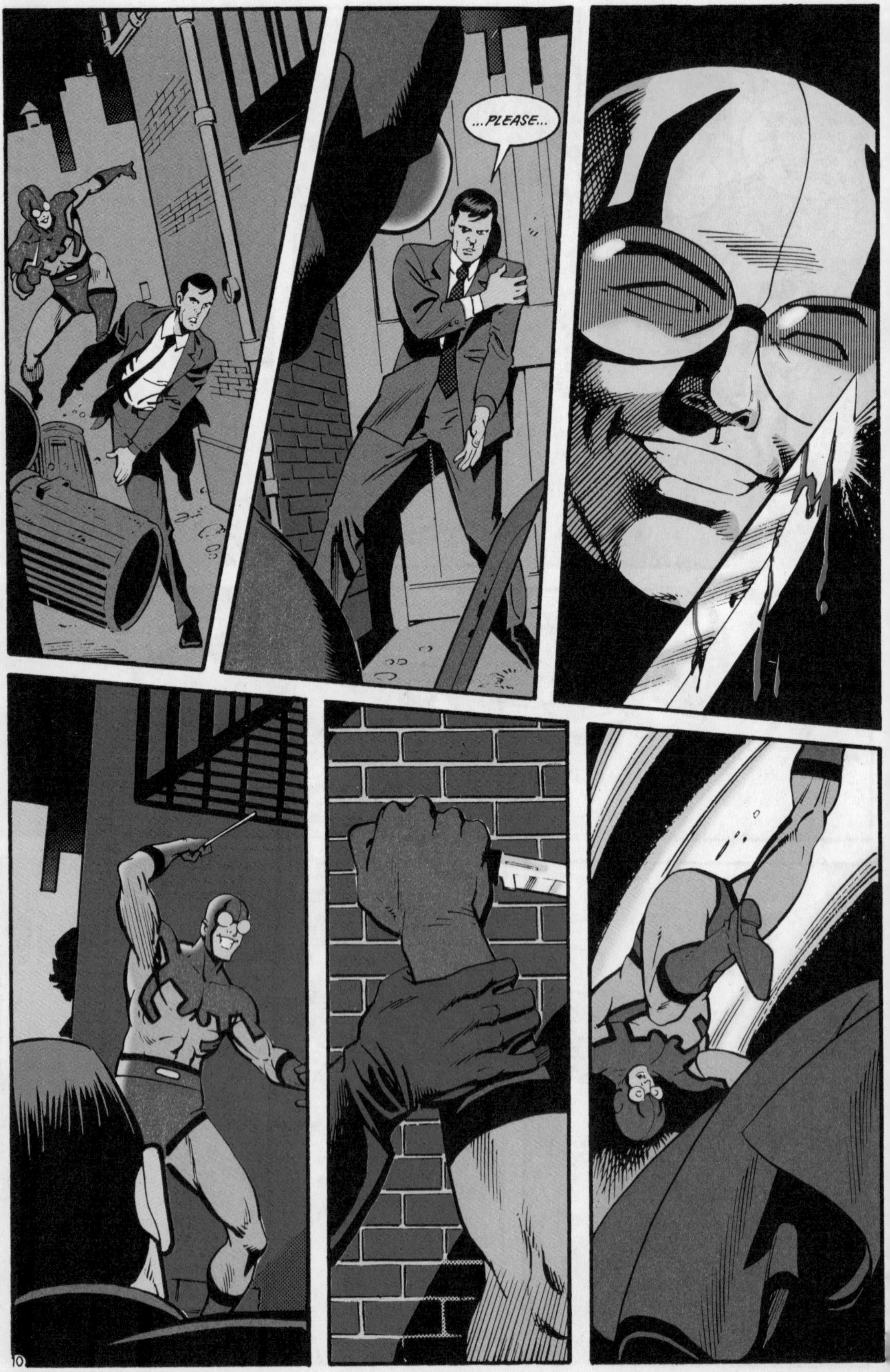
...PLEASE...
10

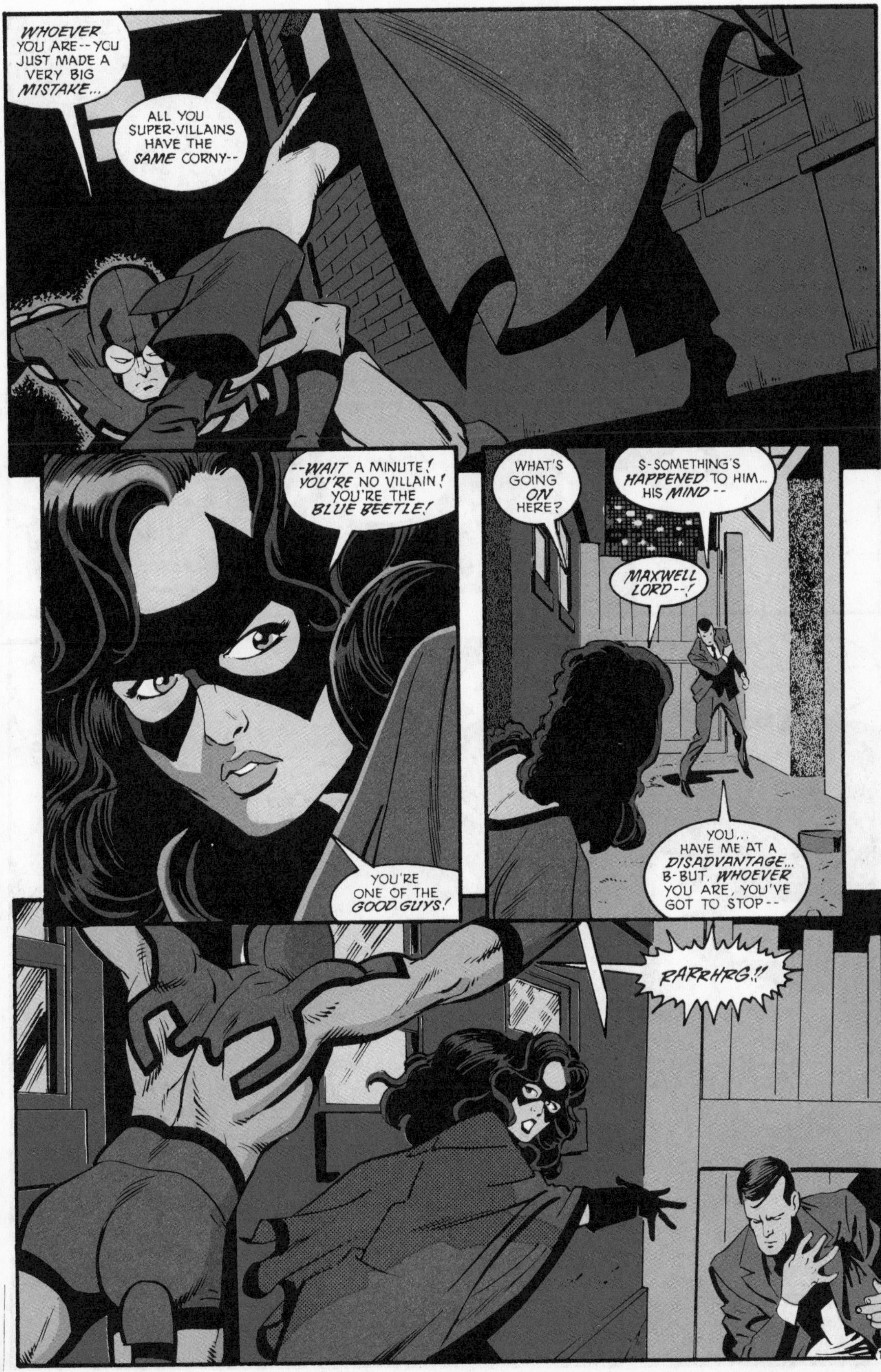
WHOEVER YOU ARE--YOU JUST MADE A VERY BIG MISTAKE...
ALL YOU SUPER-VILLAINS HAVE THE SAME CORNY--
--WAIT A MINUTE! YOU'RE NO VILLAIN! YOU'RE THE BLUE BEETLE!
YOU'RE ONE OF THE GOOD GUYS!
WHAT'S GOING ON HERE?
S-SOMETHING'S HAPPENED TO HIM... HIS MIND--
MAXWELL LORD--!
YOU... HAVE ME AT A DISADVANTAGE... B-BUT, WHOEVER YOU ARE, YOU'VE GOT TO STOP--
RARRHRG!!
11

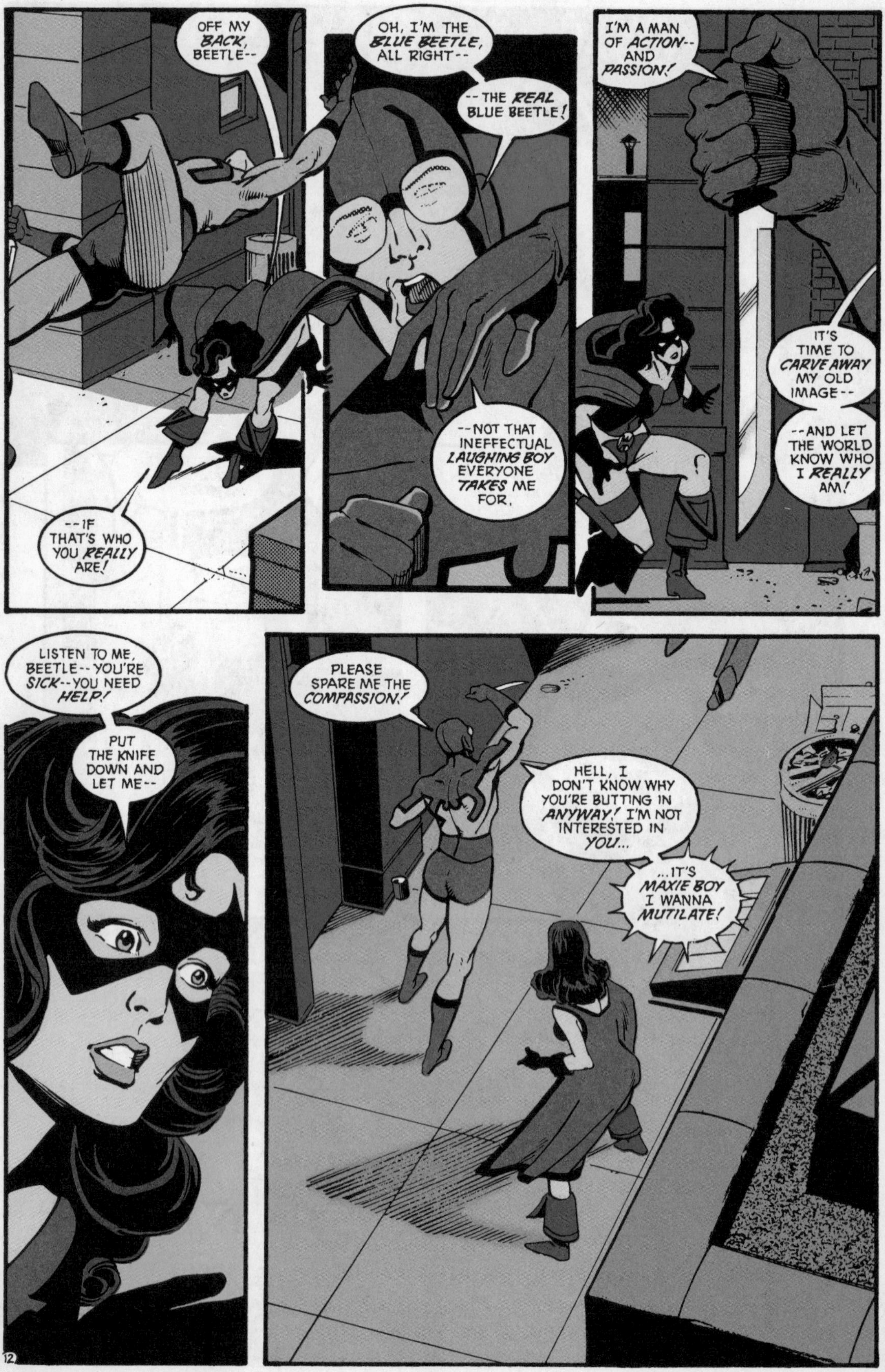
OFF MY BACK, BEETLE--
--IF THAT'S WHO YOU REALLY ARE!
OH, I'M THE BLUE BEETLE, ALL RIGHT--
--THE REAL BLUE BEETLE!
--NOT THAT INEFFECTUAL LAUGHING BOY EVERYONE TAKES ME FOR.
I'M A MAN OF ACTION--AND PASSION!
IT'S TIME TO CARVE AWAY MY OLD IMAGE--
--AND LET THE WORLD KNOW WHO I REALLY AM!
LISTEN TO ME, BEETLE--YOU'RE SICK--YOU NEED HELP!
PUT THE KNIFE DOWN AND LET ME--
12
PLEASE SPARE ME THE COMPASSION!
HELL, I DON'T KNOW WHY YOU'RE BUTTING IN ANYWAY! I'M NOT INTERESTED IN YOU...
...IT'S MAXIE BOY I WANNA MUTILATE!

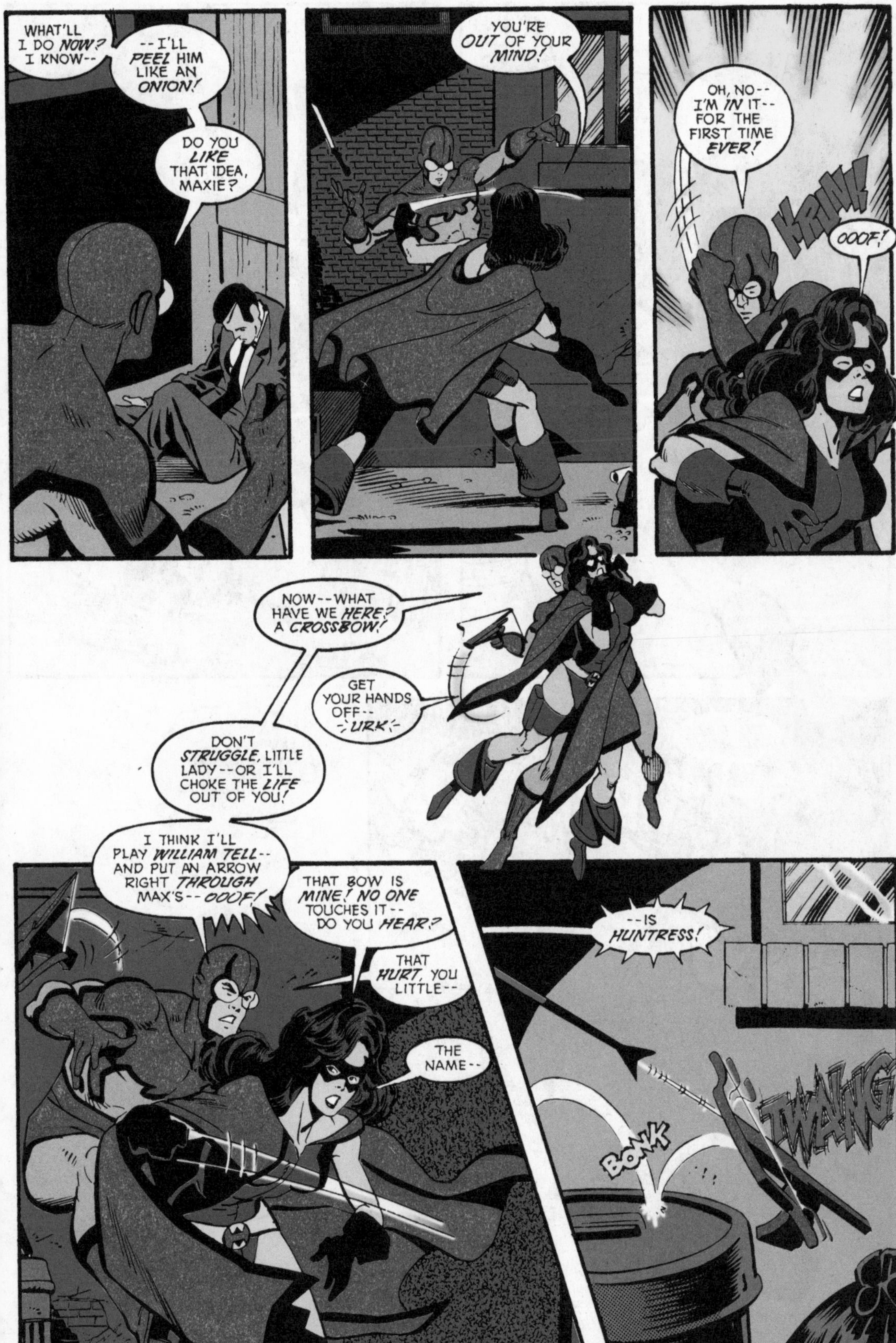

WHAT'LL I DO NOW? I KNOW--
--I'LL PEEL HIM LIKE AN ONION!
DO YOU LIKE THAT IDEA, MAXIE?
YOU'RE OUT OF YOUR MIND!
OH, NO--I'M IN IT--FOR THE FIRST TIME EVER!
KRUNK
OOOF!
NOW--WHAT HAVE WE HERE? A CROSSBOW!
GET YOUR HANDS OFF-- -URK-
DON'T STRUGGLE, LITTLE LADY--OR I'LL CHOKE THE LIFE OUT OF YOU!
I THINK I'LL PLAY WILLIAM TELL--AND PUT AN ARROW RIGHT THROUGH MAX'S--OOOF!
THAT BOW IS MINE! NO ONE TOUCHES IT--DO YOU HEAR?
THAT HURT, YOU LITTLE--
THE NAME--
--IS HUNTRESS!
BONK
TWANG
13

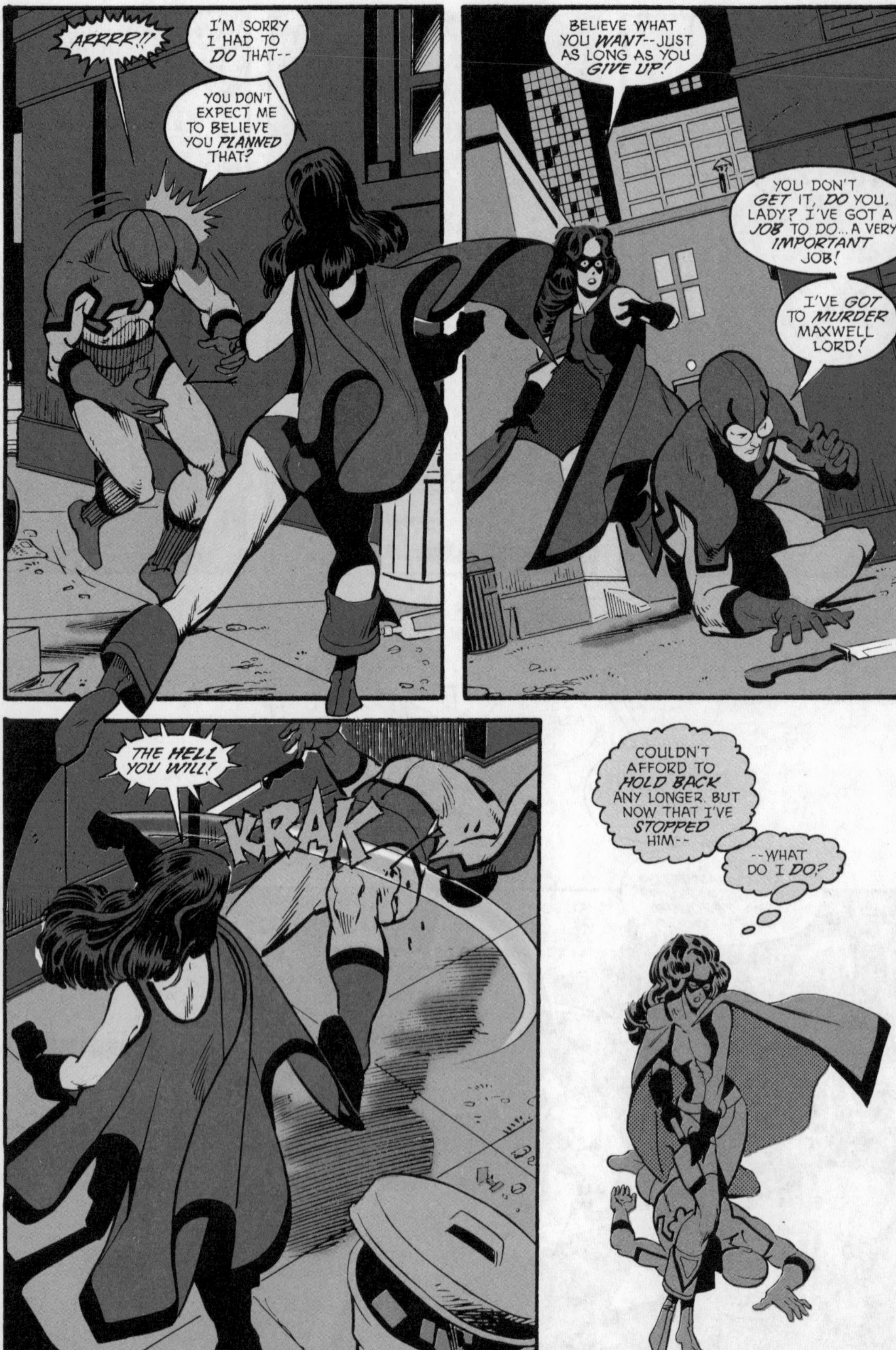
ARRRR!!
I'M SORRY I HAD TO DO THAT--
YOU DON'T EXPECT ME TO BELIEVE YOU PLANNED THAT?
BELIEVE WHAT YOU WANT--JUST AS LONG AS YOU GIVE UP!
YOU DON'T GET IT, DO YOU, LADY? I'VE GOT A JOB TO DO... A VERY IMPORTANT JOB!
I'VE GOT TO MURDER MAXWELL LORD!
THE HELL YOU WILL!
KRAK
14
COULDN'T AFFORD TO HOLD BACK ANY LONGER. BUT NOW THAT I'VE STOPPED HIM--
--WHAT DO I DO?

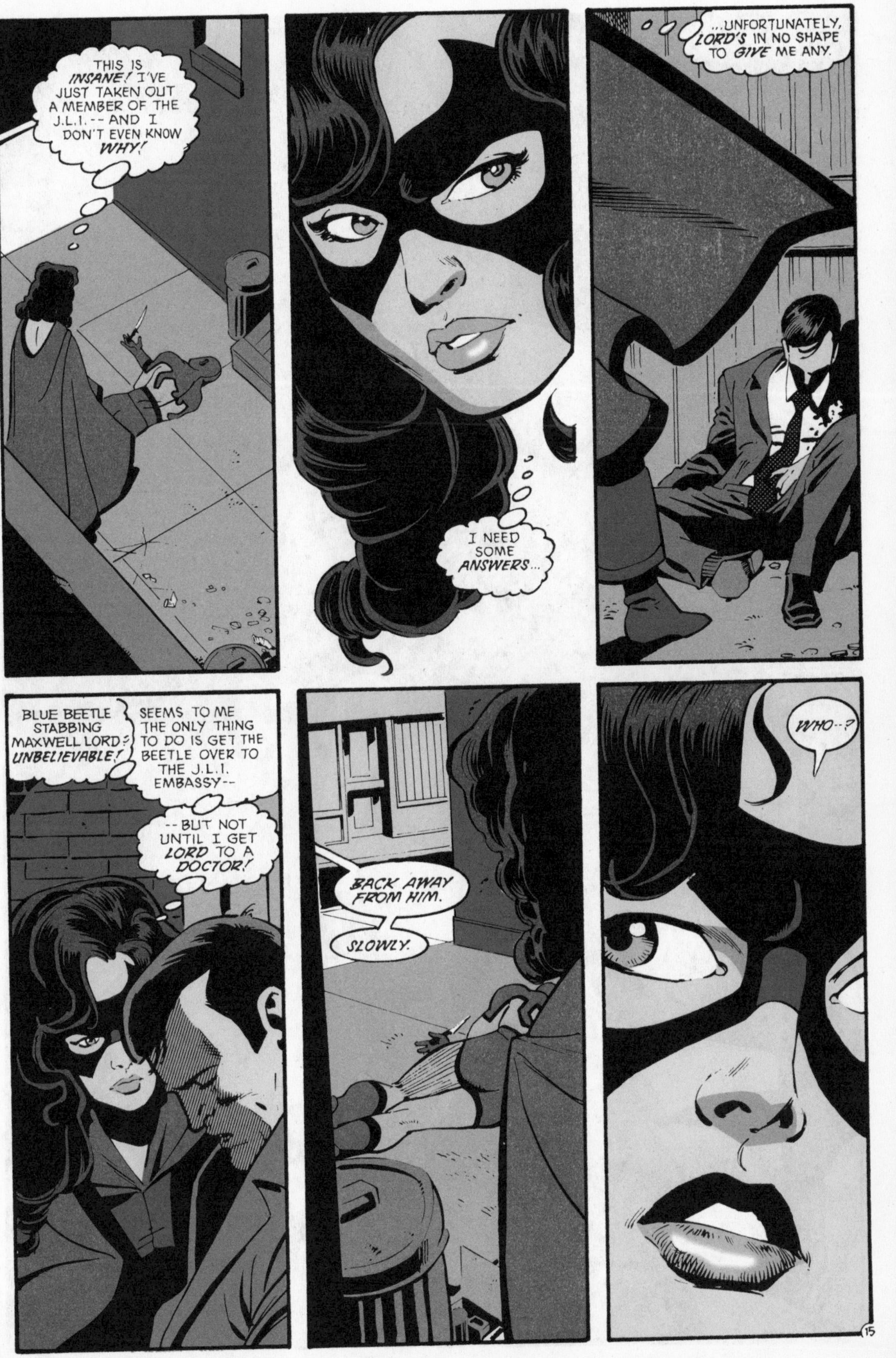
THIS IS INSANE! I'VE JUST TAKEN OUT A MEMBER OF THE J.L.I. -- AND I DON'T EVEN KNOW WHY!
I NEED SOME ANSWERS...
...UNFORTUNATELY, LORD'S IN NO SHAPE TO GIVE ME ANY.
BLUE BEETLE STABBING MAXWELL LORD? UNBELIEVABLE!
SEEMS TO ME THE ONLY THING TO DO IS GET THE BEETLE OVER TO THE J.L.I. EMBASSY--
-- BUT NOT UNTIL I GET LORD TO A DOCTOR!
BACK AWAY FROM HIM.
SLOWLY.
WHO--?
15

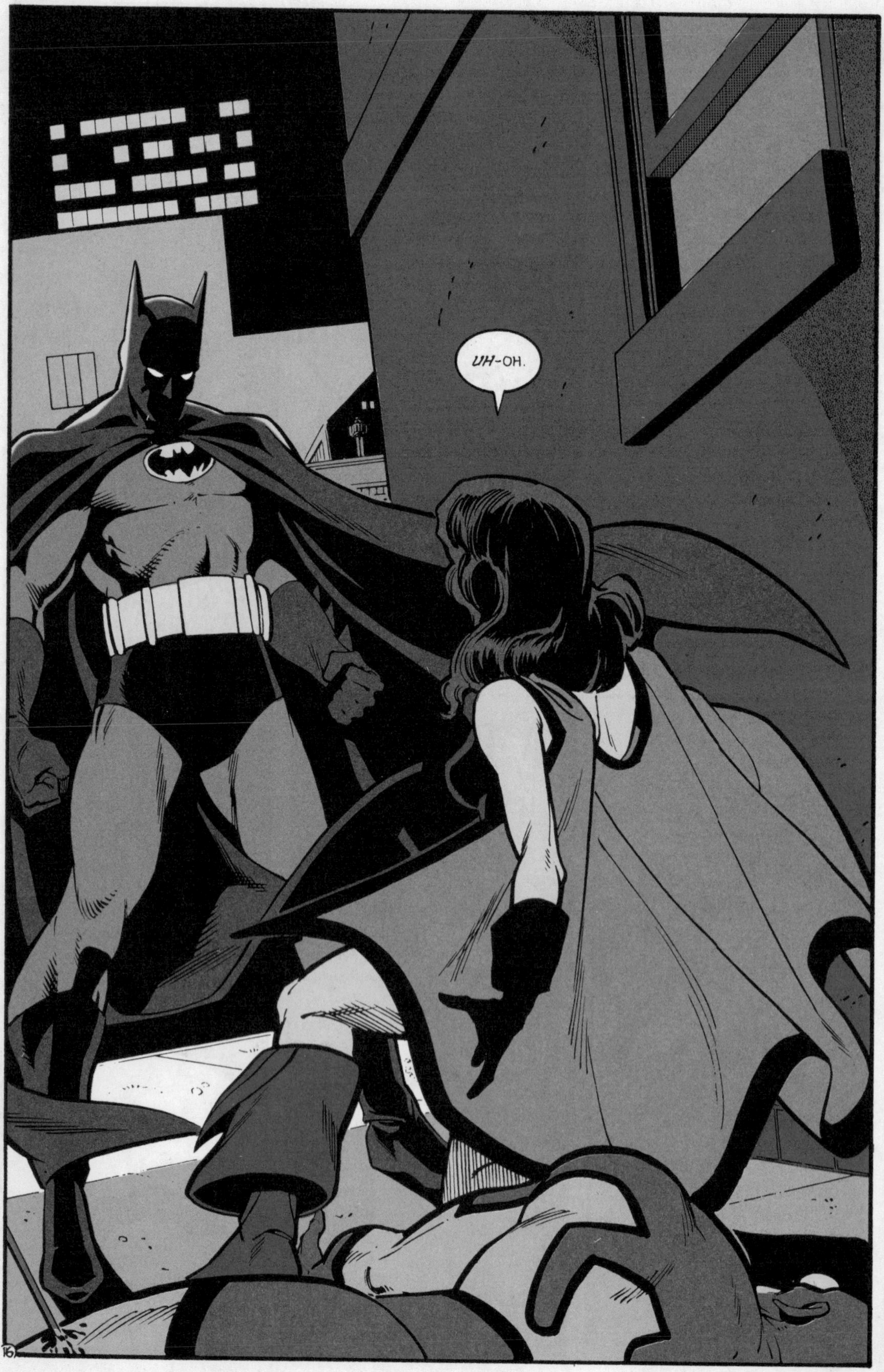
UH-OH.

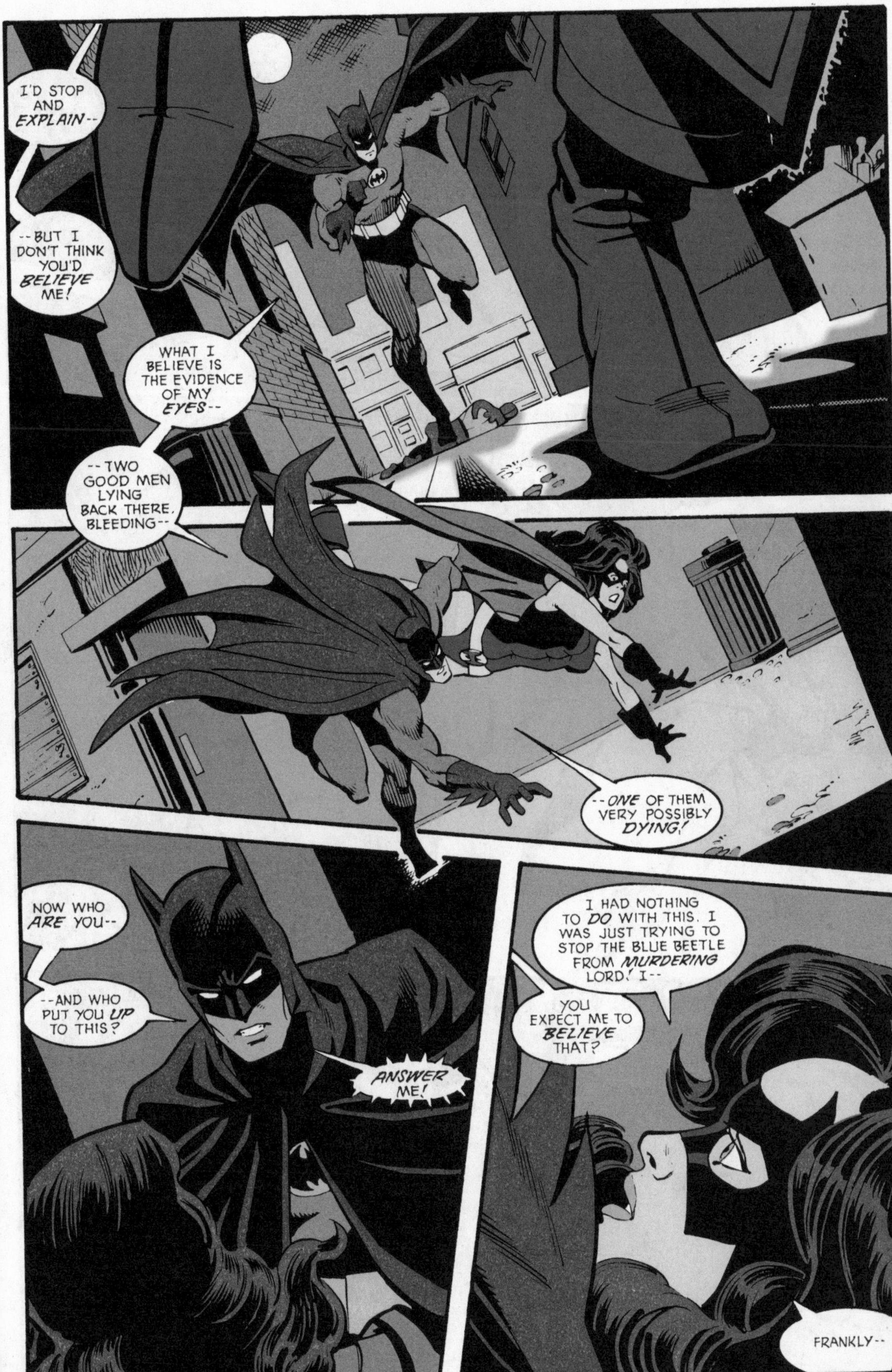

I'D STOP AND EXPLAIN--
--BUT I DON'T THINK YOU'D BELIEVE ME!
WHAT I BELIEVE IS THE EVIDENCE OF MY EYES--
--TWO GOOD MEN LYING BACK THERE, BLEEDING--
--ONE OF THEM VERY POSSIBLY DYING!
NOW WHO ARE YOU--
--AND WHO PUT YOU UP TO THIS?
ANSWER ME!
I HAD NOTHING TO DO WITH THIS. I WAS JUST TRYING TO STOP THE BLUE BEETLE FROM MURDERING LORD! I--
YOU EXPECT ME TO BELIEVE THAT?
FRANKLY--
17

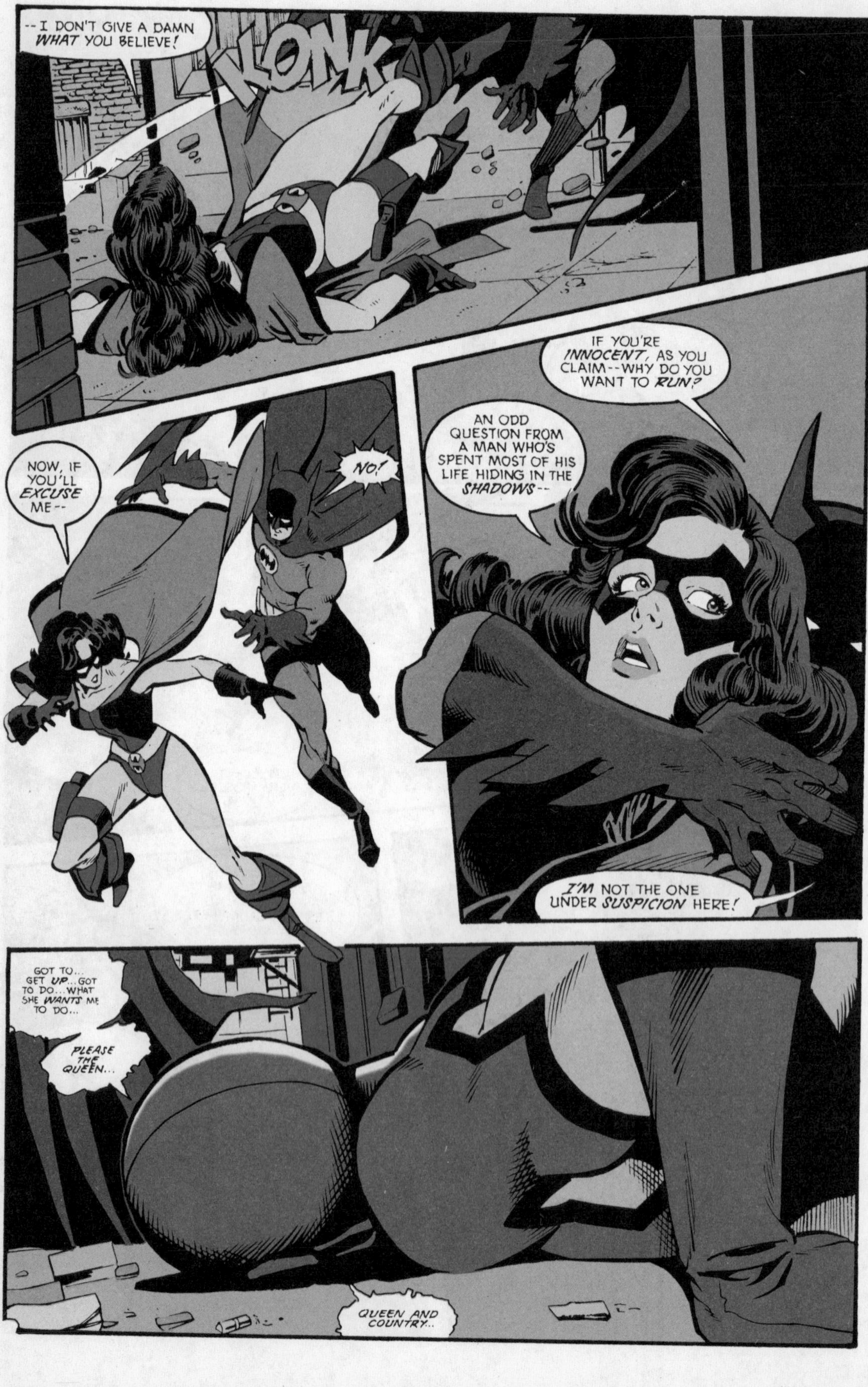

--I DON'T GIVE A DAMN WHAT YOU BELIEVE!
KONK
NOW, IF YOU'LL EXCUSE ME--
NO!
IF YOU'RE INNOCENT, AS YOU CLAIM--WHY DO YOU WANT TO RUN?
AN ODD QUESTION FROM A MAN WHO'S SPENT MOST OF HIS LIFE HIDING IN THE SHADOWS--
I'M NOT THE ONE UNDER SUSPICION HERE!
GOT TO... GET UP... GOT TO DO... WHAT SHE WANTS ME TO DO...
PLEASE THE QUEEN...
QUEEN AND COUNTRY...

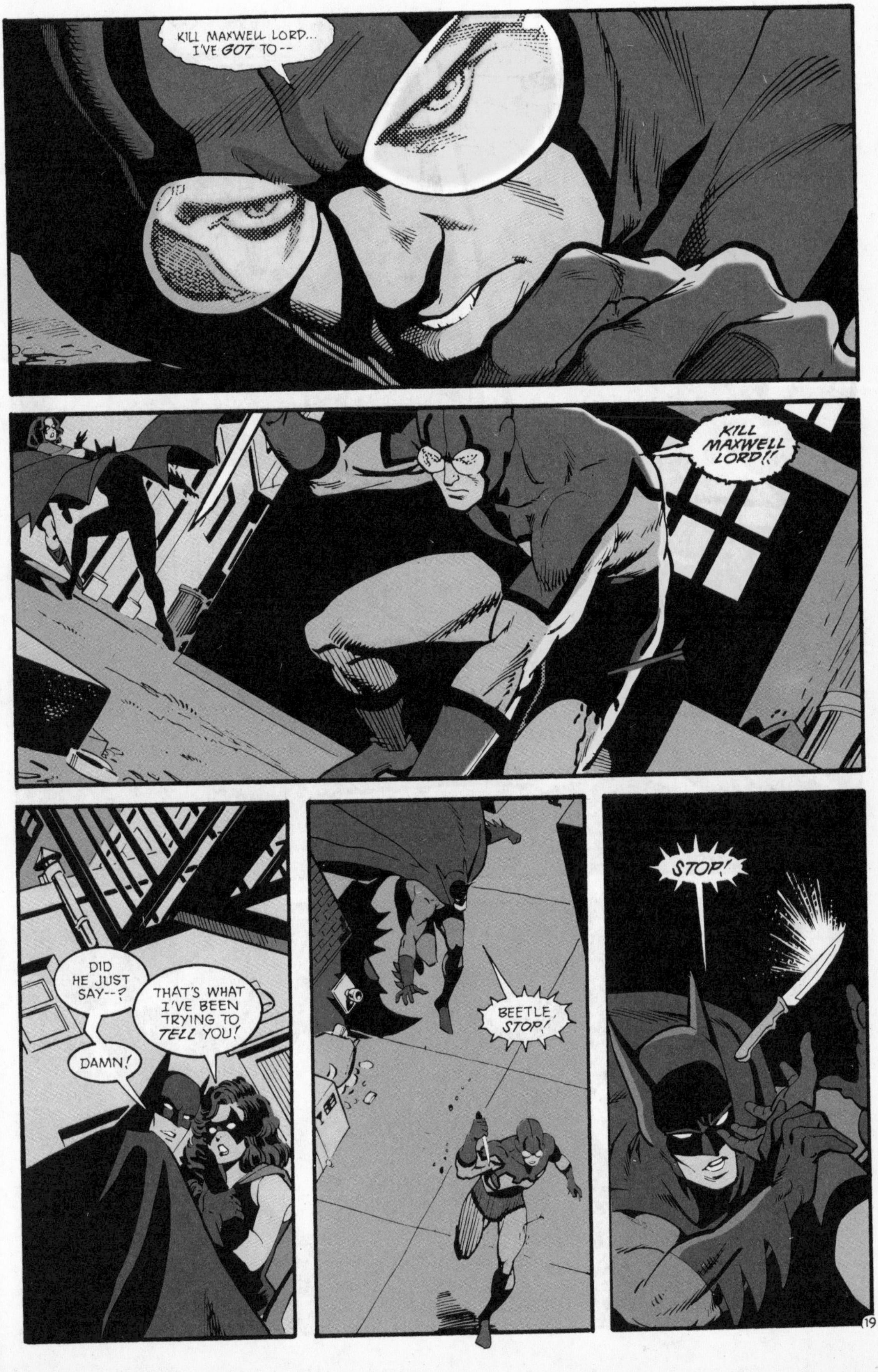
KILL MAXWELL LORD... I'VE GOT TO--
KILL MAXWELL LORD!!
DID HE JUST SAY--?
THAT'S WHAT I'VE BEEN TRYING TO TELL YOU!
DAMN!
BEETLE, STOP!
STOP!
19

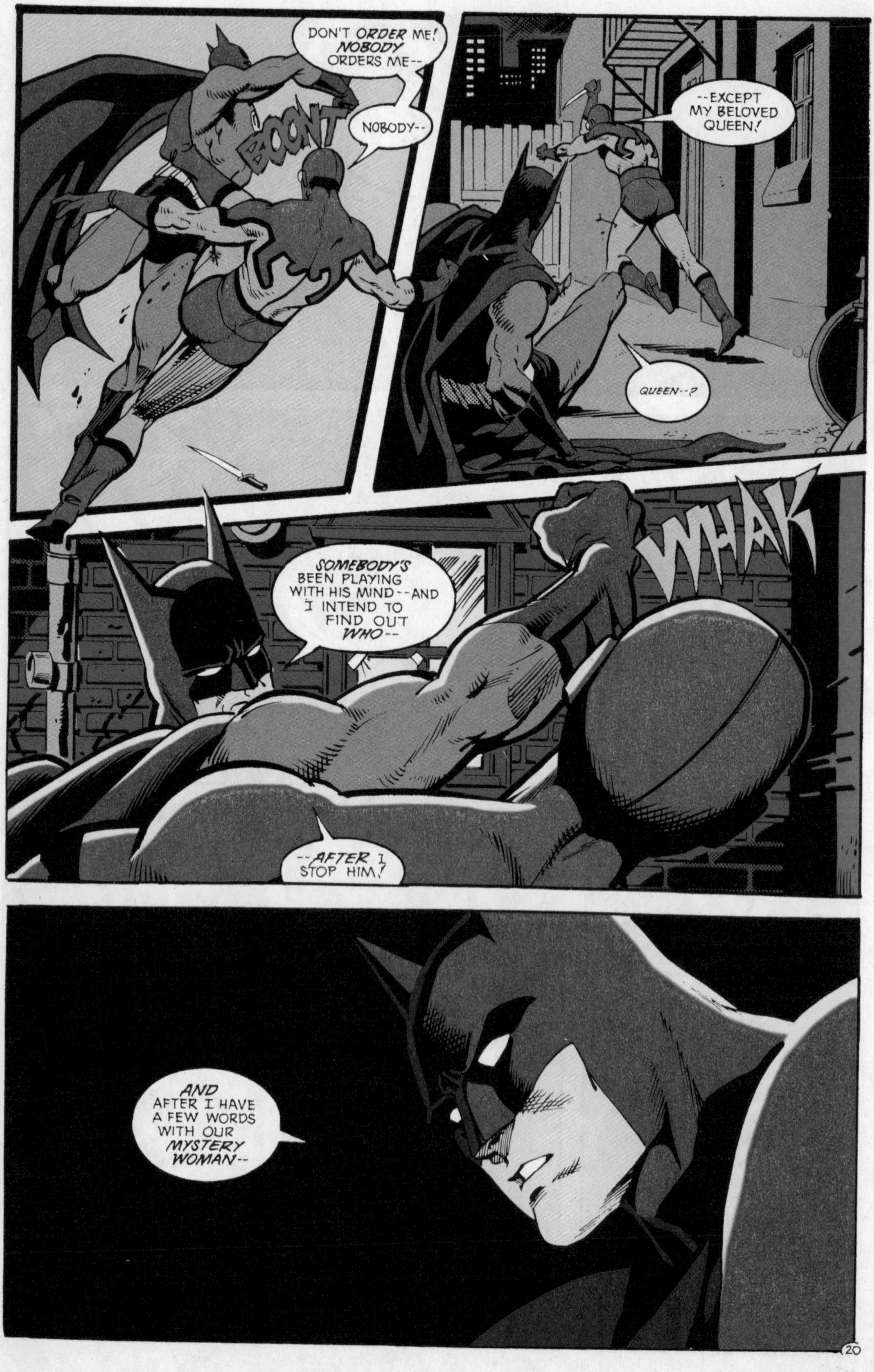
DON'T ORDER ME! NOBODY ORDERS ME--
BOONT
NOBODY--
--EXCEPT MY BELOVED QUEEN!
QUEEN--?
WHAK
SOMEBODY'S BEEN PLAYING WITH HIS MIND--AND I INTEND TO FIND OUT WHO--
--AFTER I STOP HIM!
AND AFTER I HAVE A FEW WORDS WITH OUR MYSTERY WOMAN--
20

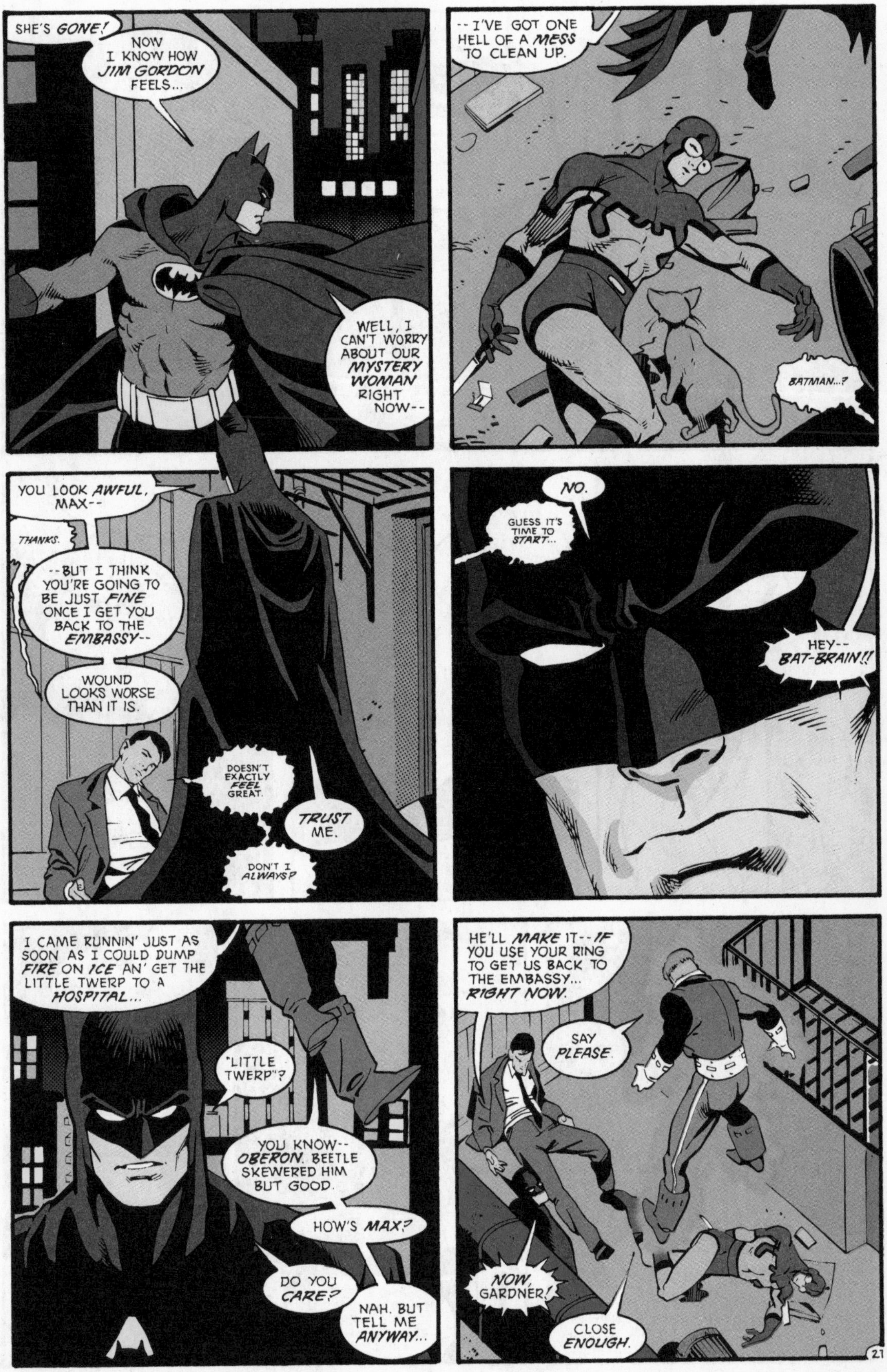
SHE'S GONE!
NOW I KNOW HOW JIM GORDON FEELS...
WELL, I CAN'T WORRY ABOUT OUR MYSTERY WOMAN RIGHT NOW--
--I'VE GOT ONE HELL OF A MESS TO CLEAN UP.
BATMAN...?
YOU LOOK AWFUL, MAX--
THANKS.
--BUT I THINK YOU'RE GOING TO BE JUST FINE ONCE I GET YOU BACK TO THE EMBASSY--
WOUND LOOKS WORSE THAN IT IS.
DOESN'T EXACTLY FEEL GREAT.
TRUST ME.
DON'T I ALWAYS?
NO.
GUESS IT'S TIME TO START...
HEY-- BAT-BRAIN!!
I CAME RUNNIN' JUST AS SOON AS I COULD DUMP FIRE ON ICE AN' GET THE LITTLE TWERP TO A HOSPITAL...
"LITTLE TWERP"?
YOU KNOW-- OBERON. BEETLE SKEWERED HIM BUT GOOD.
HOW'S MAX?
DO YOU CARE?
NAH. BUT TELL ME ANYWAY...
HE'LL MAKE IT--IF YOU USE YOUR RING TO GET US BACK TO THE EMBASSY... RIGHT NOW.
SAY PLEASE.
NOW, GARDNER!
CLOSE ENOUGH.
21

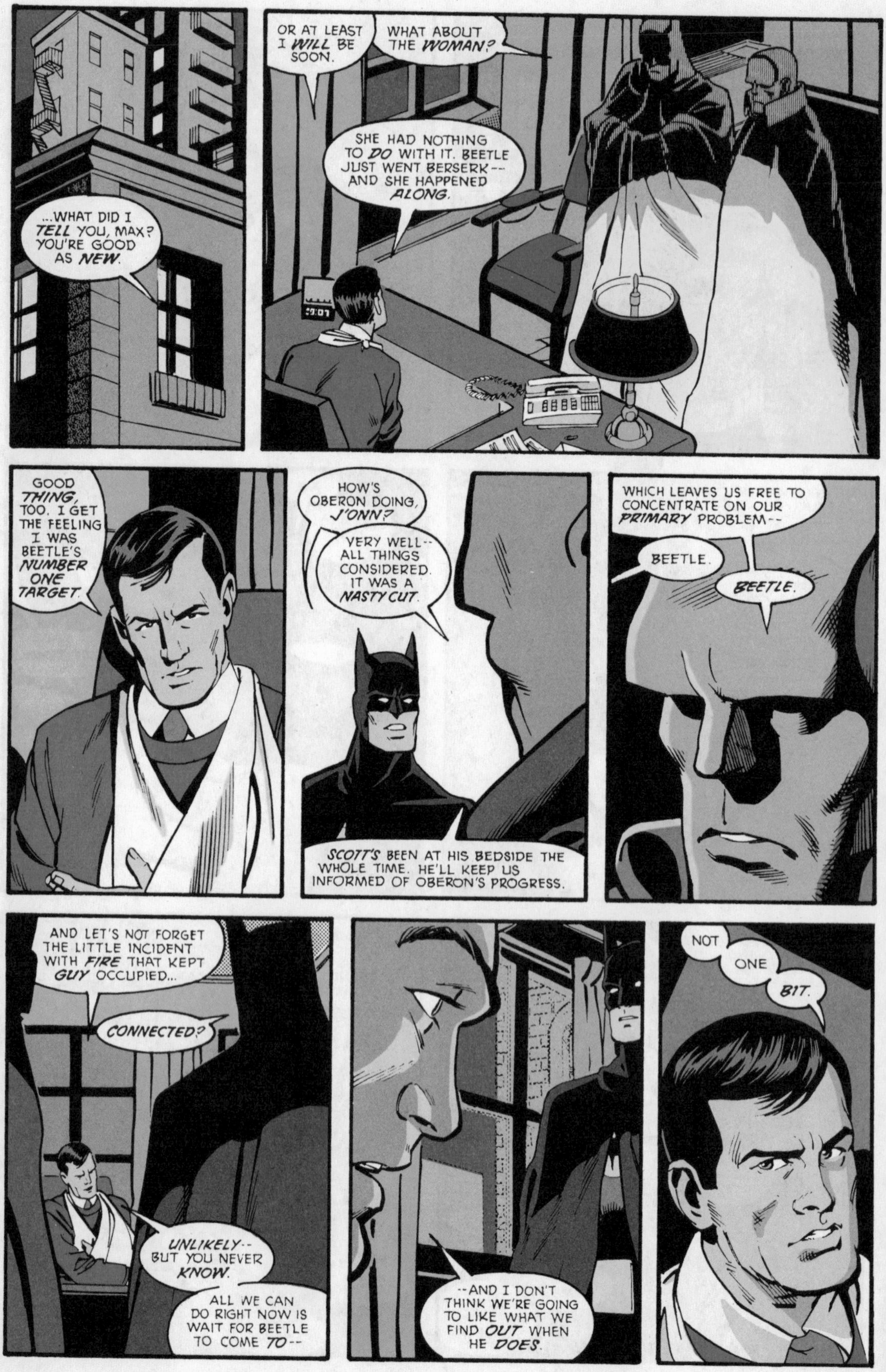
...WHAT DID I TELL YOU, MAX? YOU'RE GOOD AS NEW.
OR AT LEAST I WILL BE SOON.
WHAT ABOUT THE WOMAN?
SHE HAD NOTHING TO DO WITH IT. BEETLE JUST WENT BERSERK-- AND SHE HAPPENED ALONG.
GOOD THING, TOO. I GET THE FEELING I WAS BEETLE'S NUMBER ONE TARGET.
HOW'S OBERON DOING, J'ONN?
VERY WELL-- ALL THINGS CONSIDERED. IT WAS A NASTY CUT.
SCOTT'S BEEN AT HIS BEDSIDE THE WHOLE TIME. HE'LL KEEP US INFORMED OF OBERON'S PROGRESS.
WHICH LEAVES US FREE TO CONCENTRATE ON OUR PRIMARY PROBLEM--
BEETLE.
BEETLE.
AND LET'S NOT FORGET THE LITTLE INCIDENT WITH FIRE THAT KEPT GUY OCCUPIED...
CONNECTED?
UNLIKELY-- BUT YOU NEVER KNOW.
ALL WE CAN DO RIGHT NOW IS WAIT FOR BEETLE TO COME TO--
--AND I DON'T THINK WE'RE GOING TO LIKE WHAT WE FIND OUT WHEN HE DOES.
NOT
ONE
BIT.

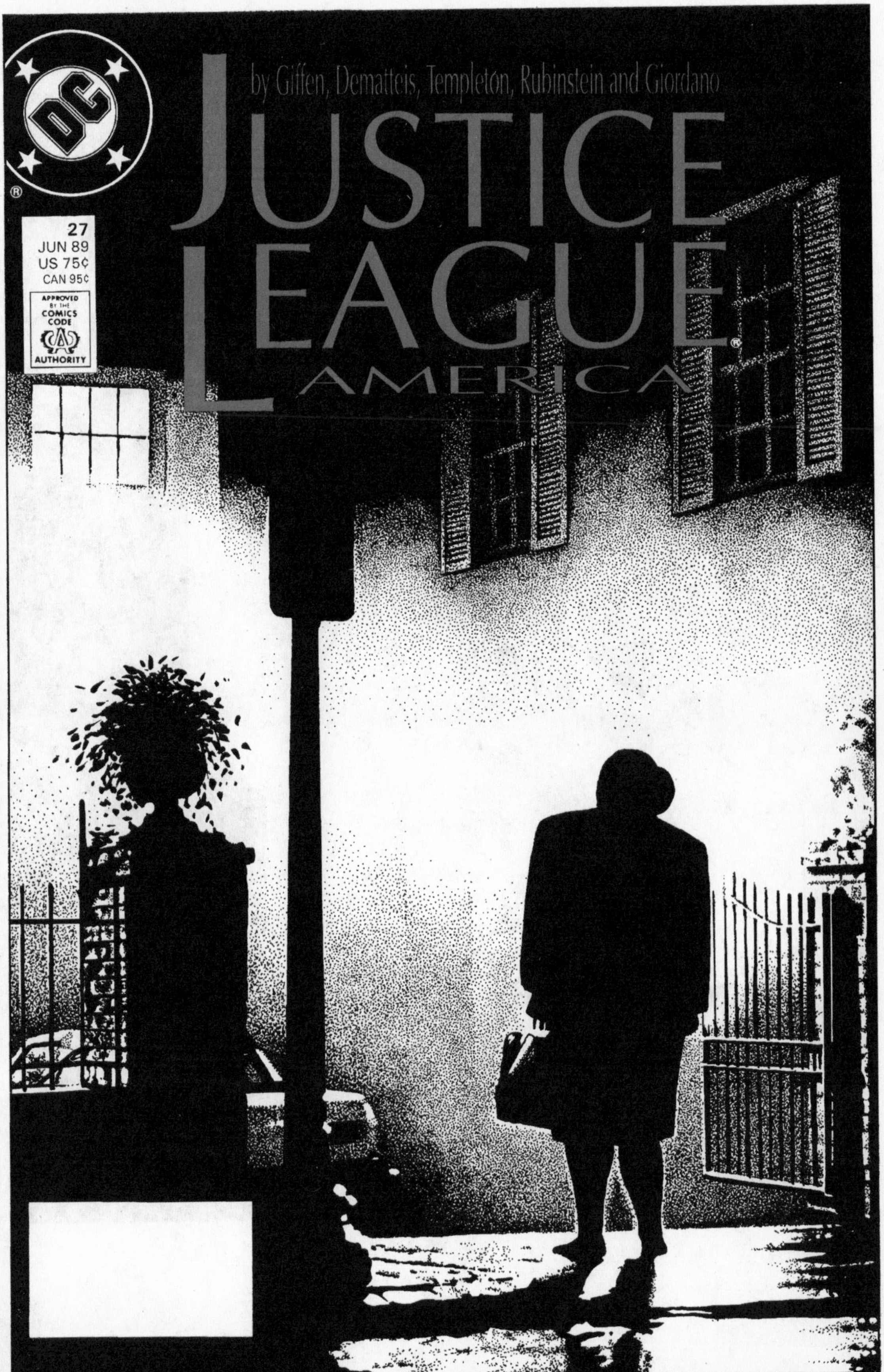

by Giffen, Dematteis, Templeton, Rubinstein and Giordano
JUSTICE LEAGUE AMERICA
27
JUN 89
US 75¢
CAN 95¢
APPROVED BY THE COMICS CODE AUTHORITY

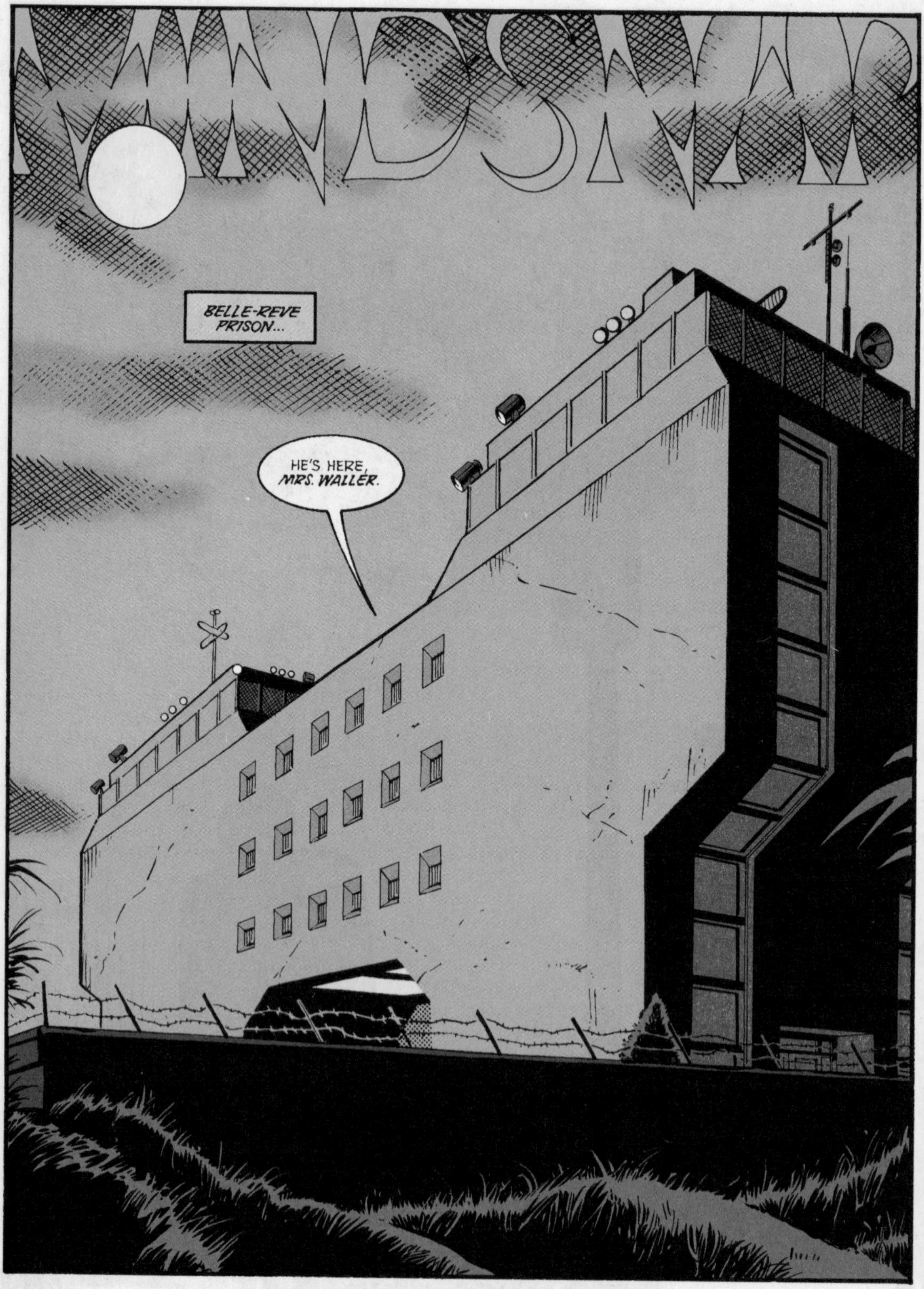
BELLE-REVE PRISON...
HE'S HERE, MRS. WALLER.

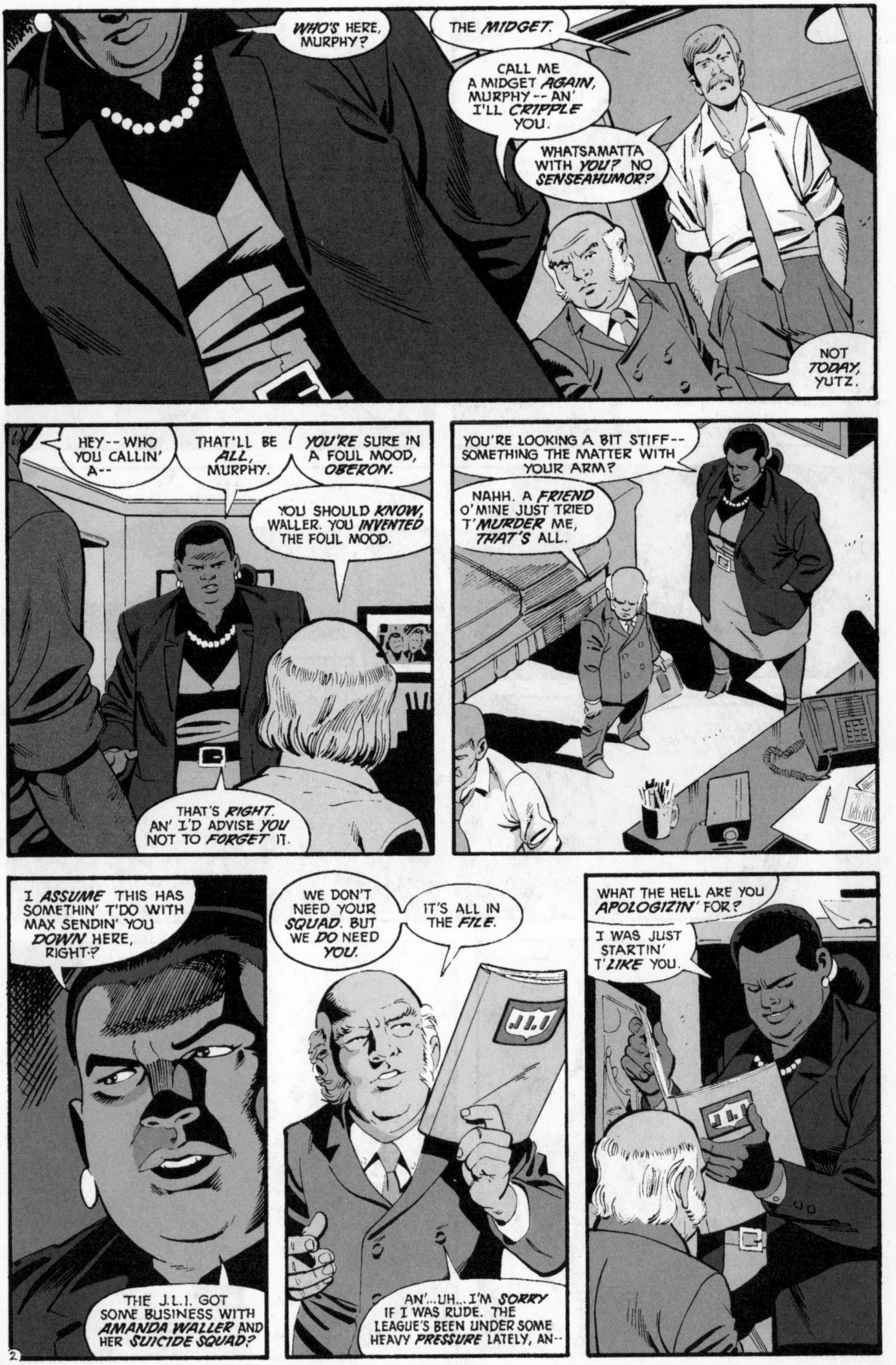

WHO'S HERE, MURPHY?
THE MIDGET.
CALL ME A MIDGET AGAIN, MURPHY--AN' I'LL CRIPPLE YOU.
WHATSAMATTA WITH YOU? NO SENSEAHUMOR?
NOT TODAY, YUTZ.
HEY--WHO YOU CALLIN' A--
THAT'LL BE ALL, MURPHY.
YOU'RE SURE IN A FOUL MOOD, OBERON.
YOU SHOULD KNOW, WALLER. YOU INVENTED THE FOUL MOOD.
THAT'S RIGHT. AN' I'D ADVISE YOU NOT TO FORGET IT.
YOU'RE LOOKING A BIT STIFF--SOMETHING THE MATTER WITH YOUR ARM?
NAHH. A FRIEND O'MINE JUST TRIED T'MURDER ME, THAT'S ALL.
I ASSUME THIS HAS SOMETHIN' T'DO WITH MAX SENDIN' YOU DOWN HERE, RIGHT?
THE J.L.I. GOT SOME BUSINESS WITH AMANDA WALLER AND HER SUICIDE SQUAD?
WE DON'T NEED YOUR SQUAD. BUT WE DO NEED YOU.
IT'S ALL IN THE FILE.
AN'...UH...I'M SORRY IF I WAS RUDE. THE LEAGUE'S BEEN UNDER SOME HEAVY PRESSURE LATELY, AN--
WHAT THE HELL ARE YOU APOLOGIZIN' FOR?
I WAS JUST STARTIN' T'LIKE YOU.
2

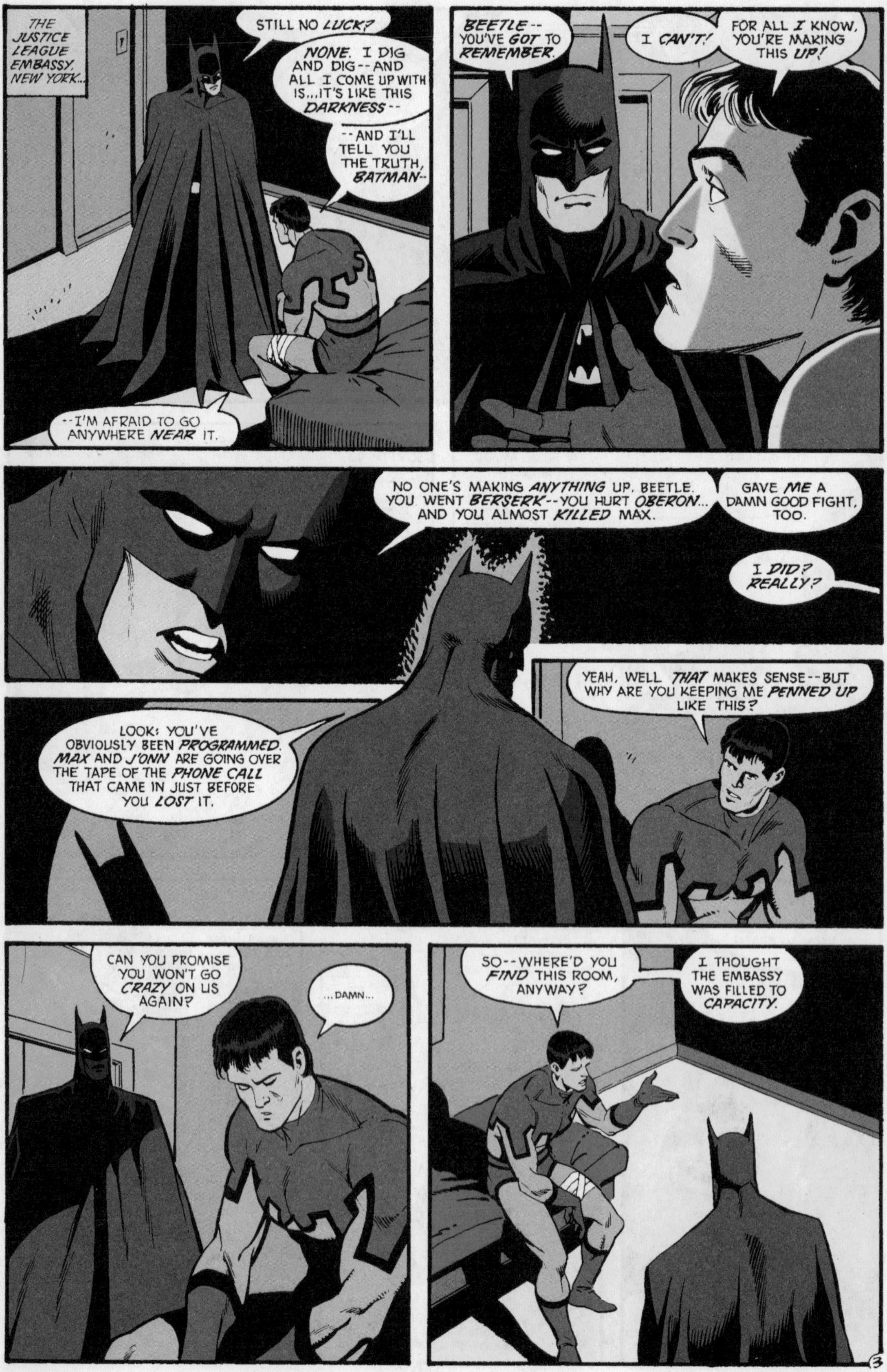
THE JUSTICE LEAGUE EMBASSY, NEW YORK...
STILL NO LUCK?
NONE. I DIG AND DIG--AND ALL I COME UP WITH IS...IT'S LIKE THIS DARKNESS--
--AND I'LL TELL YOU THE TRUTH, BATMAN--
--I'M AFRAID TO GO ANYWHERE NEAR IT.
BEETLE--YOU'VE GOT TO REMEMBER.
I CAN'T!
FOR ALL I KNOW, YOU'RE MAKING THIS UP!
NO ONE'S MAKING ANYTHING UP, BEETLE. YOU WENT BERSERK--YOU HURT OBERON... AND YOU ALMOST KILLED MAX.
GAVE ME A DAMN GOOD FIGHT, TOO.
I DID? REALLY?
YEAH, WELL THAT MAKES SENSE--BUT WHY ARE YOU KEEPING ME PENNED UP LIKE THIS?
LOOK: YOU'VE OBVIOUSLY BEEN PROGRAMMED. MAX AND J'ONN ARE GOING OVER THE TAPE OF THE PHONE CALL THAT CAME IN JUST BEFORE YOU LOST IT.
CAN YOU PROMISE YOU WON'T GO CRAZY ON US AGAIN?
...DAMN...
SO--WHERE'D YOU FIND THIS ROOM, ANYWAY?
I THOUGHT THE EMBASSY WAS FILLED TO CAPACITY.
3

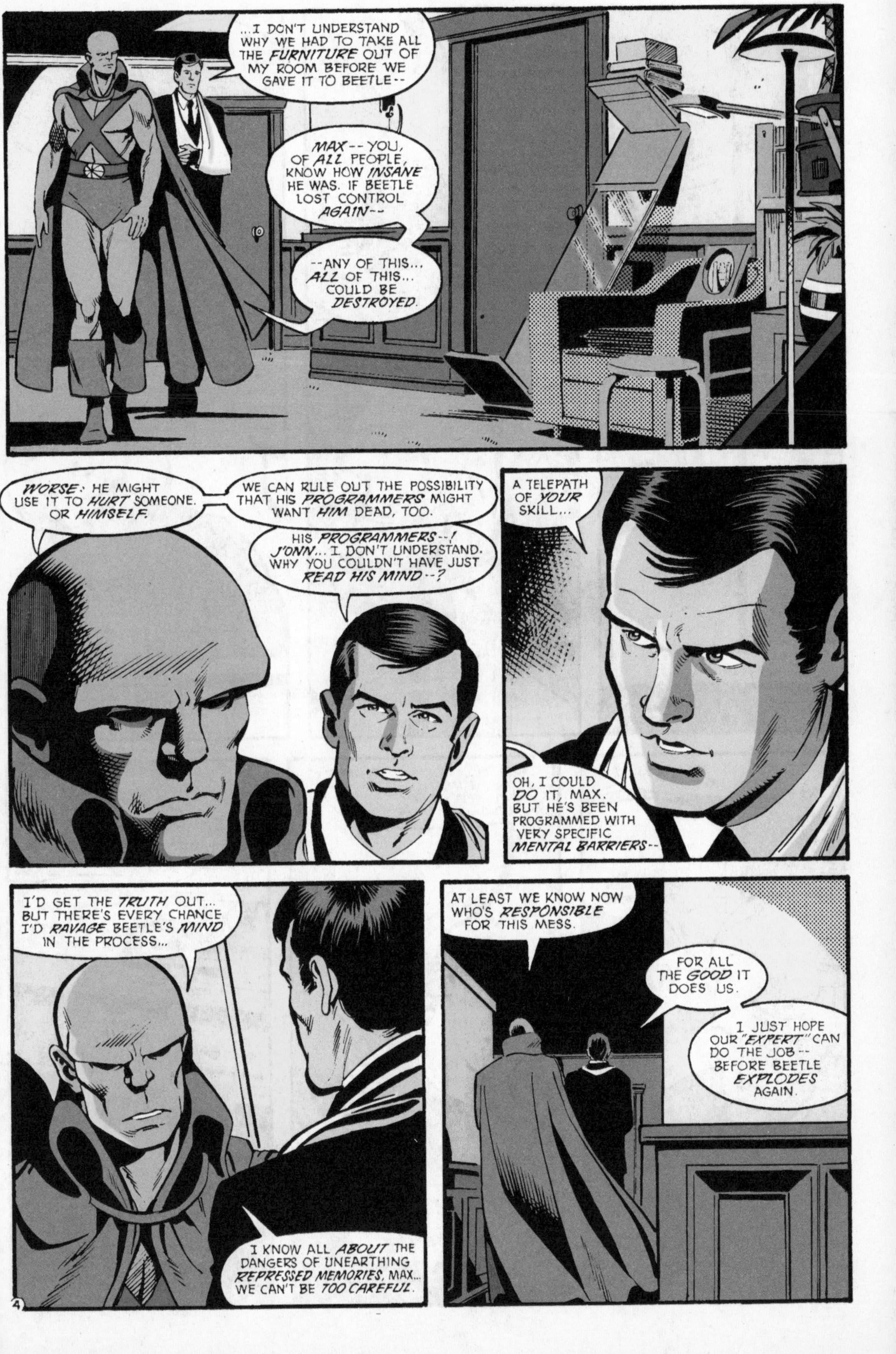
...I DON'T UNDERSTAND WHY WE HAD TO TAKE ALL THE FURNITURE OUT OF MY ROOM BEFORE WE GAVE IT TO BEETLE--
MAX--YOU, OF ALL PEOPLE, KNOW HOW INSANE HE WAS. IF BEETLE LOST CONTROL AGAIN--
--ANY OF THIS... ALL OF THIS... COULD BE DESTROYED.
WORSE: HE MIGHT USE IT TO HURT SOMEONE. OR HIMSELF.
WE CAN RULE OUT THE POSSIBILITY THAT HIS PROGRAMMERS MIGHT WANT HIM DEAD, TOO.
HIS PROGRAMMERS--! J'ONN... I DON'T UNDERSTAND. WHY YOU COULDN'T HAVE JUST READ HIS MIND--?
A TELEPATH OF YOUR SKILL...
OH, I COULD DO IT, MAX. BUT HE'S BEEN PROGRAMMED WITH VERY SPECIFIC MENTAL BARRIERS--
I'D GET THE TRUTH OUT... BUT THERE'S EVERY CHANCE I'D RAVAGE BEETLE'S MIND IN THE PROCESS...
I KNOW ALL ABOUT THE DANGERS OF UNEARTHING REPRESSED MEMORIES, MAX... WE CAN'T BE TOO CAREFUL.
4
AT LEAST WE KNOW NOW WHO'S RESPONSIBLE FOR THIS MESS.
FOR ALL THE GOOD IT DOES US.
I JUST HOPE OUR "EXPERT" CAN DO THE JOB--BEFORE BEETLE EXPLODES AGAIN.

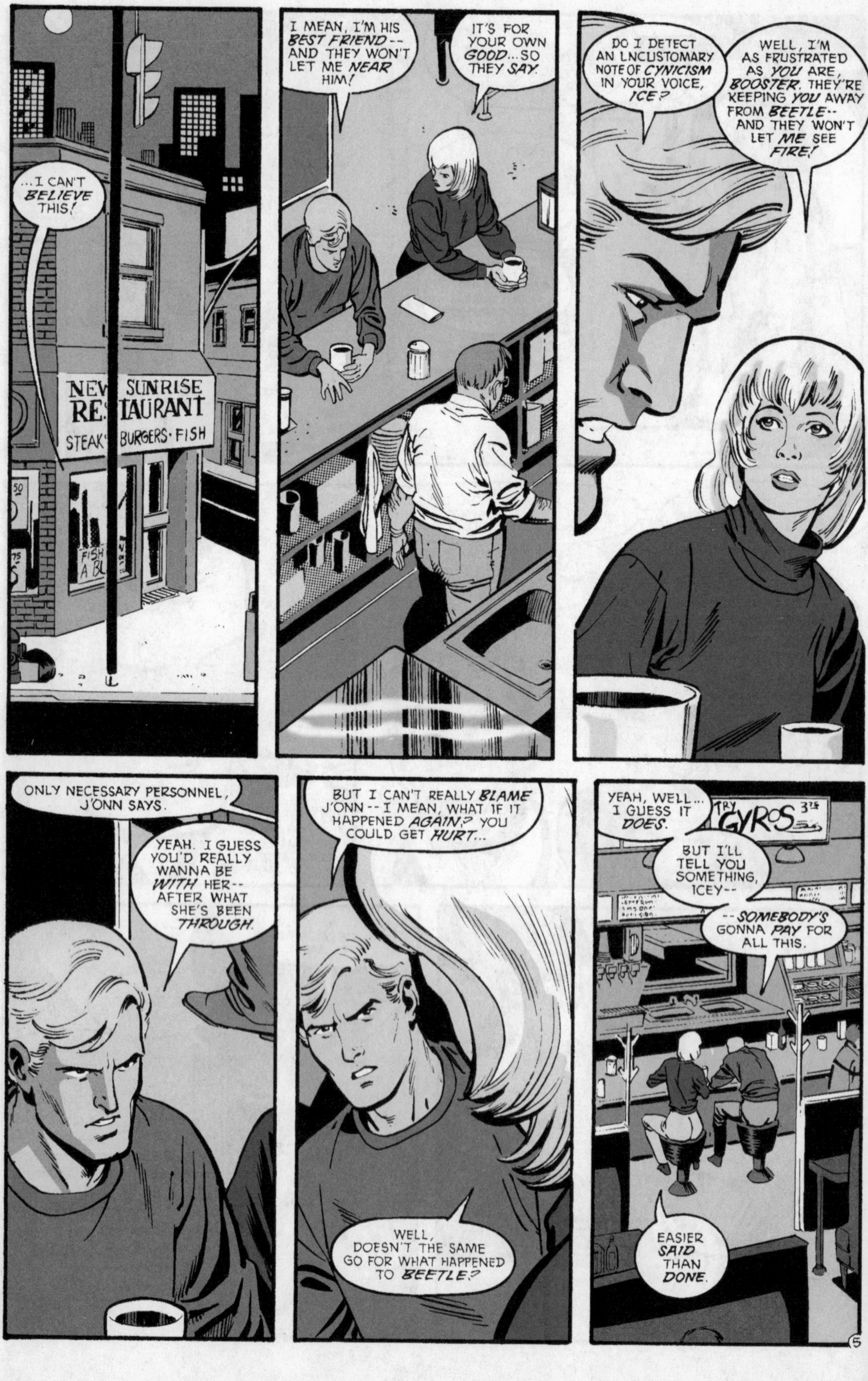
...I CAN'T BELIEVE THIS!
NEW SUNRISE RESTAURANT
STEAKS BURGERS FISH
I MEAN, I'M HIS BEST FRIEND -- AND THEY WON'T LET ME NEAR HIM!
IT'S FOR YOUR OWN GOOD... SO THEY SAY.
DO I DETECT AN UNCUSTOMARY NOTE OF CYNICISM IN YOUR VOICE, ICE?
WELL, I'M AS FRUSTRATED AS YOU ARE, BOOSTER. THEY'RE KEEPING YOU AWAY FROM BEETLE -- AND THEY WON'T LET ME SEE FIRE!
ONLY NECESSARY PERSONNEL, J'ONN SAYS.
YEAH. I GUESS YOU'D REALLY WANNA BE WITH HER -- AFTER WHAT SHE'S BEEN THROUGH.
BUT I CAN'T REALLY BLAME J'ONN -- I MEAN, WHAT IF IT HAPPENED AGAIN? YOU COULD GET HURT...
WELL, DOESN'T THE SAME GO FOR WHAT HAPPENED TO BEETLE?
YEAH, WELL... I GUESS IT DOES.
TRY GYROS
BUT I'LL TELL YOU SOMETHING, ICEY --
-- SOMEBODY'S GONNA PAY FOR ALL THIS.
EASIER SAID THAN DONE.
5

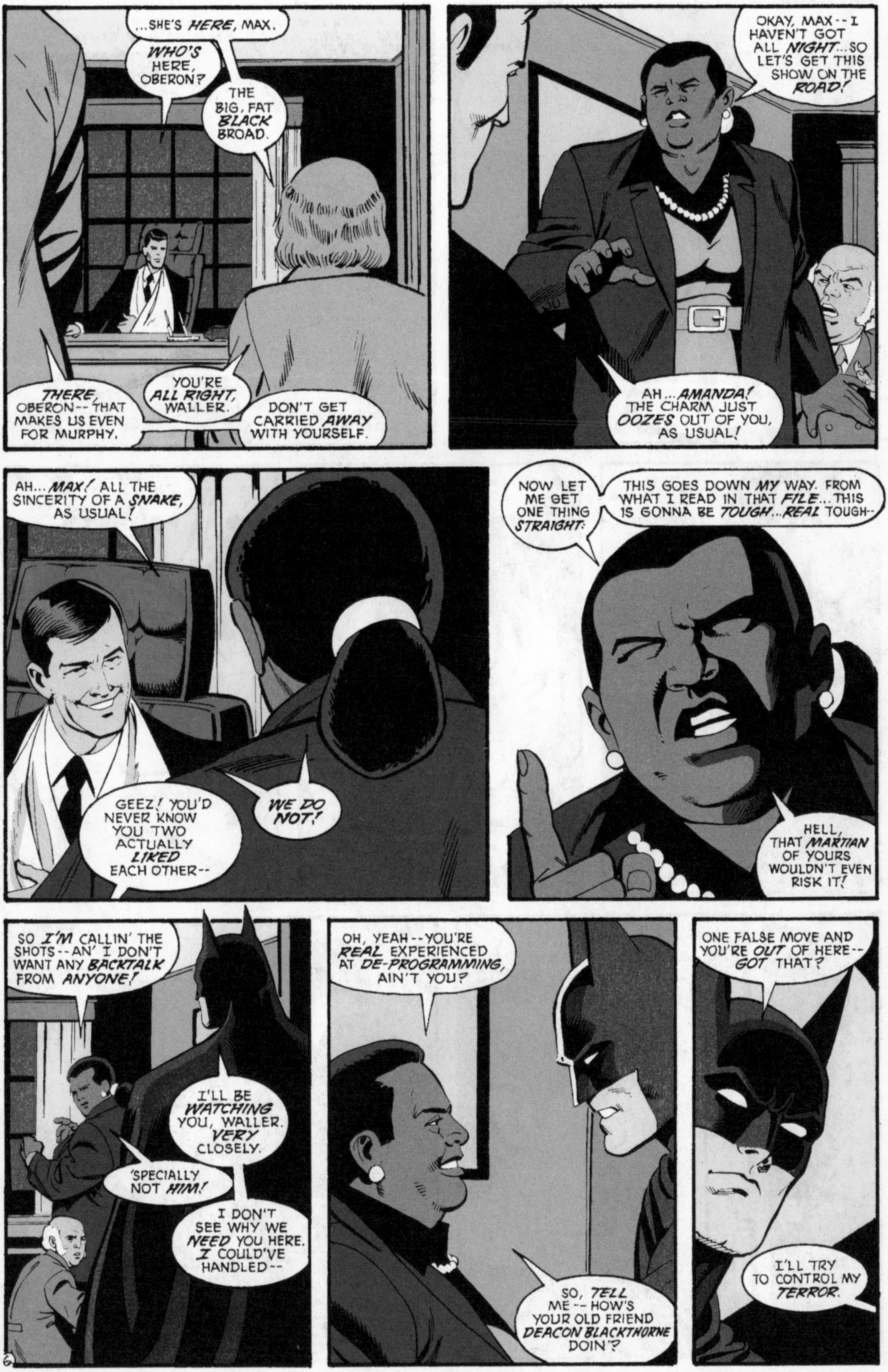
...SHE'S HERE, MAX.
WHO'S HERE, OBERON?
THE BIG, FAT BLACK BROAD.
THERE, OBERON--THAT MAKES US EVEN FOR MURPHY.
YOU'RE ALL RIGHT, WALLER.
DON'T GET CARRIED AWAY WITH YOURSELF.
OKAY, MAX--I HAVEN'T GOT ALL NIGHT...SO LET'S GET THIS SHOW ON THE ROAD!
AH...AMANDA! THE CHARM JUST OOZES OUT OF YOU, AS USUAL!
AH...MAX! ALL THE SINCERITY OF A SNAKE, AS USUAL!
GEEZ! YOU'D NEVER KNOW YOU TWO ACTUALLY LIKED EACH OTHER--
WE DO NOT!
NOW LET ME GET ONE THING STRAIGHT:
THIS GOES DOWN MY WAY. FROM WHAT I READ IN THAT FILE...THIS IS GONNA BE TOUGH...REAL TOUGH--
HELL, THAT MARTIAN OF YOURS WOULDN'T EVEN RISK IT!
SO I'M CALLIN' THE SHOTS--AN' I DON'T WANT ANY BACKTALK FROM ANYONE!
I'LL BE WATCHING YOU, WALLER. VERY CLOSELY.
'SPECIALLY NOT HIM!
I DON'T SEE WHY WE NEED YOU HERE. I COULD'VE HANDLED--
OH, YEAH--YOU'RE REAL EXPERIENCED AT DE-PROGRAMMING, AIN'T YOU?
SO, TELL ME--HOW'S YOUR OLD FRIEND DEACON BLACKTHORNE DOIN'?
ONE FALSE MOVE AND YOU'RE OUT OF HERE--GOT THAT?
I'LL TRY TO CONTROL MY TERROR.

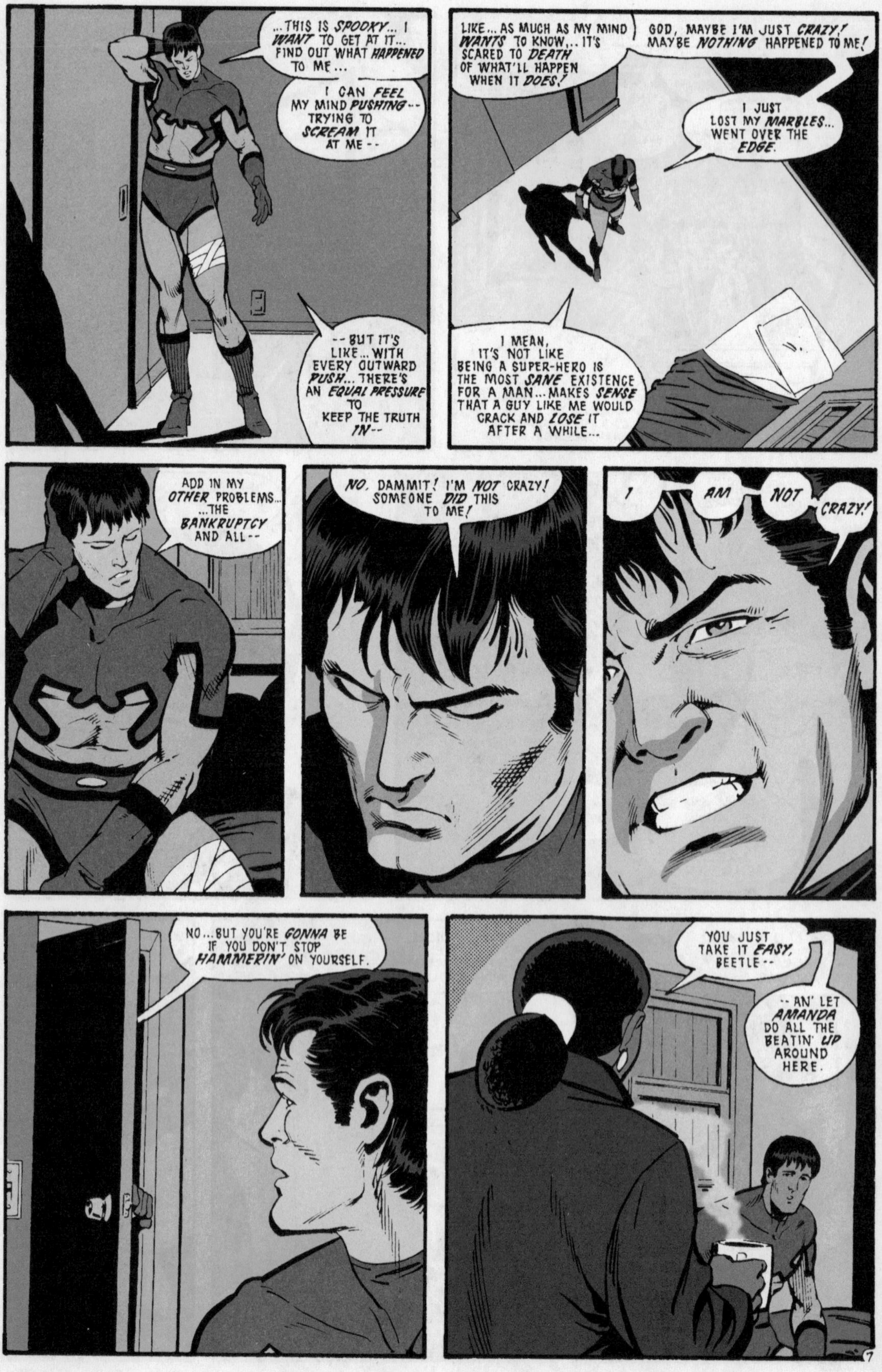

...THIS IS SPOOKY... I WANT TO GET AT IT... FIND OUT WHAT HAPPENED TO ME...
I CAN FEEL MY MIND PUSHING-- TRYING TO SCREAM IT AT ME--
--BUT IT'S LIKE... WITH EVERY OUTWARD PUSH... THERE'S AN EQUAL PRESSURE TO KEEP THE TRUTH IN--
LIKE... AS MUCH AS MY MIND WANTS TO KNOW,.. IT'S SCARED TO DEATH OF WHAT'LL HAPPEN WHEN IT DOES!
GOD, MAYBE I'M JUST CRAZY! MAYBE NOTHING HAPPENED TO ME!
I JUST LOST MY MARBLES... WENT OVER THE EDGE.
I MEAN, IT'S NOT LIKE BEING A SUPER-HERO IS THE MOST SANE EXISTENCE FOR A MAN... MAKES SENSE THAT A GUY LIKE ME WOULD CRACK AND LOSE IT AFTER A WHILE...
ADD IN MY OTHER PROBLEMS... ...THE BANKRUPTCY AND ALL--
NO, DAMMIT! I'M NOT CRAZY! SOMEONE DID THIS TO ME!
I
AM
NOT
CRAZY!
NO... BUT YOU'RE GONNA BE IF YOU DON'T STOP HAMMERIN' ON YOURSELF.
YOU JUST TAKE IT EASY, BEETLE--
--AN' LET AMANDA DO ALL THE BEATIN' UP AROUND HERE.
7

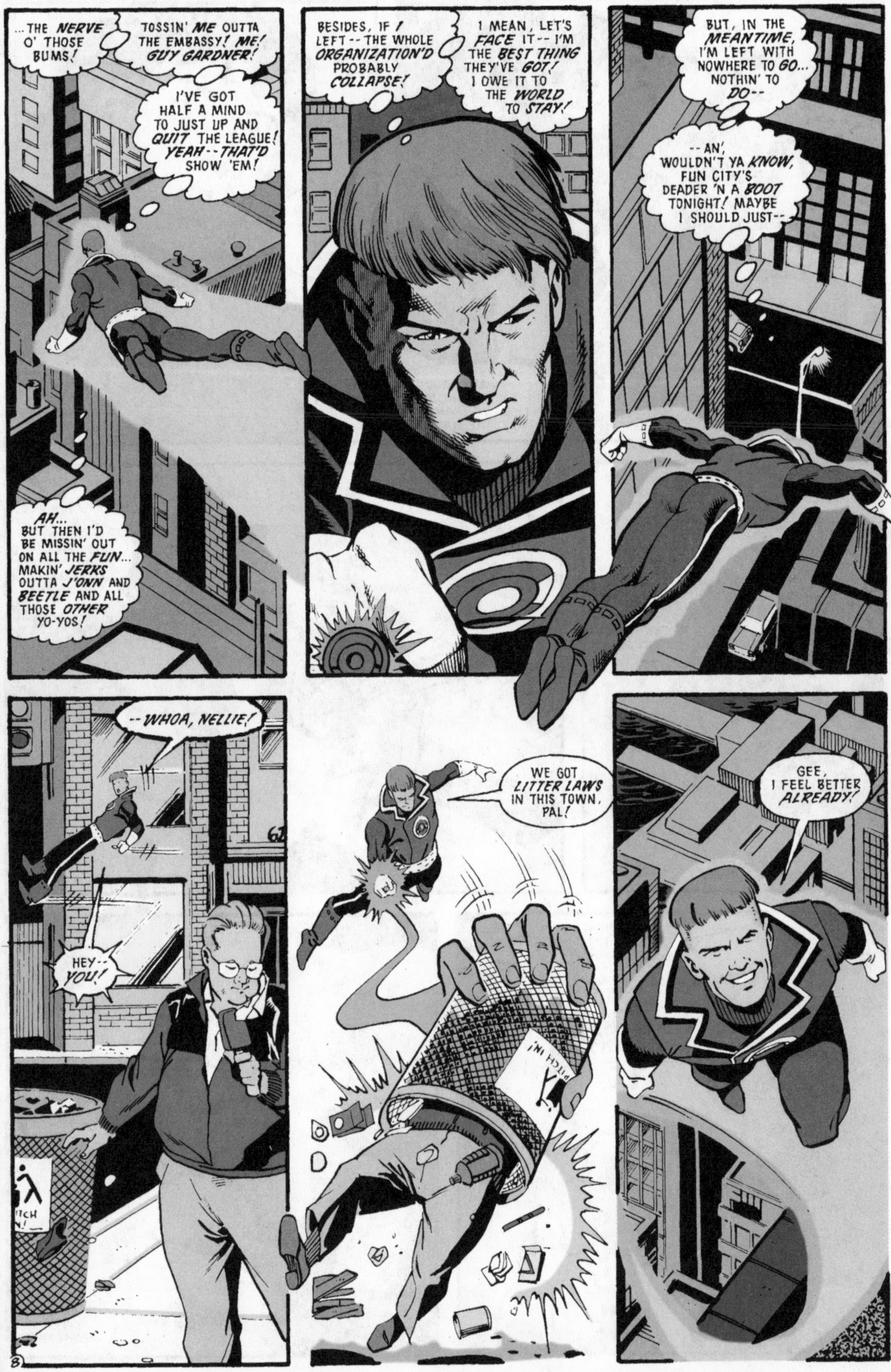
...THE NERVE O' THOSE BUMS!
TOSSIN' ME OUTTA THE EMBASSY! ME! GUY GARDNER!
I'VE GOT HALF A MIND TO JUST UP AND QUIT THE LEAGUE! YEAH--THAT'D SHOW 'EM!
AH... BUT THEN I'D BE MISSIN' OUT ON ALL THE FUN... MAKIN' JERKS OUTTA J'ONN AND BEETLE AND ALL THOSE OTHER YO-YOS!
BESIDES, IF I LEFT--THE WHOLE ORGANIZATION'D PROBABLY COLLAPSE!
I MEAN, LET'S FACE IT--I'M THE BEST THING THEY'VE GOT! I OWE IT TO THE WORLD TO STAY!
BUT, IN THE MEANTIME, I'M LEFT WITH NOWHERE TO GO... NOTHIN' TO DO--
--AN', WOULDN'T YA KNOW, FUN CITY'S DEADER 'N A BOOT TONIGHT! MAYBE I SHOULD JUST--
--WHOA, NELLIE!
HEY-- YOU!
WE GOT LITTER LAWS IN THIS TOWN, PAL!
PITCH IN!
GEE, I FEEL BETTER ALREADY!
8

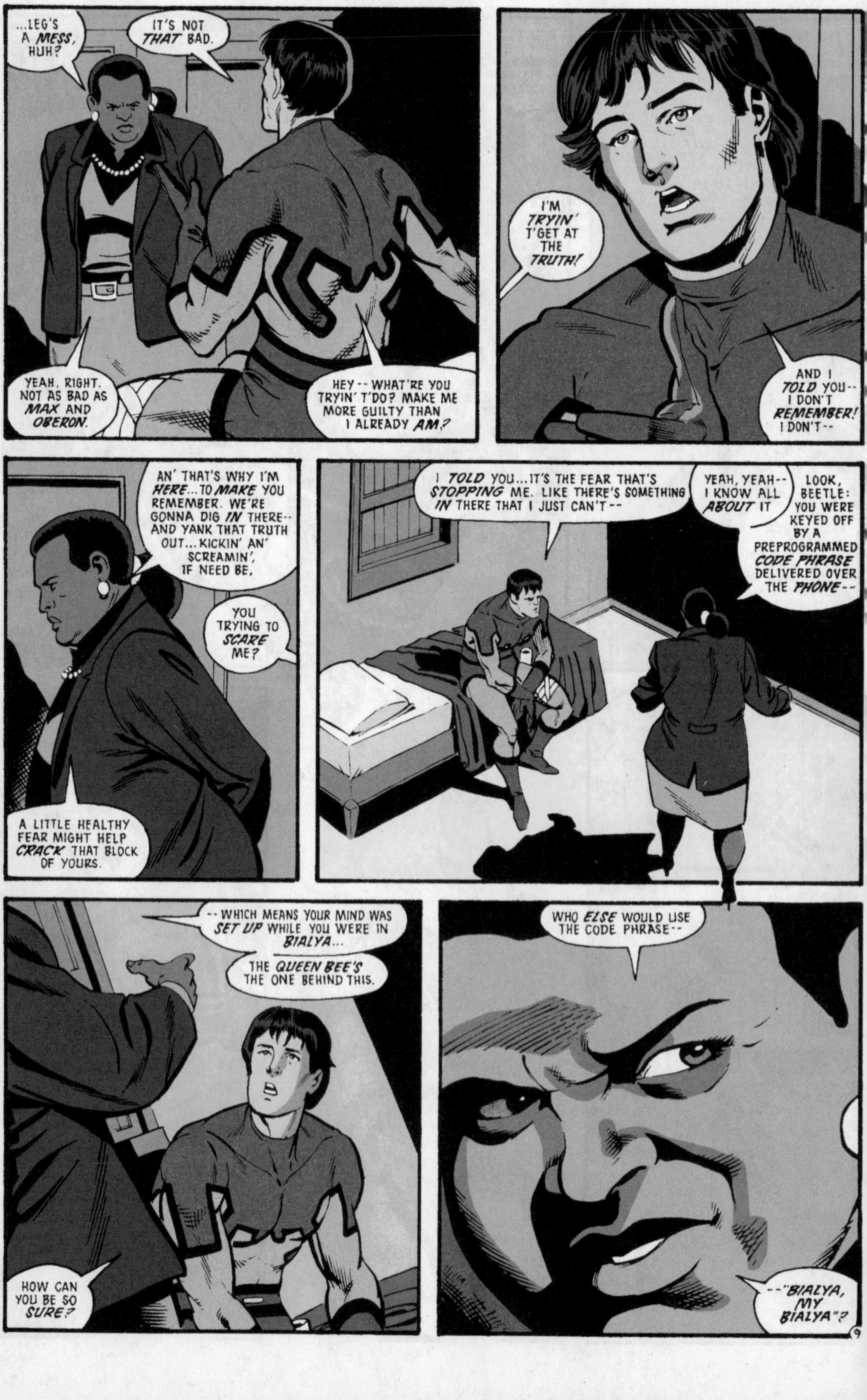
...LEG'S A MESS, HUH?
IT'S NOT THAT BAD.
YEAH, RIGHT. NOT AS BAD AS MAX AND OBERON.
HEY -- WHAT'RE YOU TRYIN' T'DO? MAKE ME MORE GUILTY THAN I ALREADY AM?
I'M TRYIN' T'GET AT THE TRUTH!
AND I TOLD YOU -- I DON'T REMEMBER! I DON'T --
AN' THAT'S WHY I'M HERE... TO MAKE YOU REMEMBER. WE'RE GONNA DIG IN THERE -- AND YANK THAT TRUTH OUT... KICKIN' AN' SCREAMIN', IF NEED BE.
YOU TRYING TO SCARE ME?
A LITTLE HEALTHY FEAR MIGHT HELP CRACK THAT BLOCK OF YOURS.
I TOLD YOU... IT'S THE FEAR THAT'S STOPPING ME. LIKE THERE'S SOMETHING IN THERE THAT I JUST CAN'T --
YEAH, YEAH -- I KNOW ALL ABOUT IT
LOOK, BEETLE: YOU WERE KEYED OFF BY A PREPROGRAMMED CODE PHRASE DELIVERED OVER THE PHONE --
-- WHICH MEANS YOUR MIND WAS SET UP WHILE YOU WERE IN BIALYA...
THE QUEEN BEE'S THE ONE BEHIND THIS.
HOW CAN YOU BE SO SURE?
WHO ELSE WOULD USE THE CODE PHRASE --
-- "BIALYA, MY BIALYA"?
9

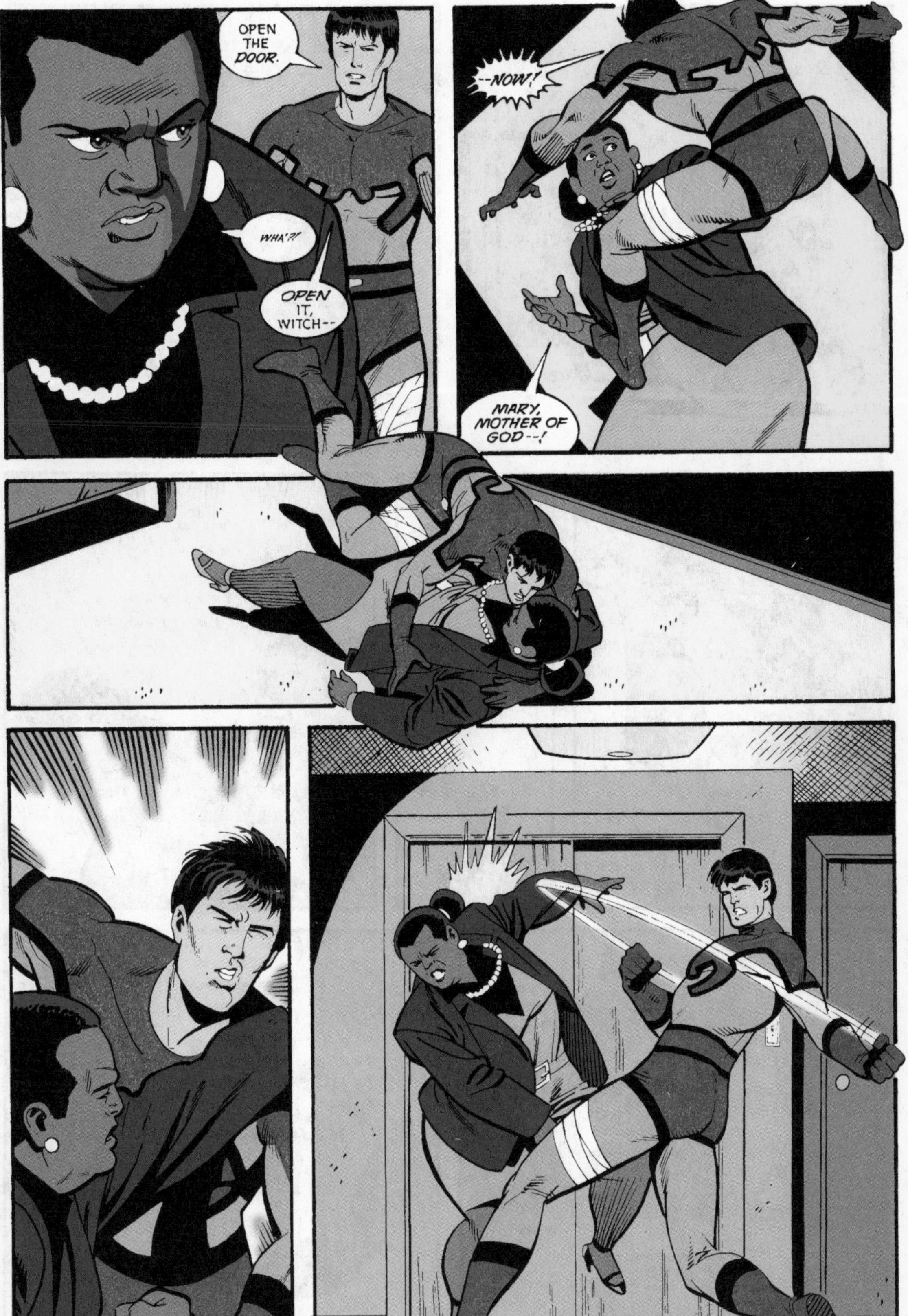

OPEN THE DOOR.
WHA'?!
OPEN IT, WITCH--
--NOW!
MARY, MOTHER OF GOD--!
10

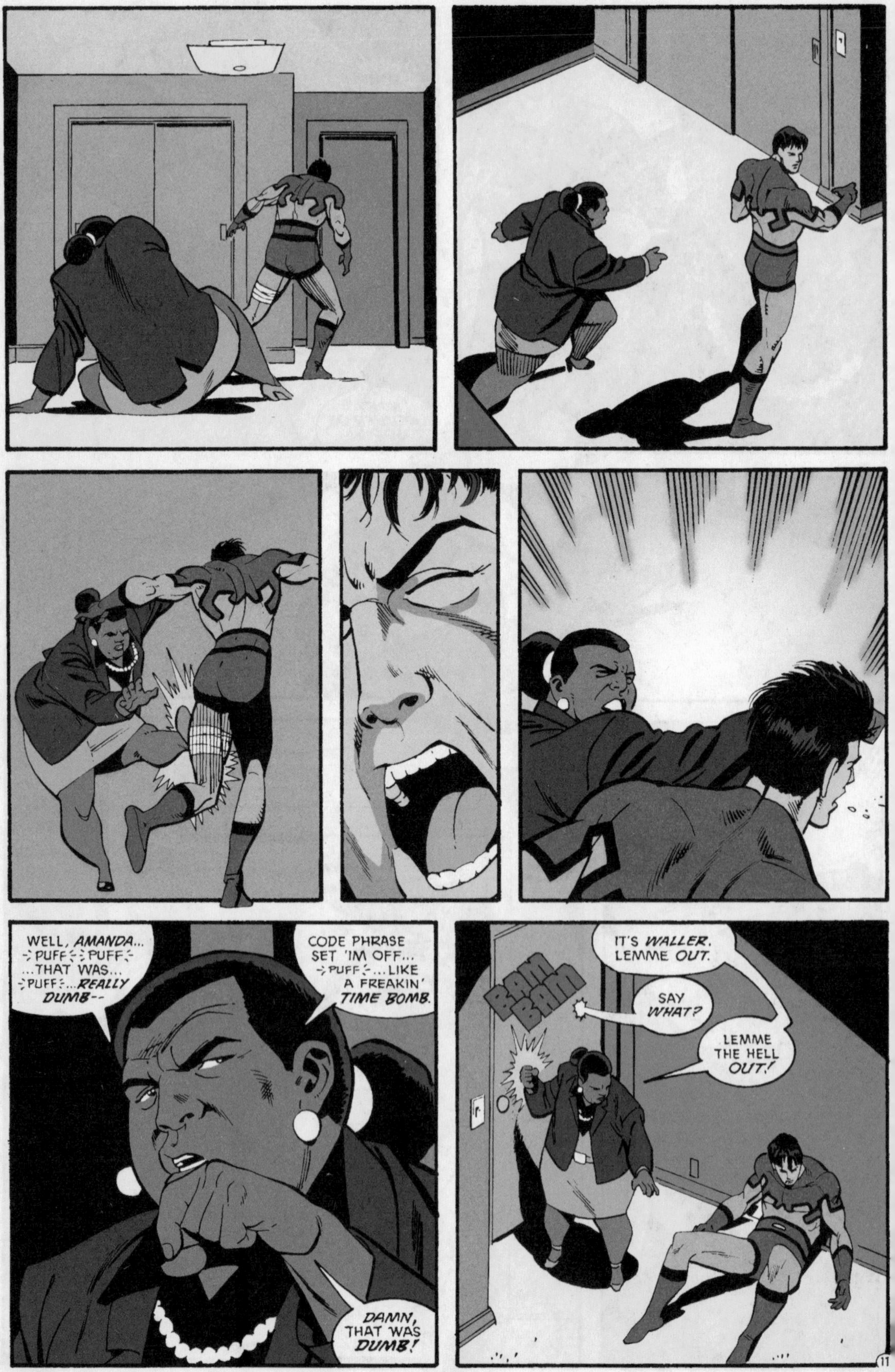

WELL, AMANDA... PUFF PUFF ...THAT WAS... PUFF ...REALLY DUMB--
CODE PHRASE SET 'IM OFF... PUFF ...LIKE A FREAKIN' TIME BOMB.
DAMN, THAT WAS DUMB!
BAM BAM
IT'S WALLER. LEMME OUT.
SAY WHAT?
LEMME THE HELL OUT!
11

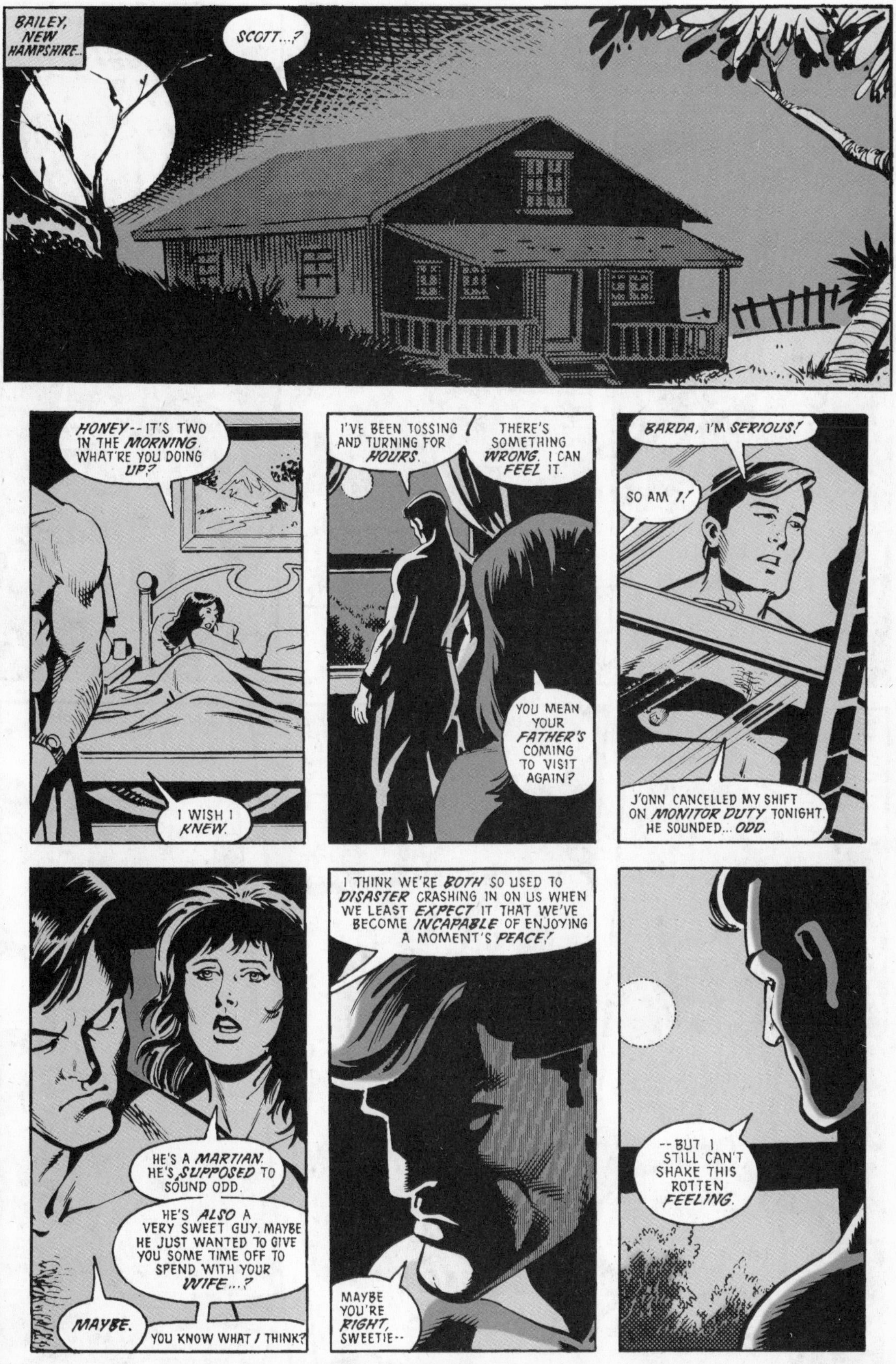
BAILEY, NEW HAMPSHIRE...
SCOTT...?
HONEY-- IT'S TWO IN THE MORNING. WHAT'RE YOU DOING UP?
I WISH I KNEW.
I'VE BEEN TOSSING AND TURNING FOR HOURS.
THERE'S SOMETHING WRONG. I CAN FEEL IT.
YOU MEAN YOUR FATHER'S COMING TO VISIT AGAIN?
BARDA, I'M SERIOUS!
SO AM I!
J'ONN CANCELLED MY SHIFT ON MONITOR DUTY TONIGHT. HE SOUNDED... ODD.
HE'S A MARTIAN. HE'S SUPPOSED TO SOUND ODD.
HE'S ALSO A VERY SWEET GUY. MAYBE HE JUST WANTED TO GIVE YOU SOME TIME OFF TO SPEND WITH YOUR WIFE...?
MAYBE.
YOU KNOW WHAT I THINK?
I THINK WE'RE BOTH SO USED TO DISASTER CRASHING IN ON US WHEN WE LEAST EXPECT IT THAT WE'VE BECOME INCAPABLE OF ENJOYING A MOMENT'S PEACE!
MAYBE YOU'RE RIGHT, SWEETIE--
--BUT I STILL CAN'T SHAKE THIS ROTTEN FEELING.

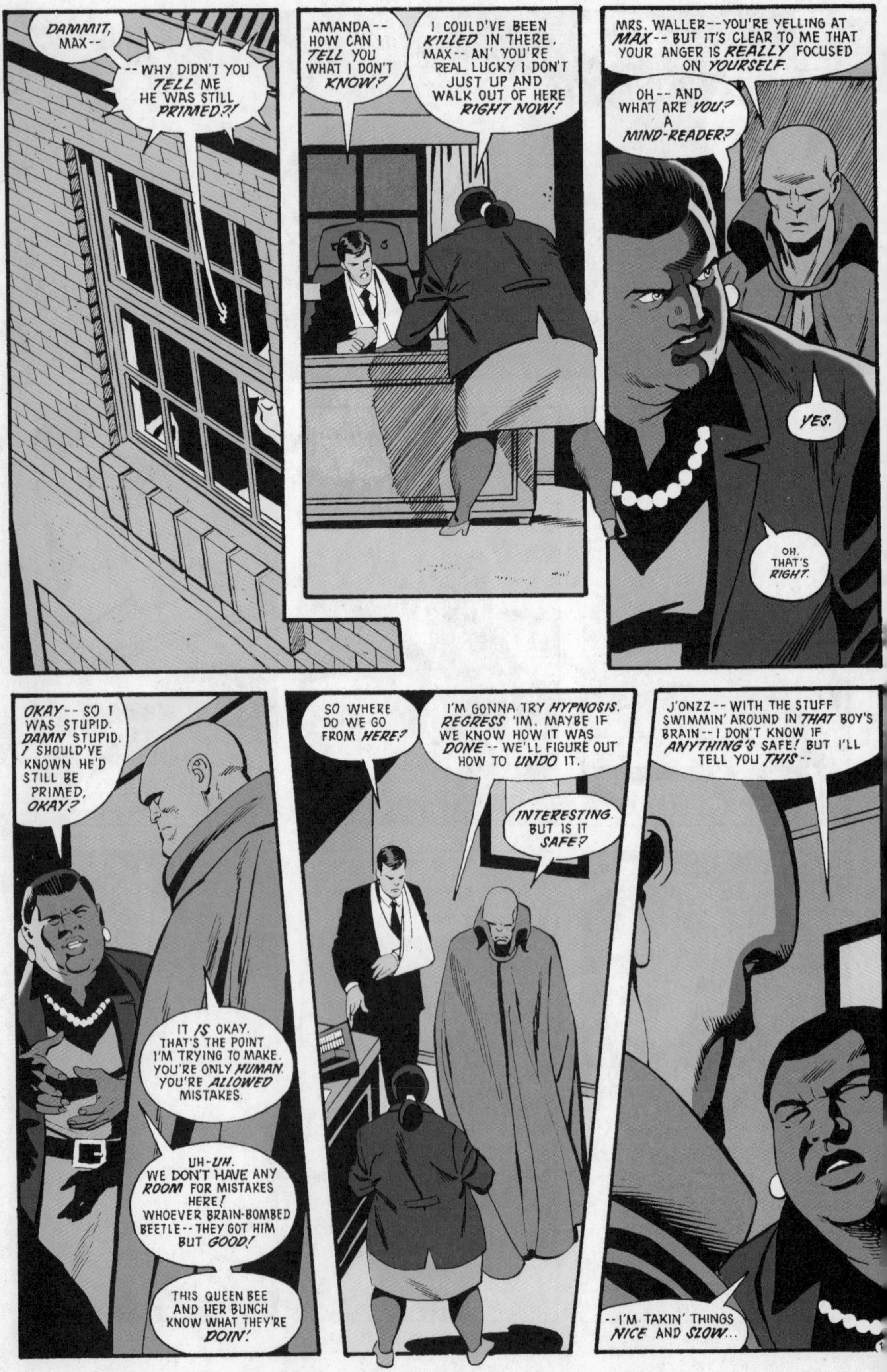
DAMMIT, MAX--
--WHY DIDN'T YOU TELL ME HE WAS STILL PRIMED?!
AMANDA-- HOW CAN I TELL YOU WHAT I DON'T KNOW?
I COULD'VE BEEN KILLED IN THERE, MAX-- AN' YOU'RE REAL LUCKY I DON'T JUST UP AND WALK OUT OF HERE RIGHT NOW!
MRS. WALLER--YOU'RE YELLING AT MAX-- BUT IT'S CLEAR TO ME THAT YOUR ANGER IS REALLY FOCUSED ON YOURSELF.
OH-- AND WHAT ARE YOU? A MIND-READER?
YES.
OH. THAT'S RIGHT.
OKAY-- SO I WAS STUPID. DAMN STUPID. I SHOULD'VE KNOWN HE'D STILL BE PRIMED, OKAY?
IT IS OKAY. THAT'S THE POINT I'M TRYING TO MAKE. YOU'RE ONLY HUMAN. YOU'RE ALLOWED MISTAKES.
UH-UH. WE DON'T HAVE ANY ROOM FOR MISTAKES HERE! WHOEVER BRAIN-BOMBED BEETLE-- THEY GOT HIM BUT GOOD!
THIS QUEEN BEE AND HER BUNCH KNOW WHAT THEY'RE DOIN'.
SO WHERE DO WE GO FROM HERE?
I'M GONNA TRY HYPNOSIS. REGRESS 'IM. MAYBE IF WE KNOW HOW IT WAS DONE -- WE'LL FIGURE OUT HOW TO UNDO IT.
INTERESTING. BUT IS IT SAFE?
J'ONZZ -- WITH THE STUFF SWIMMIN' AROUND IN THAT BOY'S BRAIN -- I DON'T KNOW IF ANYTHING'S SAFE! BUT I'LL TELL YOU THIS --
--I'M TAKIN' THINGS NICE AND SLOW...

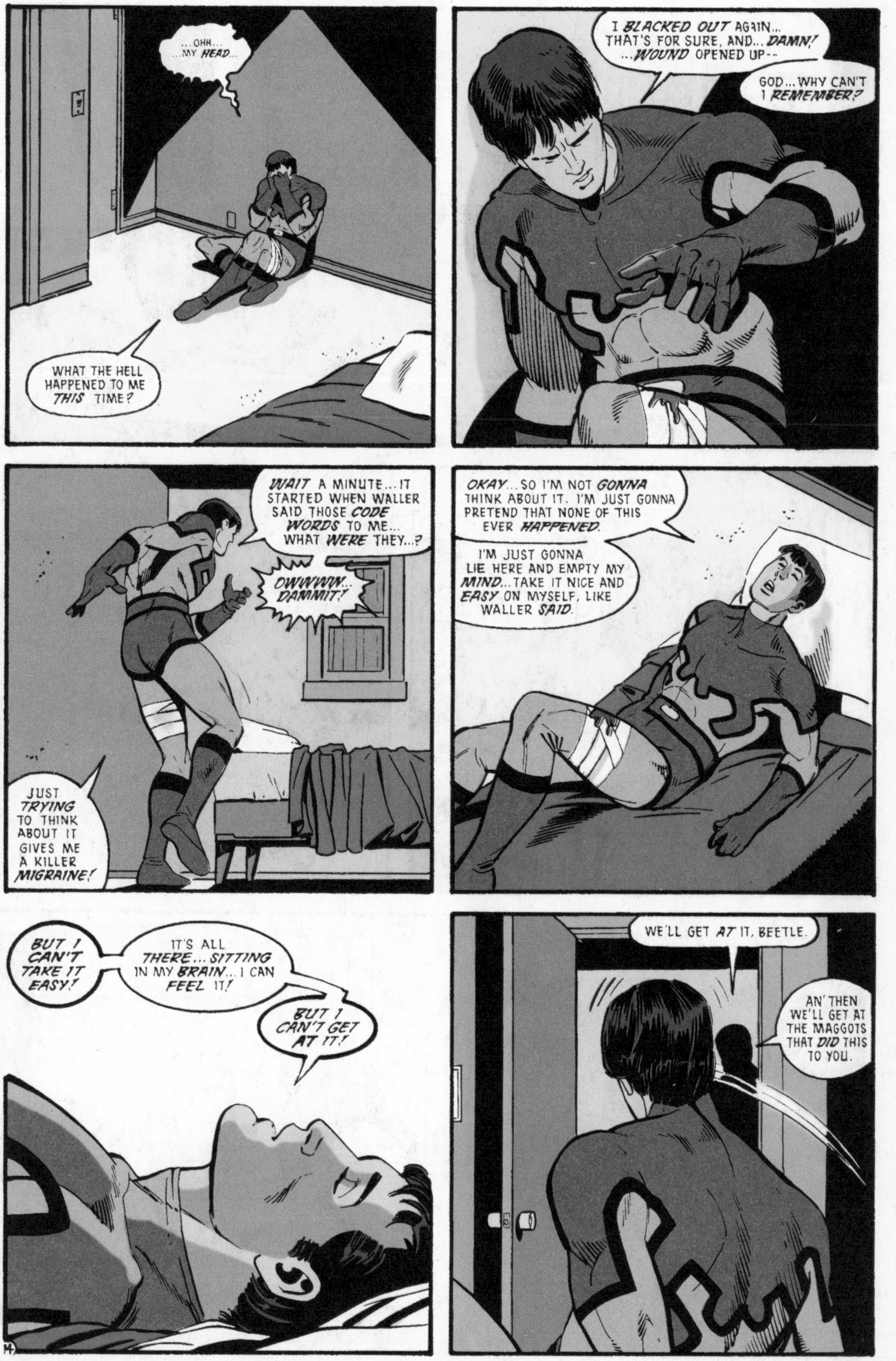
...OHH...
...MY HEAD...
WHAT THE HELL HAPPENED TO ME THIS TIME?
I BLACKED OUT AGAIN... THAT'S FOR SURE, AND... DAMN! ...WOUND OPENED UP--
GOD... WHY CAN'T I REMEMBER?
WAIT A MINUTE... IT STARTED WHEN WALLER SAID THOSE CODE WORDS TO ME... WHAT WERE THEY...?
OWWWW... DAMMIT!
JUST TRYING TO THINK ABOUT IT GIVES ME A KILLER MIGRAINE!
OKAY... SO I'M NOT GONNA THINK ABOUT IT. I'M JUST GONNA PRETEND THAT NONE OF THIS EVER HAPPENED.
I'M JUST GONNA LIE HERE AND EMPTY MY MIND... TAKE IT NICE AND EASY ON MYSELF, LIKE WALLER SAID.
BUT I CAN'T TAKE IT EASY!
IT'S ALL THERE... SITTING IN MY BRAIN... I CAN FEEL IT!
BUT I CAN'T GET AT IT!
WE'LL GET AT IT, BEETLE.
AN' THEN WE'LL GET AT THE MAGGOTS THAT DID THIS TO YOU.
14

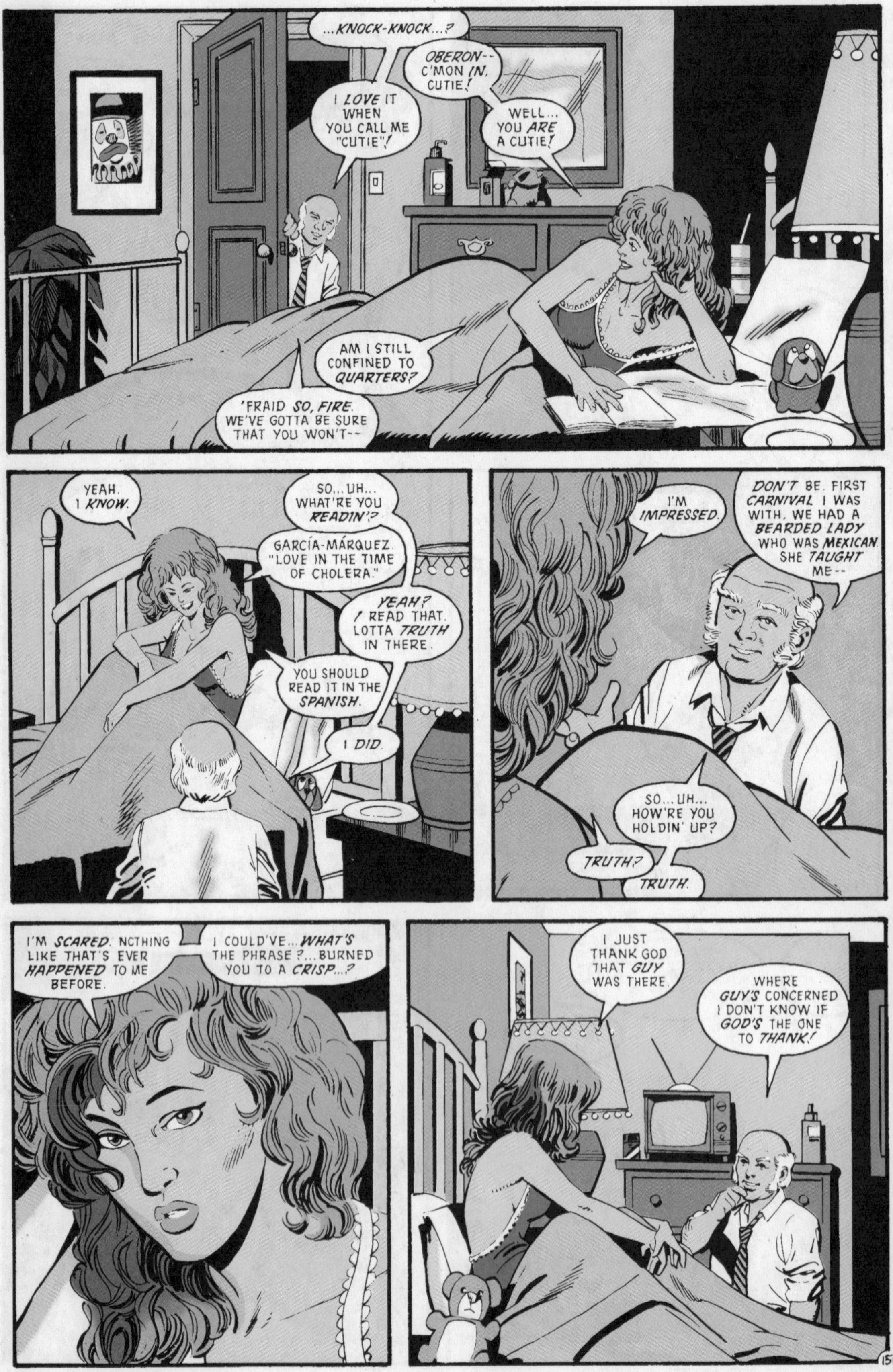
...KNOCK-KNOCK...?
OBERON-- C'MON IN, CUTIE!
I LOVE IT WHEN YOU CALL ME "CUTIE"!
WELL... YOU ARE A CUTIE!
AM I STILL CONFINED TO QUARTERS?
'FRAID SO, FIRE. WE'VE GOTTA BE SURE THAT YOU WON'T--
YEAH. I KNOW.
SO... UH... WHAT'RE YOU READIN'?
GARCÍA-MÁRQUEZ. "LOVE IN THE TIME OF CHOLERA."
YEAH? I READ THAT. LOTTA TRUTH IN THERE.
YOU SHOULD READ IT IN THE SPANISH.
I DID.
I'M IMPRESSED.
DON'T BE. FIRST CARNIVAL I WAS WITH, WE HAD A BEARDED LADY WHO WAS MEXICAN. SHE TAUGHT ME--
SO... UH... HOW'RE YOU HOLDIN' UP?
TRUTH?
TRUTH.
I'M SCARED. NOTHING LIKE THAT'S EVER HAPPENED TO ME BEFORE.
I COULD'VE... WHAT'S THE PHRASE?... BURNED YOU TO A CRISP...?
I JUST THANK GOD THAT GUY WAS THERE.
WHERE GUY'S CONCERNED I DON'T KNOW IF GOD'S THE ONE TO THANK!
15

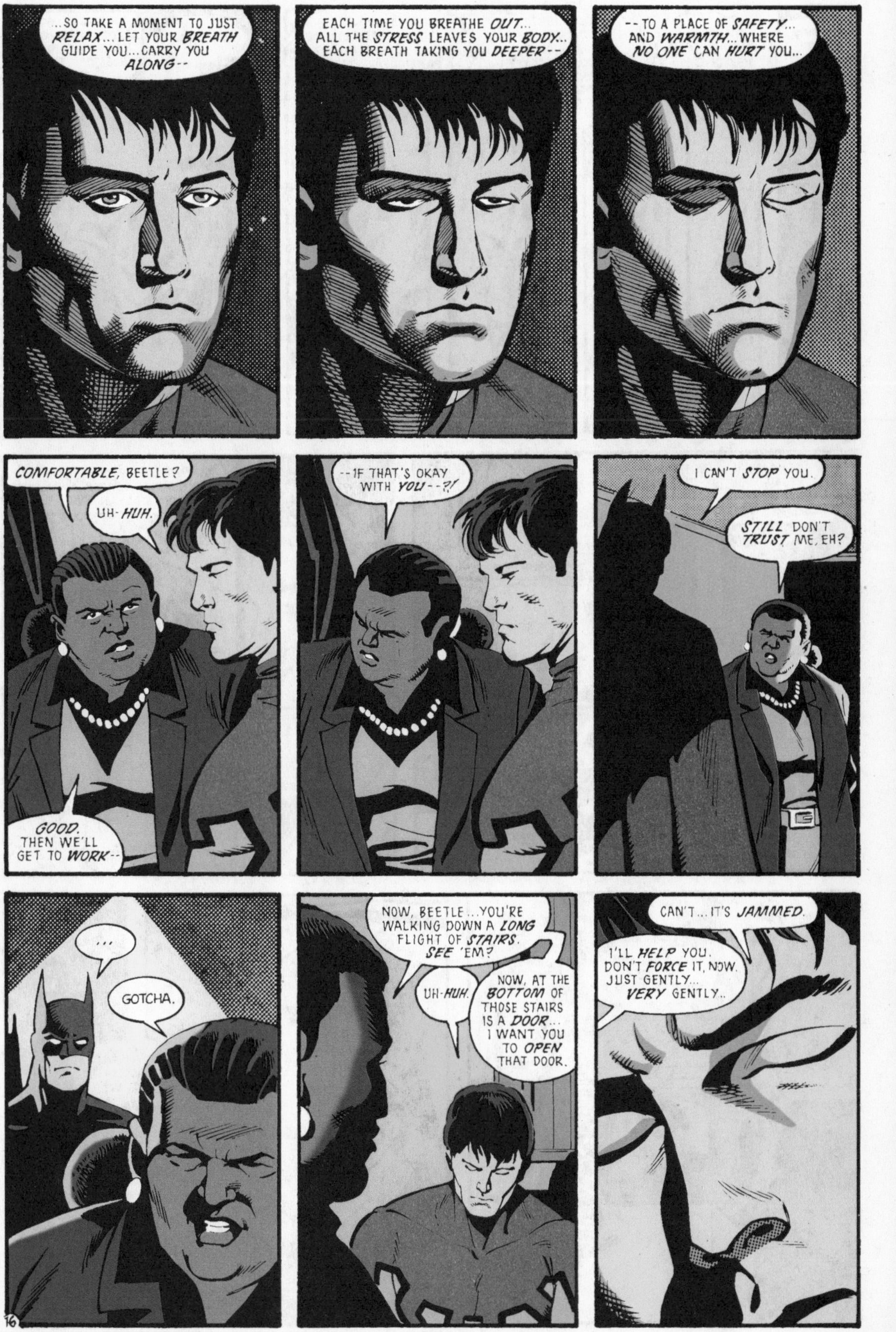
...SO TAKE A MOMENT TO JUST RELAX... LET YOUR BREATH GUIDE YOU... CARRY YOU ALONG--
EACH TIME YOU BREATHE OUT... ALL THE STRESS LEAVES YOUR BODY... EACH BREATH TAKING YOU DEEPER--
--TO A PLACE OF SAFETY... AND WARMTH... WHERE NO ONE CAN HURT YOU...
COMFORTABLE, BEETLE?
UH-HUH.
GOOD. THEN WE'LL GET TO WORK--
--IF THAT'S OKAY WITH YOU--?!
I CAN'T STOP YOU.
STILL DON'T TRUST ME, EH?
...
GOTCHA.
16
NOW, BEETLE... YOU'RE WALKING DOWN A LONG FLIGHT OF STAIRS. SEE 'EM?
UH-HUH.
NOW, AT THE BOTTOM OF THOSE STAIRS IS A DOOR... I WANT YOU TO OPEN THAT DOOR.
CAN'T... IT'S JAMMED.
I'LL HELP YOU. DON'T FORCE IT, NOW. JUST GENTLY... VERY GENTLY..

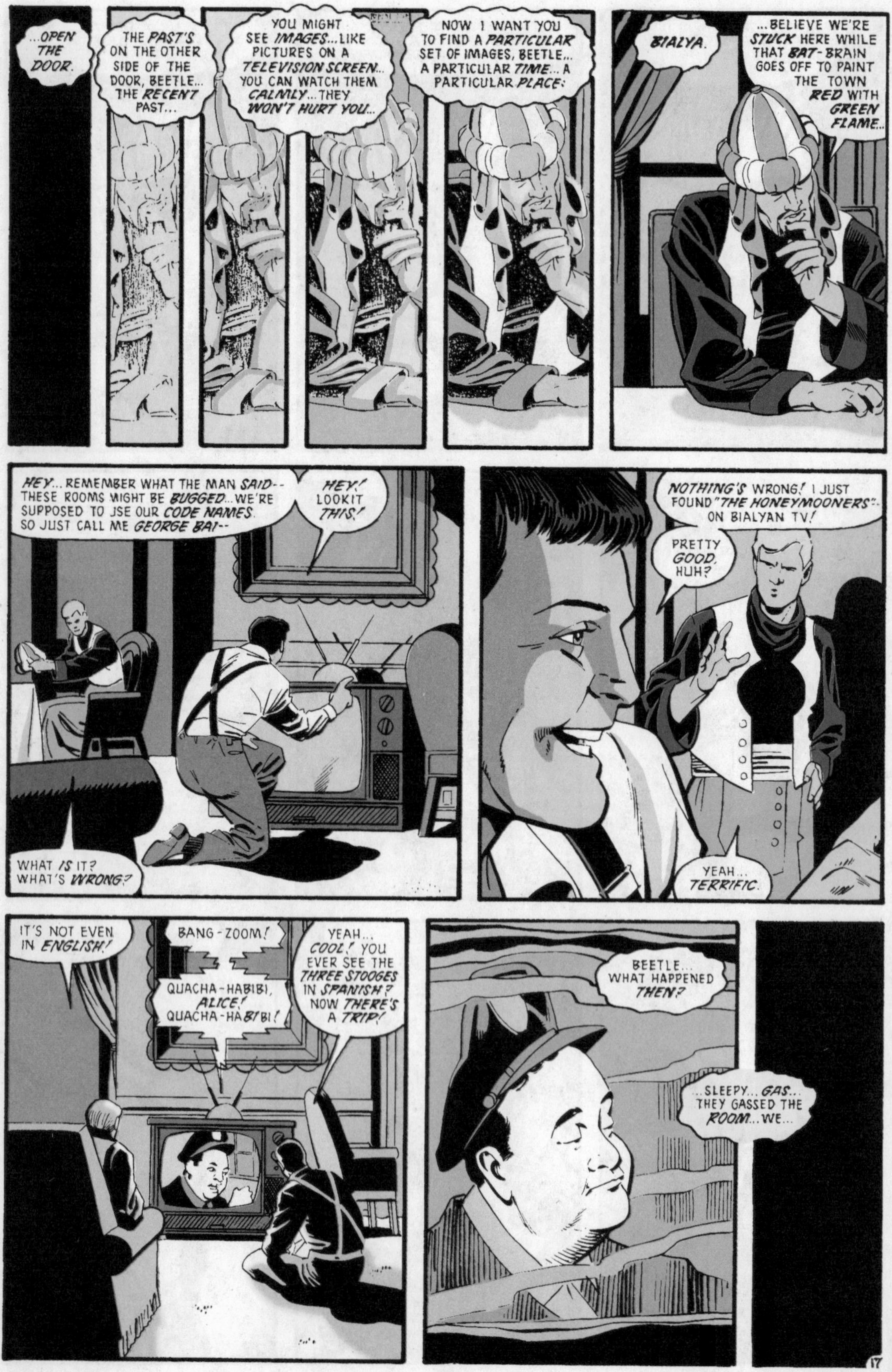
...OPEN THE DOOR.
THE PAST'S ON THE OTHER SIDE OF THE DOOR, BEETLE... THE RECENT PAST...
YOU MIGHT SEE IMAGES... LIKE PICTURES ON A TELEVISION SCREEN... YOU CAN WATCH THEM CALMLY... THEY WON'T HURT YOU...
NOW I WANT YOU TO FIND A PARTICULAR SET OF IMAGES, BEETLE... A PARTICULAR TIME... A PARTICULAR PLACE:
BIALYA.
...BELIEVE WE'RE STUCK HERE WHILE THAT BAT-BRAIN GOES OFF TO PAINT THE TOWN RED WITH GREEN FLAME...
HEY... REMEMBER WHAT THE MAN SAID-- THESE ROOMS MIGHT BE BUGGED... WE'RE SUPPOSED TO USE OUR CODE NAMES. SO JUST CALL ME GEORGE BAI--
HEY! LOOKIT THIS!
WHAT IS IT? WHAT'S WRONG?
NOTHING'S WRONG! I JUST FOUND "THE HONEYMOONERS" ON BIALYAN TV!
PRETTY GOOD, HUH?
YEAH... TERRIFIC.
IT'S NOT EVEN IN ENGLISH!
BANG-ZOOM!
QUACHA-HABIBI, ALICE! QUACHA-HABIBI!
YEAH... COOL! YOU EVER SEE THE THREE STOOGES IN SPANISH? NOW THERE'S A TRIP!
BEETLE... WHAT HAPPENED THEN?
...SLEEPY... GAS... THEY GASSED THE ROOM... WE...
17

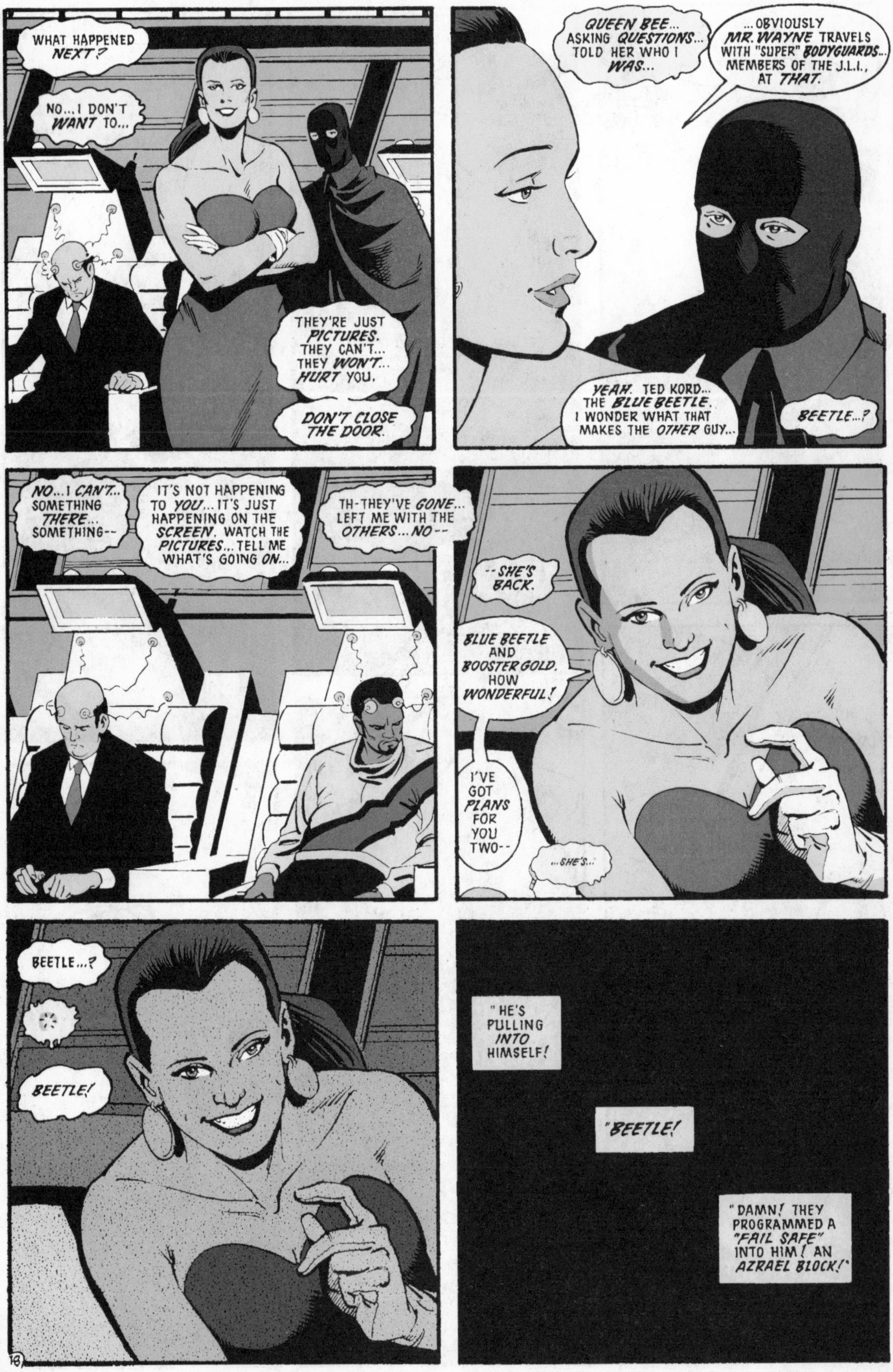
WHAT HAPPENED NEXT?
NO... I DON'T WANT TO...
THEY'RE JUST PICTURES. THEY CAN'T... THEY WON'T... HURT YOU.
DON'T CLOSE THE DOOR.
QUEEN BEE... ASKING QUESTIONS... TOLD HER WHO I WAS...
...OBVIOUSLY MR. WAYNE TRAVELS WITH "SUPER" BODYGUARDS... MEMBERS OF THE J.L.I., AT THAT.
YEAH. TED KORD... THE BLUE BEETLE. I WONDER WHAT THAT MAKES THE OTHER GUY...
BEETLE...?
NO... I CAN'T... SOMETHING THERE... SOMETHING--
IT'S NOT HAPPENING TO YOU... IT'S JUST HAPPENING ON THE SCREEN. WATCH THE PICTURES... TELL ME WHAT'S GOING ON...
TH-THEY'VE GONE... LEFT ME WITH THE OTHERS... NO--
--SHE'S BACK.
BLUE BEETLE AND BOOSTER GOLD. HOW WONDERFUL!
I'VE GOT PLANS FOR YOU TWO--
...SHE'S...
BEETLE...?
BEETLE!
"HE'S PULLING INTO HIMSELF!
"BEETLE!
"DAMN! THEY PROGRAMMED A "FAIL SAFE" INTO HIM! AN AZRAEL BLOCK!"
18

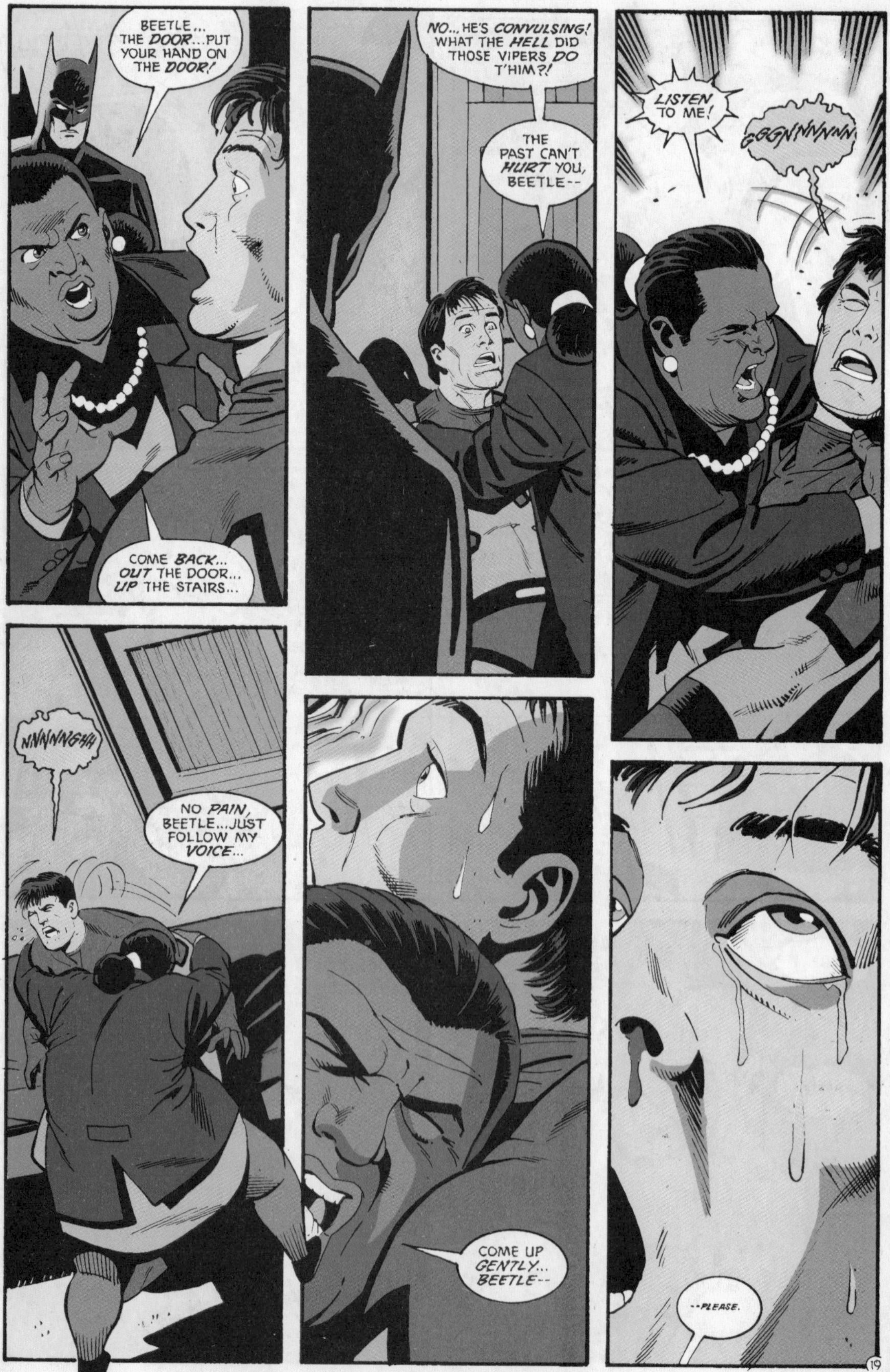
BEETLE... THE DOOR...PUT YOUR HAND ON THE DOOR!
COME BACK... OUT THE DOOR... UP THE STAIRS...
NO... HE'S CONVULSING! WHAT THE HELL DID THOSE VIPERS DO T'HIM?!
THE PAST CAN'T HURT YOU, BEETLE--
LISTEN TO ME!
GGGNNNNNN
NNNNNGHH
NO PAIN, BEETLE...JUST FOLLOW MY VOICE...
COME UP GENTLY... BEETLE--
--PLEASE.
19

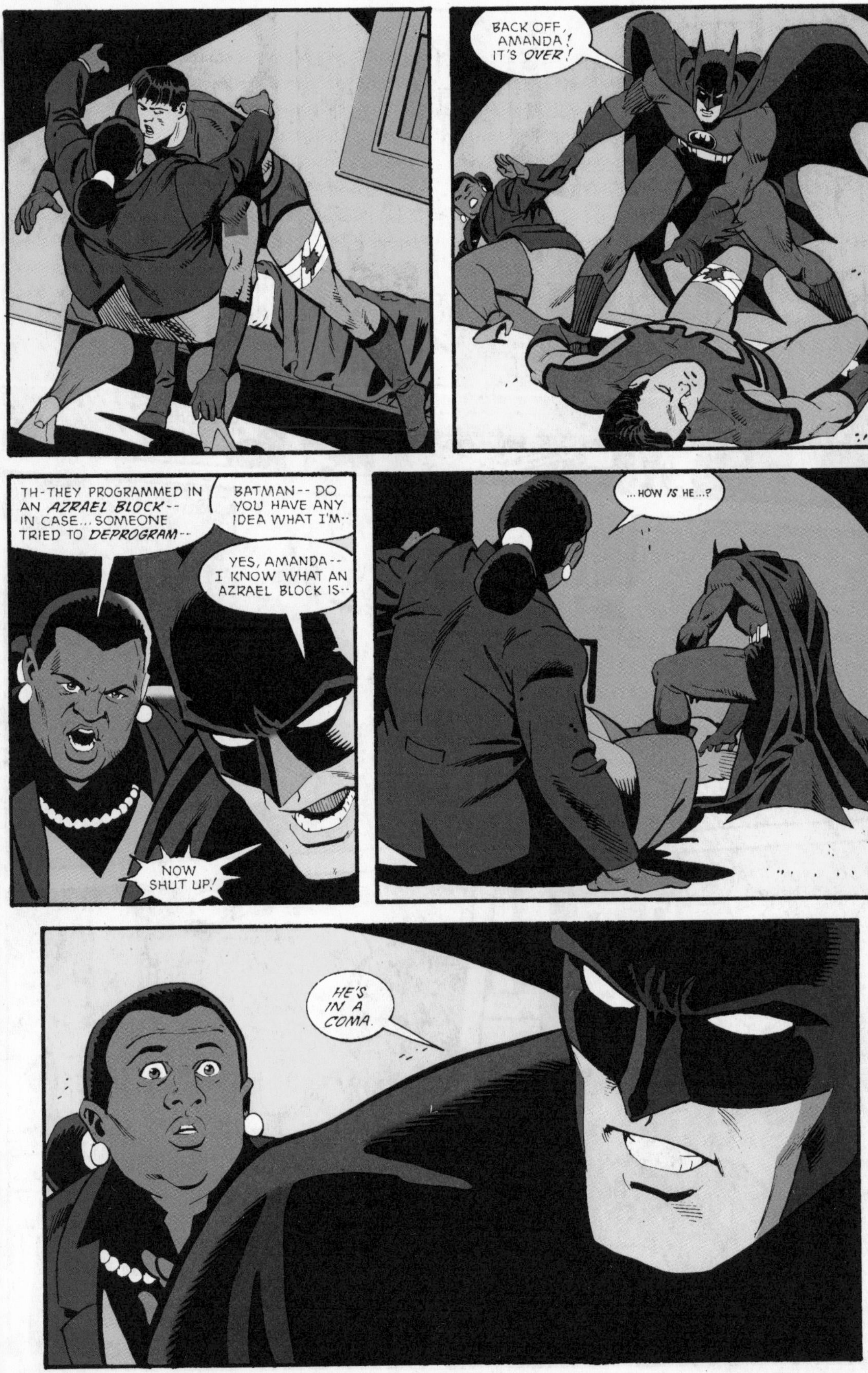
BACK OFF, AMANDA! IT'S OVER!
TH-THEY PROGRAMMED IN AN AZRAEL BLOCK-- IN CASE... SOMEONE TRIED TO DEPROGRAM--
BATMAN-- DO YOU HAVE ANY IDEA WHAT I'M--
YES, AMANDA-- I KNOW WHAT AN AZRAEL BLOCK IS--
NOW SHUT UP!
...HOW IS HE...?
HE'S IN A COMA.

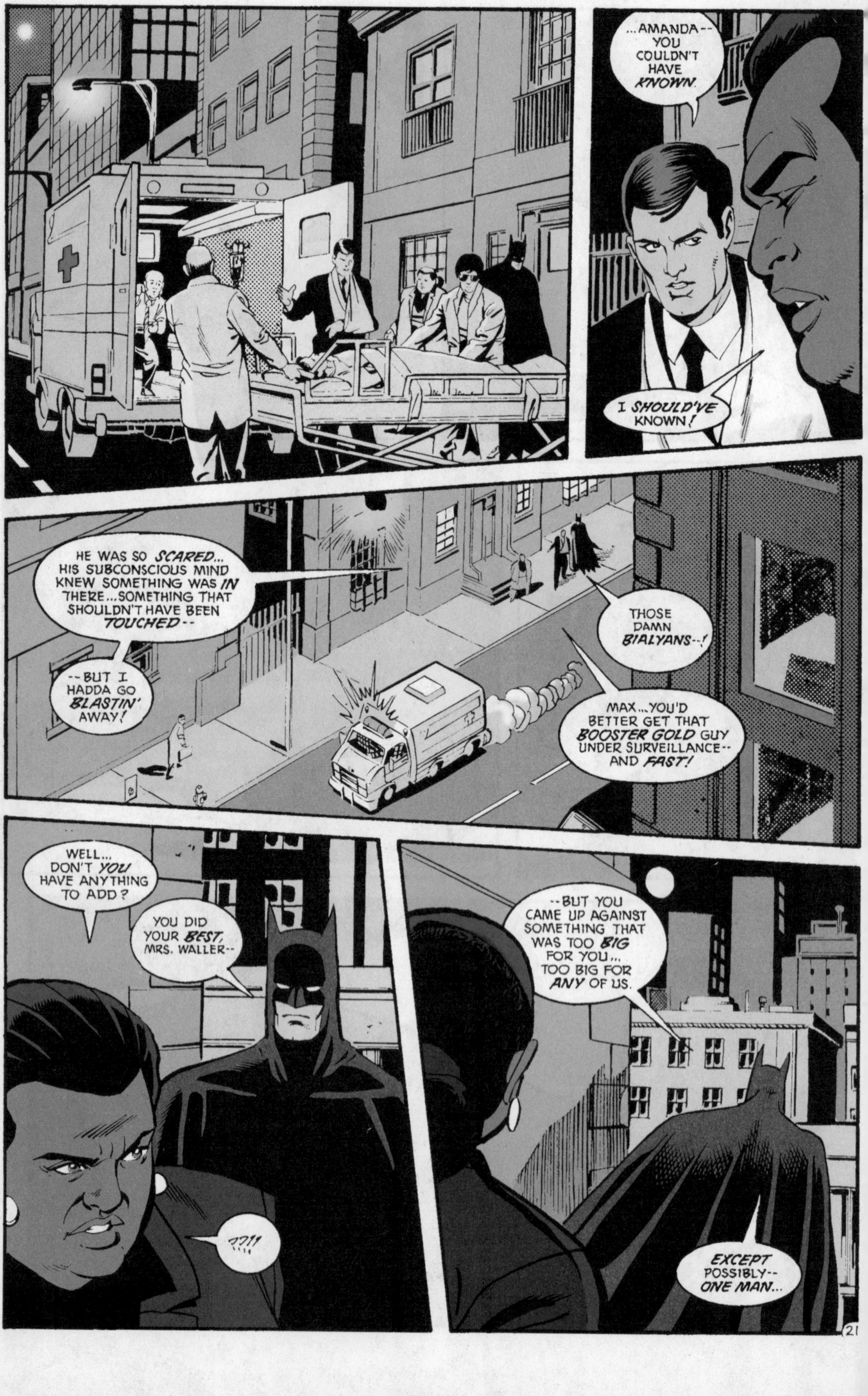

...AMANDA-- YOU COULDN'T HAVE KNOWN.
I SHOULD'VE KNOWN!
HE WAS SO SCARED... HIS SUBCONSCIOUS MIND KNEW SOMETHING WAS IN THERE...SOMETHING THAT SHOULDN'T HAVE BEEN TOUCHED--
--BUT I HADDA GO BLASTIN' AWAY!
THOSE DAMN BIALYANS--!
MAX...YOU'D BETTER GET THAT BOOSTER GOLD GUY UNDER SURVEILLANCE-- AND FAST!
WELL... DON'T YOU HAVE ANYTHING TO ADD?
YOU DID YOUR BEST, MRS. WALLER--
??!!
--BUT YOU CAME UP AGAINST SOMETHING THAT WAS TOO BIG FOR YOU... TOO BIG FOR ANY OF US.
EXCEPT POSSIBLY-- ONE MAN...
21

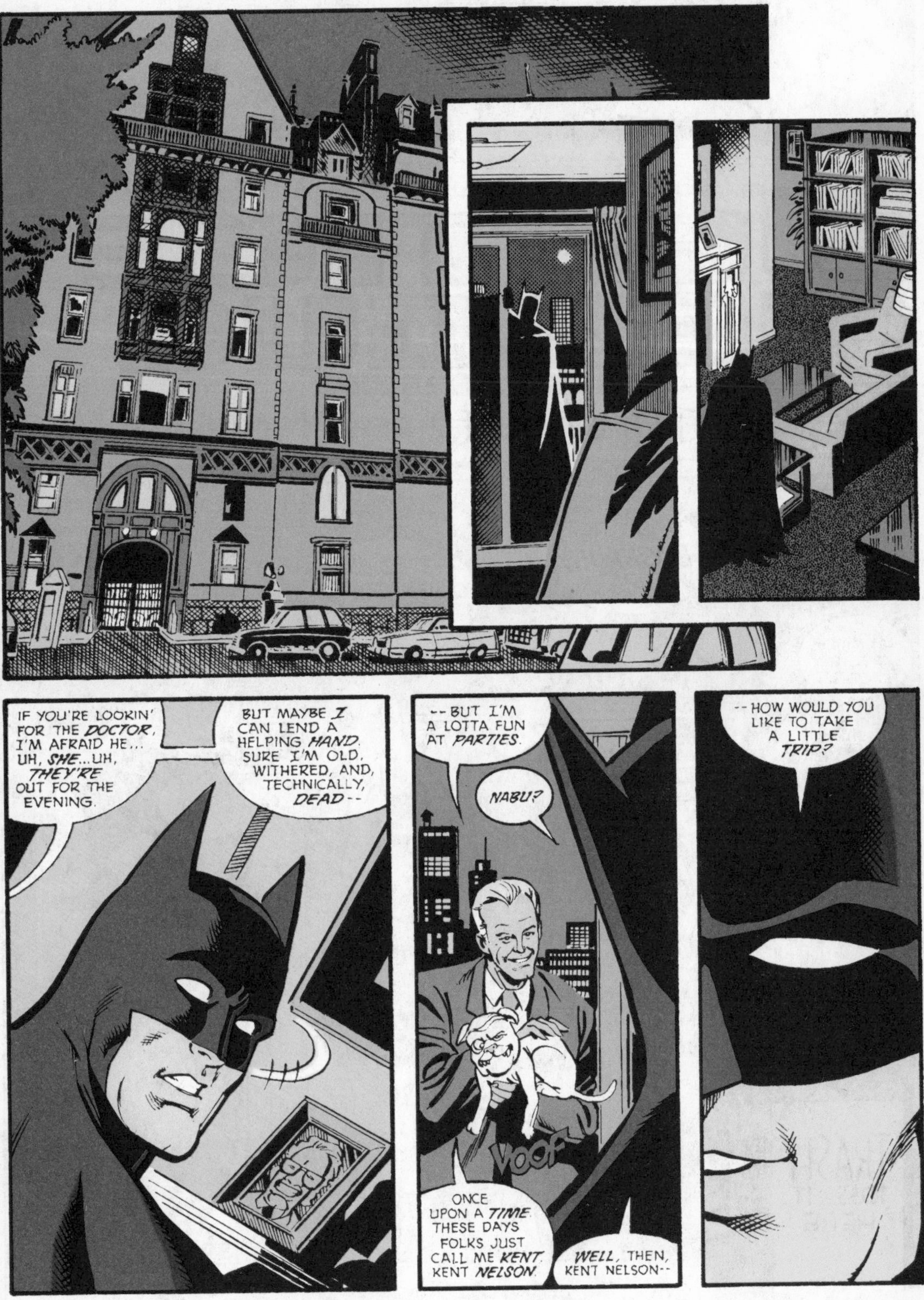
IF YOU'RE LOOKIN' FOR THE DOCTOR, I'M AFRAID HE... UH, SHE...UH, THEY'RE OUT FOR THE EVENING.
BUT MAYBE I CAN LEND A HELPING HAND. SURE I'M OLD, WITHERED, AND, TECHNICALLY, DEAD--
--BUT I'M A LOTTA FUN AT PARTIES.
NABU?
VOOF
ONCE UPON A TIME. THESE DAYS FOLKS JUST CALL ME KENT. KENT NELSON.
WELL, THEN, KENT NELSON--
--HOW WOULD YOU LIKE TO TAKE A LITTLE TRIP?

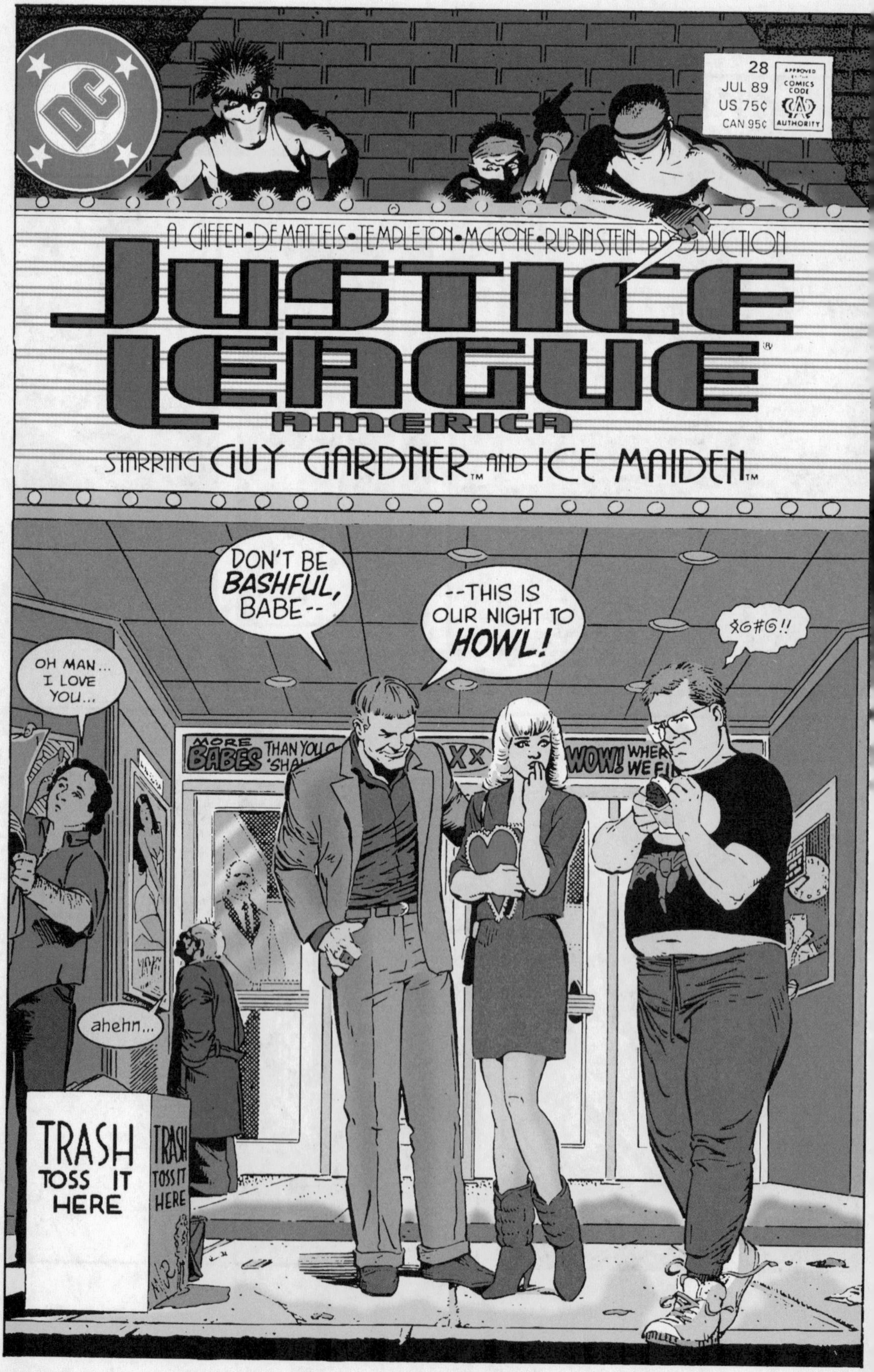
28
JUL 89
US 75¢
CAN 95¢
APPROVED BY THE COMICS CODE AUTHORITY
A GIFFEN•DEMATTEIS•TEMPLETON•MCKONE•RUBINSTEIN PRODUCTION
JUSTICE LEAGUE AMERICA
STARRING GUY GARDNER™ AND ICE MAIDEN™
DON'T BE BASHFUL, BABE--
--THIS IS OUR NIGHT TO HOWL!
$&#&!!
OH MAN... I LOVE YOU...
ahehn...
TRASH TOSS IT HERE
TRASH TOSS IT HERE

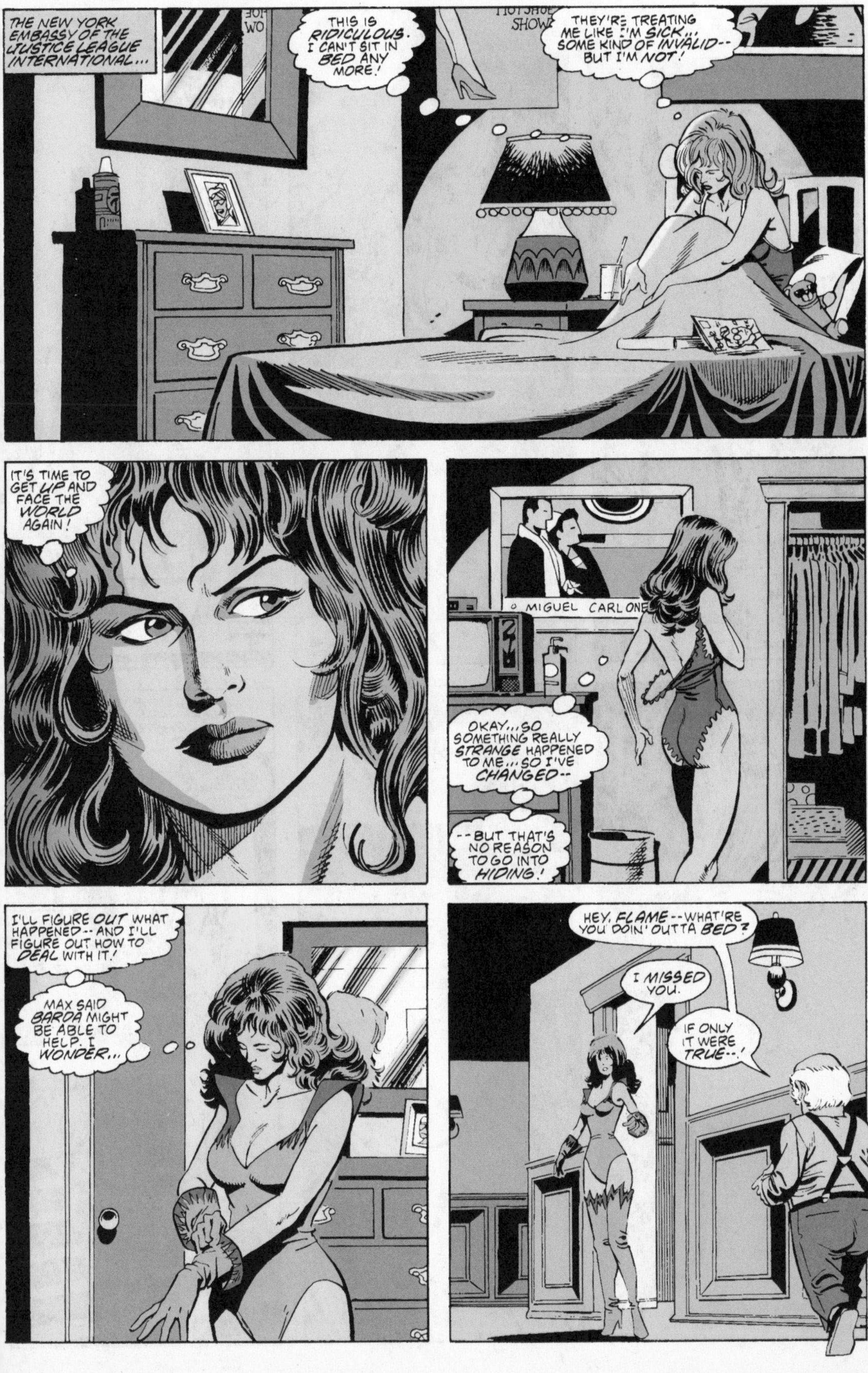
THE NEW YORK EMBASSY OF THE JUSTICE LEAGUE INTERNATIONAL...
THIS IS RIDICULOUS. I CAN'T SIT IN BED ANY MORE!
THEY'RE TREATING ME LIKE I'M SICK... SOME KIND OF INVALID-- BUT I'M NOT!
IT'S TIME TO GET UP AND FACE THE WORLD AGAIN!
MIGUEL CARLONE
OKAY... SO SOMETHING REALLY STRANGE HAPPENED TO ME... SO I'VE CHANGED--
--BUT THAT'S NO REASON TO GO INTO HIDING!
I'LL FIGURE OUT WHAT HAPPENED-- AND I'LL FIGURE OUT HOW TO DEAL WITH IT!
MAX SAID BARDA MIGHT BE ABLE TO HELP. I WONDER...
HEY, FLAME--WHAT'RE YOU DOIN' OUTTA BED?
I MISSED YOU.
IF ONLY IT WERE TRUE--!

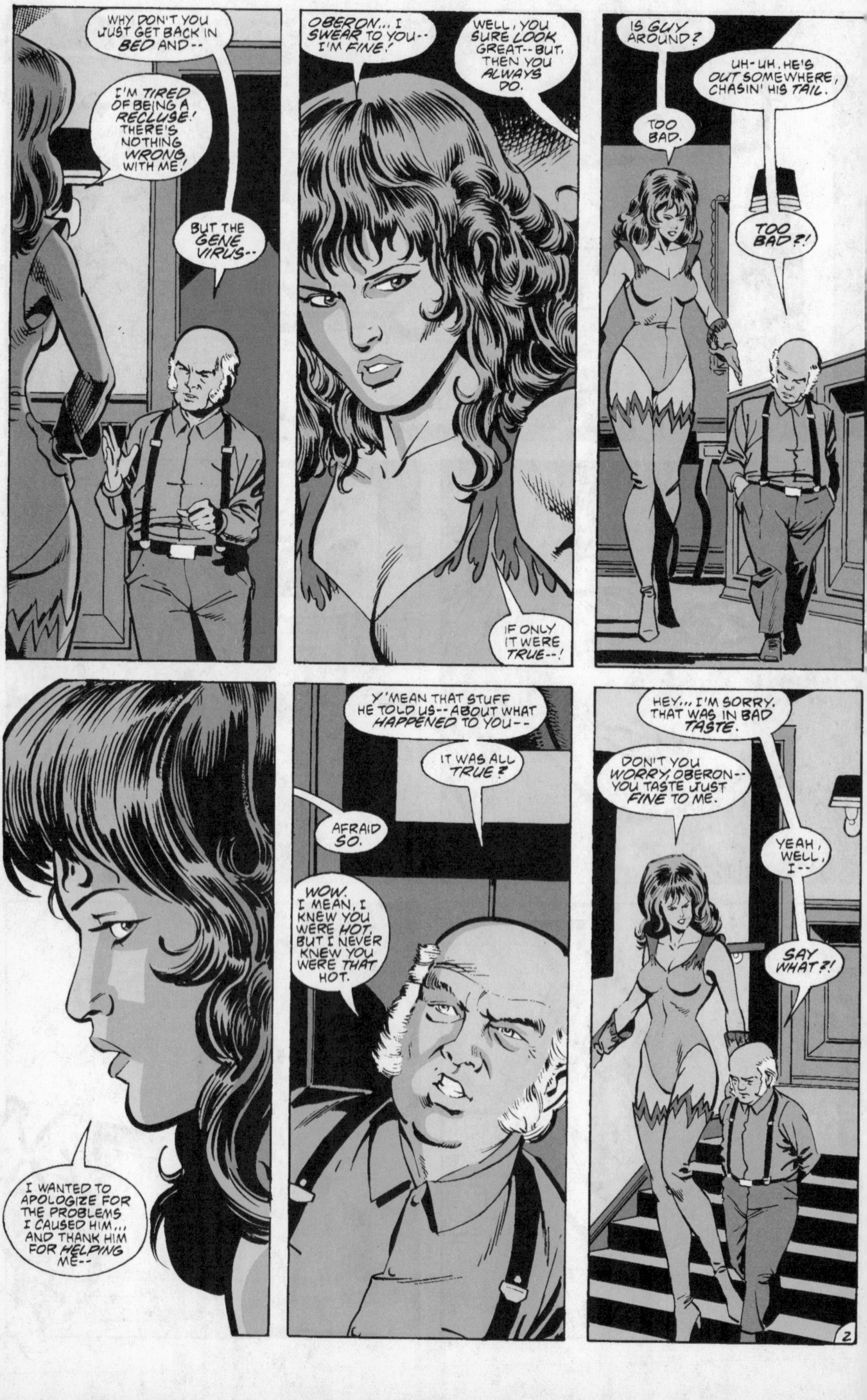
WHY DON'T YOU JUST GET BACK IN BED AND--
I'M TIRED OF BEING A RECLUSE! THERE'S NOTHING WRONG WITH ME!
BUT THE GENE VIRUS--
OBERON... I SWEAR TO YOU-- I'M FINE!
WELL, YOU SURE LOOK GREAT--BUT, THEN YOU ALWAYS DO.
IF ONLY IT WERE TRUE--!
IS GUY AROUND?
UH-UH. HE'S OUT SOMEWHERE, CHASIN' HIS TAIL.
TOO BAD.
TOO BAD?!
I WANTED TO APOLOGIZE FOR THE PROBLEMS I CAUSED HIM... AND THANK HIM FOR HELPING ME--
Y'MEAN THAT STUFF HE TOLD US--ABOUT WHAT HAPPENED TO YOU--
IT WAS ALL TRUE?
AFRAID SO.
WOW. I MEAN, I KNEW YOU WERE HOT, BUT I NEVER KNEW YOU WERE THAT HOT.
HEY... I'M SORRY. THAT WAS IN BAD TASTE.
DON'T YOU WORRY, OBERON-- YOU TASTE JUST FINE TO ME.
YEAH, WELL, I--
SAY WHAT?!
2

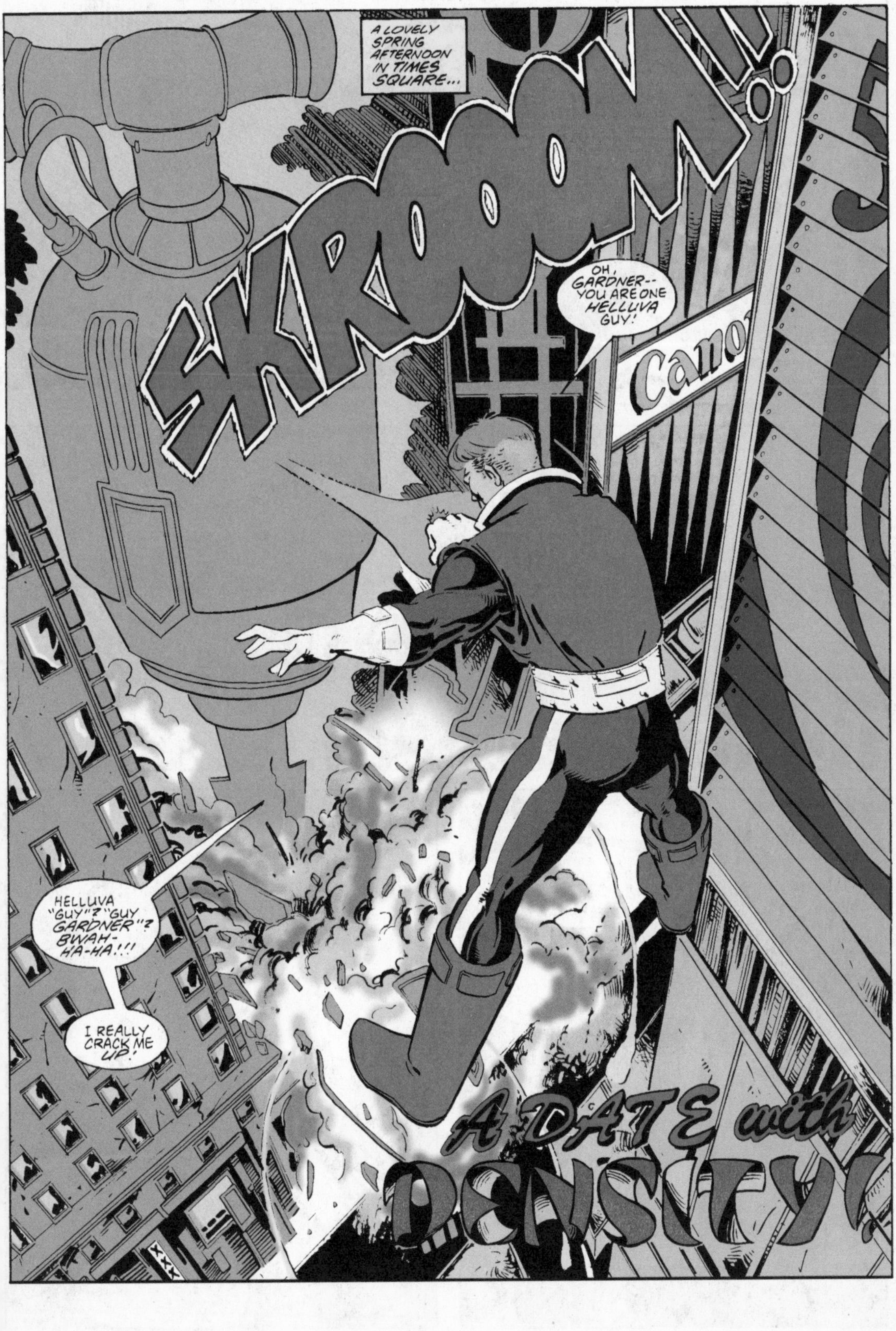
A LOVELY SPRING AFTERNOON IN TIMES SQUARE...
SKROOOM!!
OH, GARDNER-- YOU ARE ONE HELLUVA GUY!
HELLUVA "GUY"? "GUY GARDNER"? BWAH-HA-HA!!!
I REALLY CRACK ME UP!
A DATE with DENSITY!

WELL, THAT'S *ONE* BUILDING THAT WON'T BE A *FRONT* FOR DOPE-SELLERS AND FLESH-PEDDLERS ANY MORE!

NOW THAT REAGAN AIN'T *PRESIDENT,* SOMEBODY'S GOTTA BE AMERICA'S CONSCIENCE!

MAYBE I SHOULDN'T'VE FORCED ALL THOSE SCUMBOLAS OUTTA THE *BUILDING* BEFORE I *TRASHED* IT--

--LET THE RATS GO DOWN WITH THE SINKING *SHIP!*

I GUESS I'M JUST TOO *SOFT-HEARTED!*

THAT WAS *RONNIE'S* ACHILLES HEEL, TOO!

WELL, IT'S BEEN A *GOOD* DAY'S WORK.... TIME T'LAY BACK, CRACK OPEN A FEW *BREWSKIES--*

--AN' DO SOME HEAVY *READIN'!*

WHERE'D I *PUT* THAT SWIMSUIT ISSUE OF *"SPORTS ILLUSTRATED,"* ANYWAY?

...AFTERNOON, SLEEPY-- HOW'RE DOPEY AN' THE *OTHER* DWARVES?

GUY-- YOU'VE BEEN RUNNIN' THAT JOKE RAGGED FOR TWO *YEARS* NOW. DON'T YOU THINK IT'S TIME TO *STOP?*

NO.

WHY DO I *BOTHER?*

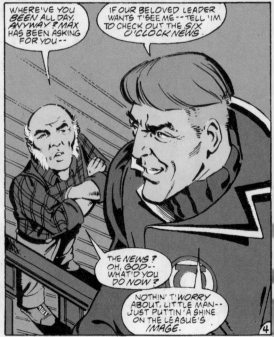

WHERE'VE YOU *BEEN* ALL DAY, ANYWAY? *MAX* HAS BEEN ASKING FOR YOU--

IF OUR BELOVED LEADER WANTS T'*SEE* ME-- TELL 'IM TO CHECK OUT THE *SIX O'CLOCK NEWS.*

THE *NEWS?* OH, *GOD*-- WHAT'D YOU *DO* NOW?

NOTHIN' T'WORRY ABOUT, LITTLE MAN-- JUST PUTTIN' A SHINE ON THE LEAGUE'S *IMAGE.*

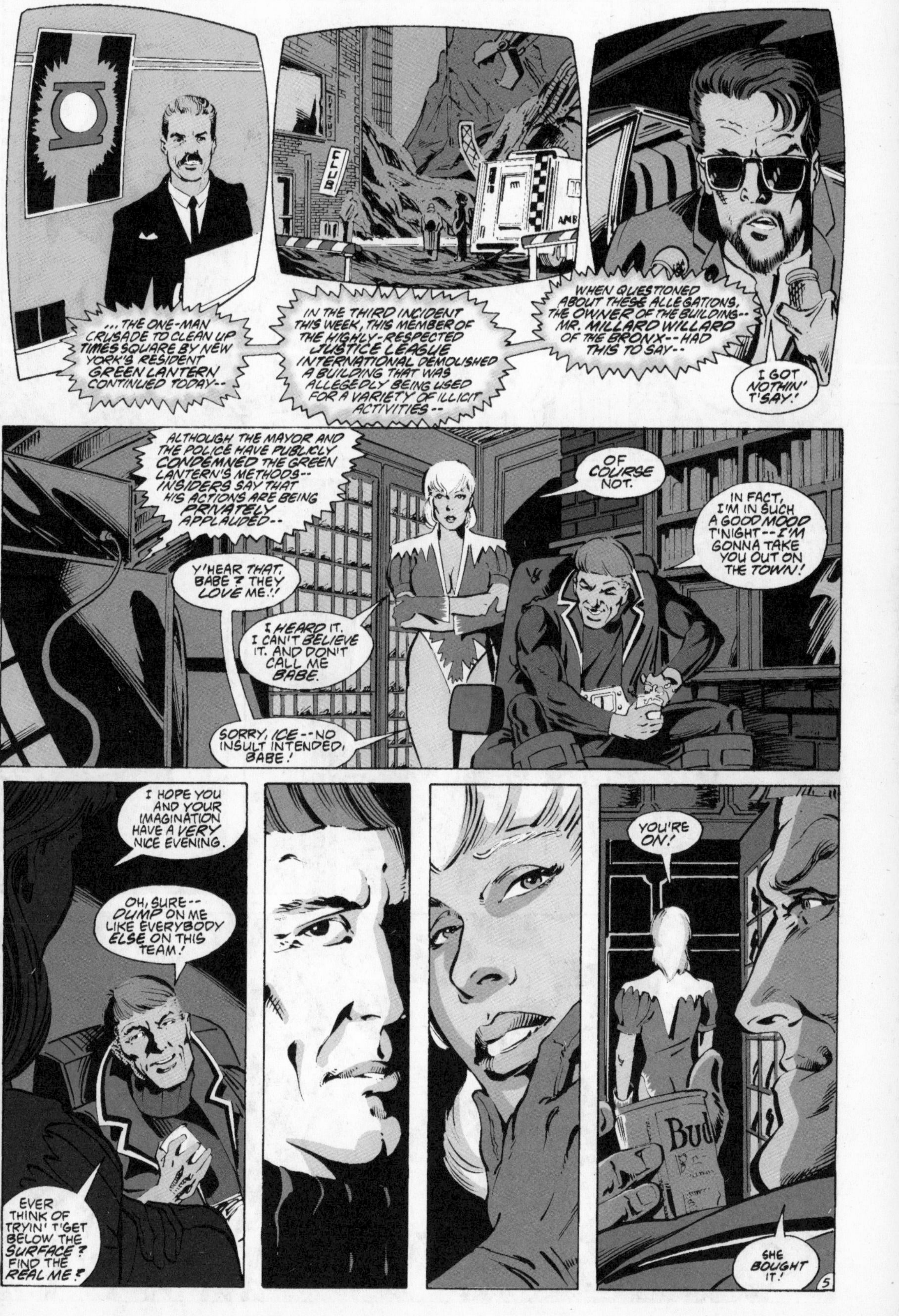

...THE ONE-MAN CRUSADE TO CLEAN UP TIMES SQUARE BY NEW YORK'S RESIDENT GREEN LANTERN CONTINUED TODAY--
IN THE THIRD INCIDENT THIS WEEK, THIS MEMBER OF THE HIGHLY-RESPECTED JUSTICE LEAGUE INTERNATIONAL DEMOLISHED A BUILDING THAT WAS ALLEGEDLY BEING USED FOR A VARIETY OF ILLICIT ACTIVITIES--
CLUB
WHEN QUESTIONED ABOUT THESE ALLEGATIONS, THE OWNER OF THE BUILDING-- MR. MILLARD WILLARD OF THE BRONX--HAD THIS TO SAY--
I GOT NOTHIN' T'SAY!
ALTHOUGH THE MAYOR AND THE POLICE HAVE PUBLICLY CONDEMNED THE GREEN LANTERN'S METHODS-- INSIDERS SAY THAT HIS ACTIONS ARE BEING PRIVATELY APPLAUDED--
Y'HEAR THAT, BABE? THEY LOVE ME!
I HEARD IT. I CAN'T BELIEVE IT. AND DON'T CALL ME BABE.
SORRY, ICE--NO INSULT INTENDED, BABE!
OF COURSE NOT.
IN FACT, I'M IN SUCH A GOOD MOOD T'NIGHT--I'M GONNA TAKE YOU OUT ON THE TOWN!
I HOPE YOU AND YOUR IMAGINATION HAVE A VERY NICE EVENING.
OH, SURE-- DUMP ON ME LIKE EVERYBODY ELSE ON THIS TEAM!
EVER THINK OF TRYIN' T'GET BELOW THE SURFACE? FIND THE REAL ME?
YOU'RE ON!
Bud
SHE BOUGHT IT!
5

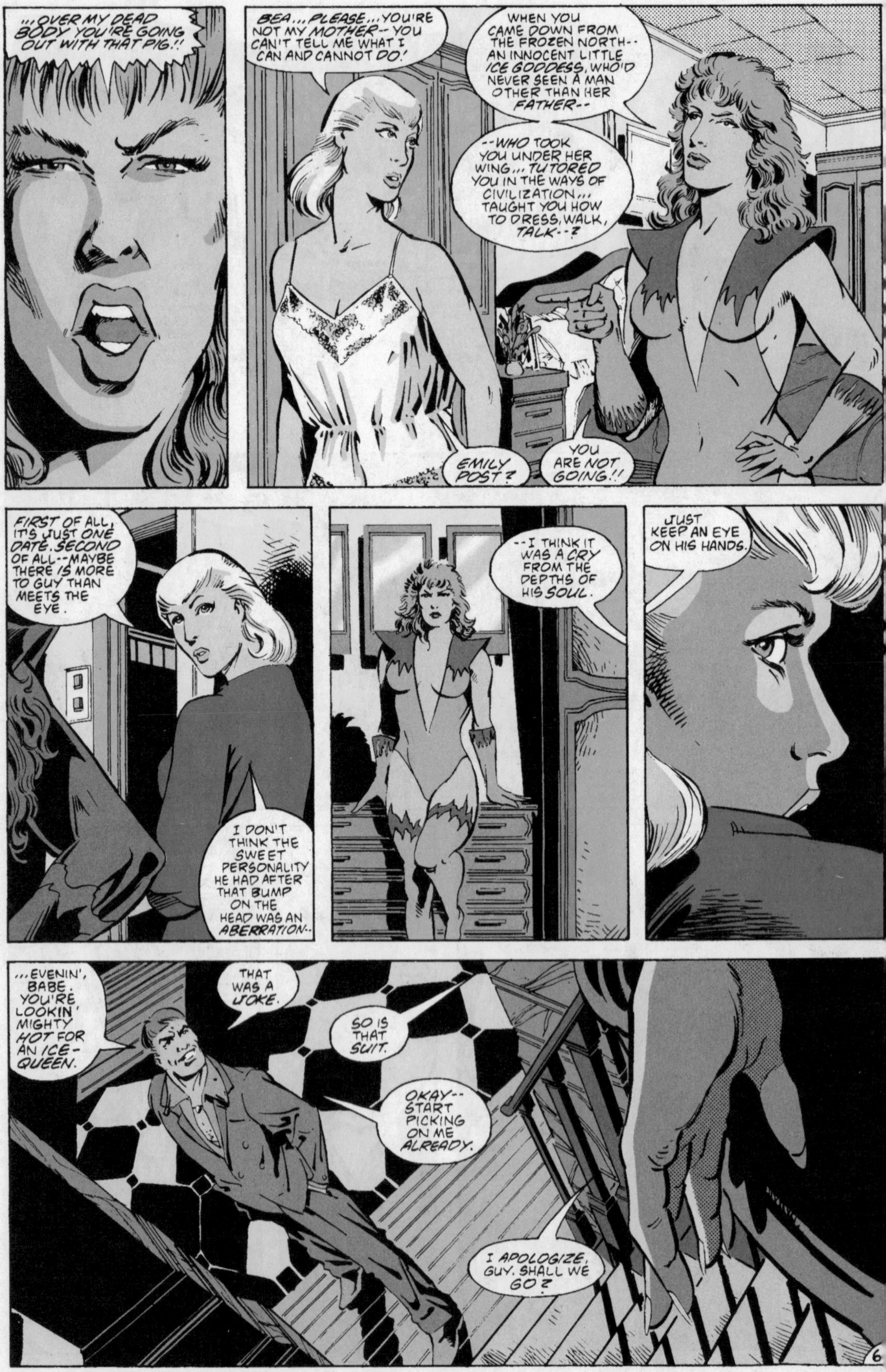
...OVER MY DEAD BODY YOU'RE GOING OUT WITH THAT PIG!!
BEA... PLEASE... YOU'RE NOT MY MOTHER-- YOU CAN'T TELL ME WHAT I CAN AND CANNOT DO!
WHEN YOU CAME DOWN FROM THE FROZEN NORTH-- AN INNOCENT LITTLE ICE GODDESS, WHO'D NEVER SEEN A MAN OTHER THAN HER FATHER--
--WHO TOOK YOU UNDER HER WING... TUTORED YOU IN THE WAYS OF CIVILIZATION... TAUGHT YOU HOW TO DRESS, WALK, TALK--?
EMILY POST?
YOU ARE NOT GOING!!
FIRST OF ALL, IT'S JUST ONE DATE. SECOND OF ALL--MAYBE THERE IS MORE TO GUY THAN MEETS THE EYE.
I DON'T THINK THE SWEET PERSONALITY HE HAD AFTER THAT BUMP ON THE HEAD WAS AN ABERRATION--
--I THINK IT WAS A CRY FROM THE DEPTHS OF HIS SOUL.
JUST KEEP AN EYE ON HIS HANDS.
...EVENIN', BABE. YOU'RE LOOKIN' MIGHTY HOT FOR AN ICE-QUEEN.
THAT WAS A JOKE.
SO IS THAT SUIT.
OKAY-- START PICKING ON ME ALREADY.
I APOLOGIZE, GUY. SHALL WE GO?
6

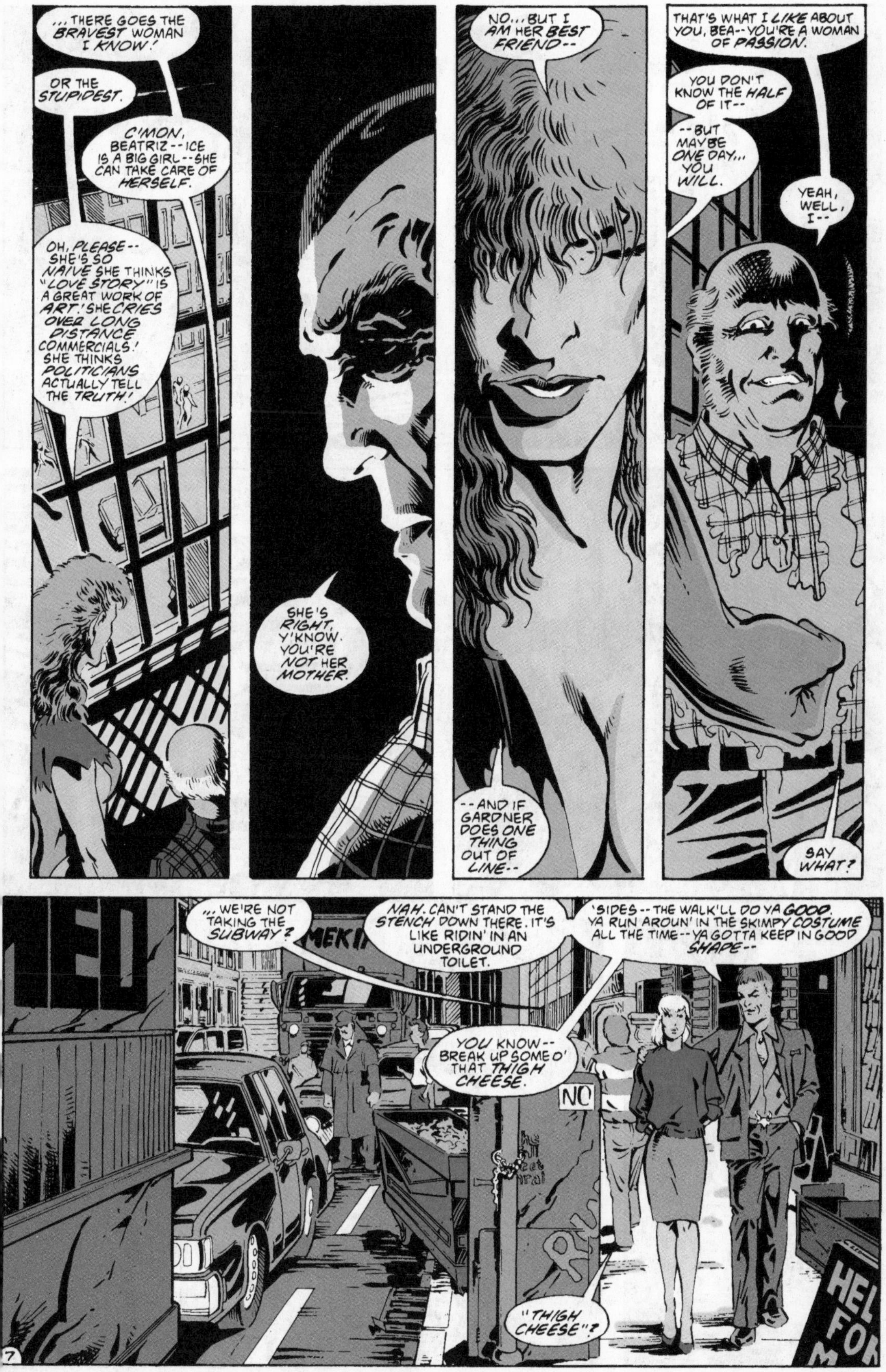

...THERE GOES THE BRAVEST WOMAN I KNOW!
OR THE STUPIDEST.
C'MON, BEATRIZ--ICE IS A BIG GIRL--SHE CAN TAKE CARE OF HERSELF.
OH, PLEASE--SHE'S SO NAIVE SHE THINKS "LOVE STORY" IS A GREAT WORK OF ART! SHE CRIES OVER LONG DISTANCE COMMERCIALS! SHE THINKS POLITICIANS ACTUALLY TELL THE TRUTH!
SHE'S RIGHT, Y'KNOW. YOU'RE NOT HER MOTHER.
NO...BUT I AM HER BEST FRIEND--
--AND IF GARDNER DOES ONE THING OUT OF LINE--
THAT'S WHAT I LIKE ABOUT YOU, BEA--YOU'RE A WOMAN OF PASSION.
YOU DON'T KNOW THE HALF OF IT--
--BUT MAYBE ONE DAY... YOU WILL.
YEAH, WELL, I--
SAY WHAT?
...WE'RE NOT TAKING THE SUBWAY?
NAH. CAN'T STAND THE STENCH DOWN THERE. IT'S LIKE RIDIN' IN AN UNDERGROUND TOILET.
'SIDES--THE WALK'LL DO YA GOOD. YA RUN AROUN' IN THE SKIMPY COSTUME ALL THE TIME--YA GOTTA KEEP IN GOOD SHAPE--
YOU KNOW--BREAK UP SOME O' THAT THIGH CHEESE.
"THIGH CHEESE"?

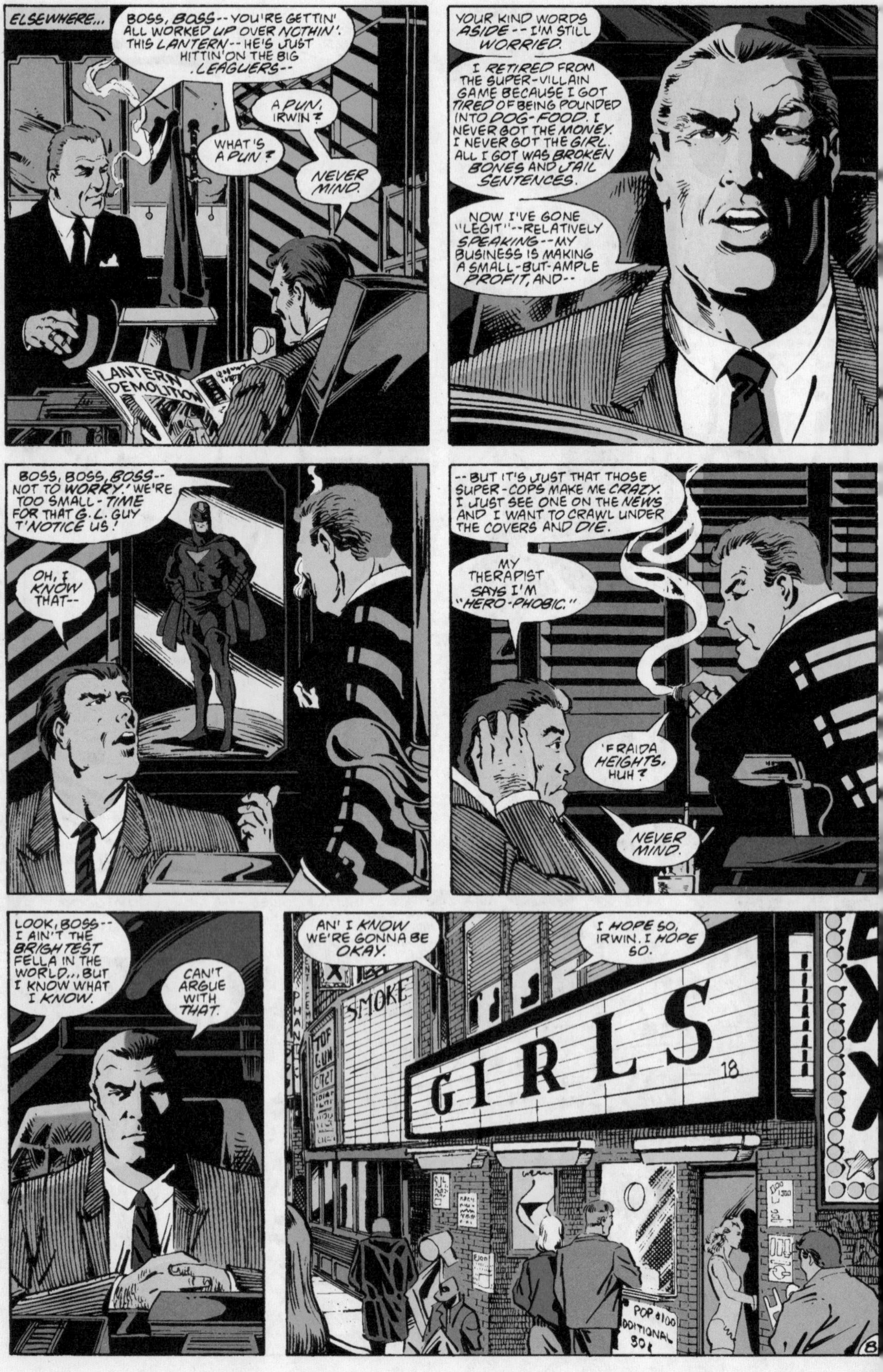
ELSEWHERE...
BOSS, BOSS--YOU'RE GETTIN' ALL WORKED UP OVER NOTHIN'. THIS LANTERN--HE'S JUST HITTIN' ON THE BIG LEAGUERS--
A PUN, IRWIN?
WHAT'S A PUN?
NEVER MIND.
LANTERN DEMOLITION
YOUR KIND WORDS ASIDE--I'M STILL WORRIED.
I RETIRED FROM THE SUPER-VILLAIN GAME BECAUSE I GOT TIRED OF BEING POUNDED INTO DOG-FOOD. I NEVER GOT THE MONEY. I NEVER GOT THE GIRL. ALL I GOT WAS BROKEN BONES AND JAIL SENTENCES.
NOW I'VE GONE "LEGIT"--RELATIVELY SPEAKING--MY BUSINESS IS MAKING A SMALL-BUT-AMPLE PROFIT, AND--
BOSS, BOSS, BOSS--NOT TO WORRY! WE'RE TOO SMALL-TIME FOR THAT G.L. GUY T'NOTICE US!
OH, I KNOW THAT--
--BUT IT'S JUST THAT THOSE SUPER-COPS MAKE ME CRAZY. I JUST SEE ONE ON THE NEWS AND I WANT TO CRAWL UNDER THE COVERS AND DIE.
MY THERAPIST SAYS I'M "HERO-PHOBIC."
'FRAIDA HEIGHTS, HUH?
NEVER MIND.
LOOK, BOSS--I AIN'T THE BRIGHTEST FELLA IN THE WORLD... BUT I KNOW WHAT I KNOW.
CAN'T ARGUE WITH THAT.
AN' I KNOW WE'RE GONNA BE OKAY.
I HOPE SO, IRWIN. I HOPE SO.
SMOKE
GIRLS
18
POP ¢100 ADDITIONAL 30¢
8

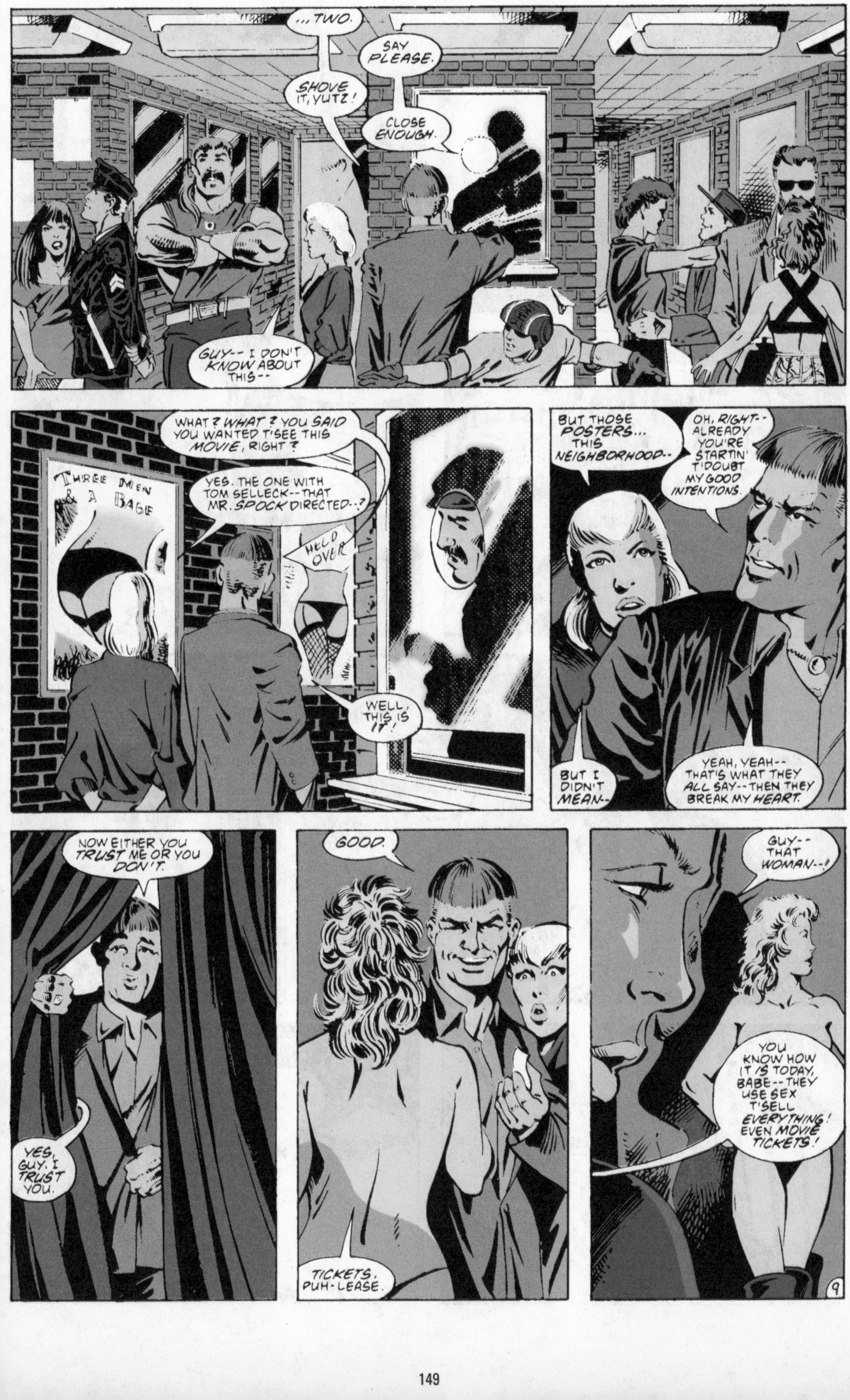
...TWO.
SAY PLEASE.
SHOVE IT, YUTZ!
CLOSE ENOUGH.
GUY-- I DON'T KNOW ABOUT THIS--
WHAT? WHAT? YOU SAID YOU WANTED T'SEE THIS MOVIE, RIGHT?
THREE MEN & A BAGE
YES. THE ONE WITH TOM SELLECK--THAT MR. SPOCK DIRECTED--?
HELD OVER
WELL, THIS IS IT!
BUT THOSE POSTERS... THIS NEIGHBORHOOD--
OH, RIGHT-- ALREADY YOU'RE STARTIN' T'DOUBT MY GOOD INTENTIONS.
BUT I DIDN'T MEAN--
YEAH, YEAH-- THAT'S WHAT THEY ALL SAY--THEN THEY BREAK MY HEART.
NOW EITHER YOU TRUST ME OR YOU DON'T.
YES, GUY. I TRUST YOU.
GOOD.
TICKETS. PUH-LEASE.
GUY-- THAT WOMAN--!
YOU KNOW HOW IT IS TODAY, BABE--THEY USE SEX T'SELL EVERYTHING! EVEN MOVIE TICKETS!
9

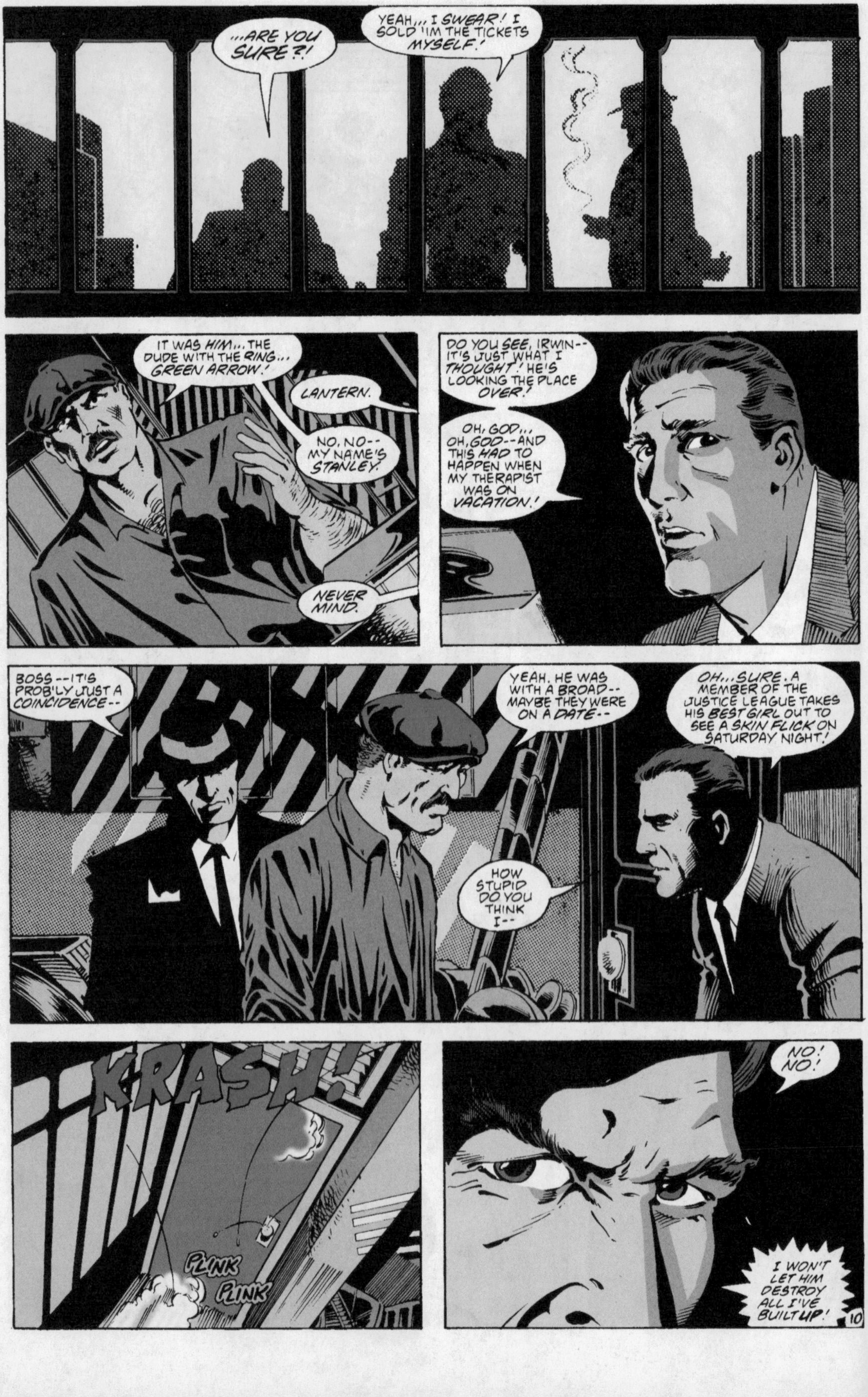
...ARE YOU SURE?!
YEAH... I SWEAR! I SOLD 'IM THE TICKETS MYSELF!
IT WAS HIM... THE DUDE WITH THE RING... GREEN ARROW!
LANTERN.
NO, NO-- MY NAME'S STANLEY.
NEVER MIND.
DO YOU SEE, IRWIN-- IT'S JUST WHAT I THOUGHT! HE'S LOOKING THE PLACE OVER!
OH, GOD... OH, GOD--AND THIS HAD TO HAPPEN WHEN MY THERAPIST WAS ON VACATION!
BOSS--IT'S PROB'LY JUST A COINCIDENCE--
YEAH. HE WAS WITH A BROAD-- MAYBE THEY WERE ON A DATE--
OH... SURE. A MEMBER OF THE JUSTICE LEAGUE TAKES HIS BEST GIRL OUT TO SEE A SKIN FLICK ON SATURDAY NIGHT!
HOW STUPID DO YOU THINK I--
KRASH!
PLINK
PLINK
NO! NO!
I WON'T LET HIM DESTROY ALL I'VE BUILT UP!
10

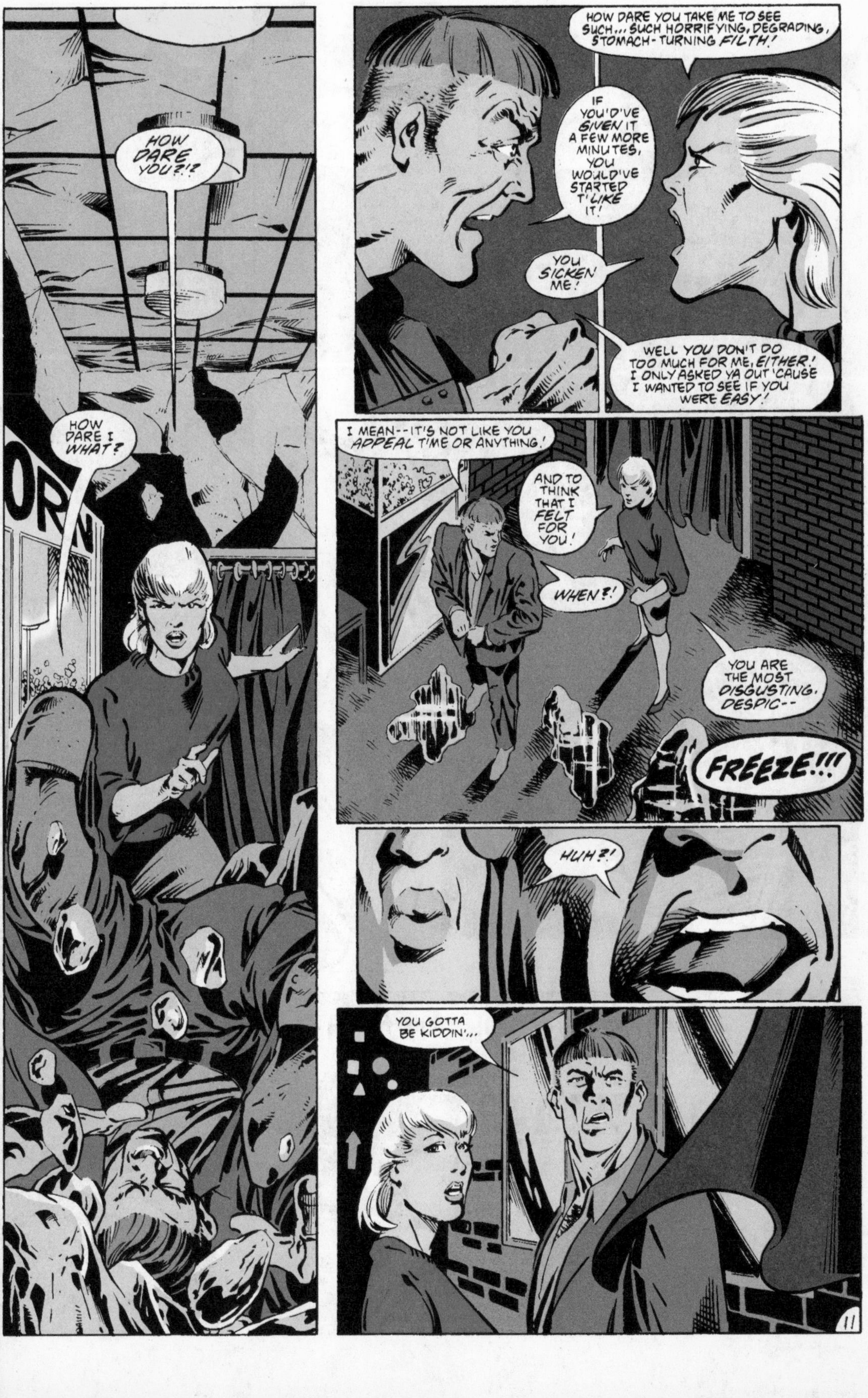
HOW DARE YOU?!?
HOW DARE I WHAT?
ORN
HOW DARE YOU TAKE ME TO SEE SUCH... SUCH HORRIFYING, DEGRADING, STOMACH-TURNING FILTH!
IF YOU'D'VE GIVEN IT A FEW MORE MINUTES, YOU WOULD'VE STARTED T'LIKE IT!
YOU SICKEN ME!
WELL YOU DON'T DO TOO MUCH FOR ME, EITHER! I ONLY ASKED YA OUT 'CAUSE I WANTED TO SEE IF YOU WERE EASY!
I MEAN--IT'S NOT LIKE YOU APPEAL T'ME OR ANYTHING!
AND TO THINK THAT I FELT FOR YOU!
WHEN?!
YOU ARE THE MOST DISGUSTING, DESPIC--
FREEZE!!!
HUH?!
YOU GOTTA BE KIDDIN'...
11

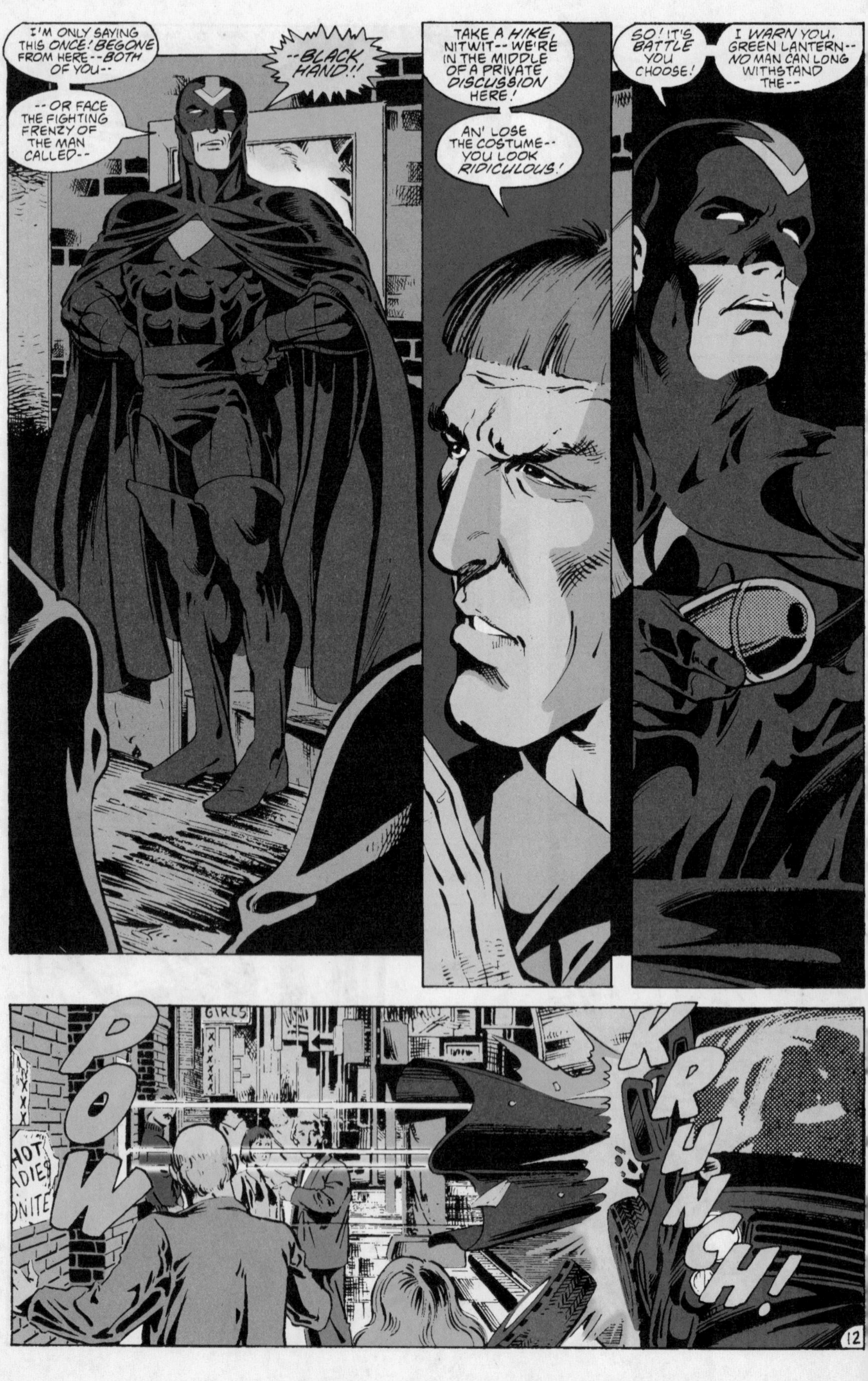

I'M ONLY SAYING THIS ONCE! BEGONE FROM HERE--BOTH OF YOU--
--OR FACE THE FIGHTING FRENZY OF THE MAN CALLED--
--BLACK HAND!!
TAKE A HIKE, NITWIT--WE'RE IN THE MIDDLE OF A PRIVATE DISCUSSION HERE!
AN' LOSE THE COSTUME--YOU LOOK RIDICULOUS!
SO! IT'S BATTLE YOU CHOOSE!
I WARN YOU, GREEN LANTERN--NO MAN CAN LONG WITHSTAND THE--
POW
KRUNCH!
GIRLS
HOT LADIES NITE
12

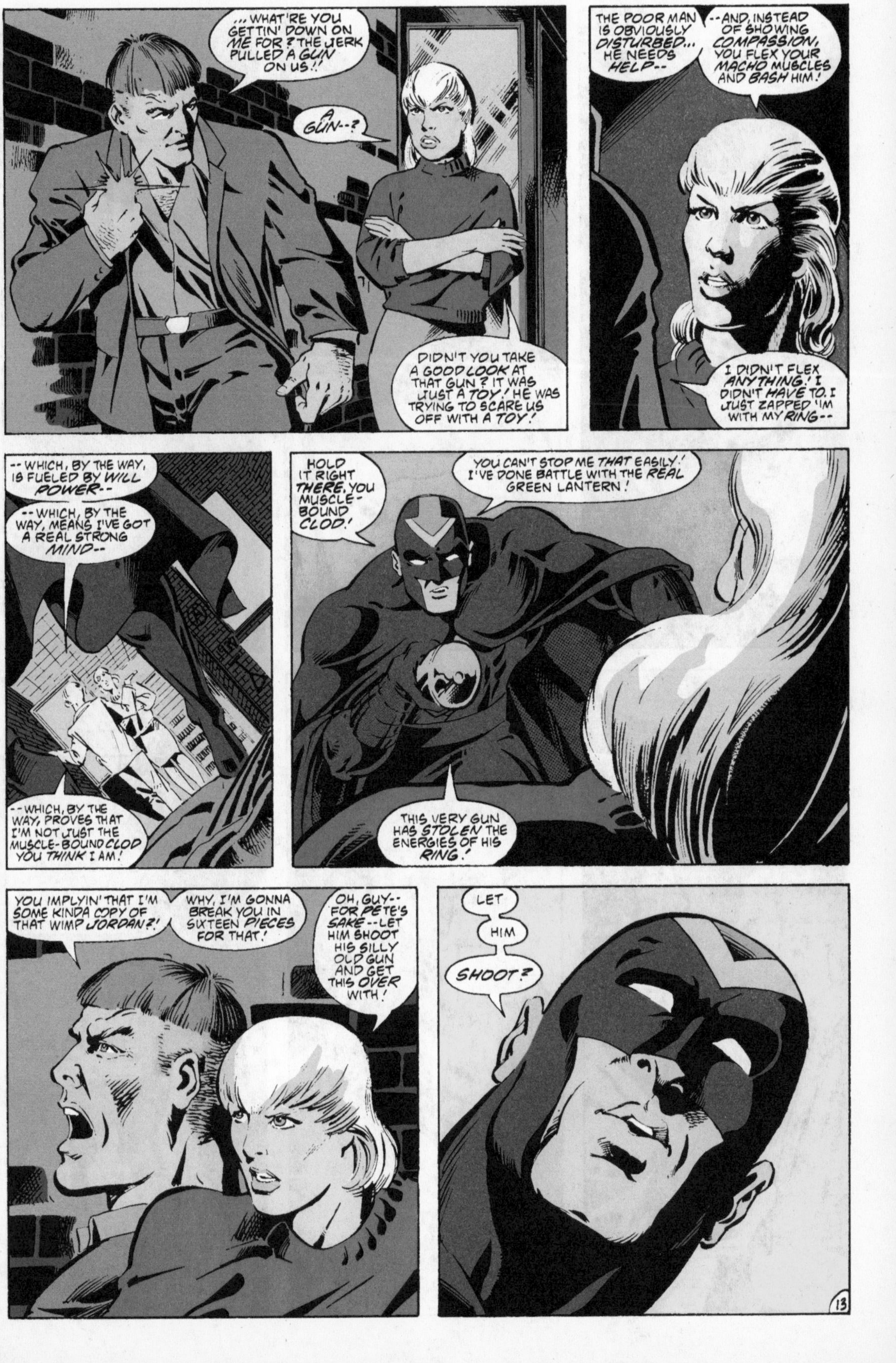
...WHAT'RE YOU GETTIN' DOWN ON ME FOR? THE JERK PULLED A GUN ON US!!
A GUN--?
DIDN'T YOU TAKE A GOOD LOOK AT THAT GUN? IT WAS JUST A TOY! HE WAS TRYING TO SCARE US OFF WITH A TOY!
THE POOR MAN IS OBVIOUSLY DISTURBED... HE NEEDS HELP--
--AND, INSTEAD OF SHOWING COMPASSION, YOU FLEX YOUR MACHO MUSCLES AND BASH HIM!
I DIDN'T FLEX ANYTHING! I DIDN'T HAVE TO. I JUST ZAPPED 'IM WITH MY RING--
--WHICH, BY THE WAY, IS FUELED BY WILL POWER--
--WHICH, BY THE WAY, MEANS I'VE GOT A REAL STRONG MIND--
--WHICH, BY THE WAY, PROVES THAT I'M NOT JUST THE MUSCLE-BOUND CLOD YOU THINK I AM!
HOLD IT RIGHT THERE, YOU MUSCLE-BOUND CLOD!
YOU CAN'T STOP ME THAT EASILY! I'VE DONE BATTLE WITH THE REAL GREEN LANTERN!
THIS VERY GUN HAS STOLEN THE ENERGIES OF HIS RING!
YOU IMPLYIN' THAT I'M SOME KINDA COPY OF THAT WIMP JORDAN?!
WHY, I'M GONNA BREAK YOU IN SIXTEEN PIECES FOR THAT!
OH, GUY-- FOR PETE'S SAKE--LET HIM SHOOT HIS SILLY OLD GUN AND GET THIS OVER WITH!
LET
HIM
SHOOT?
13

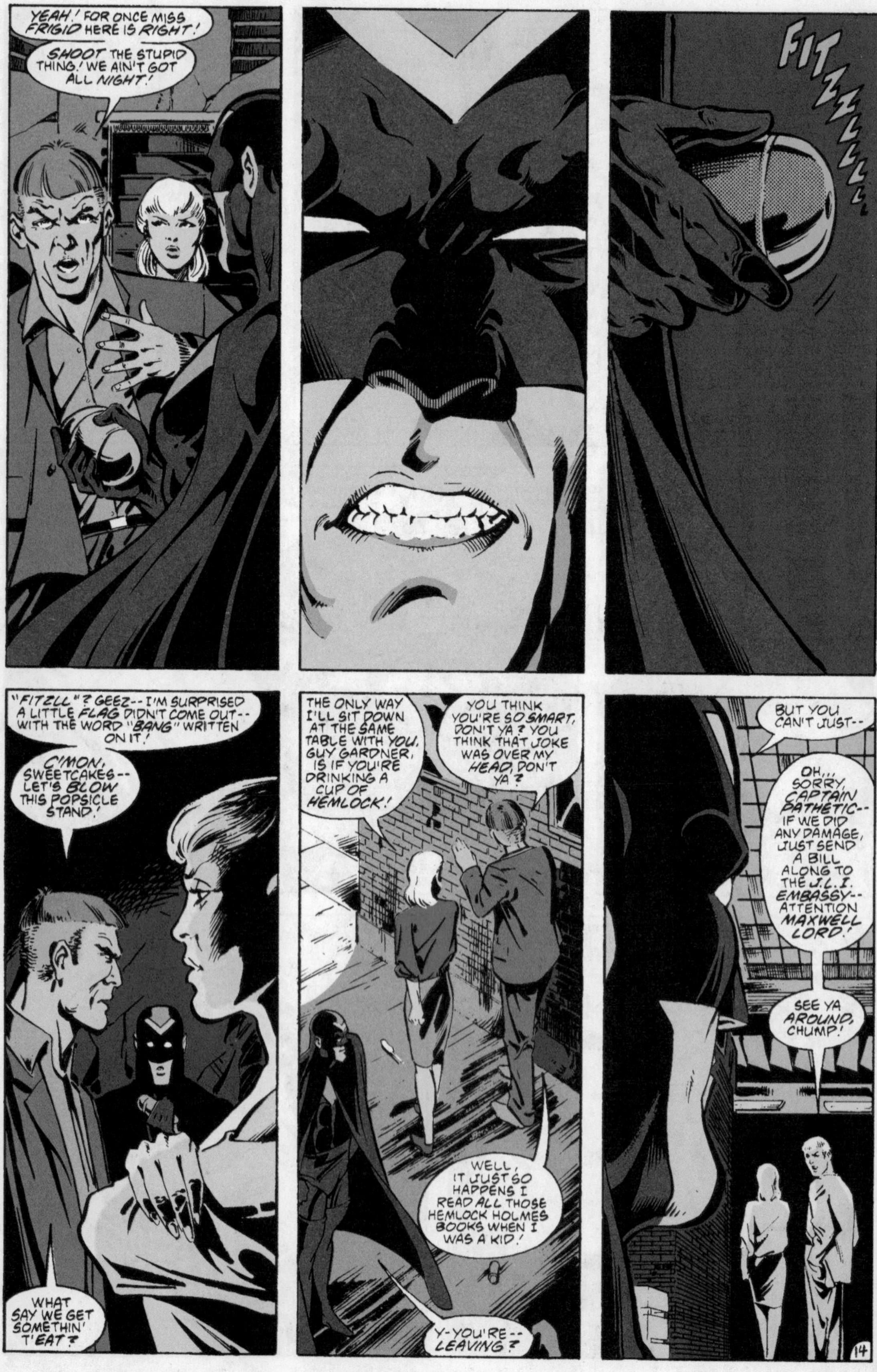
YEAH! FOR ONCE MISS FRIGID HERE IS RIGHT!
SHOOT THE STUPID THING! WE AIN'T GOT ALL NIGHT!
FITZZLLLL
"FITZLL"? GEEZ-- I'M SURPRISED A LITTLE FLAG DIDN'T COME OUT-- WITH THE WORD "BANG" WRITTEN ON IT!
C'MON, SWEETCAKES-- LET'S BLOW THIS POPSICLE STAND!
WHAT SAY WE GET SOMETHIN' T'EAT?
THE ONLY WAY I'LL SIT DOWN AT THE SAME TABLE WITH YOU, GUY GARDNER, IS IF YOU'RE DRINKING A CUP OF HEMLOCK!
YOU THINK YOU'RE SO SMART, DON'T YA? YOU THINK THAT JOKE WAS OVER MY HEAD, DON'T YA?
WELL, IT JUST SO HAPPENS I READ ALL THOSE HEMLOCK HOLMES BOOKS WHEN I WAS A KID!
Y-YOU'RE-- LEAVING?
BUT YOU CAN'T JUST--
OH,.. SORRY, CAPTAIN PATHETIC-- IF WE DID ANY DAMAGE, JUST SEND A BILL ALONG TO THE J.L.I. EMBASSY-- ATTENTION MAXWELL LORD!
SEE YA AROUND, CHUMP!
14

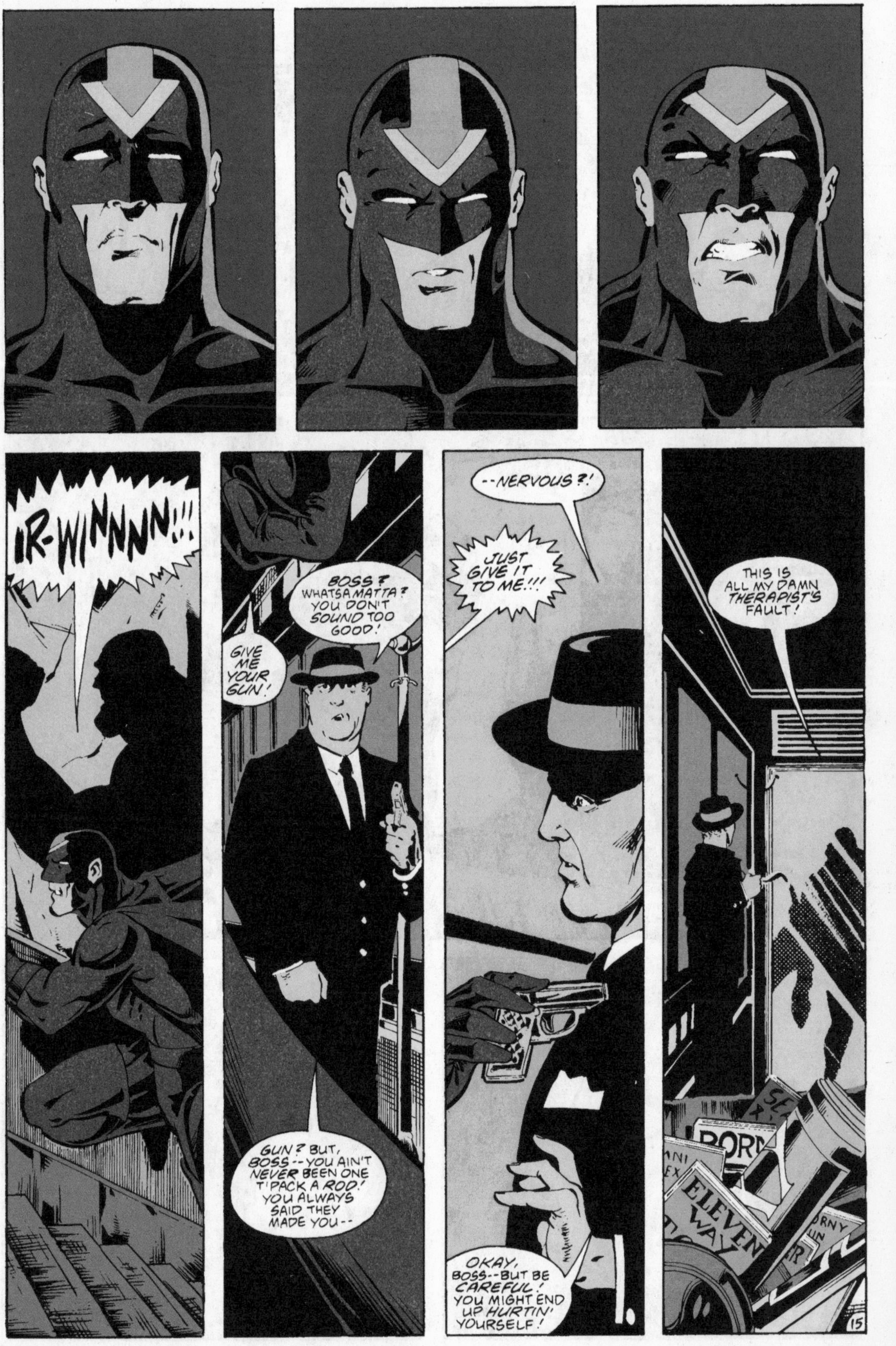

IR-WINNNN!!!
GIVE ME YOUR GUN!
BOSS? WHATSAMATTA? YOU DON'T SOUND TOO GOOD!
GUN? BUT, BOSS--YOU AIN'T NEVER BEEN ONE T'PACK A ROD! YOU ALWAYS SAID THEY MADE YOU--
--NERVOUS?!
JUST GIVE IT TO ME!!!
OKAY, BOSS--BUT BE CAREFUL! YOU MIGHT END UP HURTIN' YOURSELF!
THIS IS ALL MY DAMN THERAPIST'S FAULT!
PORN
ELEVEN WAY
15

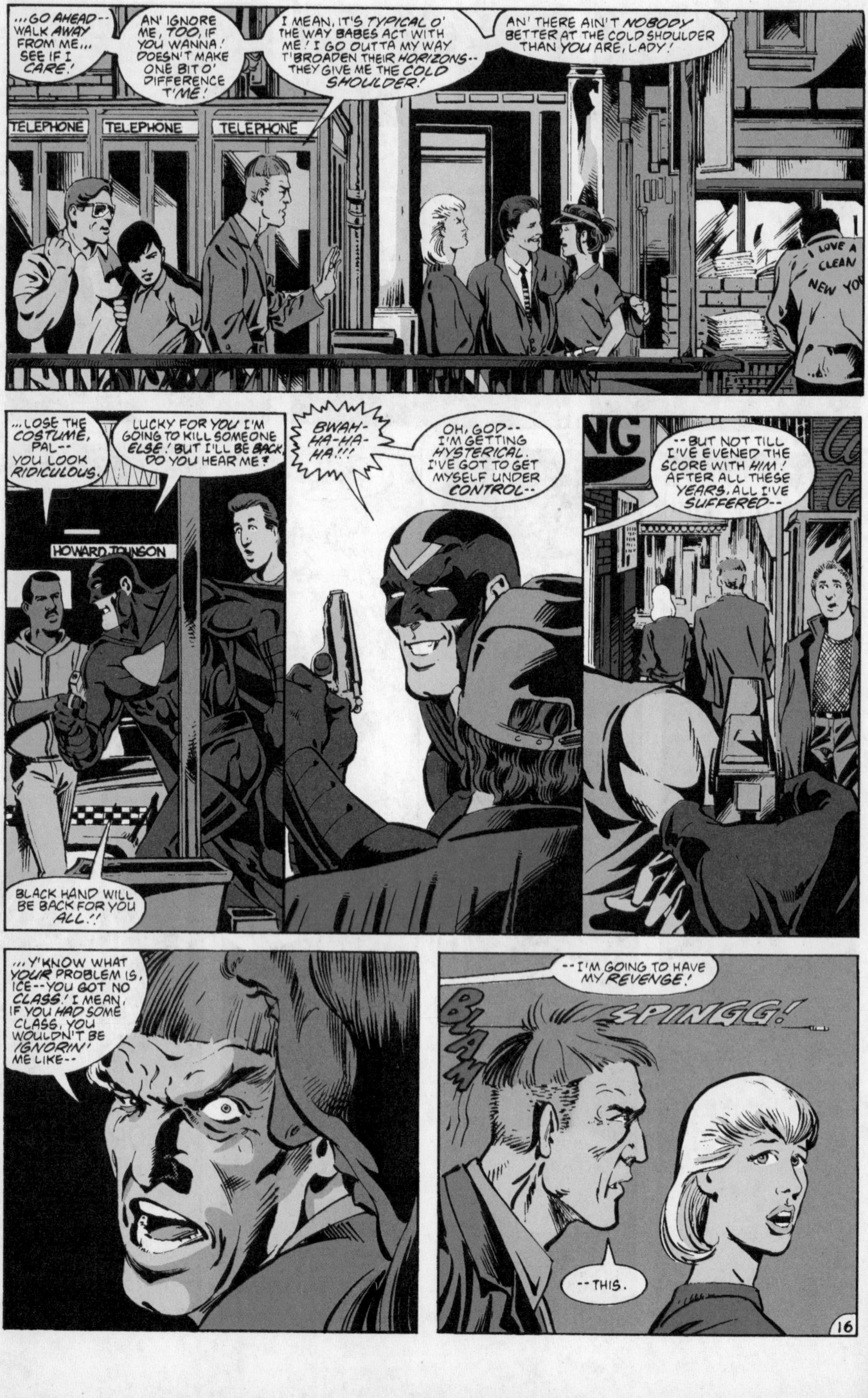
...GO AHEAD--
WALK AWAY
FROM ME...
SEE IF I
CARE!
AN' IGNORE
ME, TOO, IF
YOU WANNA!
DOESN'T MAKE
ONE BIT O'
DIFFERENCE
T'ME!
I MEAN, IT'S TYPICAL O'
THE WAY BABES ACT WITH
ME! I GO OUTTA MY WAY
T'BROADEN THEIR HORIZONS--
THEY GIVE ME THE COLD
SHOULDER!
AN' THERE AIN'T NOBODY
BETTER AT THE COLD SHOULDER
THAN YOU ARE, LADY!
TELEPHONE
TELEPHONE
TELEPHONE
I LOVE A
CLEAN
NEW YO
...LOSE THE
COSTUME,
PAL--
YOU LOOK
RIDICULOUS.
LUCKY FOR YOU I'M
GOING TO KILL SOMEONE
ELSE! BUT I'LL BE BACK.
DO YOU HEAR ME?
HOWARD JOHNSON
BLACK HAND WILL
BE BACK FOR YOU
ALL!!
BWAH-
HA-HA-
HA!!!
OH, GOD--
I'M GETTING
HYSTERICAL.
I'VE GOT TO GET
MYSELF UNDER
CONTROL--
NG
--BUT NOT TILL
I'VE EVENED THE
SCORE WITH HIM!
AFTER ALL THESE
YEARS. ALL I'VE
SUFFERED--
...Y'KNOW WHAT
YOUR PROBLEM IS,
ICE--YOU GOT NO
CLASS! I MEAN,
IF YOU HAD SOME
CLASS, YOU
WOULDN'T BE
IGNORIN'
ME LIKE--
--I'M GOING TO HAVE
MY REVENGE!
BLAM
SPINGG!
--THIS.
16

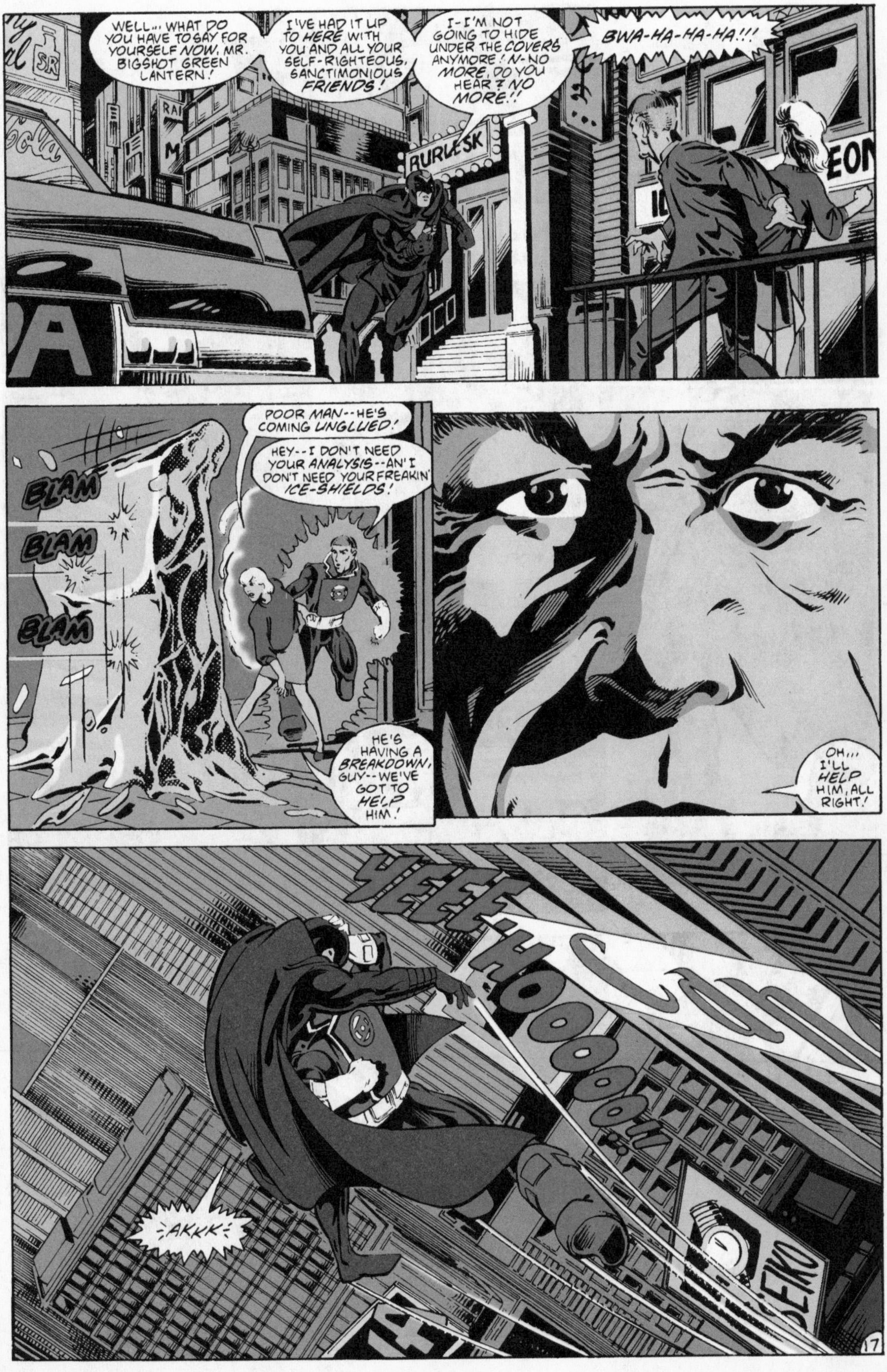
WELL... WHAT DO YOU HAVE TO SAY FOR YOURSELF NOW, MR. BIGSHOT GREEN LANTERN!
I'VE HAD IT UP TO HERE WITH YOU AND ALL YOUR SELF-RIGHTEOUS, SANCTIMONIOUS FRIENDS!
I-I'M NOT GOING TO HIDE UNDER THE COVERS ANYMORE! N-NO MORE, DO YOU HEAR? NO MORE!!
BWA-HA-HA-HA!!!
BLAM
BLAM
BLAM
POOR MAN--HE'S COMING UNGLUED!
HEY--I DON'T NEED YOUR ANALYSIS--AN' I DON'T NEED YOUR FREAKIN' ICE-SHIELDS!
HE'S HAVING A BREAKDOWN, GUY--WE'VE GOT TO HELP HIM!
OH... I'LL HELP HIM, ALL RIGHT!
YEEE-HOOOOO!!!
AKKK
17

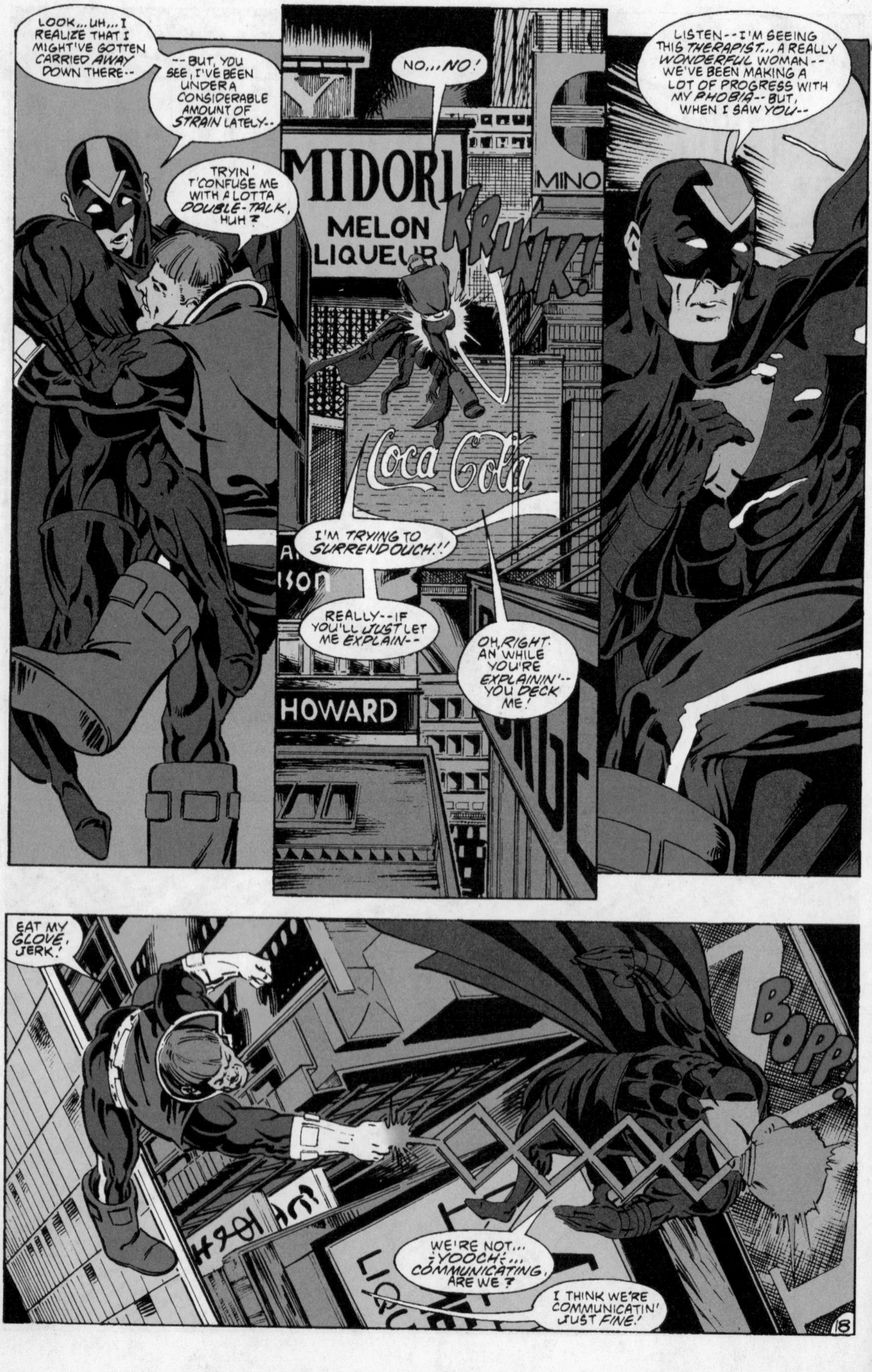

LOOK... UH... I REALIZE THAT I MIGHT'VE GOTTEN CARRIED AWAY DOWN THERE--
--BUT, YOU SEE, I'VE BEEN UNDER A CONSIDERABLE AMOUNT OF STRAIN LATELY--
TRYIN' T'CONFUSE ME WITH A LOTTA DOUBLE-TALK, HUH?
NO... NO!
MIDORI
MELON LIQUEUR
KRUNK!
Coca Cola
I'M TRYING TO SURRENDOUCH!!
REALLY--IF YOU'LL JUST LET ME EXPLAIN--
OH, RIGHT. AN' WHILE YOU'RE EXPLAININ'--YOU DECK ME!
HOWARD
MINO
LISTEN--I'M SEEING THIS THERAPIST... A REALLY WONDERFUL WOMAN--WE'VE BEEN MAKING A LOT OF PROGRESS WITH MY PHOBIA--BUT, WHEN I SAW YOU--
EAT MY GLOVE, JERK!
BOPP
WE'RE NOT... YOOCH... COMMUNICATING, ARE WE?
I THINK WE'RE COMMUNICATIN' JUST FINE!
18

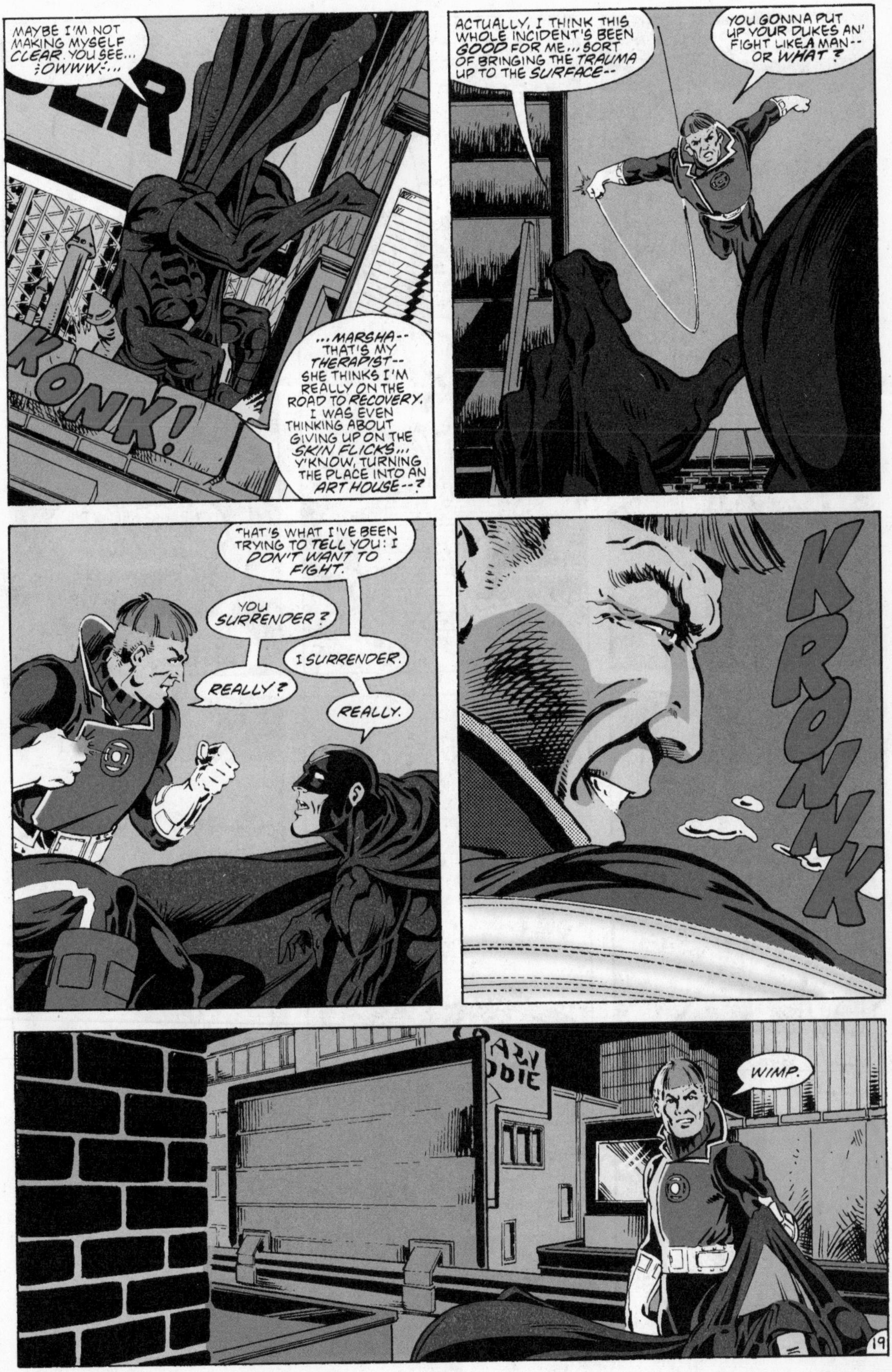
MAYBE I'M NOT MAKING MYSELF CLEAR. YOU SEE... OWWW...
KONK!
...MARSHA-- THAT'S MY THERAPIST-- SHE THINKS I'M REALLY ON THE ROAD TO RECOVERY. I WAS EVEN THINKING ABOUT GIVING UP ON THE SKIN FLICKS... Y'KNOW, TURNING THE PLACE INTO AN ART HOUSE--?
ACTUALLY, I THINK THIS WHOLE INCIDENT'S BEEN GOOD FOR ME... SORT OF BRINGING THE TRAUMA UP TO THE SURFACE--
YOU GONNA PUT UP YOUR DUKES AN' FIGHT LIKE A MAN-- OR WHAT?
THAT'S WHAT I'VE BEEN TRYING TO TELL YOU: I DON'T WANT TO FIGHT.
YOU SURRENDER?
I SURRENDER.
REALLY?
REALLY.
KRONNK
WIMP.
19

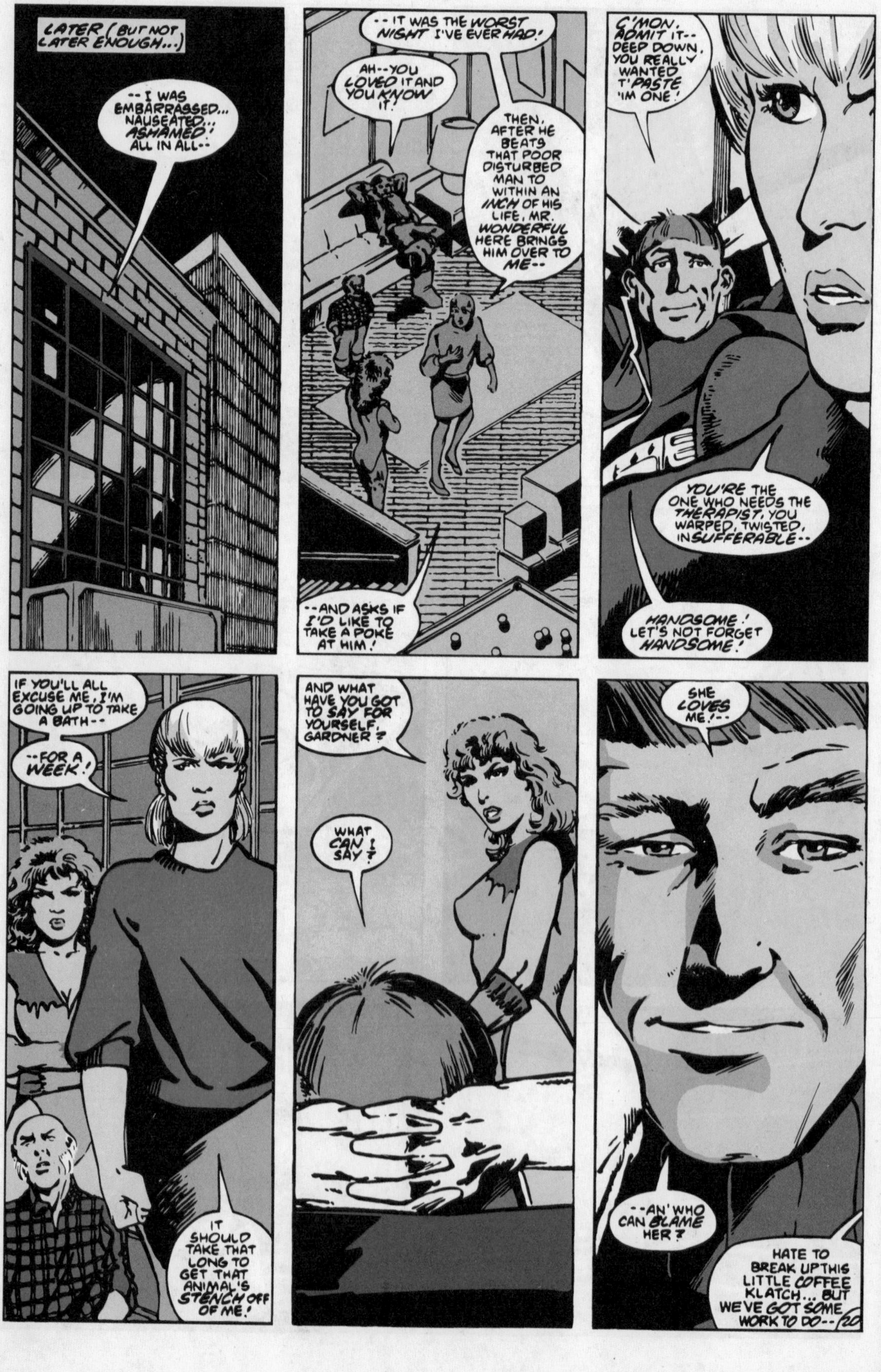
LATER (BUT NOT LATER ENOUGH...)
--I WAS EMBARRASSED... NAUSEATED... ASHAMED! ALL IN ALL--
--IT WAS THE WORST NIGHT I'VE EVER HAD!
AH--YOU LOVED IT AND YOU KNOW IT.
THEN, AFTER HE BEATS THAT POOR DISTURBED MAN TO WITHIN AN INCH OF HIS LIFE, MR. WONDERFUL HERE BRINGS HIM OVER TO ME--
--AND ASKS IF I'D LIKE TO TAKE A POKE AT HIM!
C'MON, ADMIT IT--DEEP DOWN, YOU REALLY WANTED T'PASTE 'IM ONE!
YOU'RE THE ONE WHO NEEDS THE THERAPIST, YOU WARPED, TWISTED, INSUFFERABLE--
HANDSOME! LET'S NOT FORGET HANDSOME!
IF YOU'LL ALL EXCUSE ME, I'M GOING UP TO TAKE A BATH--
--FOR A WEEK!
IT SHOULD TAKE THAT LONG TO GET THAT ANIMAL'S STENCH OFF OF ME!
AND WHAT HAVE YOU GOT TO SAY FOR YOURSELF, GARDNER?
WHAT CAN I SAY?
SHE LOVES ME!--
--AN' WHO CAN BLAME HER?
HATE TO BREAK UP THIS LITTLE COFFEE KLATCH... BUT WE'VE GOT SOME WORK TO DO--
20

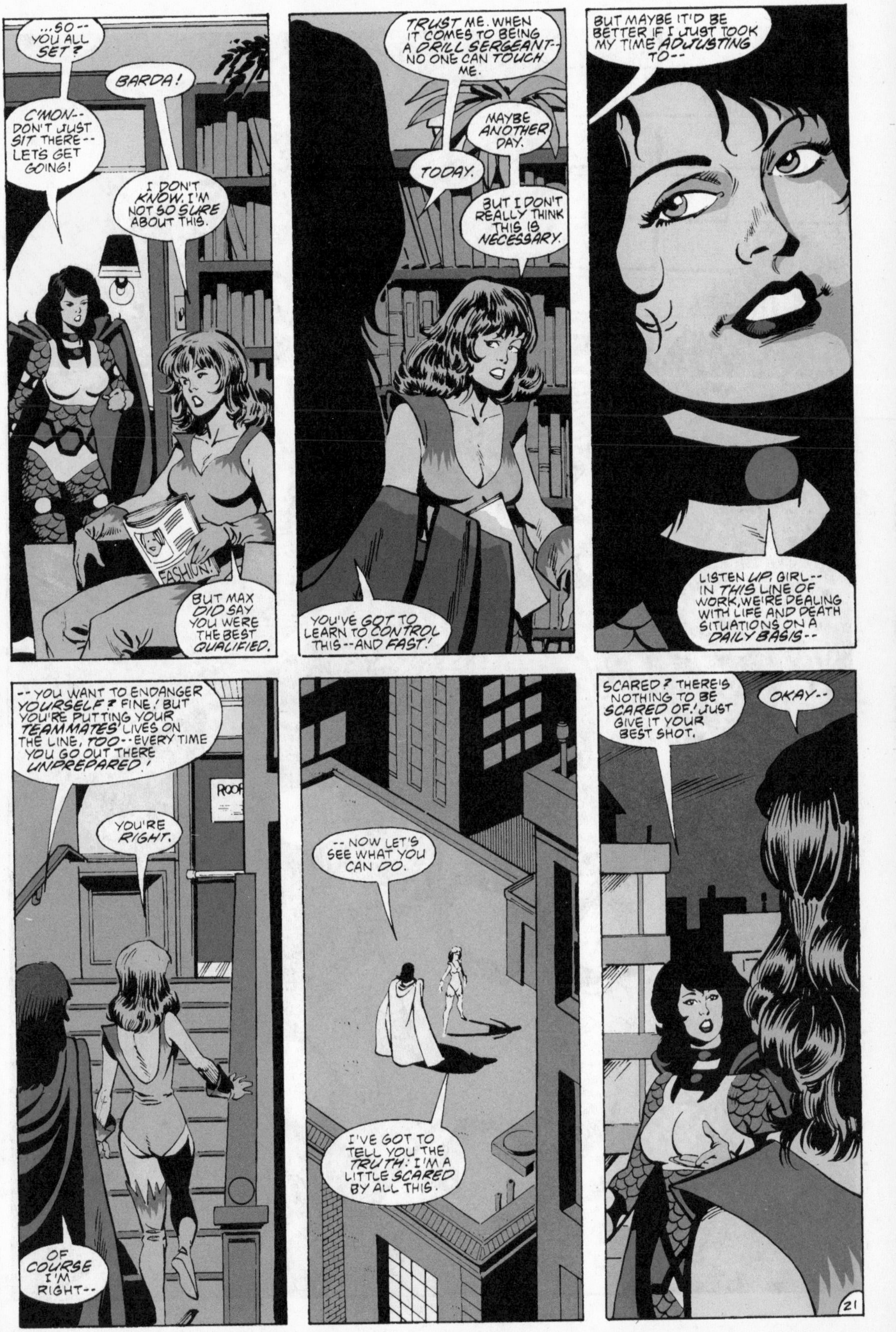
...SO -- YOU ALL SET?
BARDA!
C'MON-- DON'T JUST SIT THERE-- LET'S GET GOING!
I DON'T KNOW. I'M NOT SO SURE ABOUT THIS.
BUT MAX DID SAY YOU WERE THE BEST QUALIFIED.
FASHION
TRUST ME. WHEN IT COMES TO BEING A DRILL SERGEANT-- NO ONE CAN TOUCH ME.
MAYBE ANOTHER DAY.
TODAY.
BUT I DON'T REALLY THINK THIS IS NECESSARY.
YOU'VE GOT TO LEARN TO CONTROL THIS--AND FAST!
BUT MAYBE IT'D BE BETTER IF I JUST TOOK MY TIME ADJUSTING TO--
LISTEN UP, GIRL-- IN THIS LINE OF WORK, WE'RE DEALING WITH LIFE AND DEATH SITUATIONS ON A DAILY BASIS--
--YOU WANT TO ENDANGER YOURSELF? FINE! BUT YOU'RE PUTTING YOUR TEAMMATES' LIVES ON THE LINE, TOO--EVERY TIME YOU GO OUT THERE UNPREPARED!
ROOF
YOU'RE RIGHT.
OF COURSE I'M RIGHT--
--NOW LET'S SEE WHAT YOU CAN DO.
I'VE GOT TO TELL YOU THE TRUTH: I'M A LITTLE SCARED BY ALL THIS.
SCARED? THERE'S NOTHING TO BE SCARED OF! JUST GIVE IT YOUR BEST SHOT.
OKAY--
21

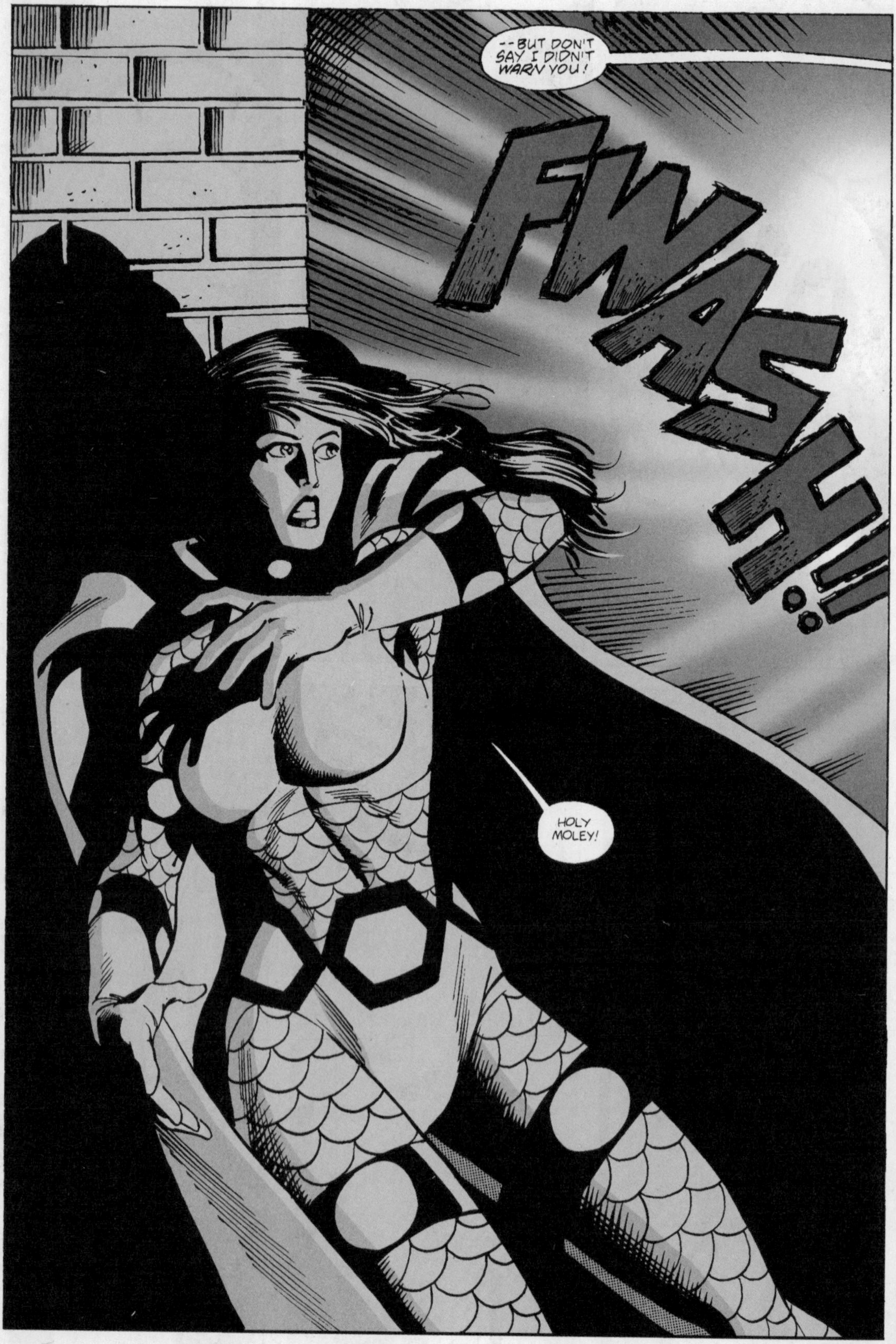
--BUT DON'T SAY I DIDN'T WARN YOU!
FWASH!!!
HOLY MOLEY!

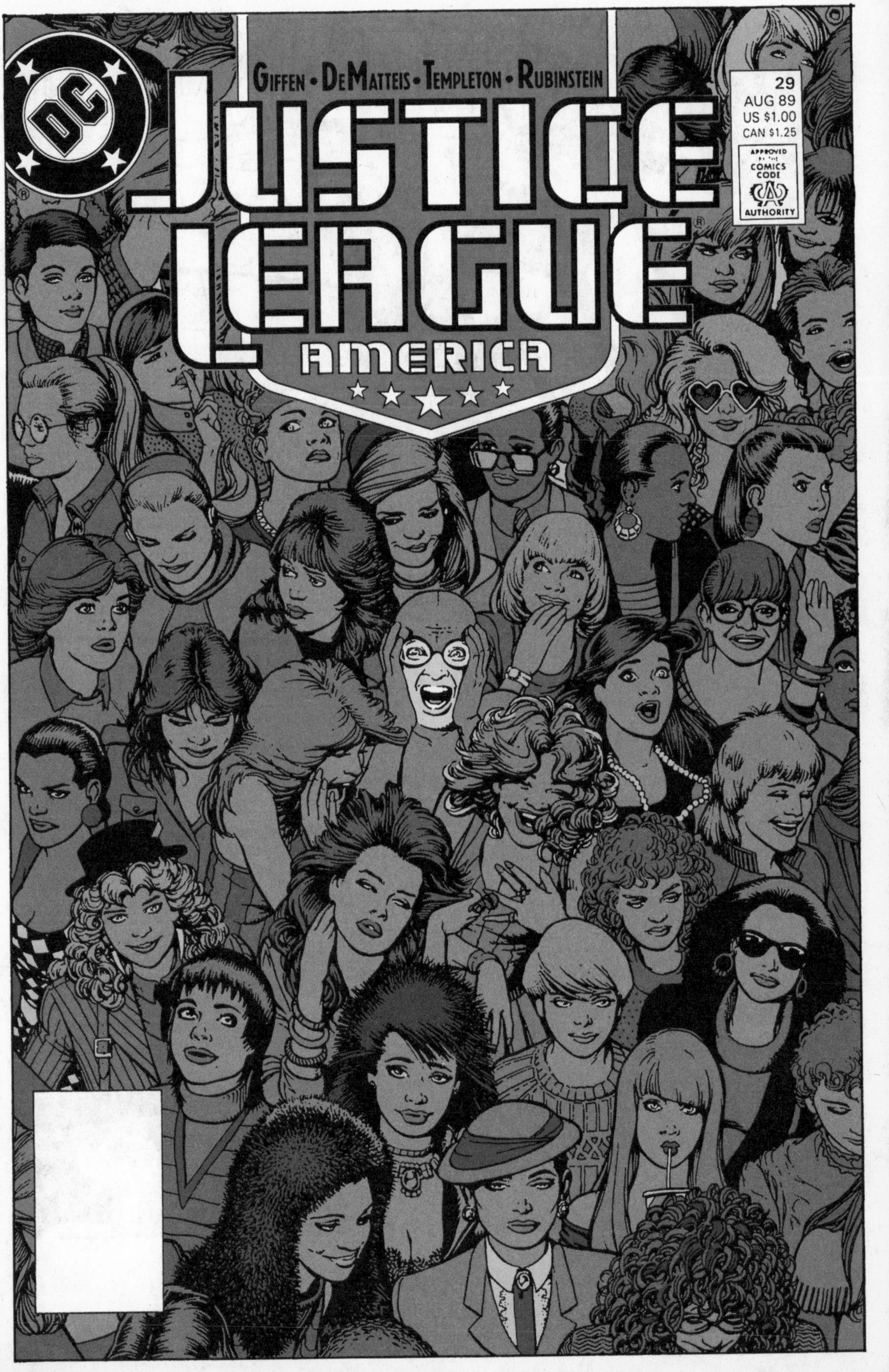
GIFFEN • DEMATTEIS • TEMPLETON • RUBINSTEIN
DC
JUSTICE LEAGUE
AMERICA
29
AUG 89
US $1.00
CAN $1.25
APPROVED BY THE COMICS CODE AUTHORITY

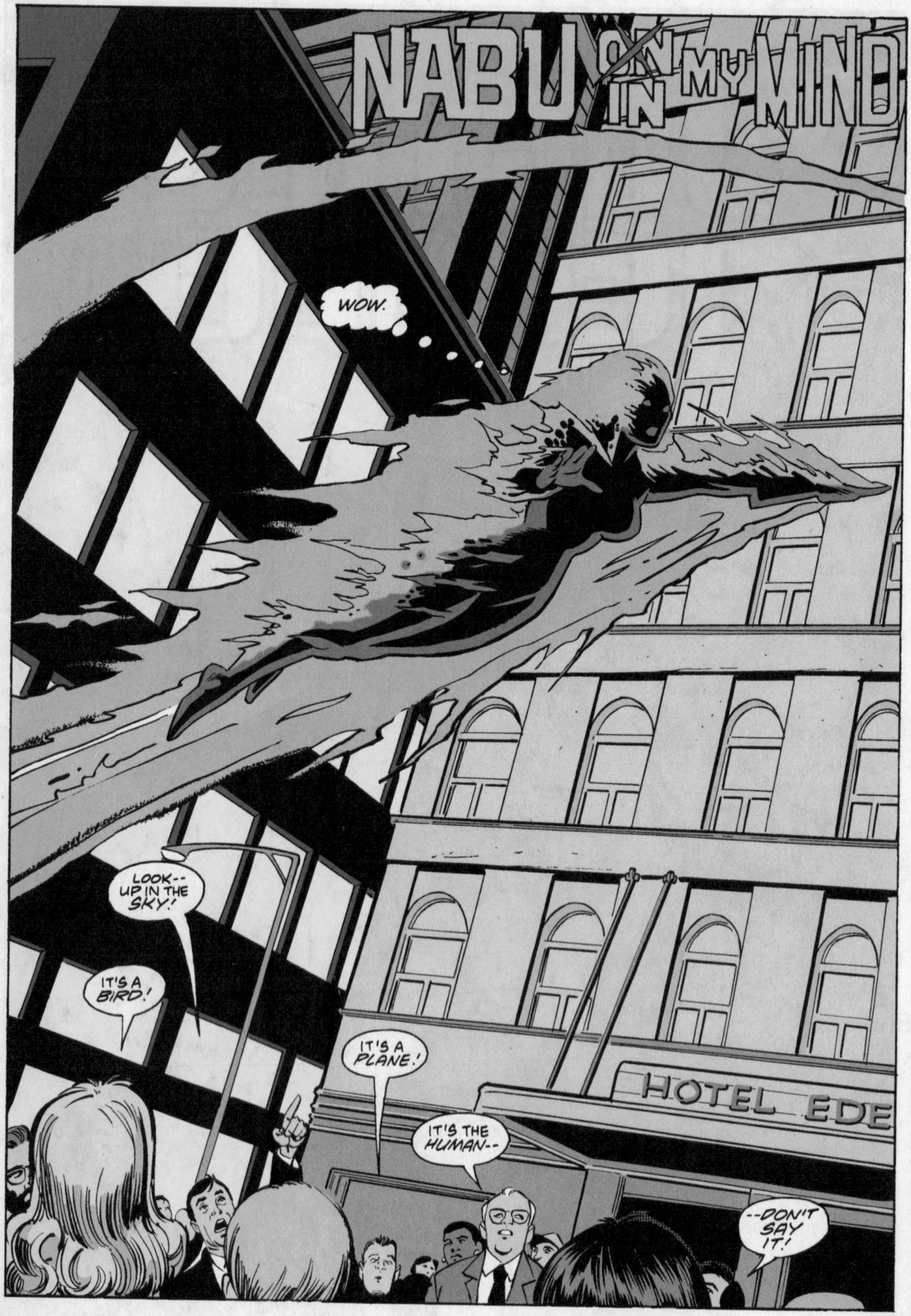
NABU ON IN MY MIND
WOW.
LOOK-- UP IN THE SKY!
IT'S A BIRD!
IT'S A PLANE!
IT'S THE HUMAN--
--DON'T SAY IT!
HOTEL EDE

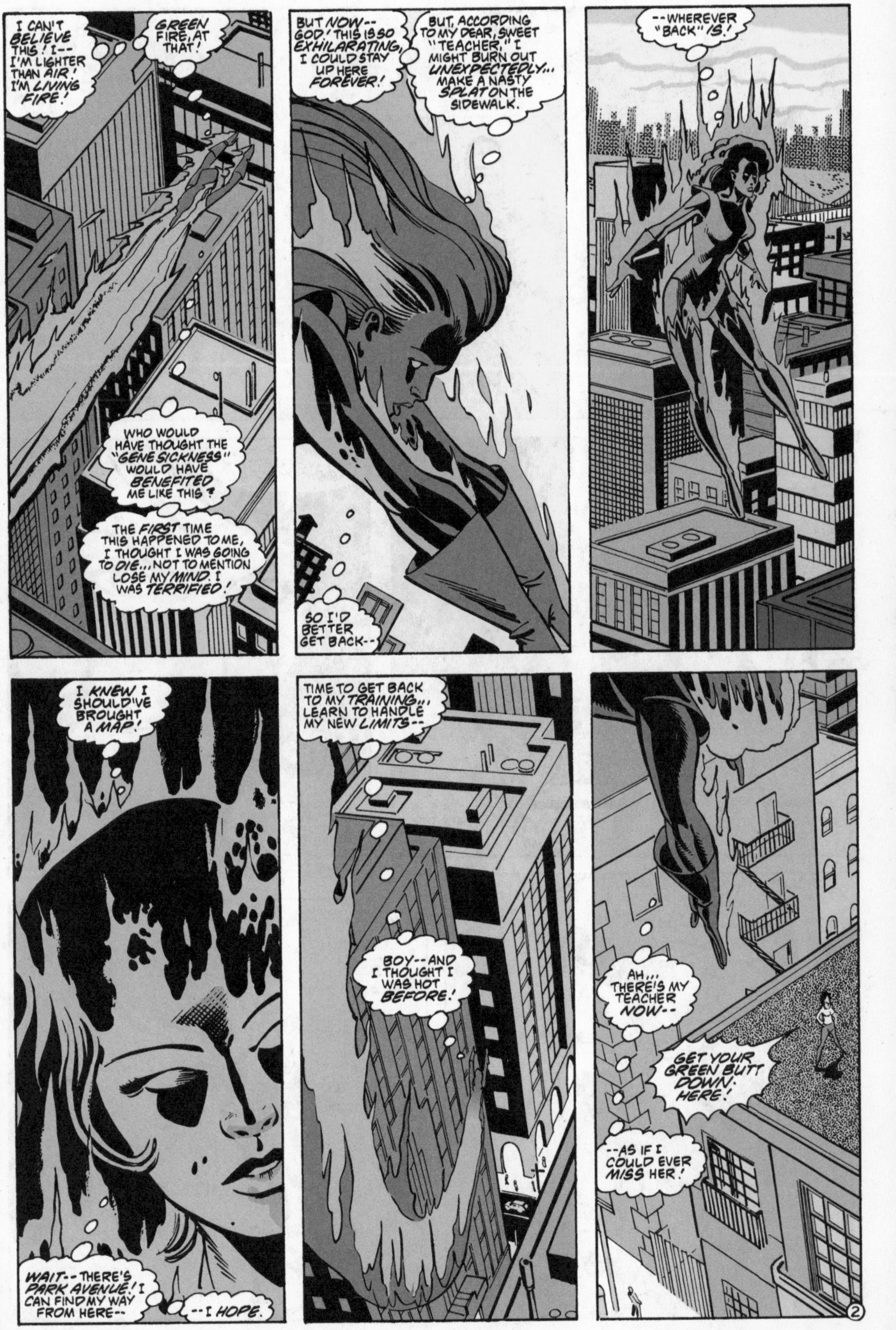
I CAN'T BELIEVE THIS! I-- I'M LIGHTER THAN AIR! I'M LIVING FIRE!
GREEN FIRE, AT THAT!
WHO WOULD HAVE THOUGHT THE "GENE SICKNESS" WOULD HAVE BENEFITED ME LIKE THIS?
THE FIRST TIME THIS HAPPENED TO ME, I THOUGHT I WAS GOING TO DIE... NOT TO MENTION LOSE MY MIND. I WAS TERRIFIED!
BUT NOW-- GOD! THIS IS SO EXHILARATING, I COULD STAY UP HERE FOREVER!
BUT, ACCORDING TO MY DEAR, SWEET "TEACHER," I MIGHT BURN OUT UNEXPECTEDLY... MAKE A NASTY SPLAT ON THE SIDEWALK.
SO I'D BETTER GET BACK--
--WHEREVER "BACK" IS!
I KNEW I SHOULD'VE BROUGHT A MAP!
WAIT-- THERE'S PARK AVENUE! I CAN FIND MY WAY FROM HERE--
--I HOPE.
TIME TO GET BACK TO MY TRAINING... LEARN TO HANDLE MY NEW LIMITS--
BOY-- AND I THOUGHT I WAS HOT BEFORE!
AH... THERE'S MY TEACHER NOW--
GET YOUR GREEN BUTT DOWN HERE!
--AS IF I COULD EVER MISS HER!
2

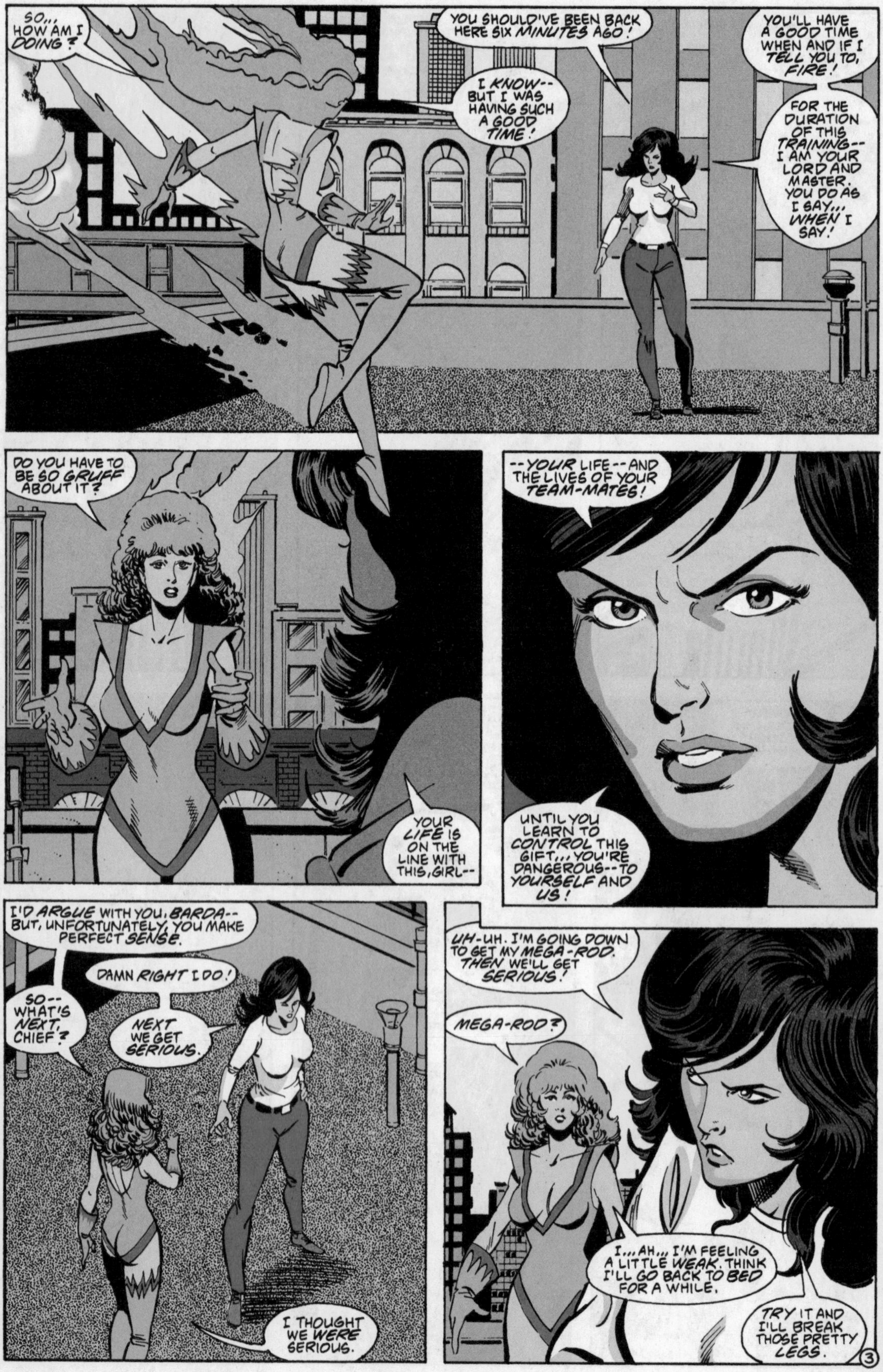

SO... HOW AM I DOING?
YOU SHOULD'VE BEEN BACK HERE SIX MINUTES AGO!
I KNOW-- BUT I WAS HAVING SUCH A GOOD TIME!
YOU'LL HAVE A GOOD TIME WHEN AND IF I TELL YOU TO, FIRE!
FOR THE DURATION OF THIS TRAINING-- I AM YOUR LORD AND MASTER. YOU DO AS I SAY... WHEN I SAY!
DO YOU HAVE TO BE SO GRUFF ABOUT IT?
YOUR LIFE IS ON THE LINE WITH THIS, GIRL--
--YOUR LIFE--AND THE LIVES OF YOUR TEAM-MATES!
UNTIL YOU LEARN TO CONTROL THIS GIFT... YOU'RE DANGEROUS--TO YOURSELF AND US!
I'D ARGUE WITH YOU, BARDA-- BUT, UNFORTUNATELY, YOU MAKE PERFECT SENSE.
DAMN RIGHT I DO!
SO-- WHAT'S NEXT, CHIEF?
NEXT WE GET SERIOUS.
I THOUGHT WE WERE SERIOUS.
UH-UH. I'M GOING DOWN TO GET MY MEGA-ROD. THEN WE'LL GET SERIOUS!
MEGA-ROD?
I... AH... I'M FEELING A LITTLE WEAK. THINK I'LL GO BACK TO BED FOR A WHILE.
TRY IT AND I'LL BREAK THOSE PRETTY LEGS.
3

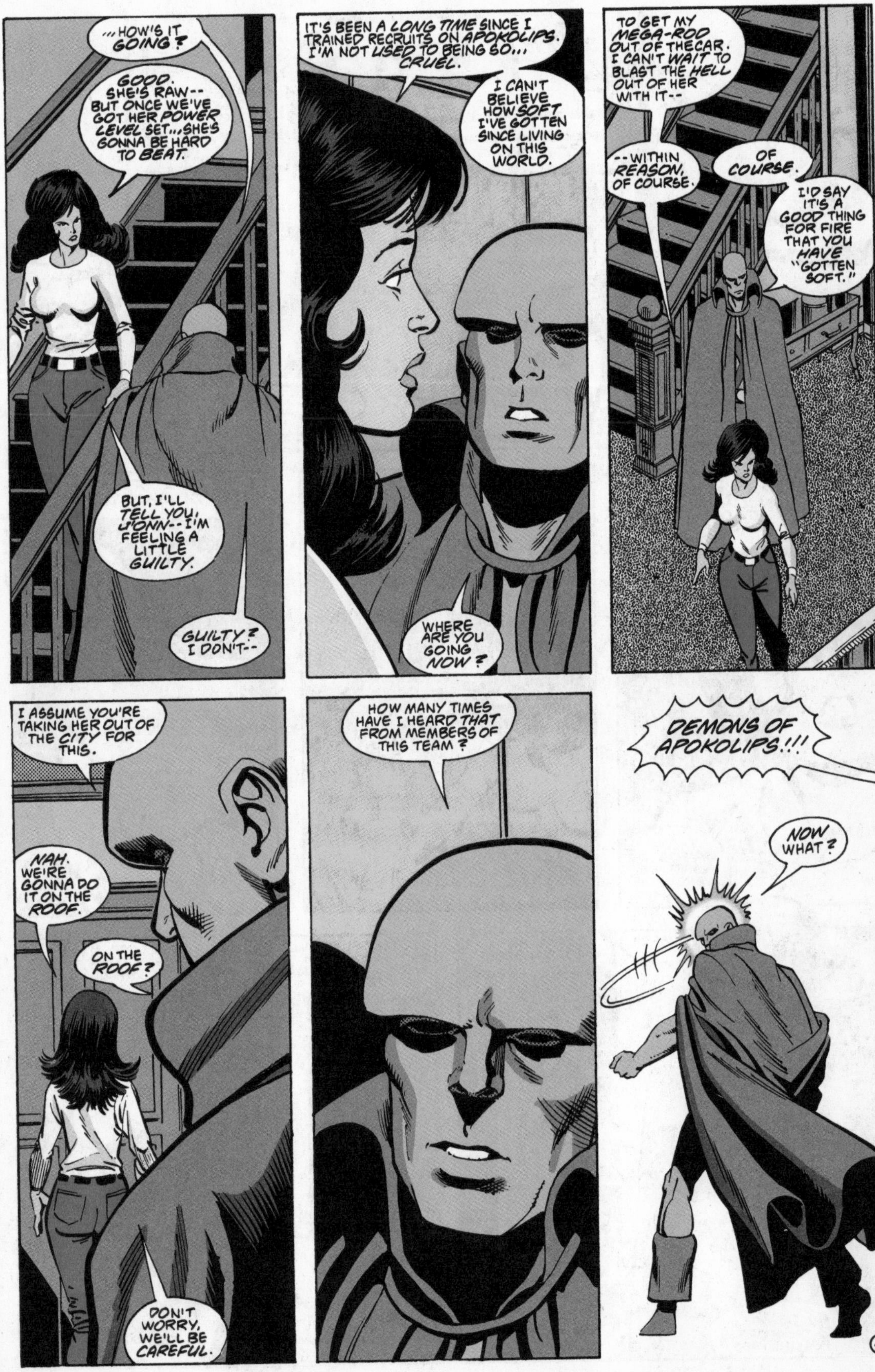
...HOW'S IT GOING?
GOOD. SHE'S RAW-- BUT ONCE WE'VE GOT HER POWER LEVEL SET... SHE'S GONNA BE HARD TO BEAT.
BUT, I'LL TELL YOU, J'ONN-- I'M FEELING A LITTLE GUILTY.
GUILTY? I DON'T--
IT'S BEEN A LONG TIME SINCE I TRAINED RECRUITS ON APOKOLIPS. I'M NOT USED TO BEING SO... CRUEL.
I CAN'T BELIEVE HOW SOFT I'VE GOTTEN SINCE LIVING ON THIS WORLD.
WHERE ARE YOU GOING NOW?
TO GET MY MEGA-ROD OUT OF THE CAR. I CAN'T WAIT TO BLAST THE HELL OUT OF HER WITH IT--
--WITHIN REASON, OF COURSE.
OF COURSE.
I'D SAY IT'S A GOOD THING FOR FIRE THAT YOU HAVE "GOTTEN SOFT."
I ASSUME YOU'RE TAKING HER OUT OF THE CITY FOR THIS.
NAH. WE'RE GONNA DO IT ON THE ROOF.
ON THE ROOF?
DON'T WORRY, WE'LL BE CAREFUL.
HOW MANY TIMES HAVE I HEARD THAT FROM MEMBERS OF THIS TEAM?
DEMONS OF APOKOLIPS!!!
NOW WHAT?
4

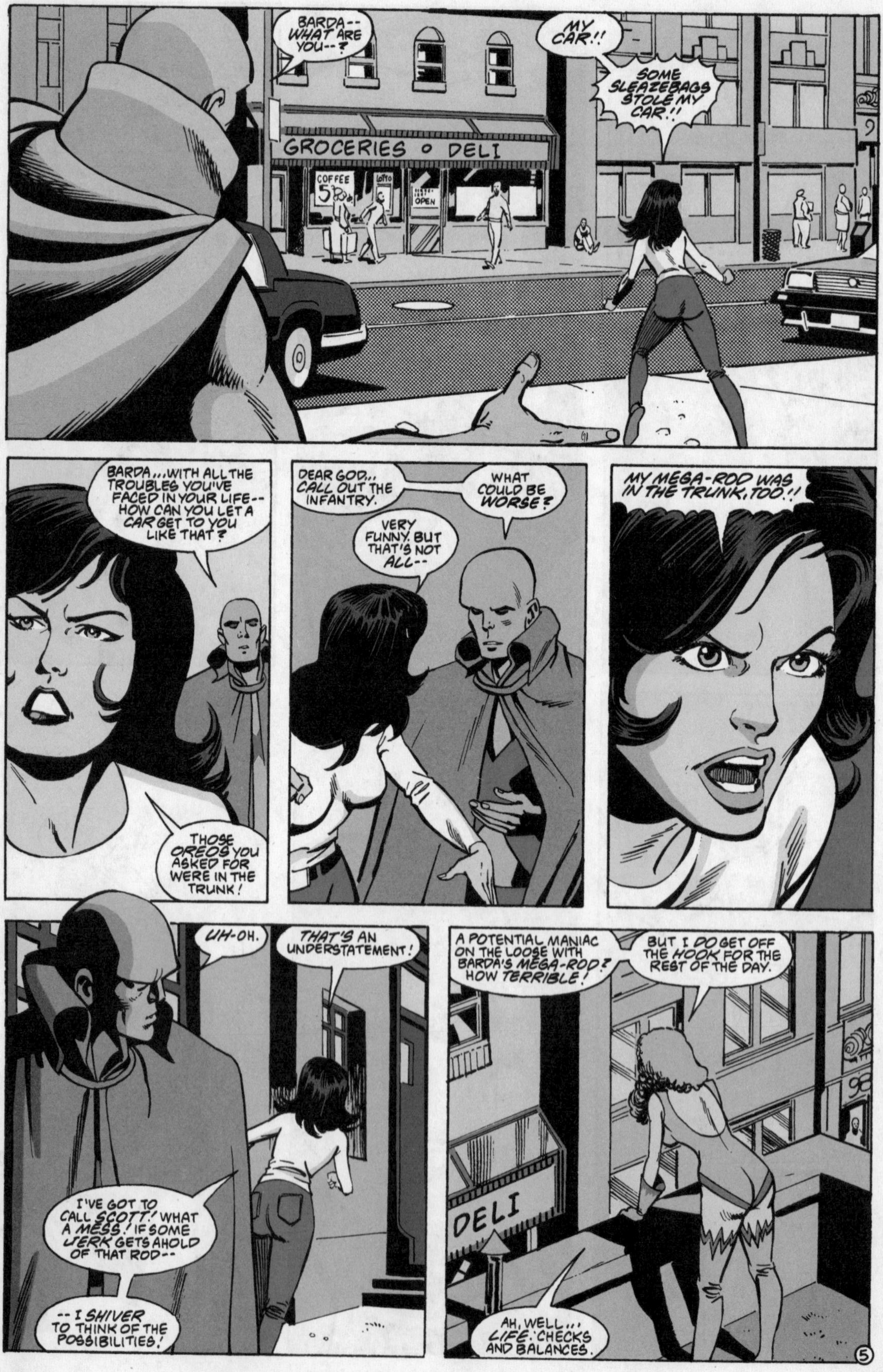
BARDA-- WHAT ARE YOU--?
MY CAR!!
SOME SLEAZEBAGS STOLE MY CAR!!
GROCERIES o DELI
COFFEE
LOTTO
OPEN
BARDA...WITH ALL THE TROUBLES YOU'VE FACED IN YOUR LIFE-- HOW CAN YOU LET A CAR GET TO YOU LIKE THAT?
THOSE OREOS YOU ASKED FOR WERE IN THE TRUNK!
DEAR GOD... CALL OUT THE INFANTRY.
WHAT COULD BE WORSE?
VERY FUNNY. BUT THAT'S NOT ALL--
MY MEGA-ROD WAS IN THE TRUNK, TOO!!
UH-OH.
THAT'S AN UNDERSTATEMENT!
I'VE GOT TO CALL SCOTT! WHAT A MESS! IF SOME JERK GETS AHOLD OF THAT ROD--
-- I SHIVER TO THINK OF THE POSSIBILITIES!
A POTENTIAL MANIAC ON THE LOOSE WITH BARDA'S MEGA-ROD? HOW TERRIBLE!
BUT I DO GET OFF THE HOOK FOR THE REST OF THE DAY.
DELI
AH, WELL... LIFE: CHECKS AND BALANCES.
5

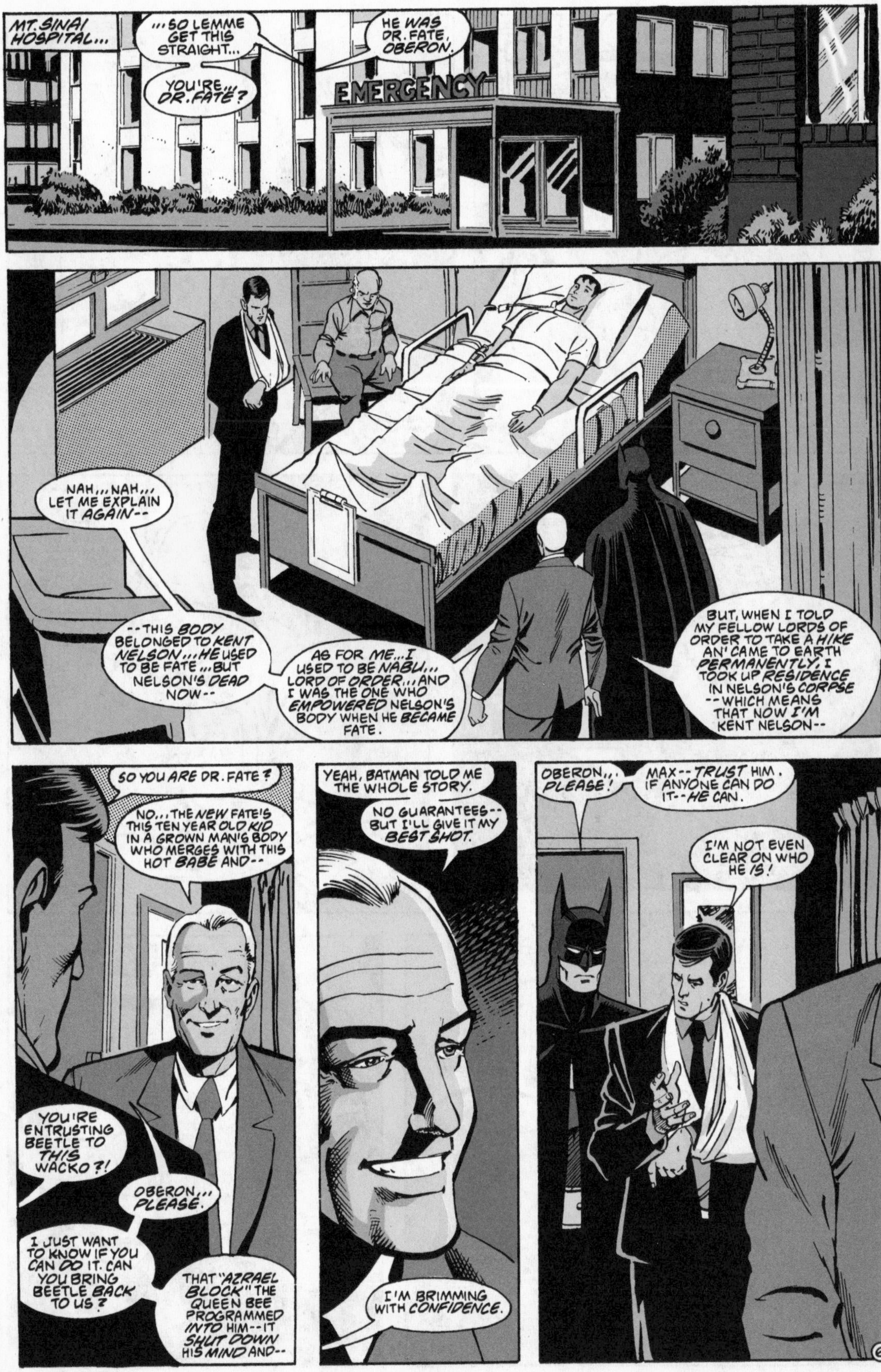
MT. SINAI HOSPITAL...
...SO LEMME GET THIS STRAIGHT...
YOU'RE... DR. FATE?
HE WAS DR. FATE, OBERON.
EMERGENCY
NAH... NAH... LET ME EXPLAIN IT AGAIN--
--THIS BODY BELONGED TO KENT NELSON... HE USED TO BE FATE... BUT NELSON'S DEAD NOW--
AS FOR ME... I USED TO BE NABU... LORD OF ORDER... AND I WAS THE ONE WHO EMPOWERED NELSON'S BODY WHEN HE BECAME FATE.
BUT, WHEN I TOLD MY FELLOW LORDS OF ORDER TO TAKE A HIKE AN' CAME TO EARTH PERMANENTLY, I TOOK UP RESIDENCE IN NELSON'S CORPSE --WHICH MEANS THAT NOW I'M KENT NELSON--
SO YOU ARE DR. FATE?
NO... THE NEW FATE'S THIS TEN YEAR OLD KID IN A GROWN MAN'S BODY WHO MERGES WITH THIS HOT BABE AND--
YOU'RE ENTRUSTING BEETLE TO THIS WACKO?!
OBERON... PLEASE.
I JUST WANT TO KNOW IF YOU CAN DO IT. CAN YOU BRING BEETLE BACK TO US?
THAT "AZRAEL BLOCK" THE QUEEN BEE PROGRAMMED INTO HIM--IT SHUT DOWN HIS MIND AND--
YEAH, BATMAN TOLD ME THE WHOLE STORY.
NO GUARANTEES-- BUT I'LL GIVE IT MY BEST SHOT.
I'M BRIMMING WITH CONFIDENCE.
OBERON... PLEASE!
MAX--TRUST HIM. IF ANYONE CAN DO IT--HE CAN.
I'M NOT EVEN CLEAR ON WHO HE IS!
6

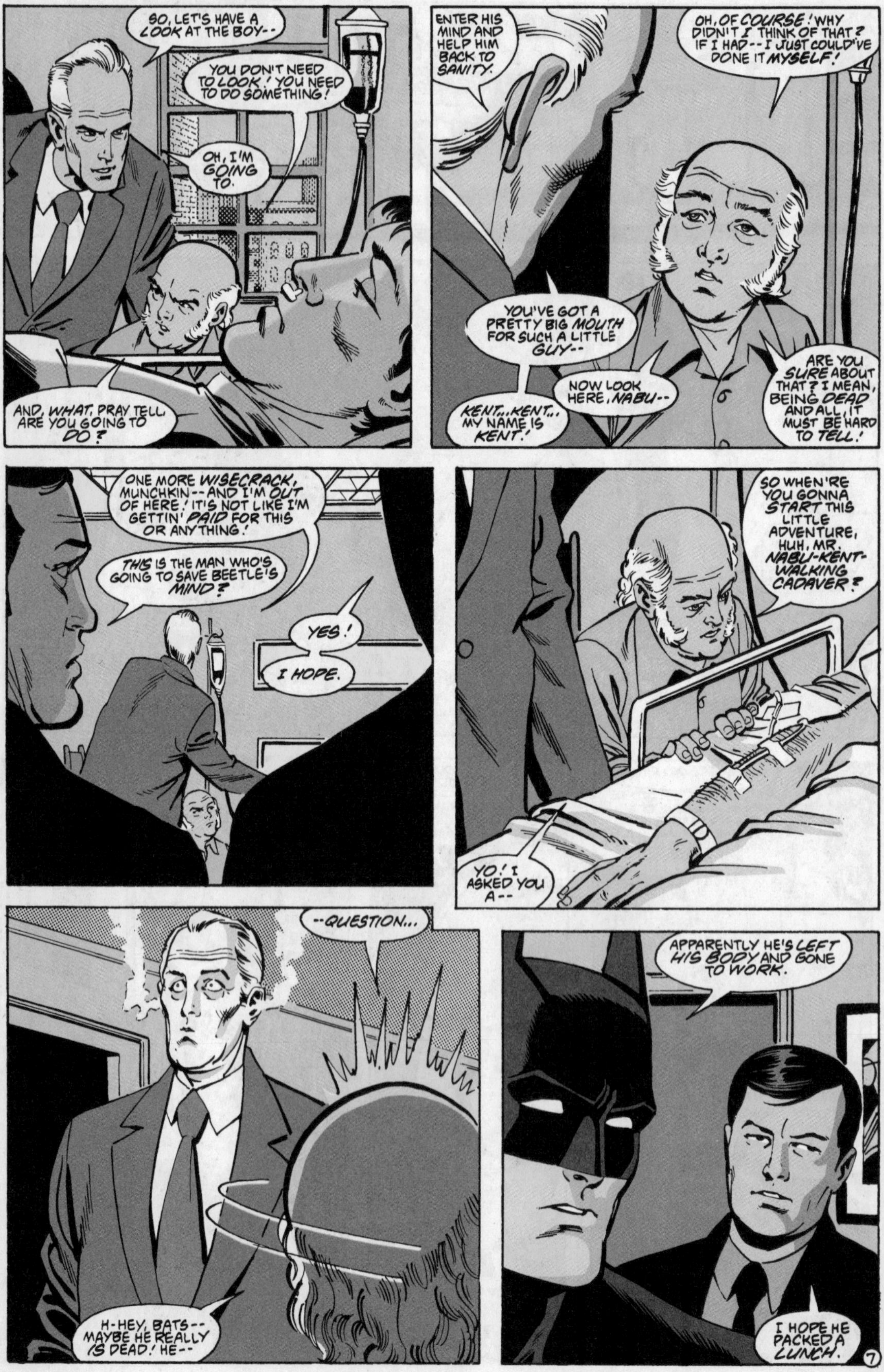
SO, LET'S HAVE A LOOK AT THE BOY--
YOU DON'T NEED TO LOOK! YOU NEED TO DO SOMETHING!
OH, I'M GOING TO.
AND, WHAT, PRAY TELL, ARE YOU GOING TO DO?
ENTER HIS MIND AND HELP HIM BACK TO SANITY.
OH, OF COURSE! WHY DIDN'T I THINK OF THAT? IF I HAD-- I JUST COULD'VE DONE IT MYSELF!
YOU'VE GOT A PRETTY BIG MOUTH FOR SUCH A LITTLE GUY--
KENT... KENT... MY NAME IS KENT!
NOW LOOK HERE, NABU--
ARE YOU SURE ABOUT THAT? I MEAN, BEING DEAD AND ALL, IT MUST BE HARD TO TELL!
ONE MORE WISECRACK, MUNCHKIN-- AND I'M OUT OF HERE! IT'S NOT LIKE I'M GETTIN' PAID FOR THIS OR ANYTHING!
THIS IS THE MAN WHO'S GOING TO SAVE BEETLE'S MIND?
YES!
I HOPE.
SO WHEN'RE YOU GONNA START THIS LITTLE ADVENTURE, HUH, MR. NABU-KENT-WALKING CADAVER?
YO! I ASKED YOU A--
--QUESTION...
H-HEY, BATS-- MAYBE HE REALLY IS DEAD! HE--
APPARENTLY HE'S LEFT HIS BODY AND GONE TO WORK.
I HOPE HE PACKED A LUNCH.
7

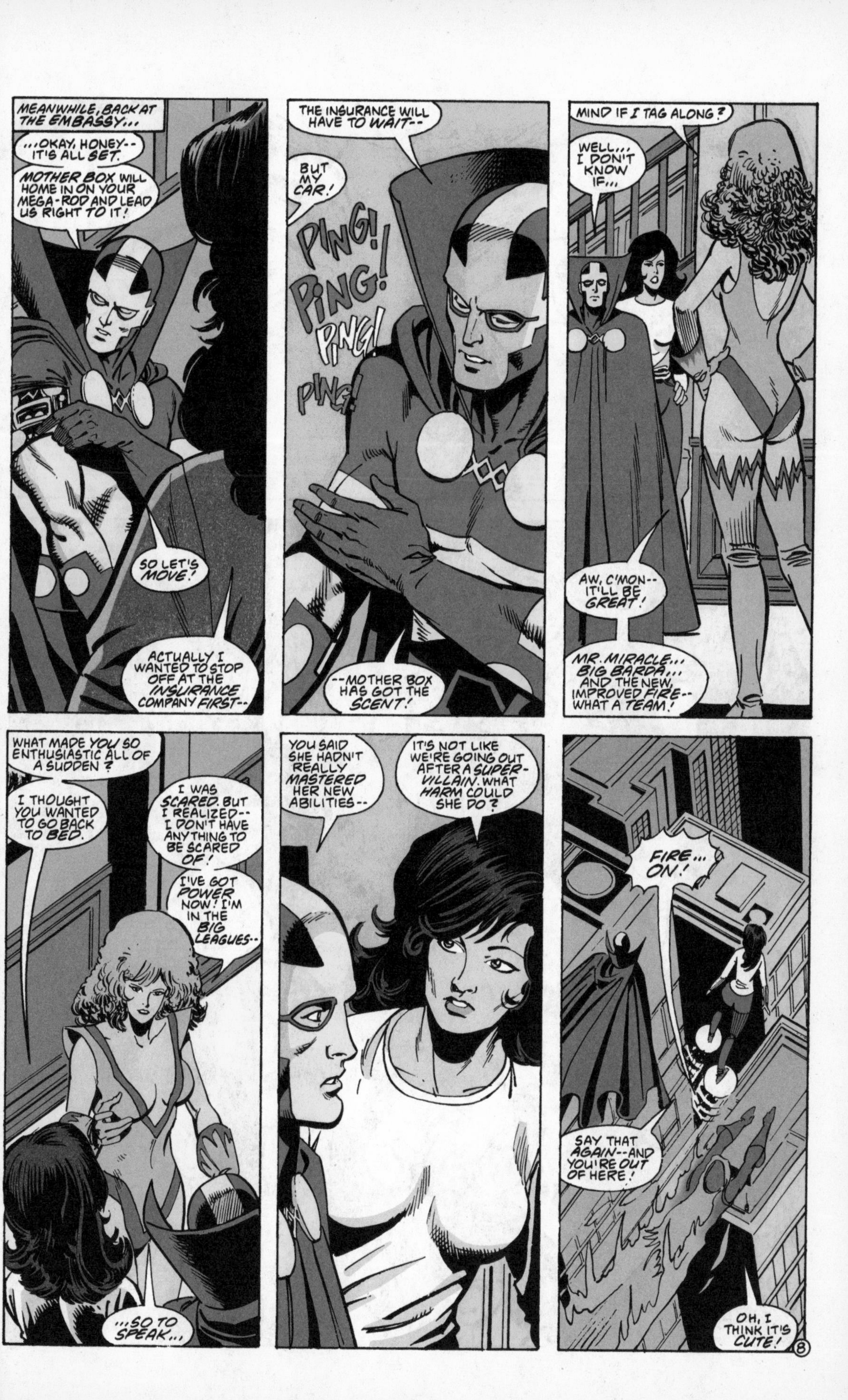
MEANWHILE, BACK AT THE EMBASSY...
...OKAY, HONEY-- IT'S ALL SET.
MOTHER BOX WILL HOME IN ON YOUR MEGA-ROD AND LEAD US RIGHT TO IT!
SO LET'S MOVE!
ACTUALLY I WANTED TO STOP OFF AT THE INSURANCE COMPANY FIRST--
THE INSURANCE WILL HAVE TO WAIT--
BUT MY CAR!
PING! PING! PING! PING!
--MOTHER BOX HAS GOT THE SCENT!
MIND IF I TAG ALONG?
WELL... I DON'T KNOW IF...
AW, C'MON-- IT'LL BE GREAT!
MR. MIRACLE... BIG BARDA... AND THE NEW, IMPROVED FIRE-- WHAT A TEAM!
WHAT MADE YOU SO ENTHUSIASTIC ALL OF A SUDDEN?
I THOUGHT YOU WANTED TO GO BACK TO BED.
I WAS SCARED. BUT I REALIZED-- I DON'T HAVE ANYTHING TO BE SCARED OF!
I'VE GOT POWER NOW! I'M IN THE BIG LEAGUES--
...SO TO SPEAK...
YOU SAID SHE HADN'T REALLY MASTERED HER NEW ABILITIES--
IT'S NOT LIKE WE'RE GOING OUT AFTER A SUPER-VILLAIN. WHAT HARM COULD SHE DO?
FIRE... ON!
SAY THAT AGAIN--AND YOU'RE OUT OF HERE!
OH, I THINK IT'S CUTE!
8

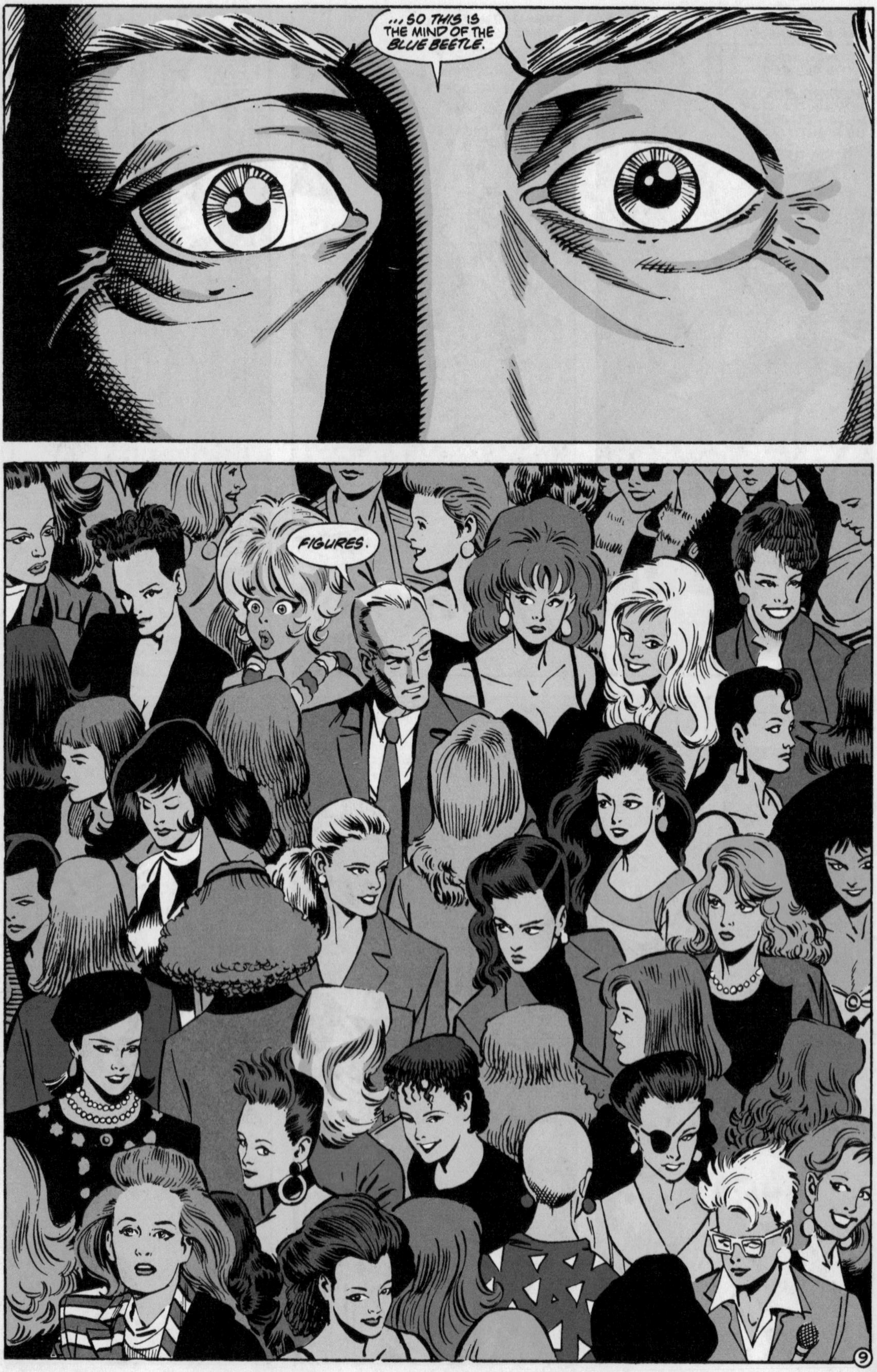
...SO THIS IS THE MIND OF THE BLUE BEETLE.
FIGURES.
9

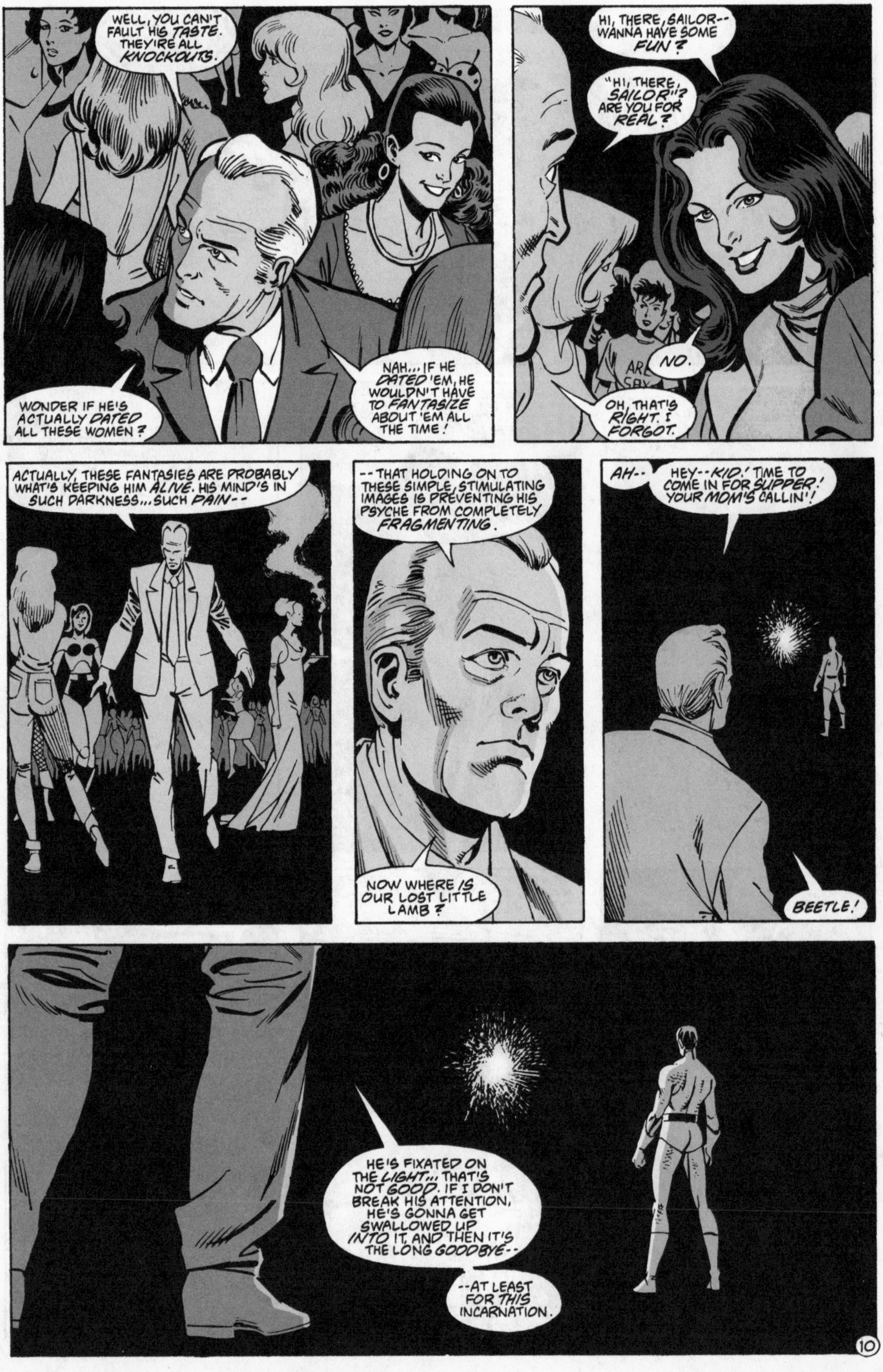
WELL, YOU CAN'T FAULT HIS TASTE. THEY'RE ALL KNOCKOUTS.
WONDER IF HE'S ACTUALLY DATED ALL THESE WOMEN?
NAH... IF HE DATED 'EM, HE WOULDN'T HAVE TO FANTASIZE ABOUT 'EM ALL THE TIME!
HI, THERE, SAILOR-- WANNA HAVE SOME FUN?
"HI, THERE, SAILOR"? ARE YOU FOR REAL?
NO.
OH, THAT'S RIGHT. I FORGOT.
ACTUALLY, THESE FANTASIES ARE PROBABLY WHAT'S KEEPING HIM ALIVE. HIS MIND'S IN SUCH DARKNESS... SUCH PAIN--
--THAT HOLDING ON TO THESE SIMPLE, STIMULATING IMAGES IS PREVENTING HIS PSYCHE FROM COMPLETELY FRAGMENTING.
NOW WHERE IS OUR LOST LITTLE LAMB?
AH--
HEY--KID! TIME TO COME IN FOR SUPPER! YOUR MOM'S CALLIN'!
BEETLE!
HE'S FIXATED ON THE LIGHT... THAT'S NOT GOOD. IF I DON'T BREAK HIS ATTENTION, HE'S GONNA GET SWALLOWED UP INTO IT, AND THEN IT'S THE LONG GOODBYE--
--AT LEAST FOR THIS INCARNATION.
10

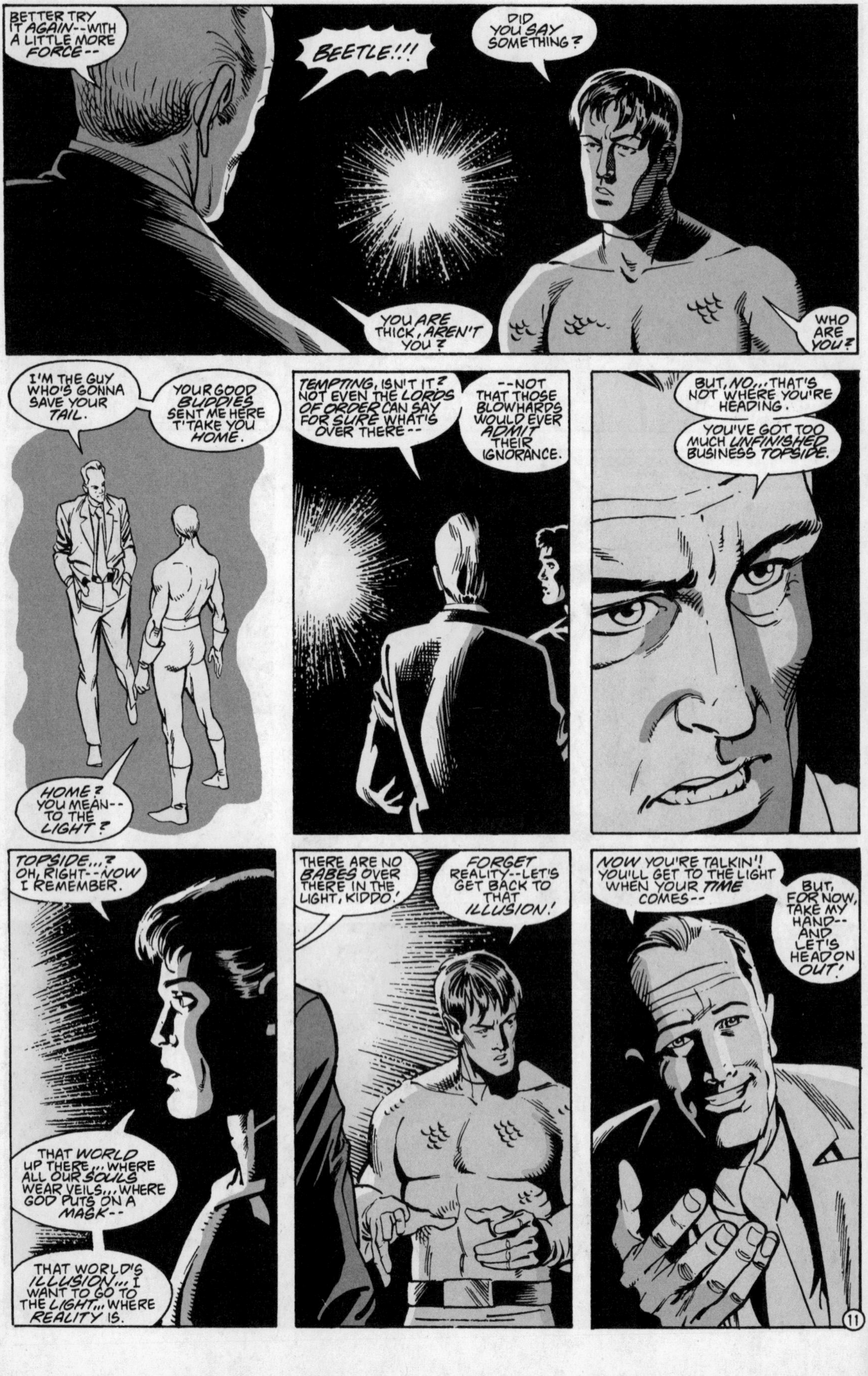
BETTER TRY IT AGAIN--WITH A LITTLE MORE FORCE--
BEETLE!!!
DID YOU SAY SOMETHING?
YOU ARE THICK, AREN'T YOU?
WHO ARE YOU?
I'M THE GUY WHO'S GONNA SAVE YOUR TAIL.
YOUR GOOD BUDDIES SENT ME HERE T'TAKE YOU HOME.
HOME? YOU MEAN-- TO THE LIGHT?
TEMPTING, ISN'T IT? NOT EVEN THE LORDS OF ORDER CAN SAY FOR SURE WHAT'S OVER THERE--
--NOT THAT THOSE BLOWHARDS WOULD EVER ADMIT THEIR IGNORANCE.
BUT, NO...THAT'S NOT WHERE YOU'RE HEADING.
YOU'VE GOT TOO MUCH UNFINISHED BUSINESS TOPSIDE.
TOPSIDE...? OH, RIGHT--NOW I REMEMBER.
THAT WORLD UP THERE... WHERE ALL OUR SOULS WEAR VEILS... WHERE GOD PUTS ON A MASK--
THAT WORLD'S ILLUSION... I WANT TO GO TO THE LIGHT... WHERE REALITY IS.
THERE ARE NO BABES OVER THERE IN THE LIGHT, KIDDO!
FORGET REALITY--LET'S GET BACK TO THAT ILLUSION!
NOW YOU'RE TALKIN'! YOU'LL GET TO THE LIGHT WHEN YOUR TIME COMES--
BUT, FOR NOW, TAKE MY HAND-- AND LET'S HEAD ON OUT!
11

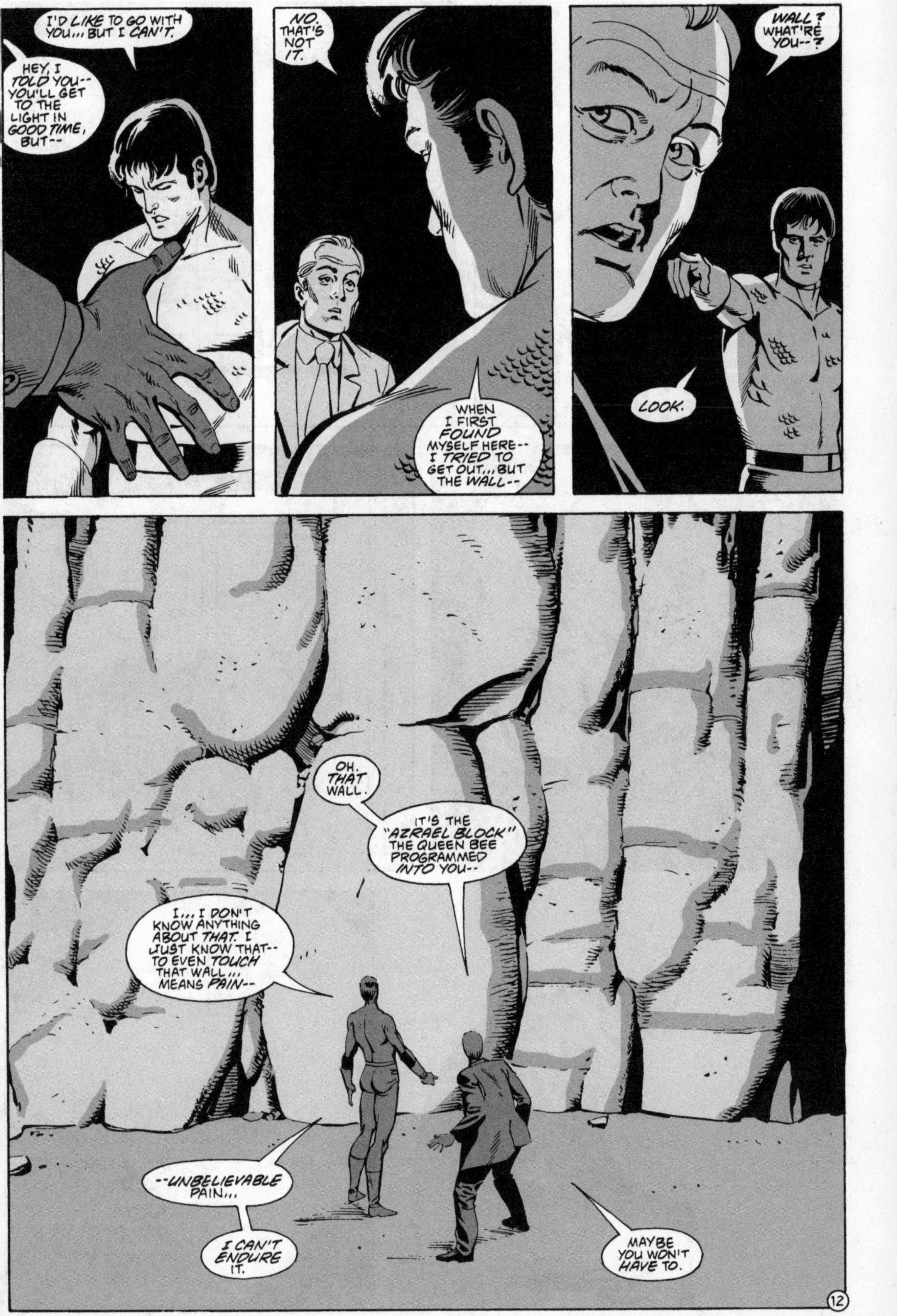
I'D LIKE TO GO WITH YOU... BUT I CAN'T.
HEY, I TOLD YOU-- YOU'LL GET TO THE LIGHT IN GOOD TIME, BUT--
NO. THAT'S NOT IT.
WHEN I FIRST FOUND MYSELF HERE-- I TRIED TO GET OUT... BUT THE WALL--
WALL? WHAT'RE YOU--?
LOOK.
OH. THAT WALL.
IT'S THE "AZRAEL BLOCK" THE QUEEN BEE PROGRAMMED INTO YOU--
I... I DON'T KNOW ANYTHING ABOUT THAT. I JUST KNOW THAT-- TO EVEN TOUCH THAT WALL... MEANS PAIN--
--UNBELIEVABLE PAIN...
I CAN'T ENDURE IT.
MAYBE YOU WON'T HAVE TO.
12

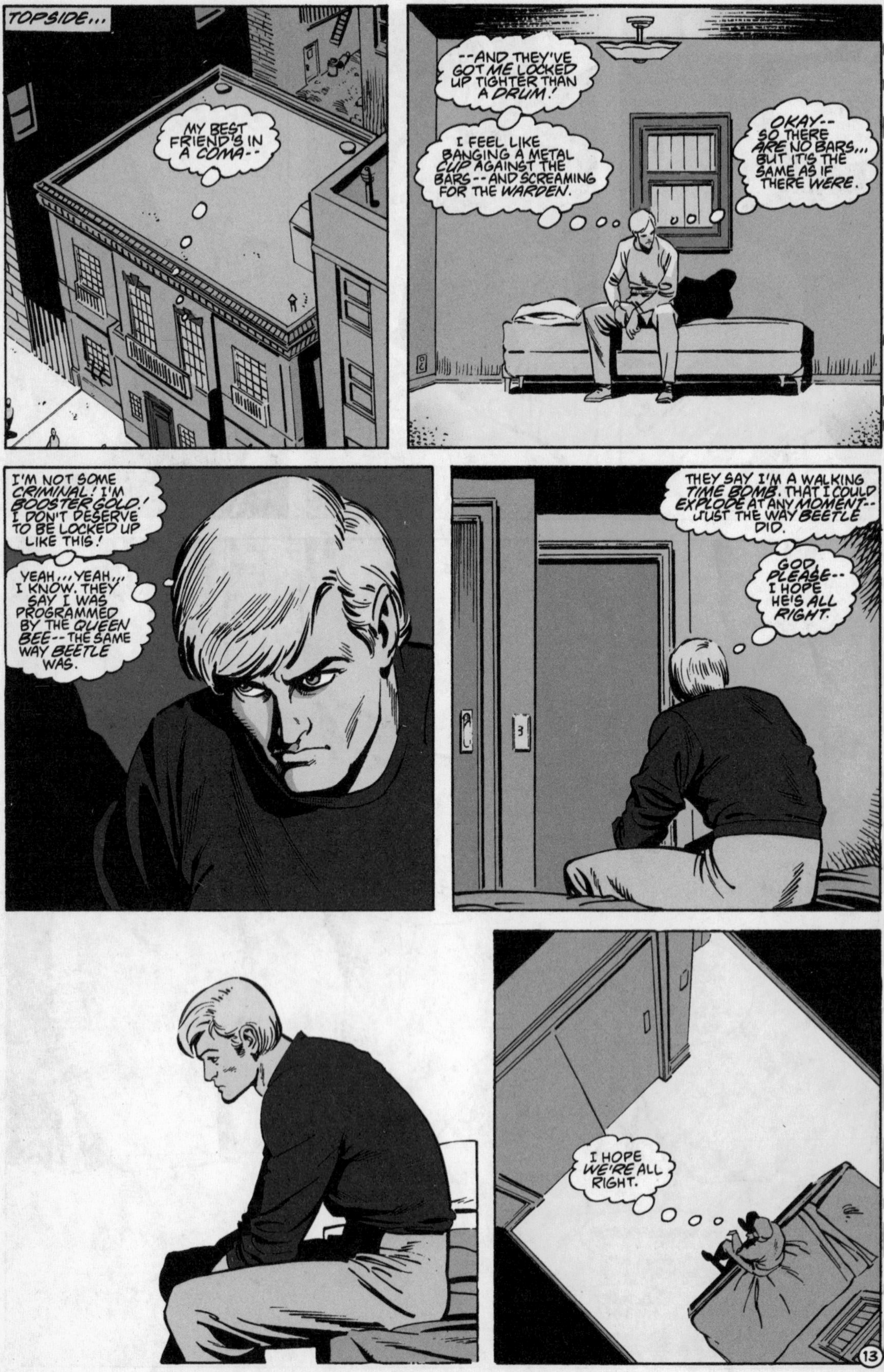
TOPSIDE...
MY BEST FRIEND'S IN A COMA--
--AND THEY'VE GOT ME LOCKED UP TIGHTER THAN A DRUM!
I FEEL LIKE BANGING A METAL CUP AGAINST THE BARS--AND SCREAMING FOR THE WARDEN.
OKAY-- SO THERE ARE NO BARS... BUT IT'S THE SAME AS IF THERE WERE.
I'M NOT SOME CRIMINAL! I'M BOOSTER GOLD! I DON'T DESERVE TO BE LOCKED UP LIKE THIS!
YEAH...YEAH... I KNOW. THEY SAY I WAS PROGRAMMED BY THE QUEEN BEE--THE SAME WAY BEETLE WAS.
THEY SAY I'M A WALKING TIME BOMB. THAT I COULD EXPLODE AT ANY MOMENT-- JUST THE WAY BEETLE DID.
GOD, PLEASE-- I HOPE HE'S ALL RIGHT.
I HOPE WE'RE ALL RIGHT.
13

"...THIS HAS BEEN GOIN' ON TOO LONG.

I AGREE.

BEETLE'S LIFE IS AT STAKE HERE-- SOME CRACKPOT IS MESSING WITH HIS MIND--

--AND WE'RE JUST SUPPOSED TO STAND HERE AND LET IT GO ON INDEFINITELY?

YES.

UNLESS, OF COURSE, YOU'VE GOT A BETTER IDEA?

YOU KNOW I DON'T! EVERY DOCTOR THAT'S LOOKED AT HIM HAS SAID IT'S HOPELESS-- THAT IT'S JUST A MATTER OF TIME TILL HE DIES!

THEN WE WAIT.

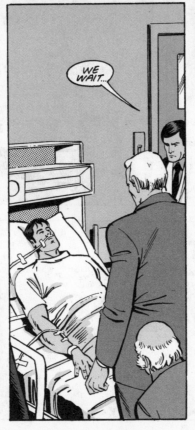

WE WAIT...

...AND JUST HOPE FOR THE BEST.

14

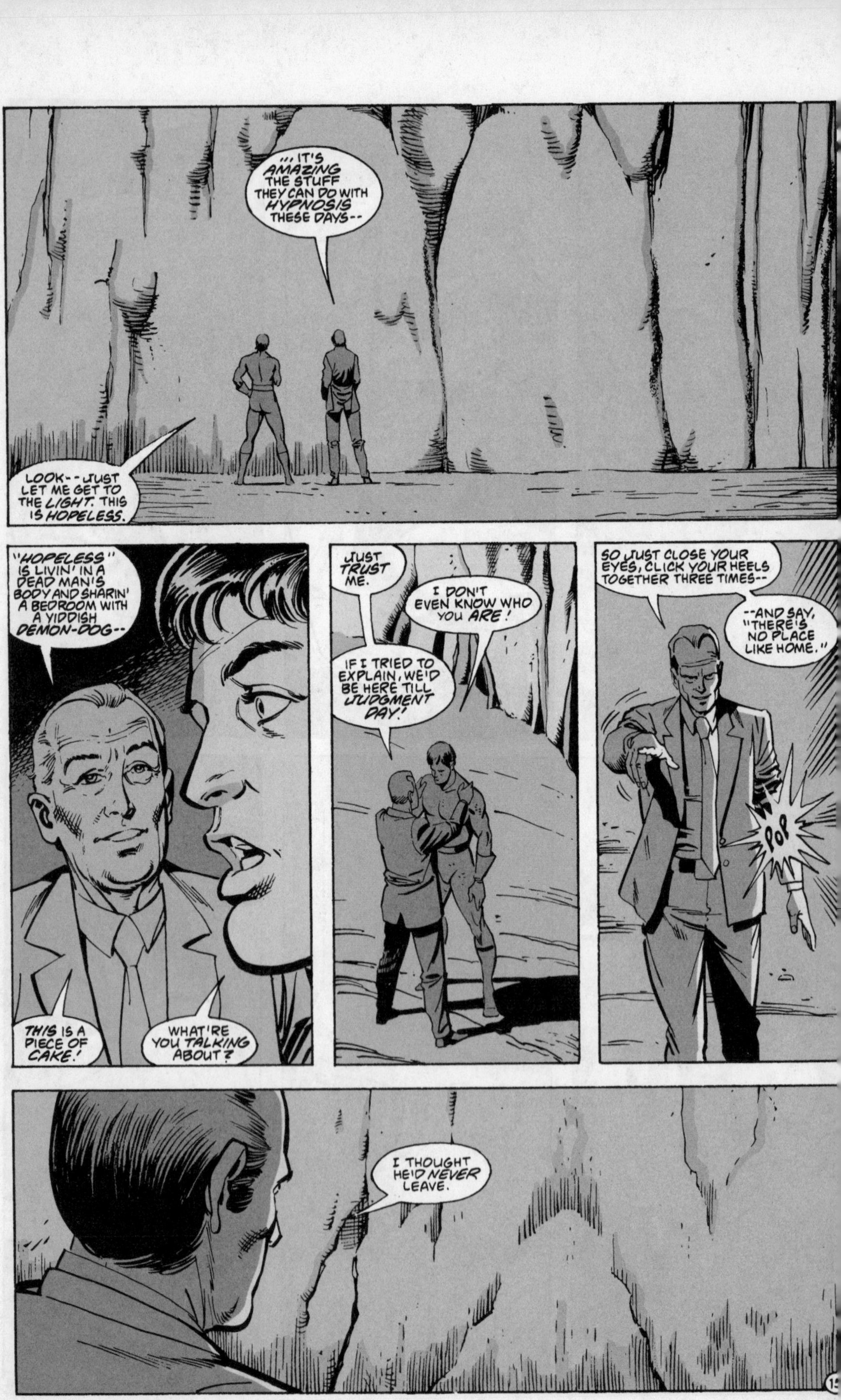

...IT'S AMAZING THE STUFF THEY CAN DO WITH HYPNOSIS THESE DAYS--
LOOK--JUST LET ME GET TO THE LIGHT. THIS IS HOPELESS.
"HOPELESS" IS LIVIN' IN A DEAD MAN'S BODY AND SHARIN' A BEDROOM WITH A YIDDISH DEMON-DOG--
THIS IS A PIECE OF CAKE!
WHAT'RE YOU TALKING ABOUT?
JUST TRUST ME.
I DON'T EVEN KNOW WHO YOU ARE!
IF I TRIED TO EXPLAIN, WE'D BE HERE TILL JUDGMENT DAY!
SO JUST CLOSE YOUR EYES, CLICK YOUR HEELS TOGETHER THREE TIMES--
--AND SAY, "THERE'S NO PLACE LIKE HOME."
POP
I THOUGHT HE'D NEVER LEAVE.

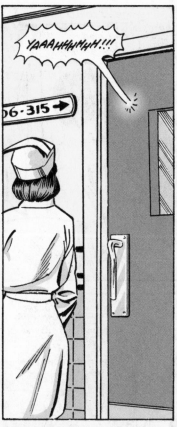

YAAAHHHHH!!!

06·315 →

I'M OLD! I'M OLD!

THAT WITCH WALLER--WHAT'D SHE DO TO ME?!?

BEETLE... IS THAT YOU?

OF COURSE IT'S ME! AT LEAST I THINK IT'S ME!

BUT WHAT HAPPENED? HOW DID WALLER--

WALLER HAD NOTHIN' T'DO WITH IT. IT WAS THAT NUTTY OLD MAN.

"OLD MAN"?

WAIT A MINUTE! THE LIGHT... THE OLD MAN... IT--

IT WAS REAL.

MY GOD-- HE TRADED BODIES WITH ME!

OF COURSE HE WOULD! I'M YOUNG... VIRILE... HANDSOME BEYOND WORDS!

WHAT AN EVIL SCHEME! WHAT A MONSTROUS--

BEETLE--LOOK AT THE BED.

THE BED? WHAT ARE YOU--?

THAT'S ME! OR IS IT HIM?

IS HE ALIVE? AM I ALIVE?! I DON'T UNDERSTAND ANY OF THIS!

I WANT MY MOTHER!!

16

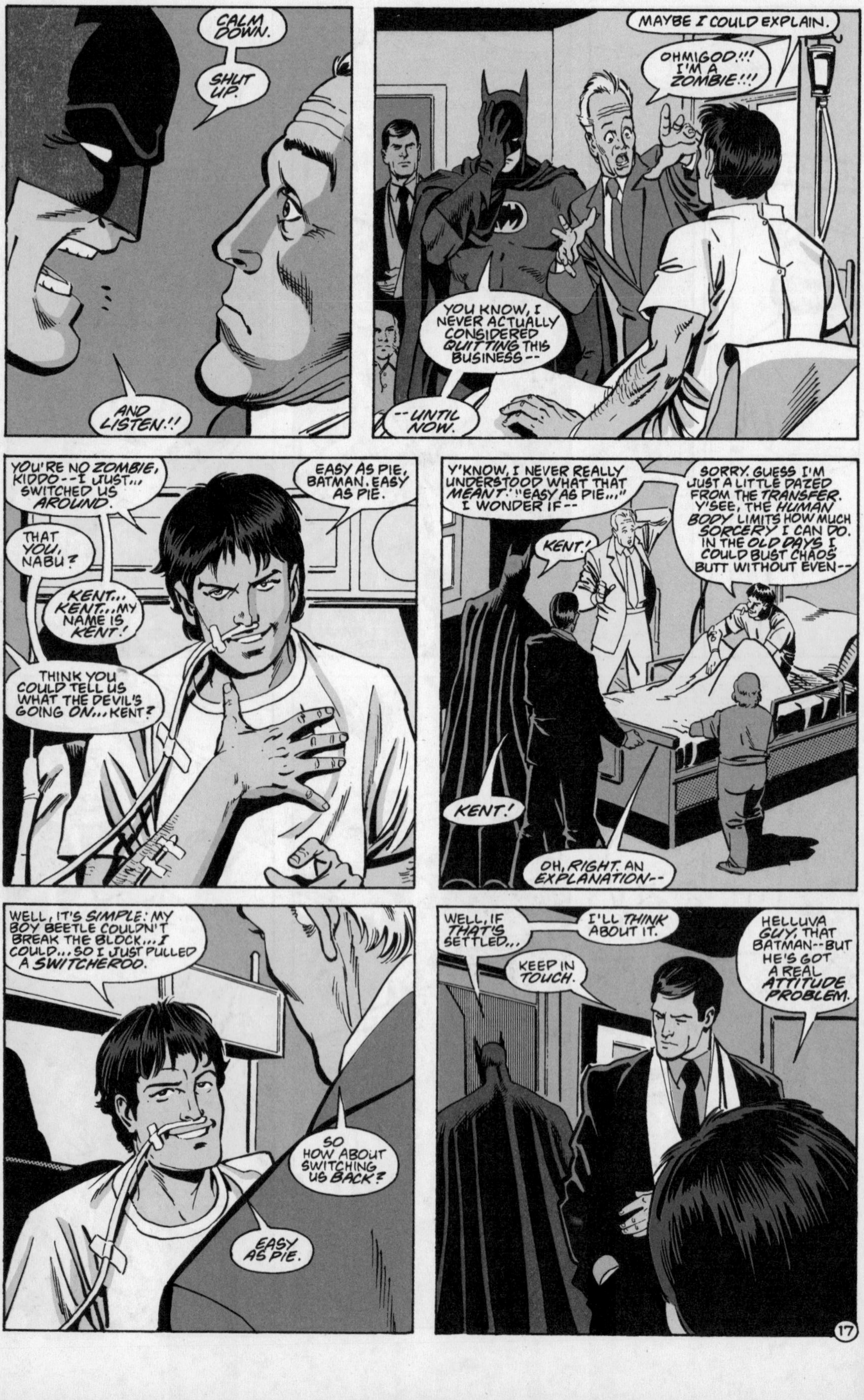
CALM DOWN.
SHUT UP.
AND LISTEN!!
MAYBE I COULD EXPLAIN.
OHMIGOD!!! I'M A ZOMBIE!!!
YOU KNOW, I NEVER ACTUALLY CONSIDERED QUITTING THIS BUSINESS --
-- UNTIL NOW.
YOU'RE NO ZOMBIE, KIDDO -- I JUST... SWITCHED US AROUND.
EASY AS PIE, BATMAN. EASY AS PIE.
THAT YOU, NABU?
KENT... KENT... MY NAME IS KENT!
THINK YOU COULD TELL US WHAT THE DEVIL'S GOING ON... KENT?
Y'KNOW, I NEVER REALLY UNDERSTOOD WHAT THAT MEANT: "EASY AS PIE..." I WONDER IF --
KENT!
SORRY. GUESS I'M JUST A LITTLE DAZED FROM THE TRANSFER. Y'SEE, THE HUMAN BODY LIMITS HOW MUCH SORCERY I CAN DO. IN THE OLD DAYS I COULD BUST CHAOS' BUTT WITHOUT EVEN --
KENT!
OH, RIGHT. AN EXPLANATION --
WELL, IT'S SIMPLE: MY BOY BEETLE COULDN'T BREAK THE BLOCK... I COULD... SO I JUST PULLED A SWITCHEROO.
SO HOW ABOUT SWITCHING US BACK?
EASY AS PIE.
WELL, IF THAT'S SETTLED...
I'LL THINK ABOUT IT.
KEEP IN TOUCH.
HELLUVA GUY, THAT BATMAN -- BUT HE'S GOT A REAL ATTITUDE PROBLEM.
17

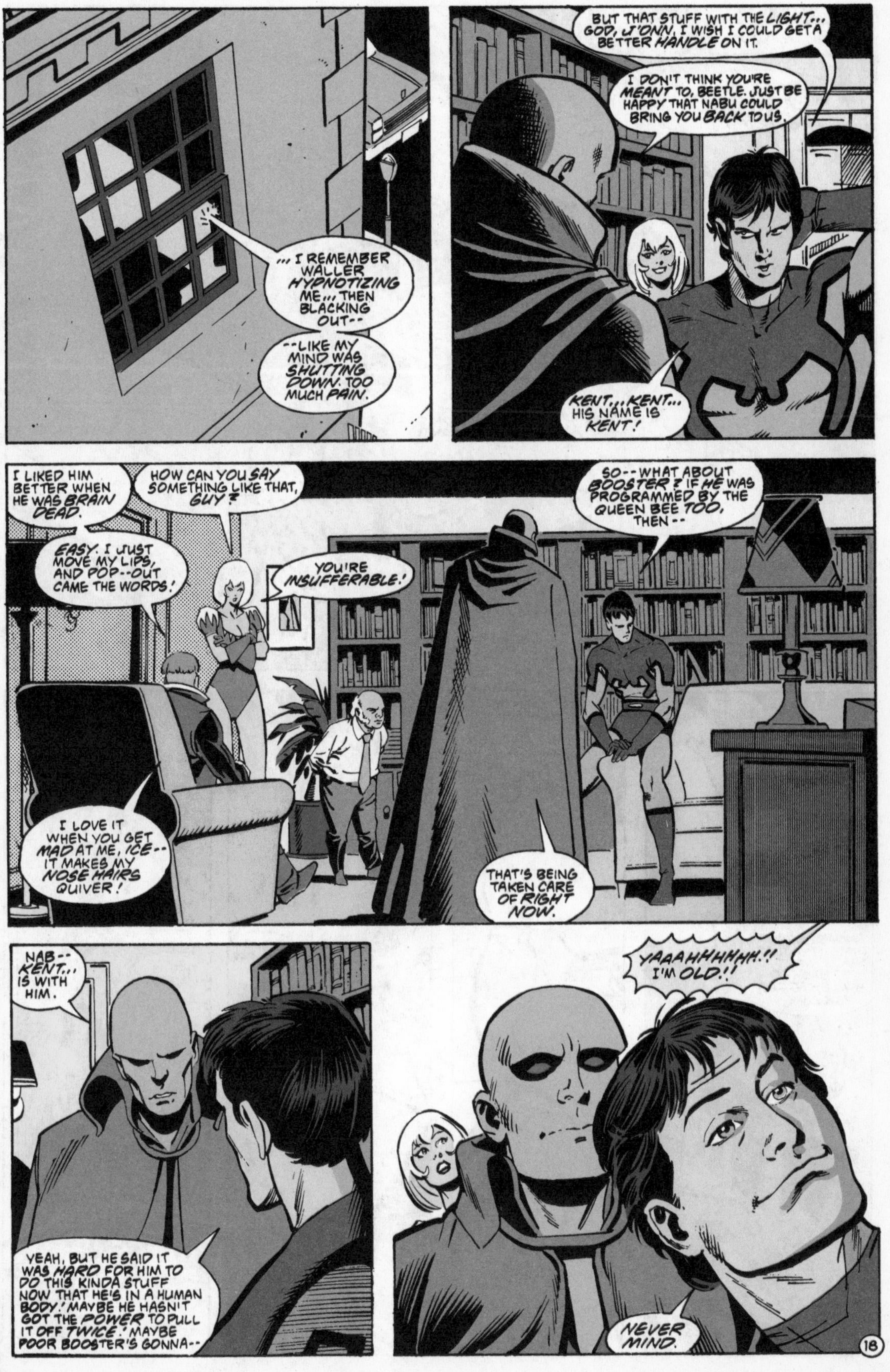
...I REMEMBER WALLER HYPNOTIZING ME... THEN BLACKING OUT--
--LIKE MY MIND WAS SHUTTING DOWN. TOO MUCH PAIN.
BUT THAT STUFF WITH THE LIGHT... GOD, J'ONN, I WISH I COULD GET A BETTER HANDLE ON IT.
I DON'T THINK YOU'RE MEANT TO, BEETLE. JUST BE HAPPY THAT NABU COULD BRING YOU BACK TO US.
KENT... KENT... HIS NAME IS KENT!
I LIKED HIM BETTER WHEN HE WAS BRAIN DEAD.
HOW CAN YOU SAY SOMETHING LIKE THAT, GUY?
EASY. I JUST MOVE MY LIPS, AND POP--OUT CAME THE WORDS!
YOU'RE INSUFFERABLE!
I LOVE IT WHEN YOU GET MAD AT ME, ICE-- IT MAKES MY NOSE HAIRS QUIVER!
SO--WHAT ABOUT BOOSTER? IF HE WAS PROGRAMMED BY THE QUEEN BEE TOO, THEN--
THAT'S BEING TAKEN CARE OF RIGHT NOW.
NAB-- KENT... IS WITH HIM.
YEAH, BUT HE SAID IT WAS HARD FOR HIM TO DO THIS KINDA STUFF NOW THAT HE'S IN A HUMAN BODY! MAYBE HE HASN'T GOT THE POWER TO PULL IT OFF TWICE! MAYBE POOR BOOSTER'S GONNA--
YAAAHHHHHH!! I'M OLD!!
NEVER MIND.
18

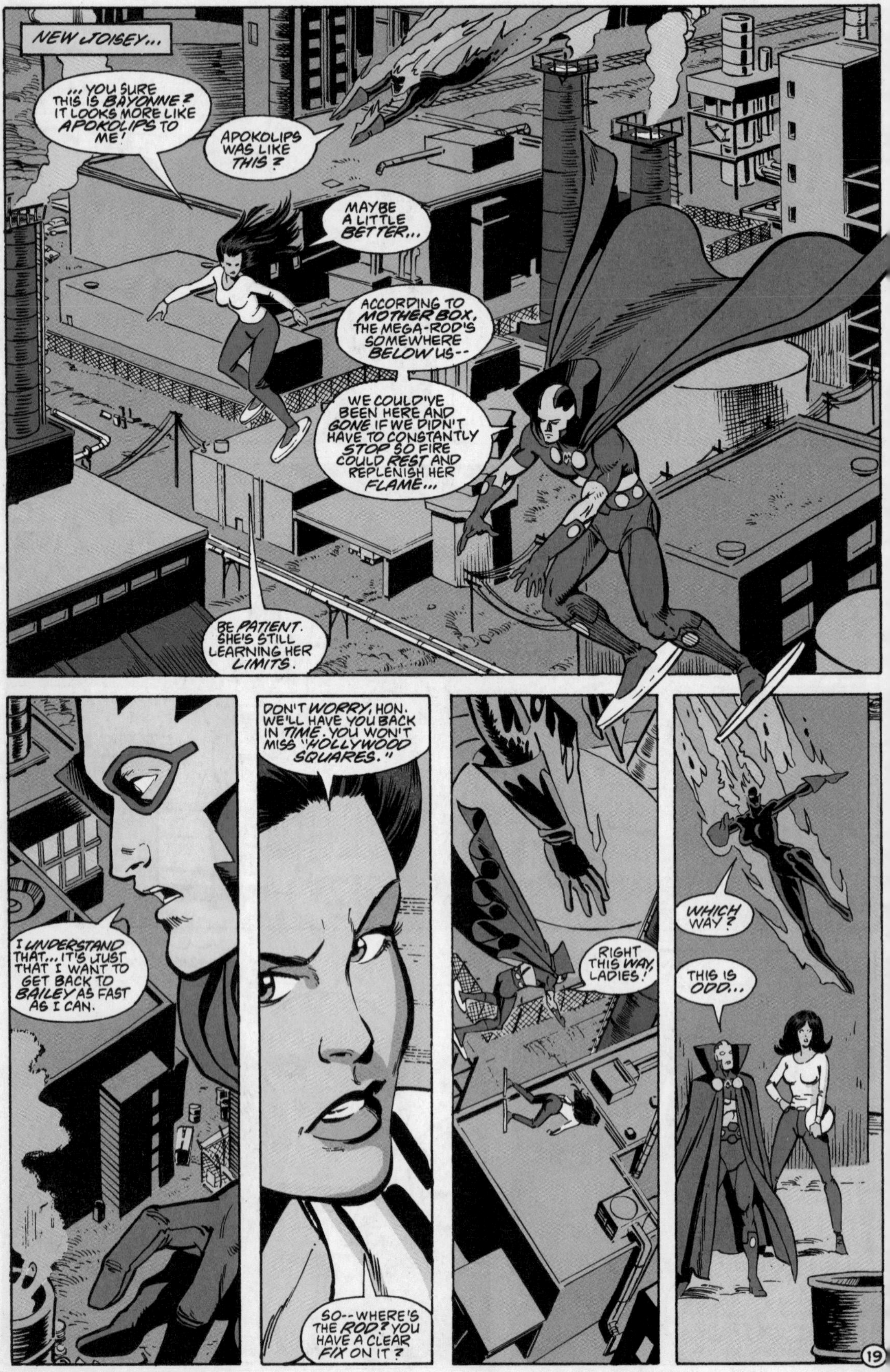

NEW JOISEY...
...YOU SURE THIS IS BAYONNE? IT LOOKS MORE LIKE APOKOLIPS TO ME!
APOKOLIPS WAS LIKE THIS?
MAYBE A LITTLE BETTER...
ACCORDING TO MOTHER BOX, THE MEGA-ROD'S SOMEWHERE BELOW US--
WE COULD'VE BEEN HERE AND GONE IF WE DIDN'T HAVE TO CONSTANTLY STOP SO FIRE COULD REST AND REPLENISH HER FLAME...
BE PATIENT. SHE'S STILL LEARNING HER LIMITS.
I UNDERSTAND THAT... IT'S JUST THAT I WANT TO GET BACK TO BAILEY AS FAST AS I CAN.
DON'T WORRY, HON. WE'LL HAVE YOU BACK IN TIME. YOU WON'T MISS "HOLLYWOOD SQUARES."
SO--WHERE'S THE ROD? YOU HAVE A CLEAR FIX ON IT?
RIGHT THIS WAY, LADIES!
WHICH WAY?
THIS IS ODD...
19

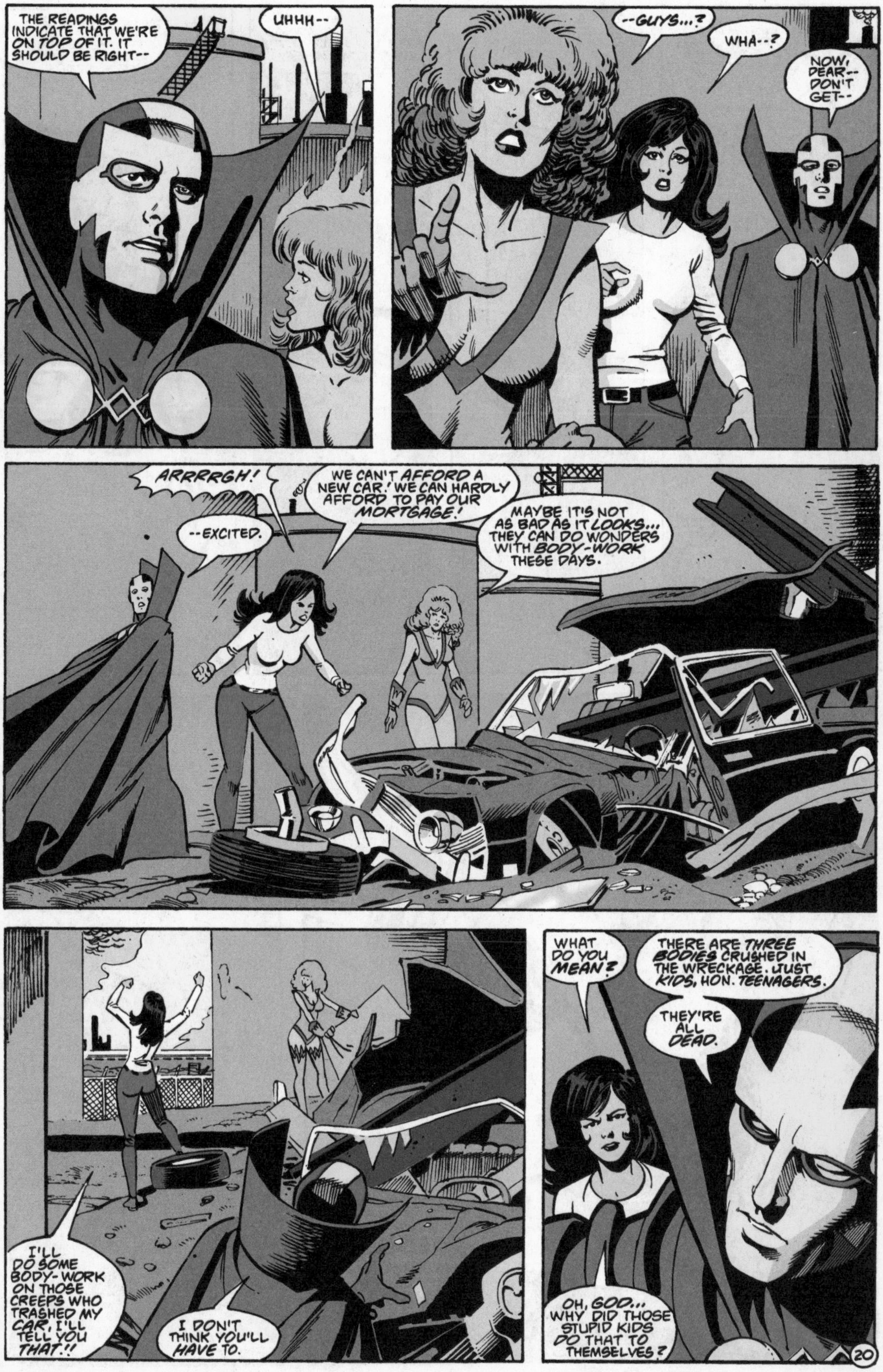
THE READINGS INDICATE THAT WE'RE ON TOP OF IT. IT SHOULD BE RIGHT--
UHHH--
--GUYS...?
WHA--?
NOW, DEAR-- DON'T GET--
ARRRRGH!
--EXCITED.
WE CAN'T AFFORD A NEW CAR! WE CAN HARDLY AFFORD TO PAY OUR MORTGAGE!
MAYBE IT'S NOT AS BAD AS IT LOOKS... THEY CAN DO WONDERS WITH BODY-WORK THESE DAYS.
I'LL DO SOME BODY-WORK ON THOSE CREEPS WHO TRASHED MY CAR, I'LL TELL YOU THAT!!
I DON'T THINK YOU'LL HAVE TO.
WHAT DO YOU MEAN?
THERE ARE THREE BODIES CRUSHED IN THE WRECKAGE. JUST KIDS, HON. TEENAGERS.
THEY'RE ALL DEAD.
OH, GOD... WHY DID THOSE STUPID KIDS DO THAT TO THEMSELVES?
20

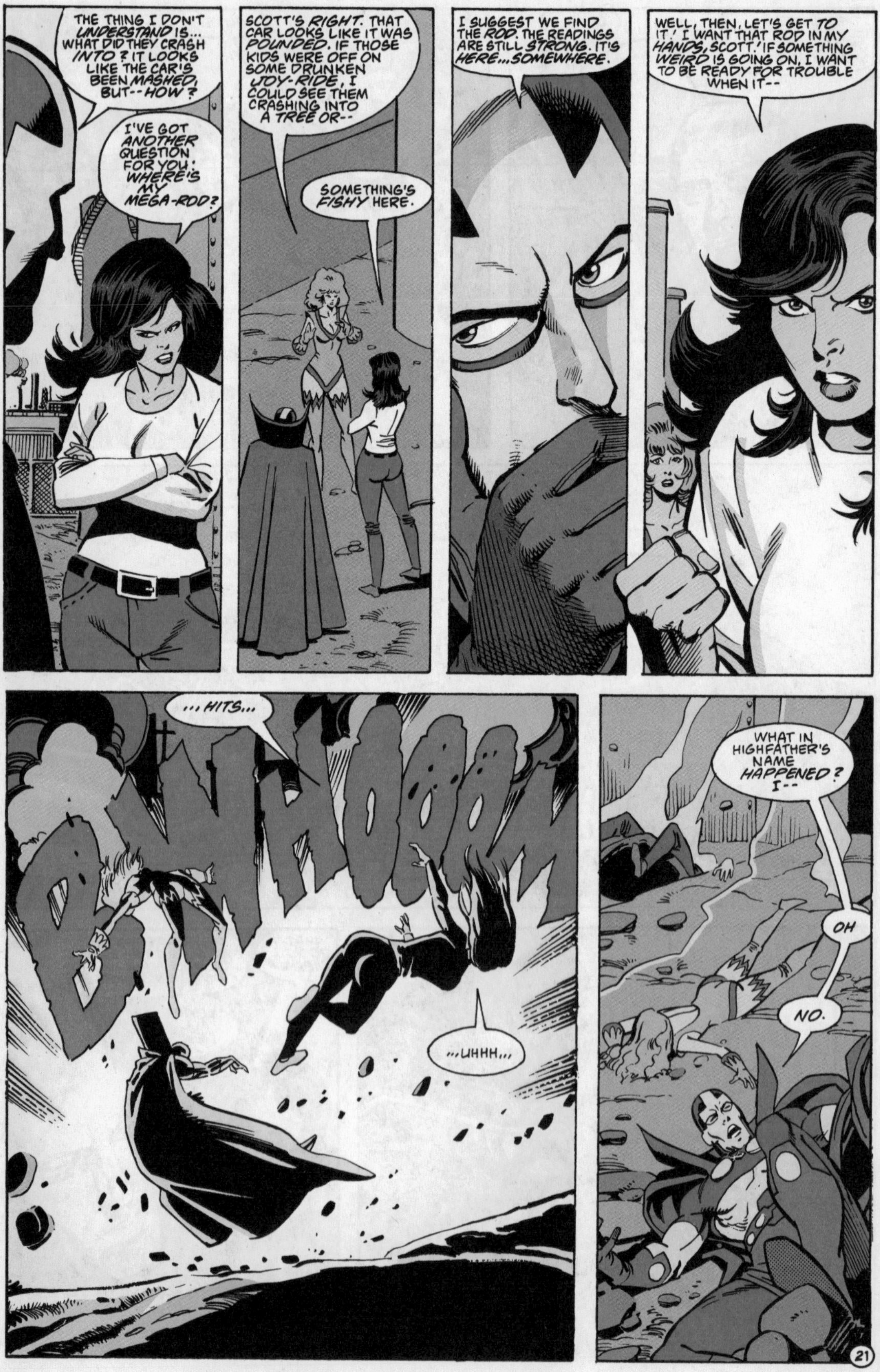

THE THING I DON'T UNDERSTAND IS... WHAT DID THEY CRASH INTO? IT LOOKS LIKE THE CAR'S BEEN MASHED, BUT--HOW?
I'VE GOT ANOTHER QUESTION FOR YOU: WHERE'S MY MEGA-ROD?
SCOTT'S RIGHT. THAT CAR LOOKS LIKE IT WAS POUNDED. IF THOSE KIDS WERE OFF ON SOME DRUNKEN JOY-RIDE, I COULD SEE THEM CRASHING INTO A TREE OR--
SOMETHING'S FISHY HERE.
I SUGGEST WE FIND THE ROD. THE READINGS ARE STILL STRONG. IT'S HERE...SOMEWHERE.
WELL, THEN, LET'S GET TO IT! I WANT THAT ROD IN MY HANDS, SCOTT! IF SOMETHING WEIRD IS GOING ON, I WANT TO BE READY FOR TROUBLE WHEN IT--
...HITS...
...UHHH...
WHAT IN HIGHFATHER'S NAME HAPPENED? I--
OH
NO.

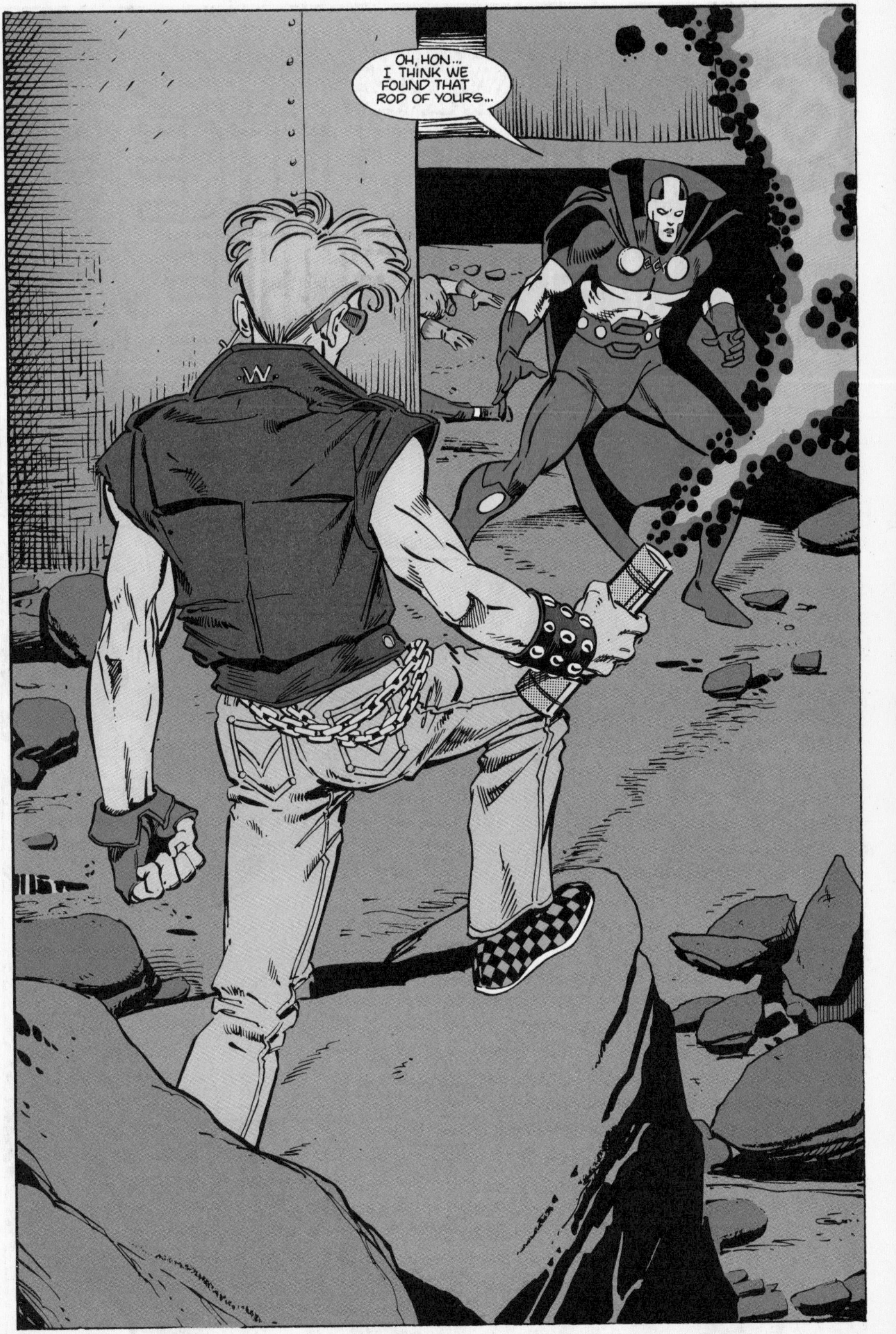
OH, HON...
I THINK WE
FOUND THAT
ROD OF YOURS...

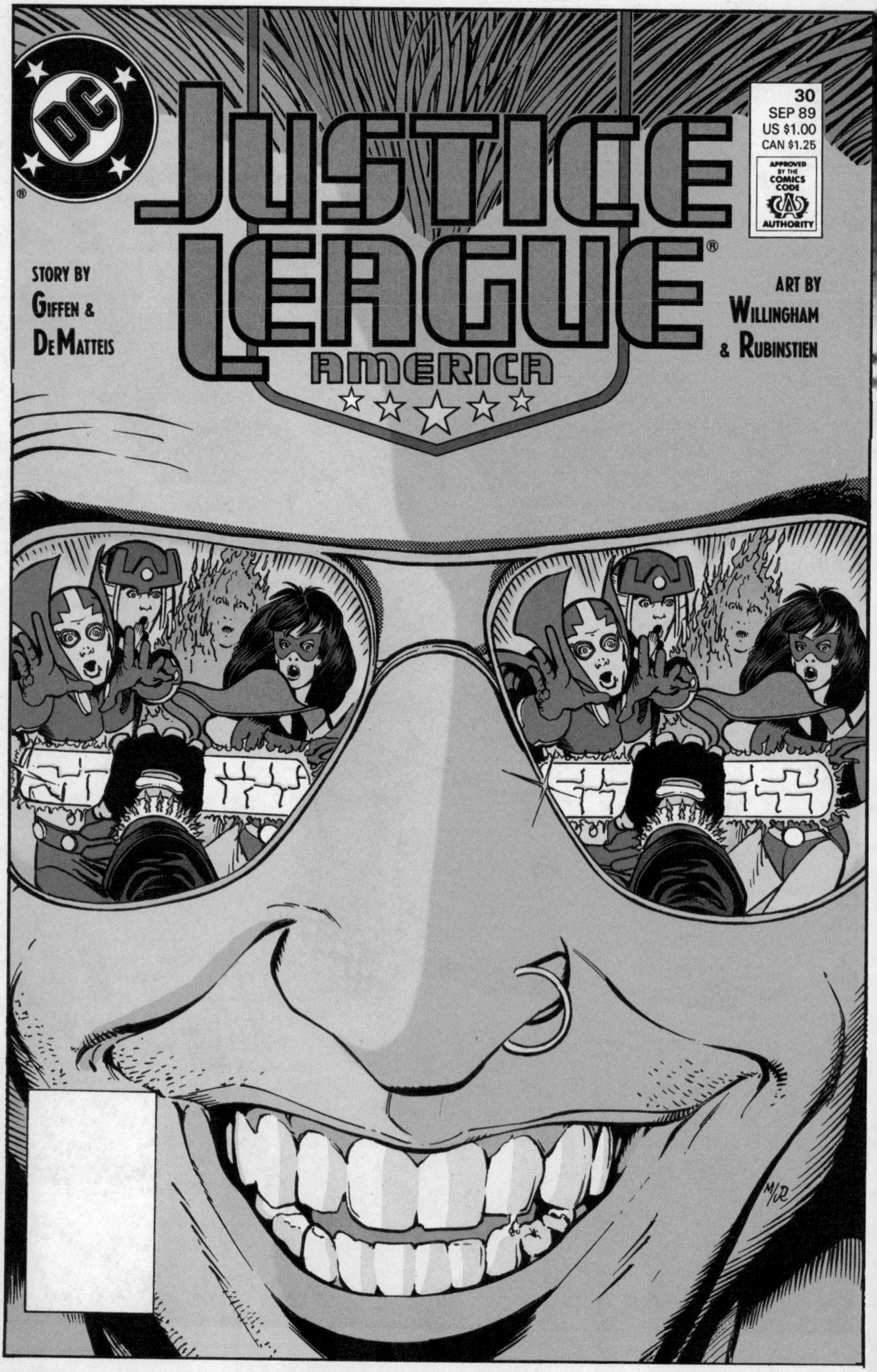
DC
JUSTICE LEAGUE AMERICA
30
SEP 89
US $1.00
CAN $1.25
APPROVED BY THE COMICS CODE AUTHORITY
STORY BY
GIFFEN &
DEMATTEIS
ART BY
WILLINGHAM
& RUBINSTIEN

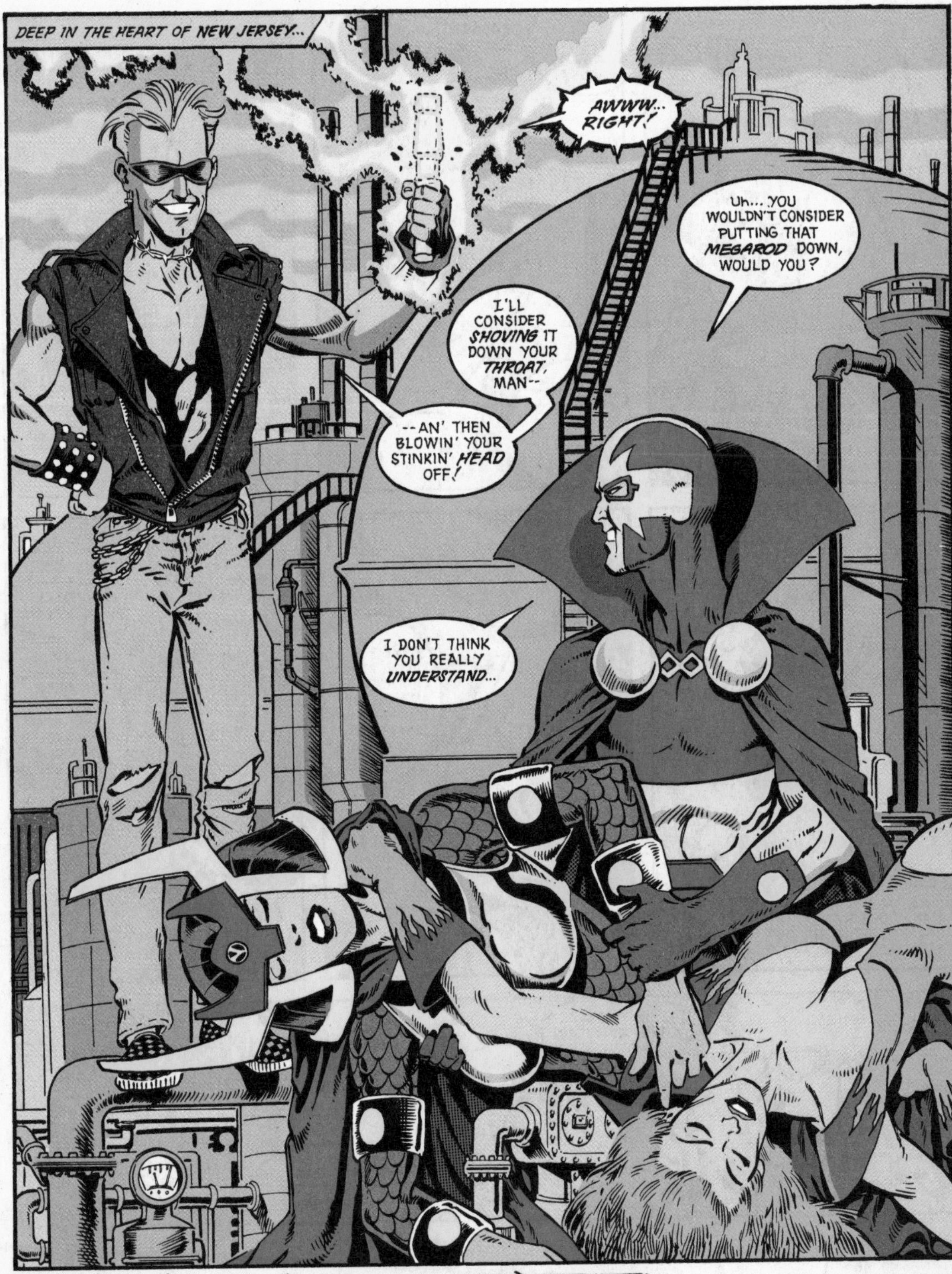
DEEP IN THE HEART OF NEW JERSEY...
AWWW... RIGHT!
Uh... YOU WOULDN'T CONSIDER PUTTING THAT MEGAROD DOWN, WOULD YOU?
I'LL CONSIDER SHOVING IT DOWN YOUR THROAT, MAN--
--AN' THEN BLOWIN' YOUR STINKIN' HEAD OFF!
I DON'T THINK YOU REALLY UNDERSTAND...

TEENAGE BIKER MEGA-DEATH!

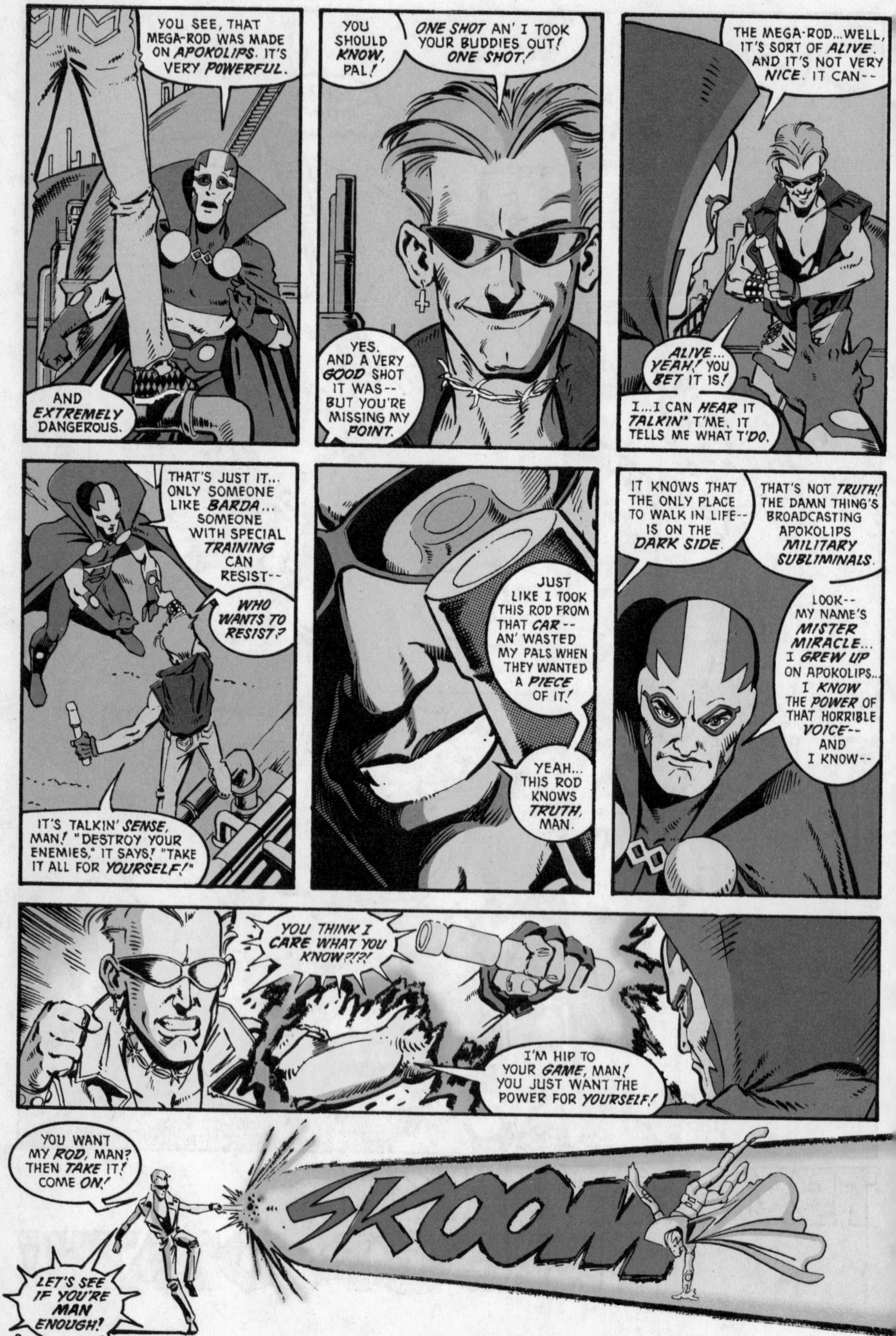

YOU SEE, THAT MEGA-ROD WAS MADE ON APOKOLIPS. IT'S VERY POWERFUL.
AND EXTREMELY DANGEROUS.
YOU SHOULD KNOW, PAL!
ONE SHOT AN' I TOOK YOUR BUDDIES OUT! ONE SHOT!
YES. AND A VERY GOOD SHOT IT WAS-- BUT YOU'RE MISSING MY POINT.
THE MEGA-ROD...WELL, IT'S SORT OF ALIVE. AND IT'S NOT VERY NICE. IT CAN--
ALIVE... YEAH! YOU BET IT IS!
I...I CAN HEAR IT TALKIN' T'ME, IT TELLS ME WHAT T'DO.
THAT'S JUST IT... ONLY SOMEONE LIKE BARDA... SOMEONE WITH SPECIAL TRAINING CAN RESIST--
WHO WANTS TO RESIST?
IT'S TALKIN' SENSE, MAN! "DESTROY YOUR ENEMIES," IT SAYS! "TAKE IT ALL FOR YOURSELF!"
JUST LIKE I TOOK THIS ROD FROM THAT CAR-- AN' WASTED MY PALS WHEN THEY WANTED A PIECE OF IT!
YEAH... THIS ROD KNOWS TRUTH, MAN.
IT KNOWS THAT THE ONLY PLACE TO WALK IN LIFE-- IS ON THE DARK SIDE.
THAT'S NOT TRUTH! THE DAMN THING'S BROADCASTING APOKOLIPS MILITARY SUBLIMINALS.
LOOK-- MY NAME'S MISTER MIRACLE... I GREW UP ON APOKOLIPS... I KNOW THE POWER OF THAT HORRIBLE VOICE-- AND I KNOW--
YOU THINK I CARE WHAT YOU KNOW?!?!
I'M HIP TO YOUR GAME, MAN! YOU JUST WANT THE POWER FOR YOURSELF!
YOU WANT MY ROD, MAN? THEN TAKE IT! COME ON!
SKOOM
LET'S SEE IF YOU'RE MAN ENOUGH!
2.

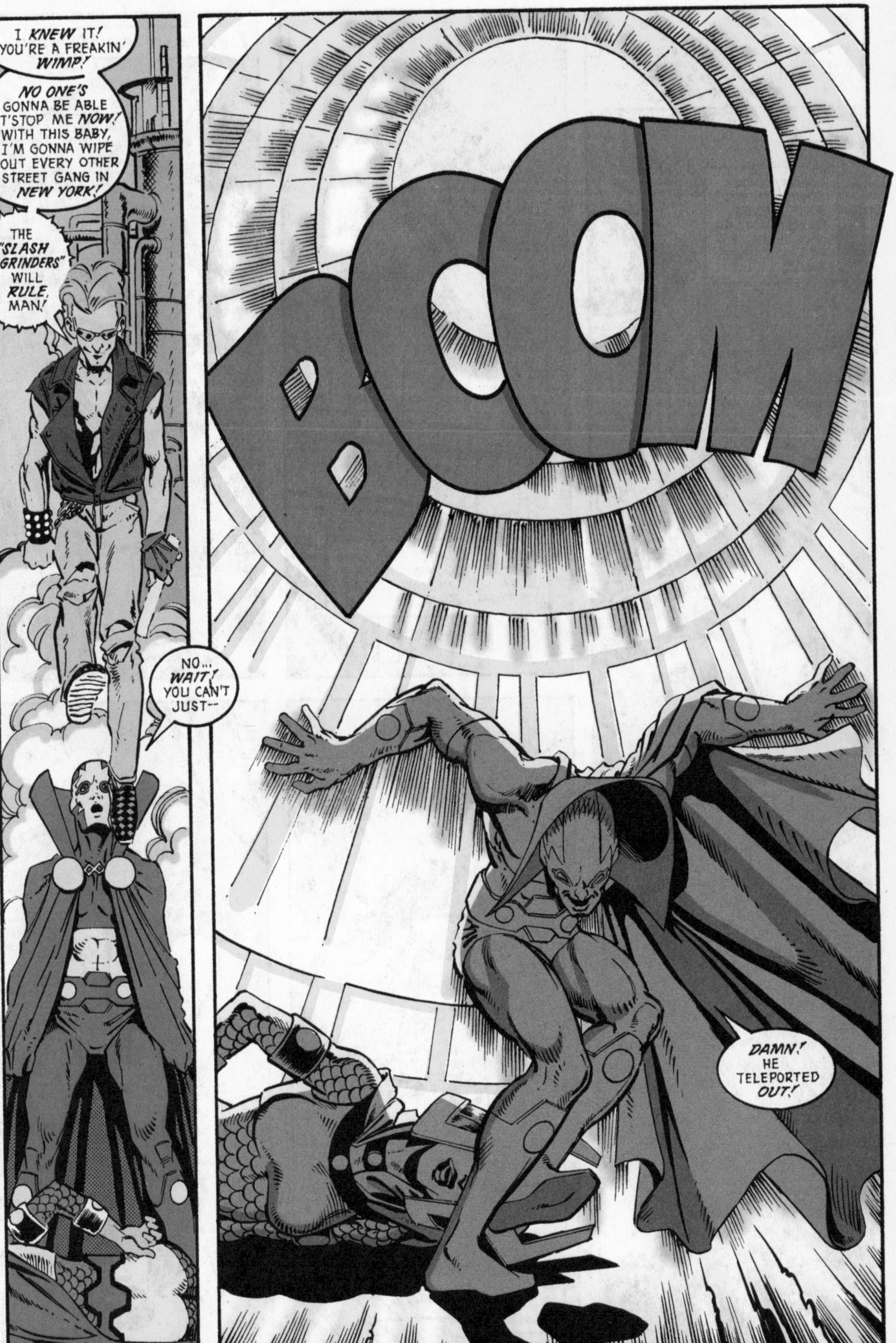
I KNEW IT! YOU'RE A FREAKIN' WIMP!
NO ONE'S GONNA BE ABLE T'STOP ME NOW! WITH THIS BABY, I'M GONNA WIPE OUT EVERY OTHER STREET GANG IN NEW YORK!
THE "SLASH GRINDERS" WILL RULE, MAN!
NO... WAIT! YOU CAN'T JUST--
BOOM
DAMN! HE TELEPORTED OUT!
3

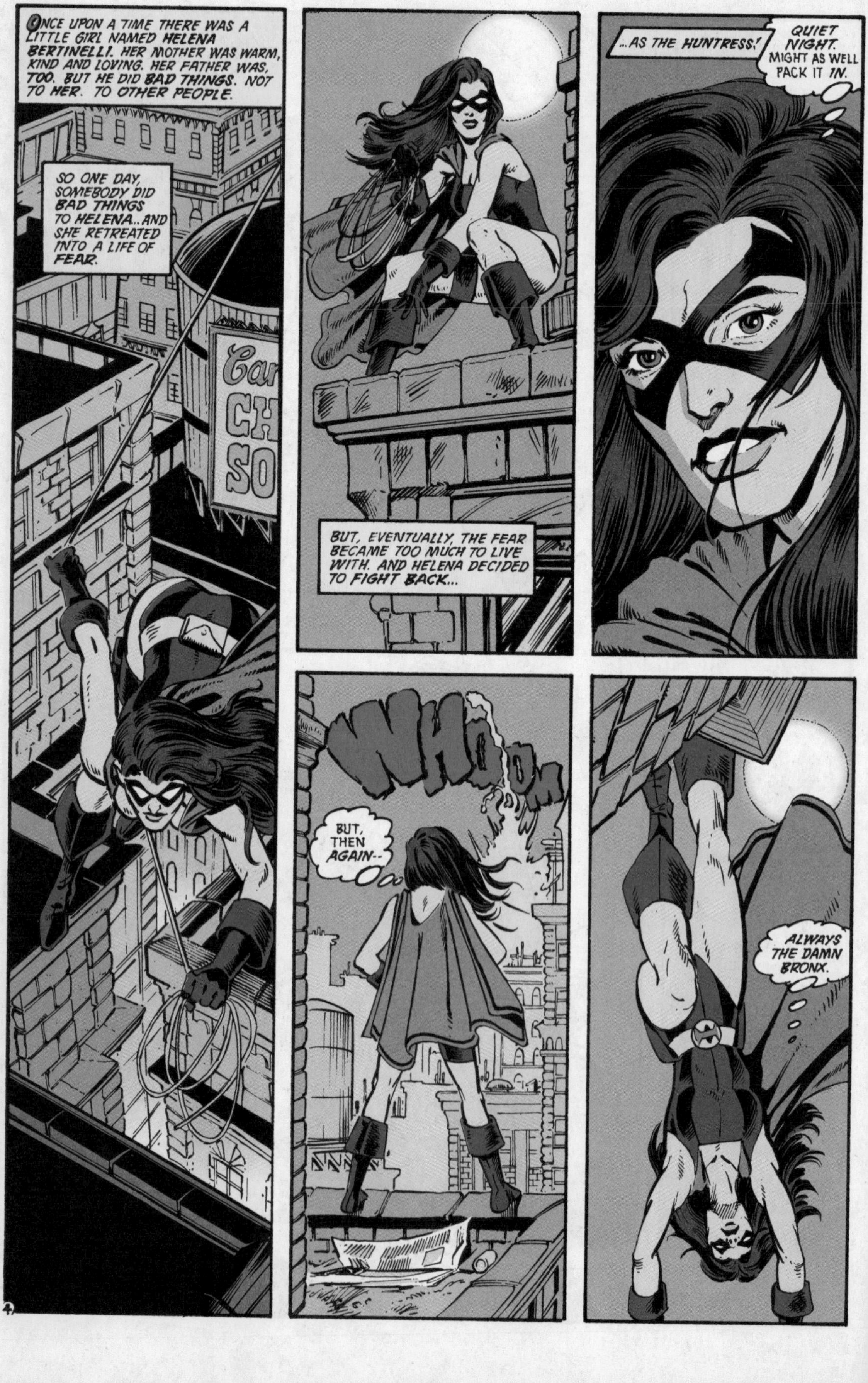
ONCE UPON A TIME THERE WAS A LITTLE GIRL NAMED HELENA BERTINELLI. HER MOTHER WAS WARM, KIND AND LOVING. HER FATHER WAS, TOO. BUT HE DID BAD THINGS. NOT TO HER. TO OTHER PEOPLE.
SO ONE DAY, SOMEBODY DID BAD THINGS TO HELENA... AND SHE RETREATED INTO A LIFE OF FEAR.
BUT, EVENTUALLY, THE FEAR BECAME TOO MUCH TO LIVE WITH. AND HELENA DECIDED TO FIGHT BACK...
...AS THE HUNTRESS!
QUIET NIGHT. MIGHT AS WELL PACK IT IN.
WHOOM
BUT, THEN AGAIN--
ALWAYS THE DAMN BRONX.

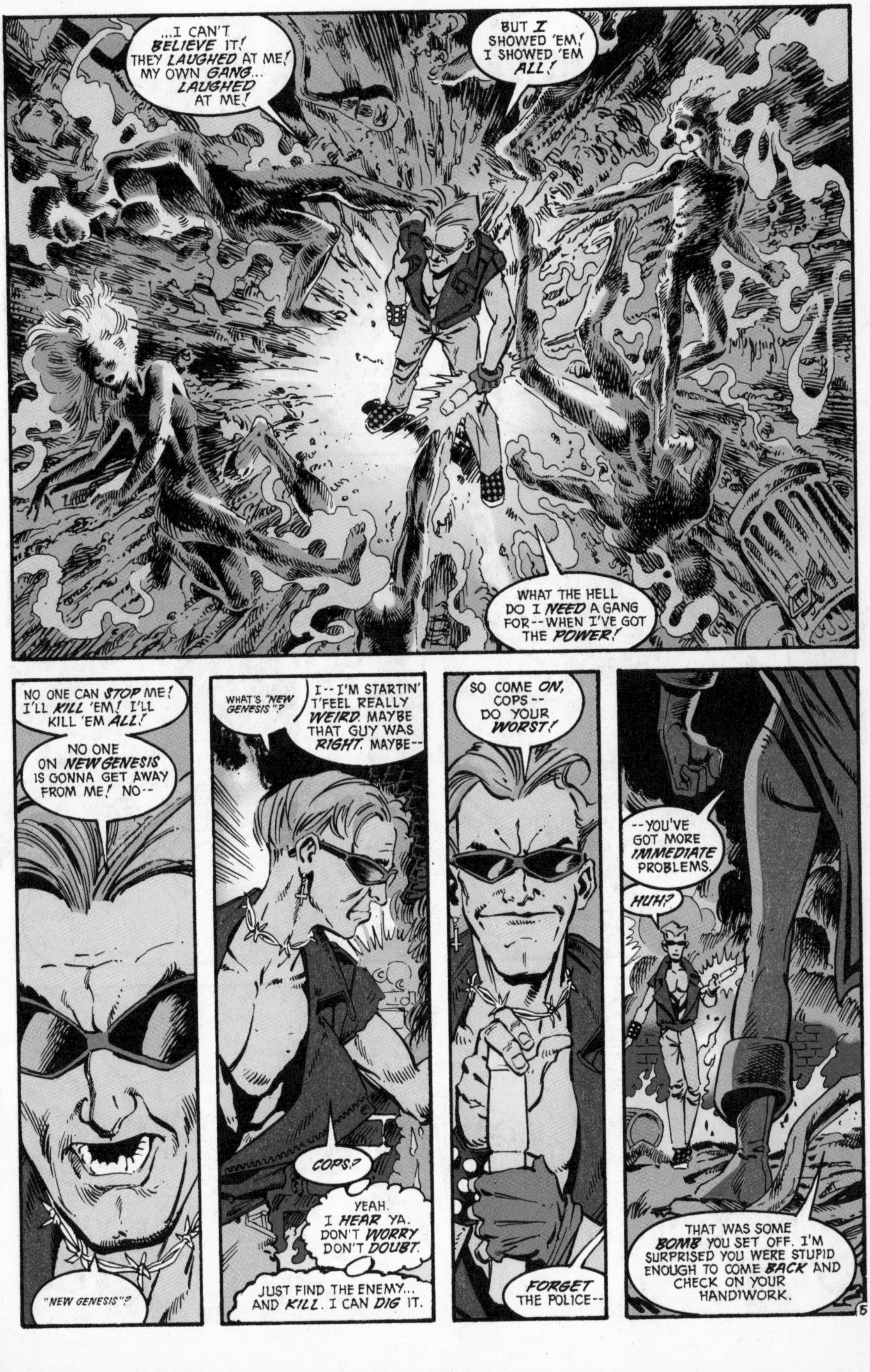
...I CAN'T BELIEVE IT! THEY LAUGHED AT ME! MY OWN GANG... LAUGHED AT ME!
BUT I SHOWED 'EM! I SHOWED 'EM ALL!
WHAT THE HELL DO I NEED A GANG FOR--WHEN I'VE GOT THE POWER!
NO ONE CAN STOP ME! I'LL KILL 'EM! I'LL KILL 'EM ALL!
NO ONE ON NEW GENESIS IS GONNA GET AWAY FROM ME! NO--
"NEW GENESIS"?
WHAT'S "NEW GENESIS"?
I--I'M STARTIN' T'FEEL REALLY WEIRD. MAYBE THAT GUY WAS RIGHT. MAYBE--
COPS?
YEAH. I HEAR YA. DON'T WORRY. DON'T DOUBT.
JUST FIND THE ENEMY... AND KILL. I CAN DIG IT.
SO COME ON, COPS--DO YOUR WORST!
FORGET THE POLICE--
--YOU'VE GOT MORE IMMEDIATE PROBLEMS.
HUH?
THAT WAS SOME BOMB YOU SET OFF. I'M SURPRISED YOU WERE STUPID ENOUGH TO COME BACK AND CHECK ON YOUR HANDIWORK.
5

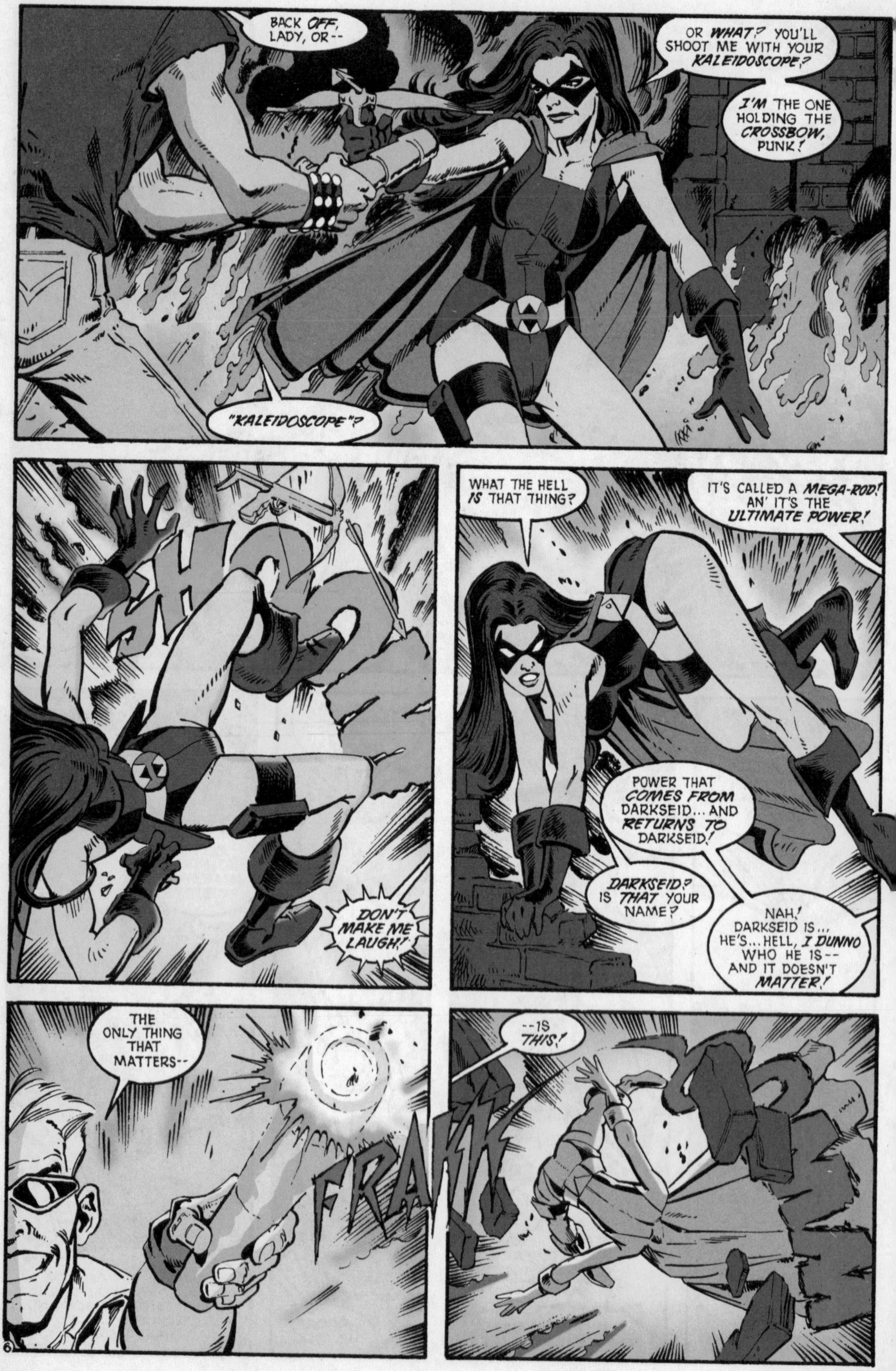

BACK *OFF*, LADY, OR--
OR *WHAT?* YOU'LL SHOOT ME WITH YOUR *KALEIDOSCOPE?*
I'M THE ONE HOLDING THE *CROSSBOW*, PUNK!
"*KALEIDOSCOPE*"?
SHOOM
DON'T MAKE ME LAUGH!
WHAT THE HELL *IS* THAT THING?
IT'S CALLED A *MEGA-ROD!* AN' IT'S THE *ULTIMATE POWER!*
POWER THAT *COMES FROM* DARKSEID... AND *RETURNS TO* DARKSEID!
DARKSEID? IS *THAT* YOUR NAME?
NAH! DARKSEID IS... HE'S... HELL, *I DUNNO* WHO HE IS -- AND IT DOESN'T *MATTER!*
THE ONLY THING THAT MATTERS--
FRAKK
--IS *THIS!*
6

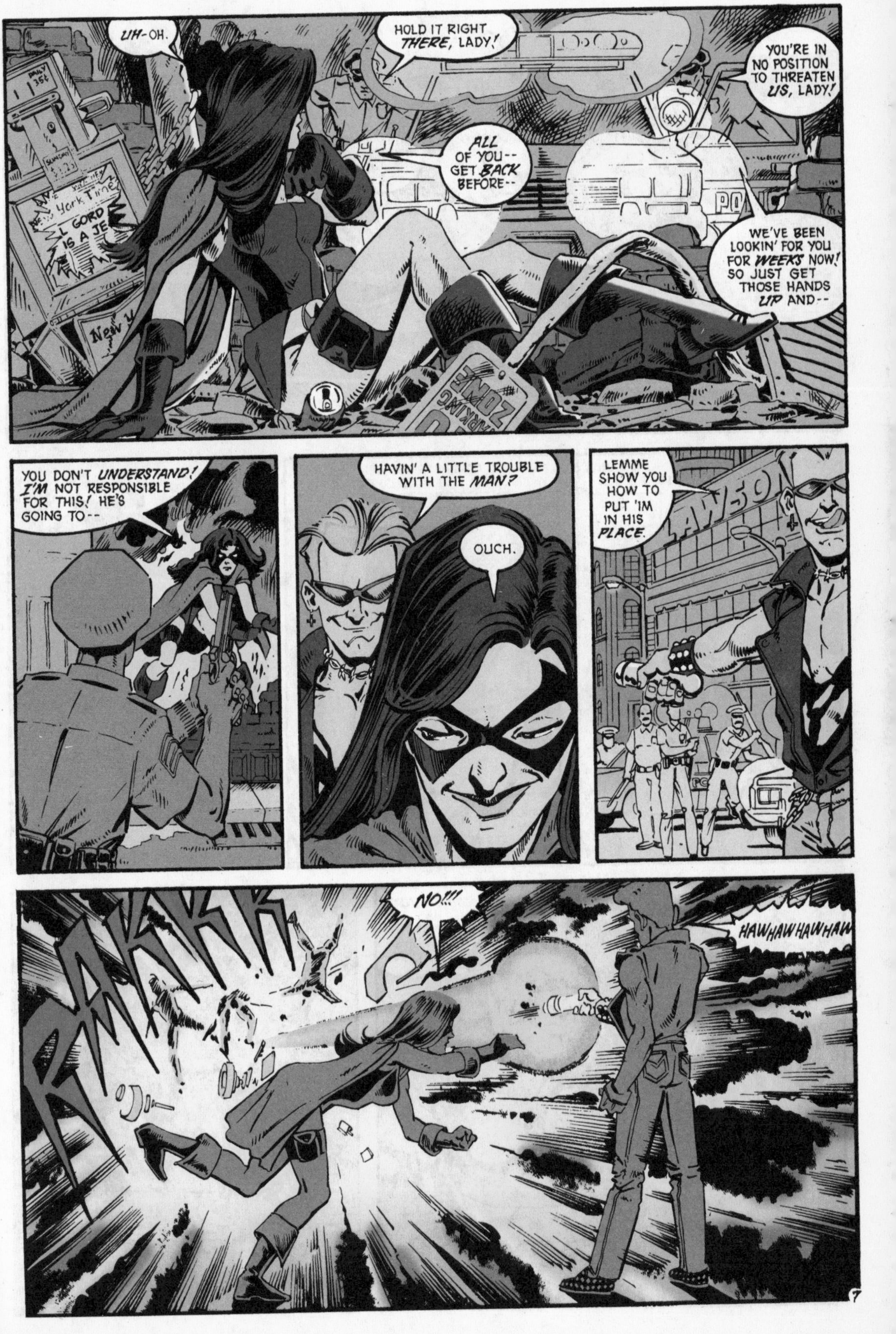
UH-OH.
HOLD IT RIGHT THERE, LADY!
YOU'RE IN NO POSITION TO THREATEN US, LADY!
ALL OF YOU-- GET BACK BEFORE--
WE'VE BEEN LOOKIN' FOR YOU FOR WEEKS NOW! SO JUST GET THOSE HANDS UP AND--
YOU DON'T UNDERSTAND! I'M NOT RESPONSIBLE FOR THIS! HE'S GOING TO--
HAVIN' A LITTLE TROUBLE WITH THE MAN?
OUCH.
LEMME SHOW YOU HOW TO PUT 'IM IN HIS PLACE.
NO!!!
HAWHAWHAWHAW
7

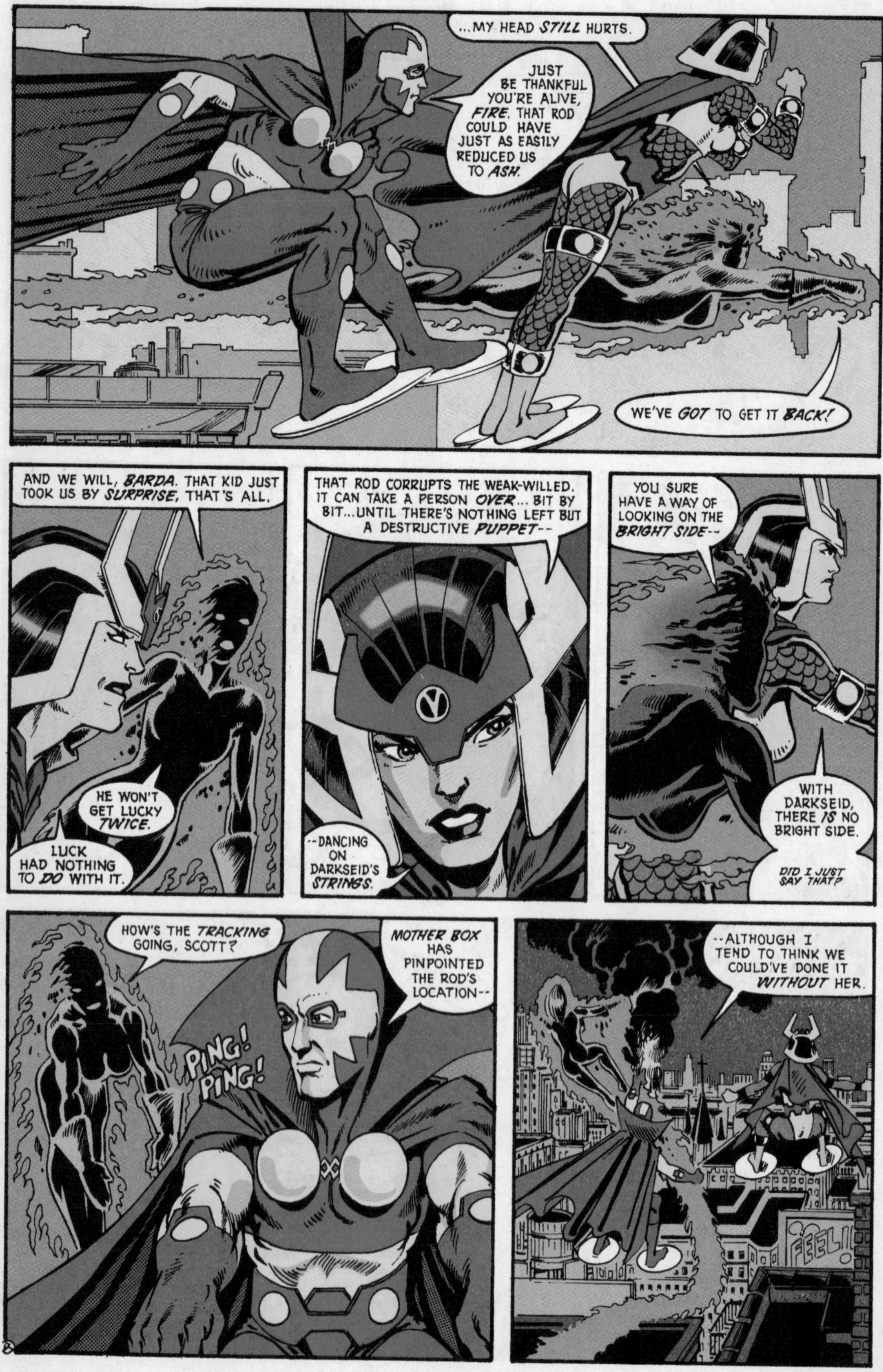
...MY HEAD STILL HURTS.
JUST BE THANKFUL YOU'RE ALIVE, FIRE. THAT ROD COULD HAVE JUST AS EASILY REDUCED US TO ASH.
WE'VE GOT TO GET IT BACK!
AND WE WILL, BARDA. THAT KID JUST TOOK US BY SURPRISE, THAT'S ALL.
HE WON'T GET LUCKY TWICE.
LUCK HAD NOTHING TO DO WITH IT.
THAT ROD CORRUPTS THE WEAK-WILLED. IT CAN TAKE A PERSON OVER... BIT BY BIT...UNTIL THERE'S NOTHING LEFT BUT A DESTRUCTIVE PUPPET--
--DANCING ON DARKSEID'S STRINGS.
YOU SURE HAVE A WAY OF LOOKING ON THE BRIGHT SIDE--
WITH DARKSEID, THERE IS NO BRIGHT SIDE.
DID I JUST SAY THAT?
HOW'S THE TRACKING GOING, SCOTT?
MOTHER BOX HAS PINPOINTED THE ROD'S LOCATION--
PING! PING!
--ALTHOUGH I TEND TO THINK WE COULD'VE DONE IT WITHOUT HER.
FEEL!

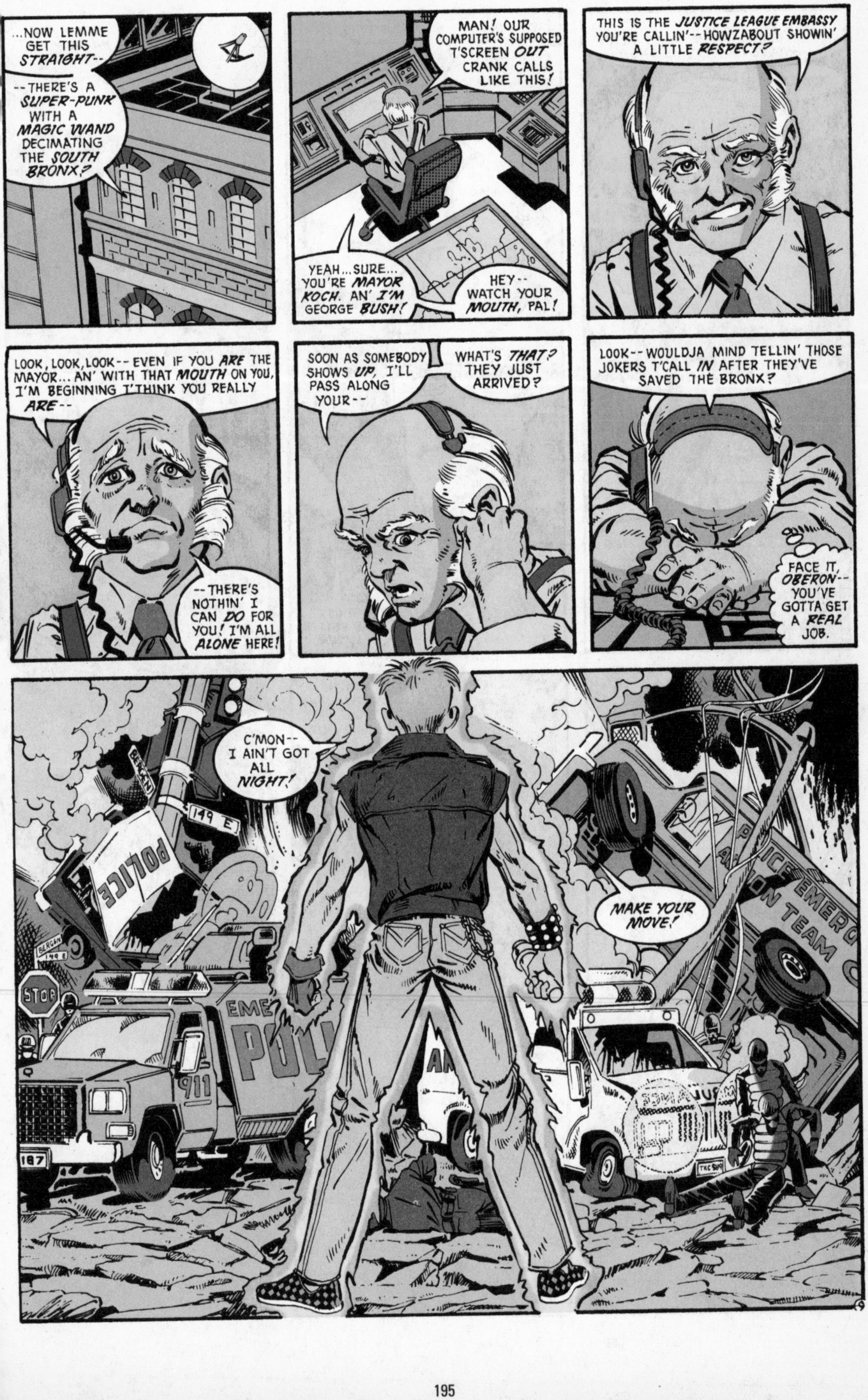
...NOW LEMME GET THIS STRAIGHT--
--THERE'S A SUPER-PUNK WITH A MAGIC WAND DECIMATING THE SOUTH BRONX?
MAN! OUR COMPUTER'S SUPPOSED T'SCREEN OUT CRANK CALLS LIKE THIS!
YEAH... SURE... YOU'RE MAYOR KOCH. AN' I'M GEORGE BUSH!
HEY-- WATCH YOUR MOUTH, PAL!
THIS IS THE JUSTICE LEAGUE EMBASSY YOU'RE CALLIN'--HOWZABOUT SHOWIN' A LITTLE RESPECT?
LOOK, LOOK, LOOK-- EVEN IF YOU ARE THE MAYOR... AN' WITH THAT MOUTH ON YOU, I'M BEGINNING T'THINK YOU REALLY ARE--
--THERE'S NOTHIN' I CAN DO FOR YOU! I'M ALL ALONE HERE!
SOON AS SOMEBODY SHOWS UP, I'LL PASS ALONG YOUR--
WHAT'S THAT? THEY JUST ARRIVED?
LOOK--WOULDJA MIND TELLIN' THOSE JOKERS T'CALL IN AFTER THEY'VE SAVED THE BRONX?
FACE IT, OBERON-- YOU'VE GOTTA GET A REAL JOB.
C'MON-- I AIN'T GOT ALL NIGHT!
MAKE YOUR MOVE!
149 E
STOP
911
187
9

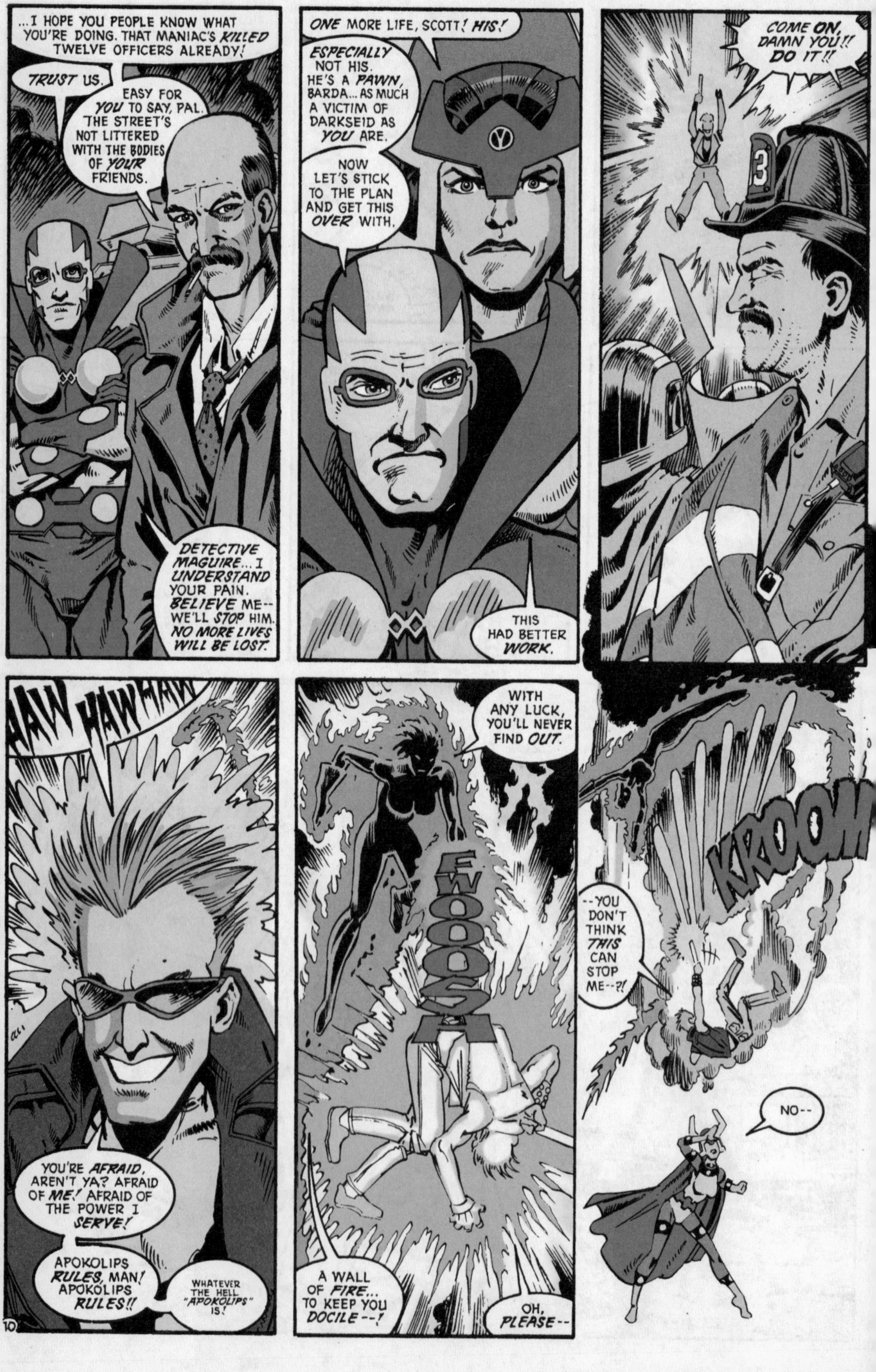

...I HOPE YOU PEOPLE KNOW WHAT YOU'RE DOING. THAT MANIAC'S KILLED TWELVE OFFICERS ALREADY!
TRUST US.
EASY FOR YOU TO SAY, PAL. THE STREET'S NOT LITTERED WITH THE BODIES OF YOUR FRIENDS.
DETECTIVE MAGUIRE... I UNDERSTAND YOUR PAIN. BELIEVE ME-- WE'LL STOP HIM. NO MORE LIVES WILL BE LOST.
ONE MORE LIFE, SCOTT! HIS!
ESPECIALLY NOT HIS. HE'S A PAWN, BARDA... AS MUCH A VICTIM OF DARKSEID AS YOU ARE.
NOW LET'S STICK TO THE PLAN AND GET THIS OVER WITH.
THIS HAD BETTER WORK.
COME ON, DAMN YOU!! DO IT!!
HAW HAW HAW
YOU'RE AFRAID, AREN'T YA? AFRAID OF ME! AFRAID OF THE POWER I SERVE!
APOKOLIPS RULES, MAN! APOKOLIPS RULES!!
WHATEVER THE HELL "APOKOLIPS" IS!
10
WITH ANY LUCK, YOU'LL NEVER FIND OUT.
FWOOOSH
A WALL OF FIRE... TO KEEP YOU DOCILE--!
OH, PLEASE--
KROOM
--YOU DON'T THINK THIS CAN STOP ME--?!
NO--

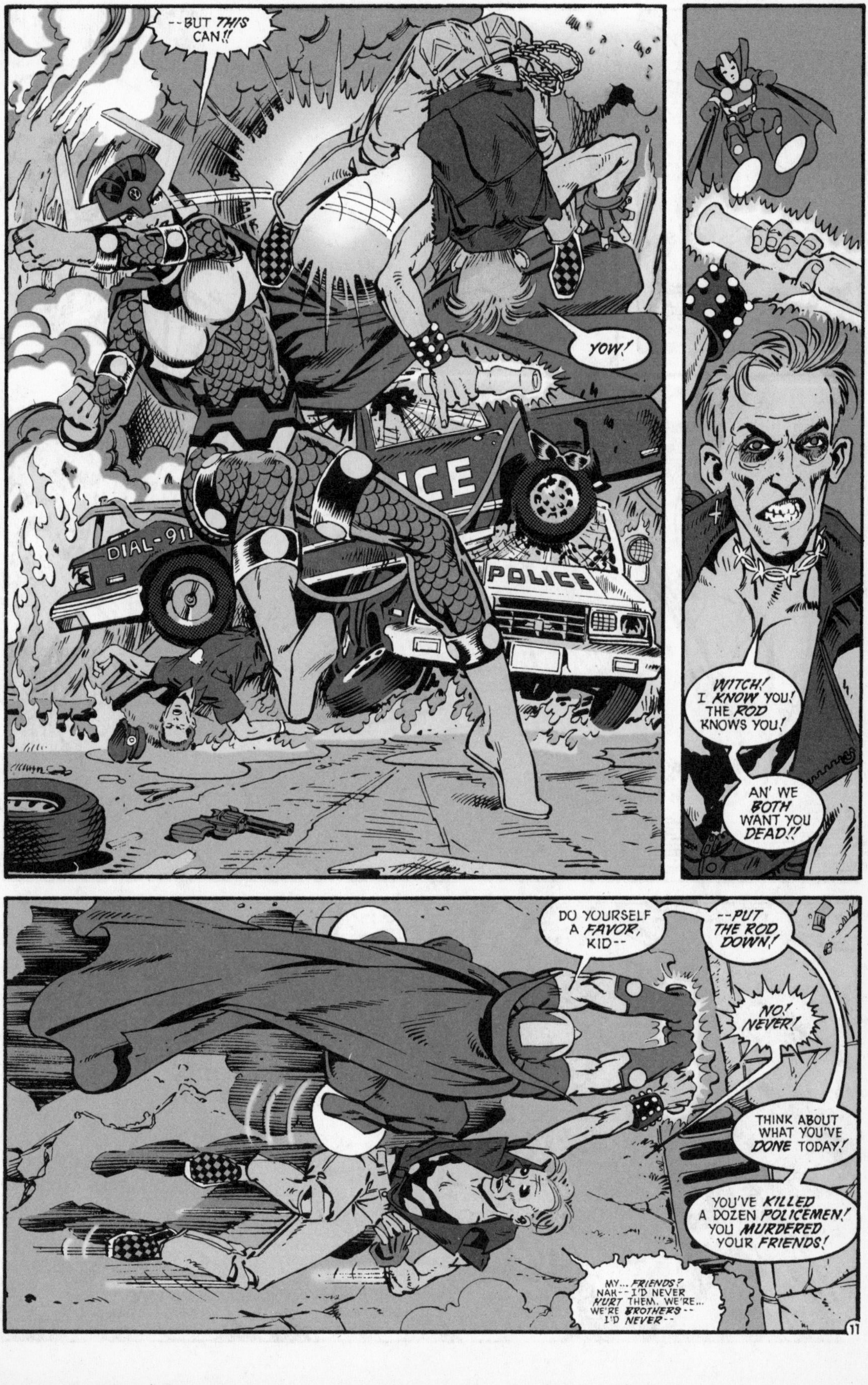
--BUT THIS CAN!!
YOW!
POLICE
DIAL-911
POLICE
WITCH! I KNOW YOU! THE ROD KNOWS YOU!
AN' WE BOTH WANT YOU DEAD!!
DO YOURSELF A FAVOR, KID--
--PUT THE ROD DOWN!
NO! NEVER!
THINK ABOUT WHAT YOU'VE DONE TODAY!
YOU'VE KILLED A DOZEN POLICEMEN! YOU MURDERED YOUR FRIENDS!
MY... FRIENDS? NAH--I'D NEVER HURT THEM. WE'RE... WE'RE BROTHERS--I'D NEVER--
11

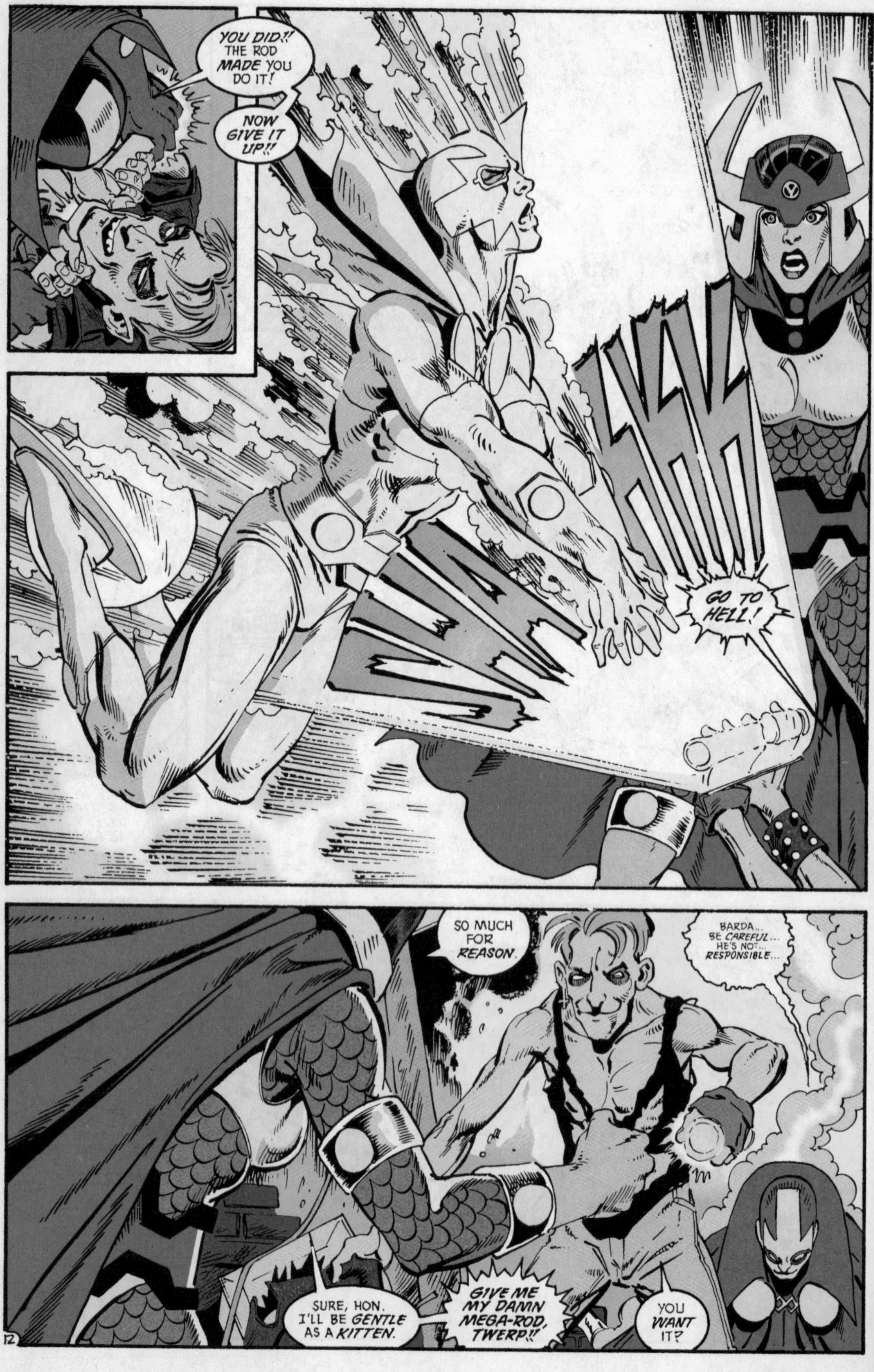
YOU DID!! THE ROD MADE YOU DO IT!
NOW GIVE IT UP!!
HHHH
GO TO HELL!
SO MUCH FOR REASON.
BARDA... BE CAREFUL... HE'S NOT... RESPONSIBLE...
SURE, HON. I'LL BE GENTLE AS A KITTEN.
GIVE ME MY DAMN MEGA-ROD, TWERP!!
YOU WANT IT?
12

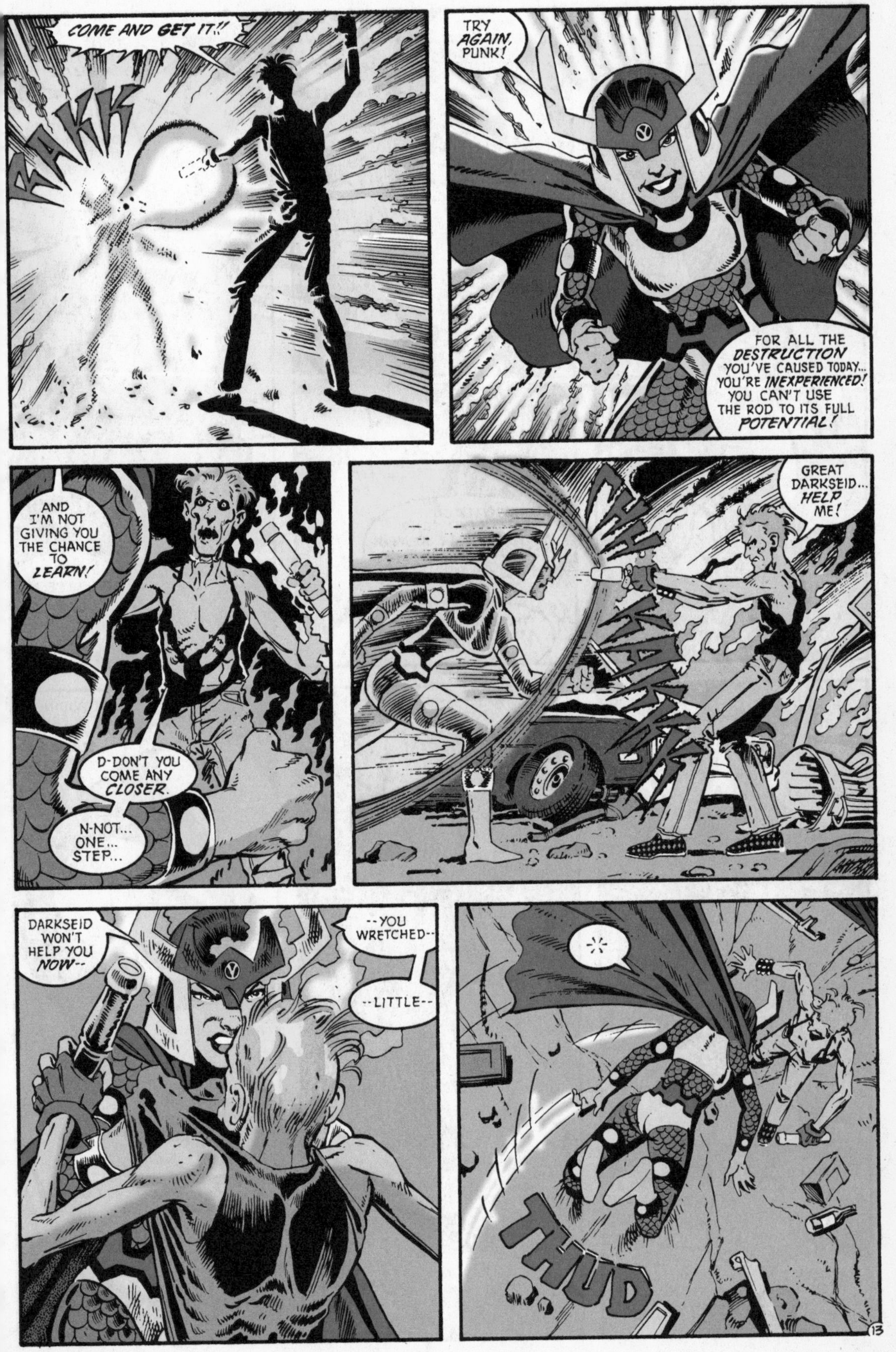
COME AND GET IT!!
BAKK
TRY AGAIN, PUNK!
FOR ALL THE DESTRUCTION YOU'VE CAUSED TODAY... YOU'RE INEXPERIENCED! YOU CAN'T USE THE ROD TO ITS FULL POTENTIAL!
AND I'M NOT GIVING YOU THE CHANCE TO LEARN!
D-DON'T YOU COME ANY CLOSER.
N-NOT... ONE... STEP...
GREAT DARKSEID... HELP ME!
CHAKKAKK
DARKSEID WON'T HELP YOU NOW--
--YOU WRETCHED--
--LITTLE--
THUD
13

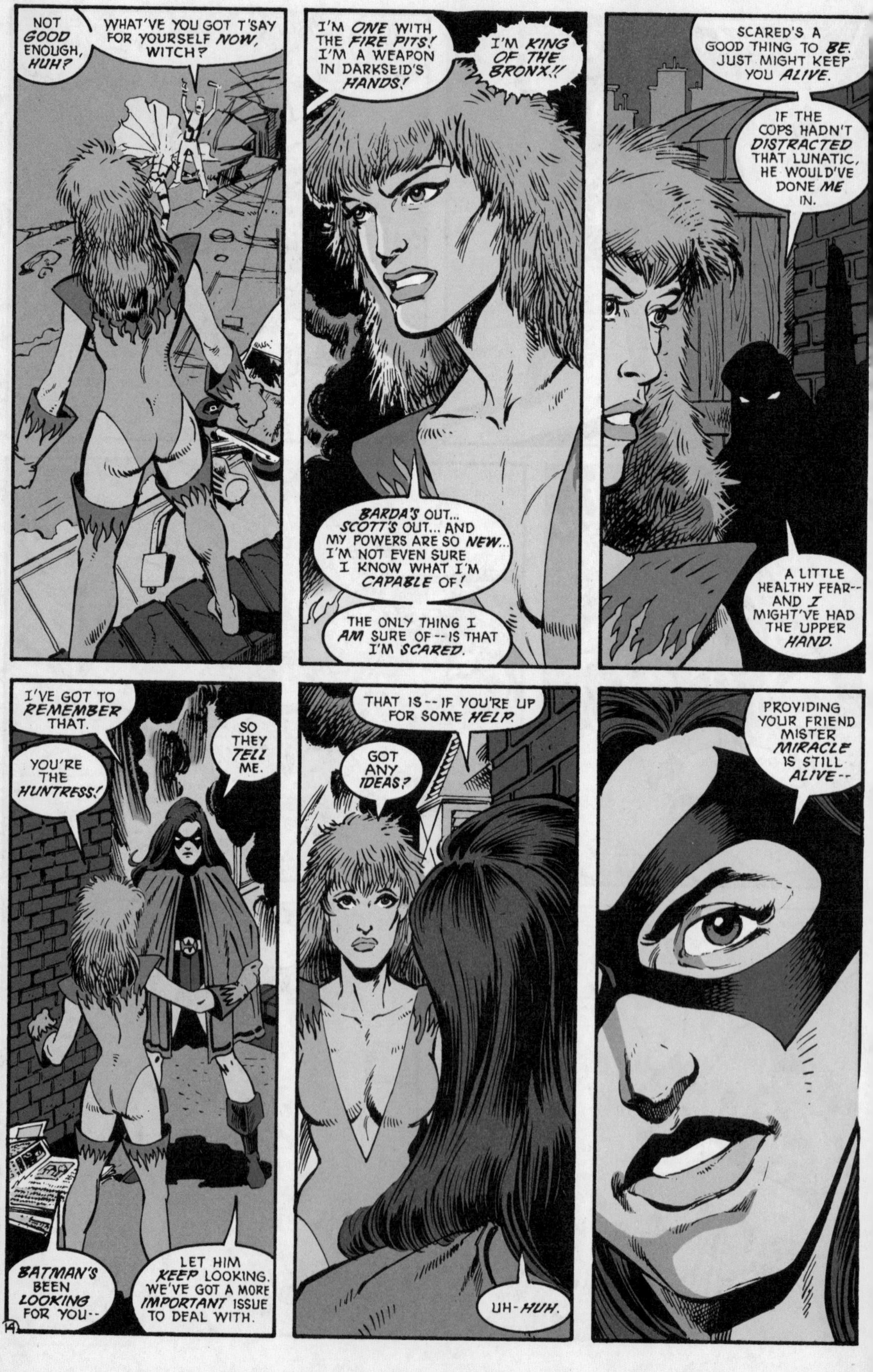
NOT GOOD ENOUGH, HUH?
WHAT'VE YOU GOT T'SAY FOR YOURSELF NOW, WITCH?
I'M ONE WITH THE FIRE PITS! I'M A WEAPON IN DARKSEID'S HANDS!
I'M KING OF THE BRONX!!
BARDA'S OUT... SCOTT'S OUT... AND MY POWERS ARE SO NEW... I'M NOT EVEN SURE I KNOW WHAT I'M CAPABLE OF!
THE ONLY THING I AM SURE OF -- IS THAT I'M SCARED.
SCARED'S A GOOD THING TO BE. JUST MIGHT KEEP YOU ALIVE.
IF THE COPS HADN'T DISTRACTED THAT LUNATIC, HE WOULD'VE DONE ME IN.
A LITTLE HEALTHY FEAR-- AND I MIGHT'VE HAD THE UPPER HAND.
I'VE GOT TO REMEMBER THAT.
SO THEY TELL ME.
YOU'RE THE HUNTRESS!
BATMAN'S BEEN LOOKING FOR YOU--
LET HIM KEEP LOOKING. WE'VE GOT A MORE IMPORTANT ISSUE TO DEAL WITH.
14
THAT IS -- IF YOU'RE UP FOR SOME HELP.
GOT ANY IDEAS?
UH-HUH.
PROVIDING YOUR FRIEND MISTER MIRACLE IS STILL ALIVE--

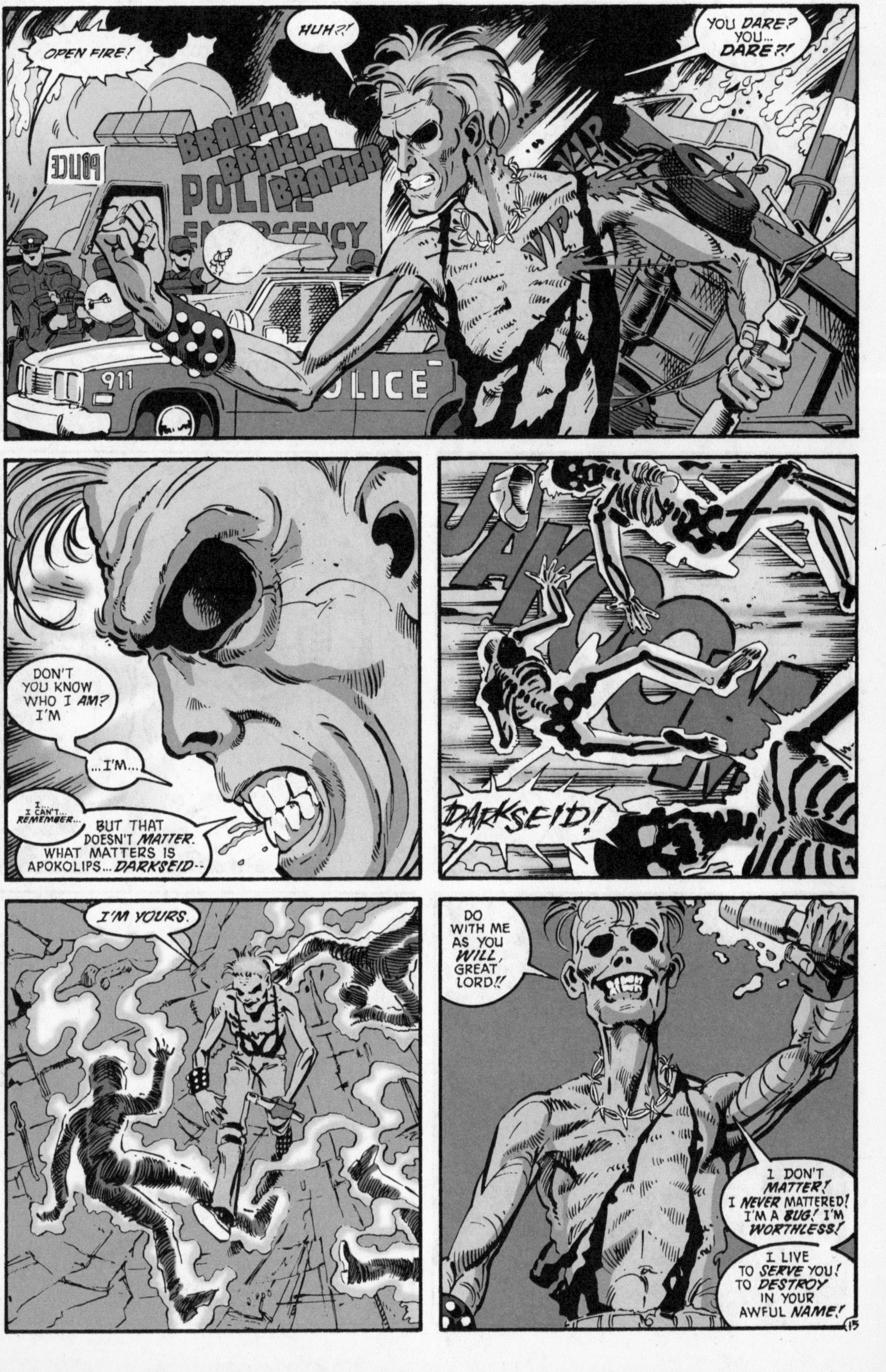
OPEN FIRE!
HUH?!
YOU DARE? YOU... DARE?!
BRAKKA BRAKKA BRAKKA
POLICE EMERGENCY
911
POLICE
DON'T YOU KNOW WHO I AM? I'M
...I'M...
I... I CAN'T... REMEMBER...
BUT THAT DOESN'T MATTER. WHAT MATTERS IS APOKOLIPS... DARKSEID--
DARKSEID!
I'M YOURS.
DO WITH ME AS YOU WILL, GREAT LORD!!
I DON'T MATTER! I NEVER MATTERED! I'M A BUG! I'M WORTHLESS!
I LIVE TO SERVE YOU! TO DESTROY IN YOUR AWFUL NAME!
15

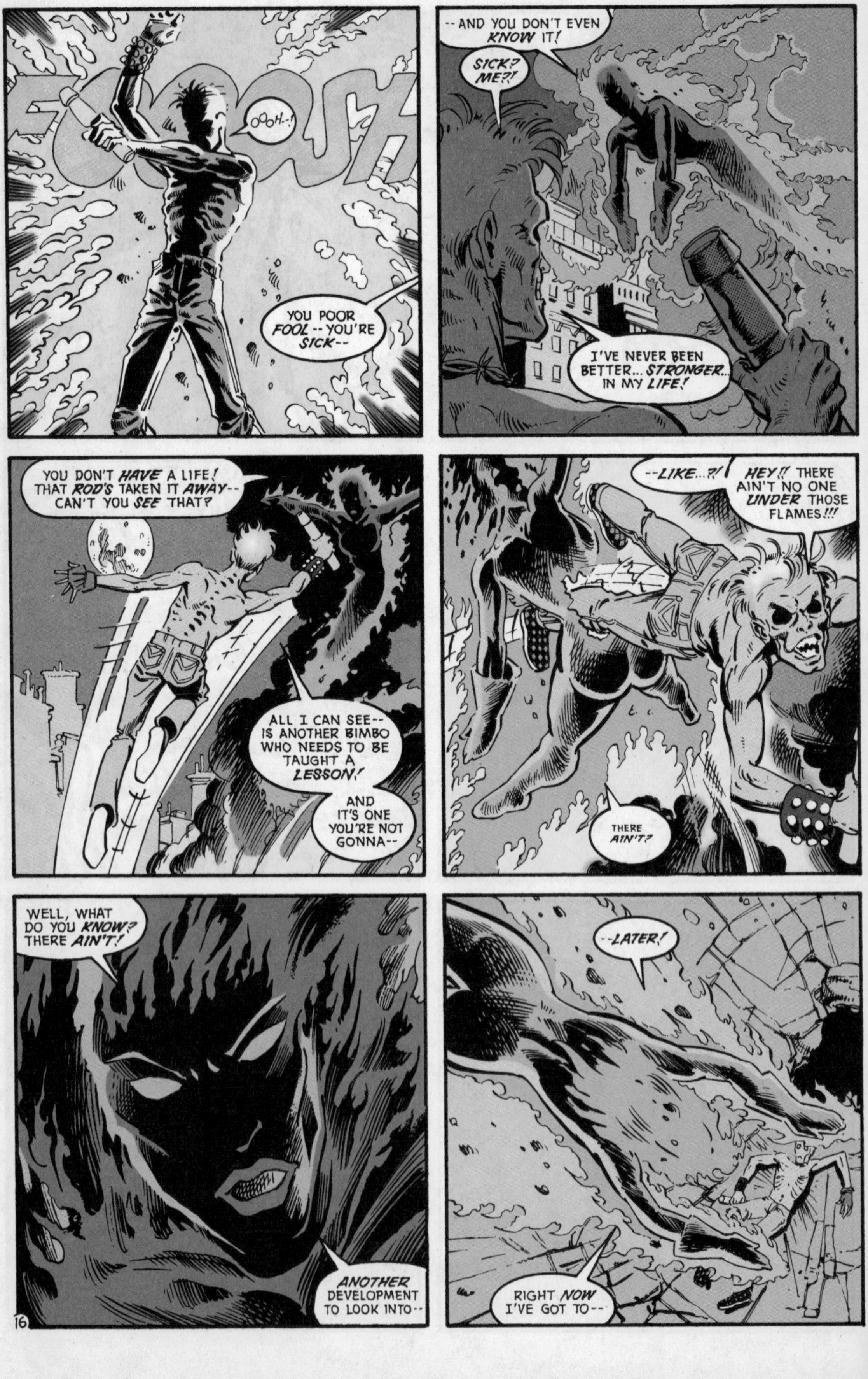
FOOSH!
OOOH--!
YOU POOR FOOL -- YOU'RE SICK--
-- AND YOU DON'T EVEN KNOW IT!
SICK?! ME?!
I'VE NEVER BEEN BETTER... STRONGER... IN MY LIFE!
YOU DON'T HAVE A LIFE! THAT ROD'S TAKEN IT AWAY-- CAN'T YOU SEE THAT?
ALL I CAN SEE-- IS ANOTHER BIMBO WHO NEEDS TO BE TAUGHT A LESSON!
AND IT'S ONE YOU'RE NOT GONNA--
--LIKE...?!
HEY!! THERE AIN'T NO ONE UNDER THOSE FLAMES!!!
THERE AIN'T?
WELL, WHAT DO YOU KNOW? THERE AIN'T!
ANOTHER DEVELOPMENT TO LOOK INTO--
16
--LATER!
RIGHT NOW I'VE GOT TO--

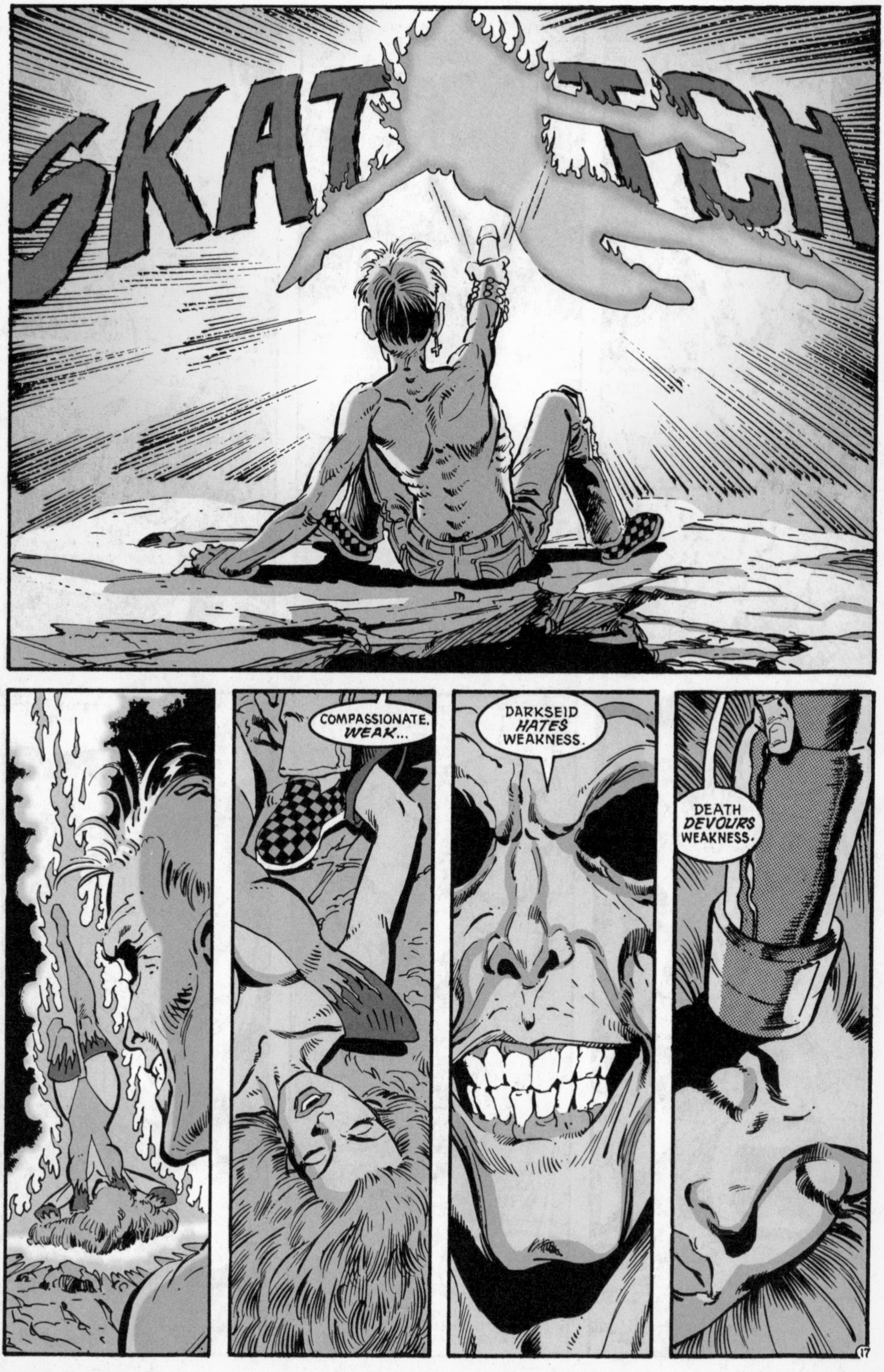
SKAT TCH
COMPASSIONATE, WEAK...
DARKSEID HATES WEAKNESS.
DEATH DEVOURS WEAKNESS.
17

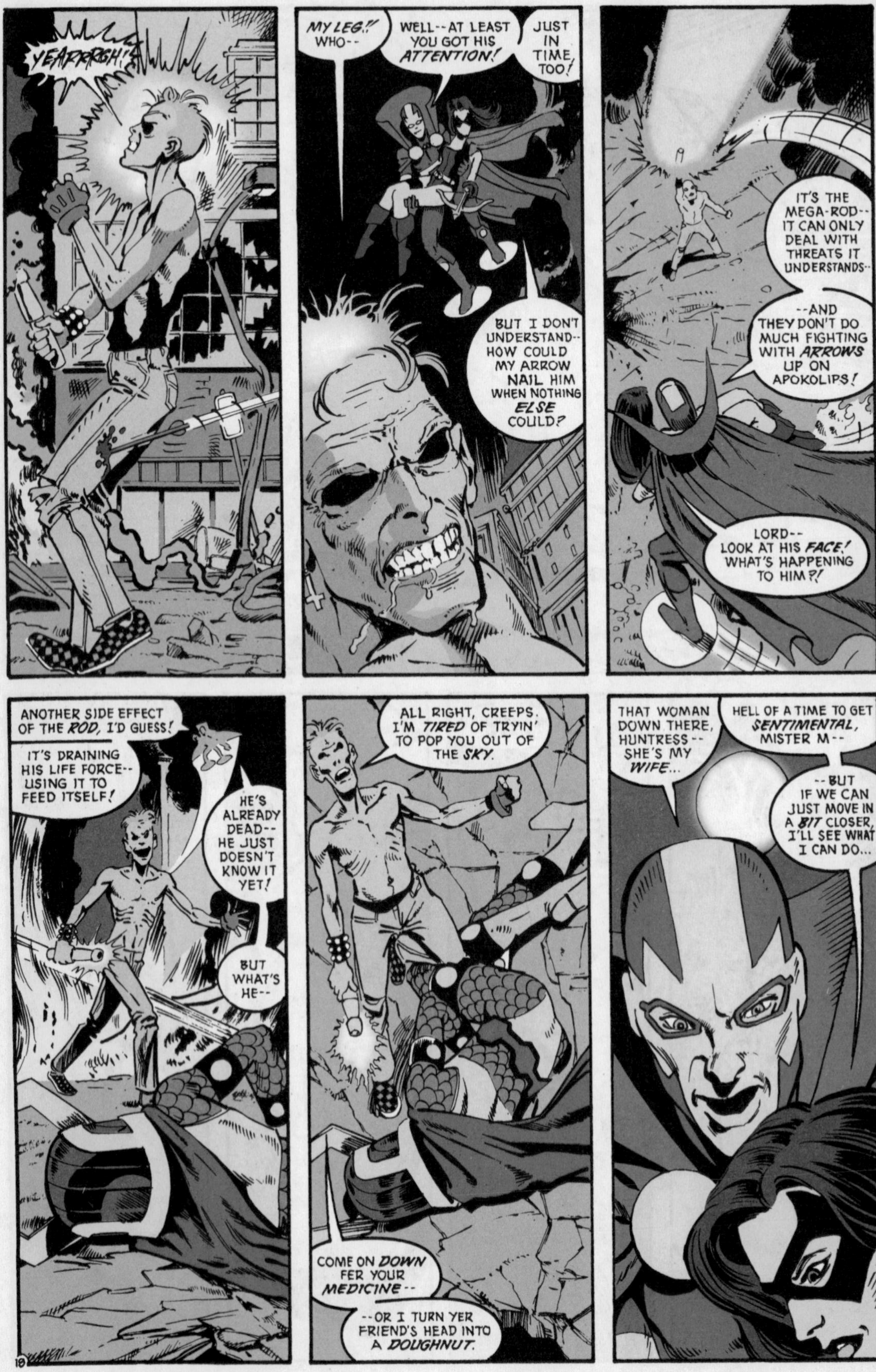
YEARRRGH!
MY LEG!? WHO--
WELL--AT LEAST YOU GOT HIS ATTENTION!
JUST IN TIME, TOO!
BUT I DON'T UNDERSTAND--HOW COULD MY ARROW NAIL HIM WHEN NOTHING ELSE COULD?
IT'S THE MEGA-ROD--IT CAN ONLY DEAL WITH THREATS IT UNDERSTANDS--
--AND THEY DON'T DO MUCH FIGHTING WITH ARROWS UP ON APOKOLIPS!
LORD--LOOK AT HIS FACE! WHAT'S HAPPENING TO HIM?!
ANOTHER SIDE EFFECT OF THE ROD, I'D GUESS!
IT'S DRAINING HIS LIFE FORCE--USING IT TO FEED ITSELF!
HE'S ALREADY DEAD--HE JUST DOESN'T KNOW IT YET!
BUT WHAT'S HE--
18
ALL RIGHT, CREEPS. I'M TIRED OF TRYIN' TO POP YOU OUT OF THE SKY.
COME ON DOWN FER YOUR MEDICINE--
--OR I TURN YER FRIEND'S HEAD INTO A DOUGHNUT.
THAT WOMAN DOWN THERE, HUNTRESS--SHE'S MY WIFE...
HELL OF A TIME TO GET SENTIMENTAL, MISTER M--
--BUT IF WE CAN JUST MOVE IN A BIT CLOSER, I'LL SEE WHAT I CAN DO...

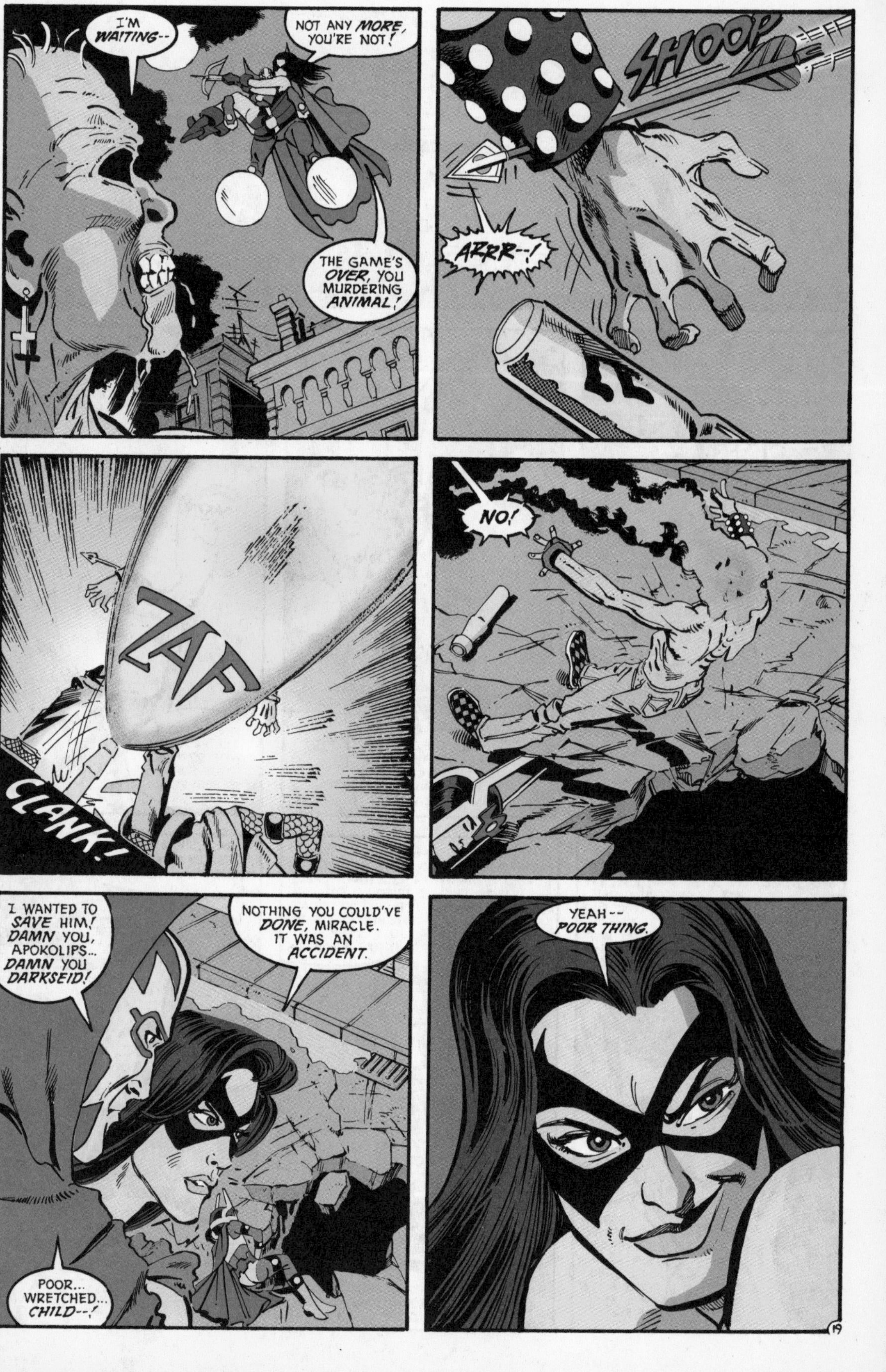
I'M WAITING--
NOT ANY MORE, YOU'RE NOT!
THE GAME'S OVER, YOU MURDERING ANIMAL!
SHOOP
ARRR--!
ZAF
CLANK!
NO!
I WANTED TO SAVE HIM! DAMN YOU, APOKOLIPS... DAMN YOU DARKSEID!
NOTHING YOU COULD'VE DONE, MIRACLE. IT WAS AN ACCIDENT.
POOR... WRETCHED... CHILD--!
YEAH-- POOR THING.
19

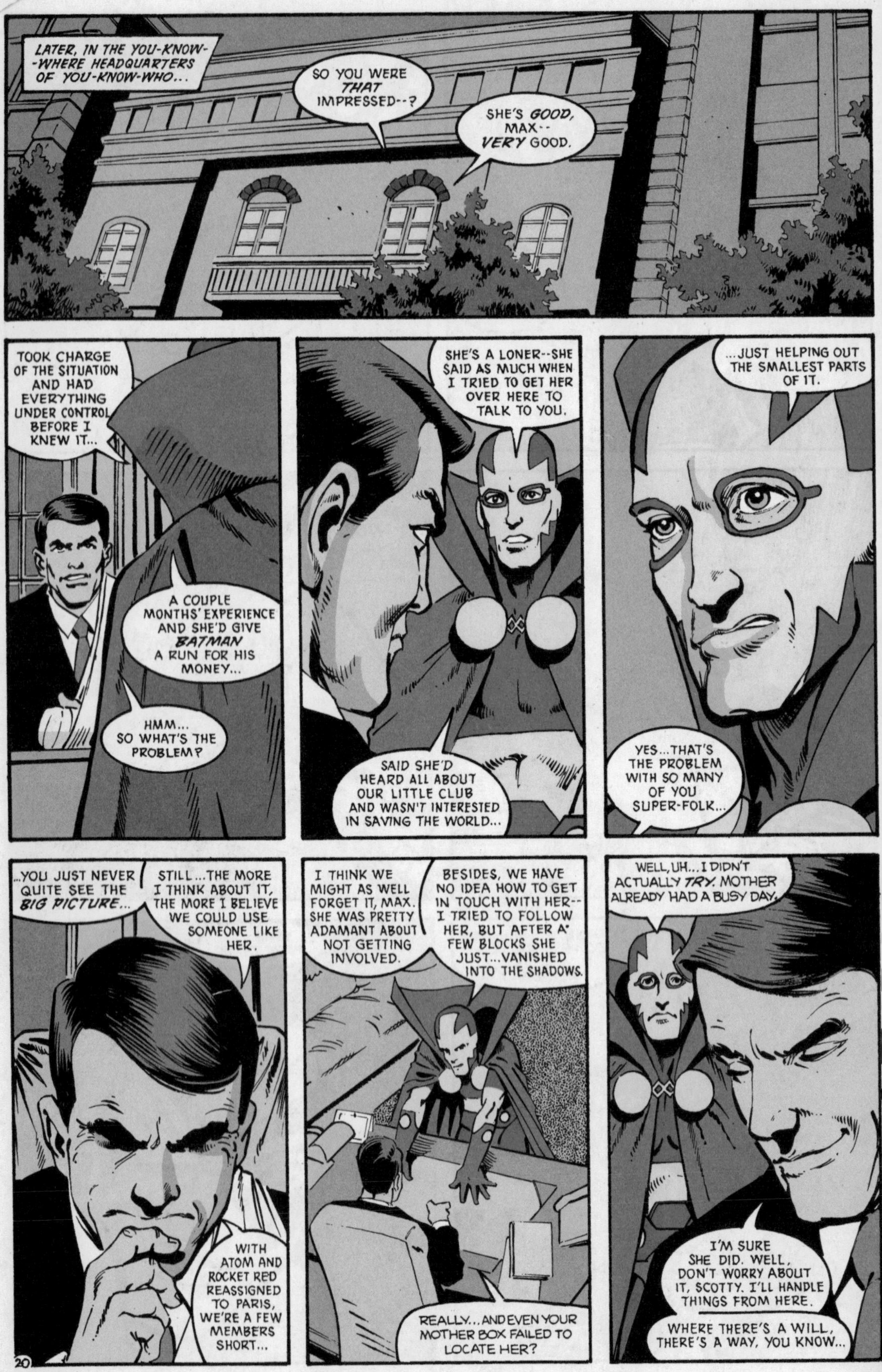

LATER, IN THE YOU-KNOW--WHERE HEADQUARTERS OF YOU-KNOW-WHO...
SO YOU WERE THAT IMPRESSED--?
SHE'S GOOD, MAX-- VERY GOOD.
TOOK CHARGE OF THE SITUATION AND HAD EVERYTHING UNDER CONTROL BEFORE I KNEW IT...
A COUPLE MONTHS' EXPERIENCE AND SHE'D GIVE BATMAN A RUN FOR HIS MONEY...
HMM... SO WHAT'S THE PROBLEM?
SHE'S A LONER--SHE SAID AS MUCH WHEN I TRIED TO GET HER OVER HERE TO TALK TO YOU.
SAID SHE'D HEARD ALL ABOUT OUR LITTLE CLUB AND WASN'T INTERESTED IN SAVING THE WORLD...
...JUST HELPING OUT THE SMALLEST PARTS OF IT.
YES...THAT'S THE PROBLEM WITH SO MANY OF YOU SUPER-FOLK...
...YOU JUST NEVER QUITE SEE THE BIG PICTURE...
STILL...THE MORE I THINK ABOUT IT, THE MORE I BELIEVE WE COULD USE SOMEONE LIKE HER.
WITH ATOM AND ROCKET RED REASSIGNED TO PARIS, WE'RE A FEW MEMBERS SHORT...
20
I THINK WE MIGHT AS WELL FORGET IT, MAX. SHE WAS PRETTY ADAMANT ABOUT NOT GETTING INVOLVED.
BESIDES, WE HAVE NO IDEA HOW TO GET IN TOUCH WITH HER--I TRIED TO FOLLOW HER, BUT AFTER A FEW BLOCKS SHE JUST...VANISHED INTO THE SHADOWS.
REALLY...AND EVEN YOUR MOTHER BOX FAILED TO LOCATE HER?
WELL, UH...I DIDN'T ACTUALLY TRY. MOTHER ALREADY HAD A BUSY DAY.
I'M SURE SHE DID. WELL, DON'T WORRY ABOUT IT, SCOTTY. I'LL HANDLE THINGS FROM HERE.
WHERE THERE'S A WILL, THERE'S A WAY, YOU KNOW...

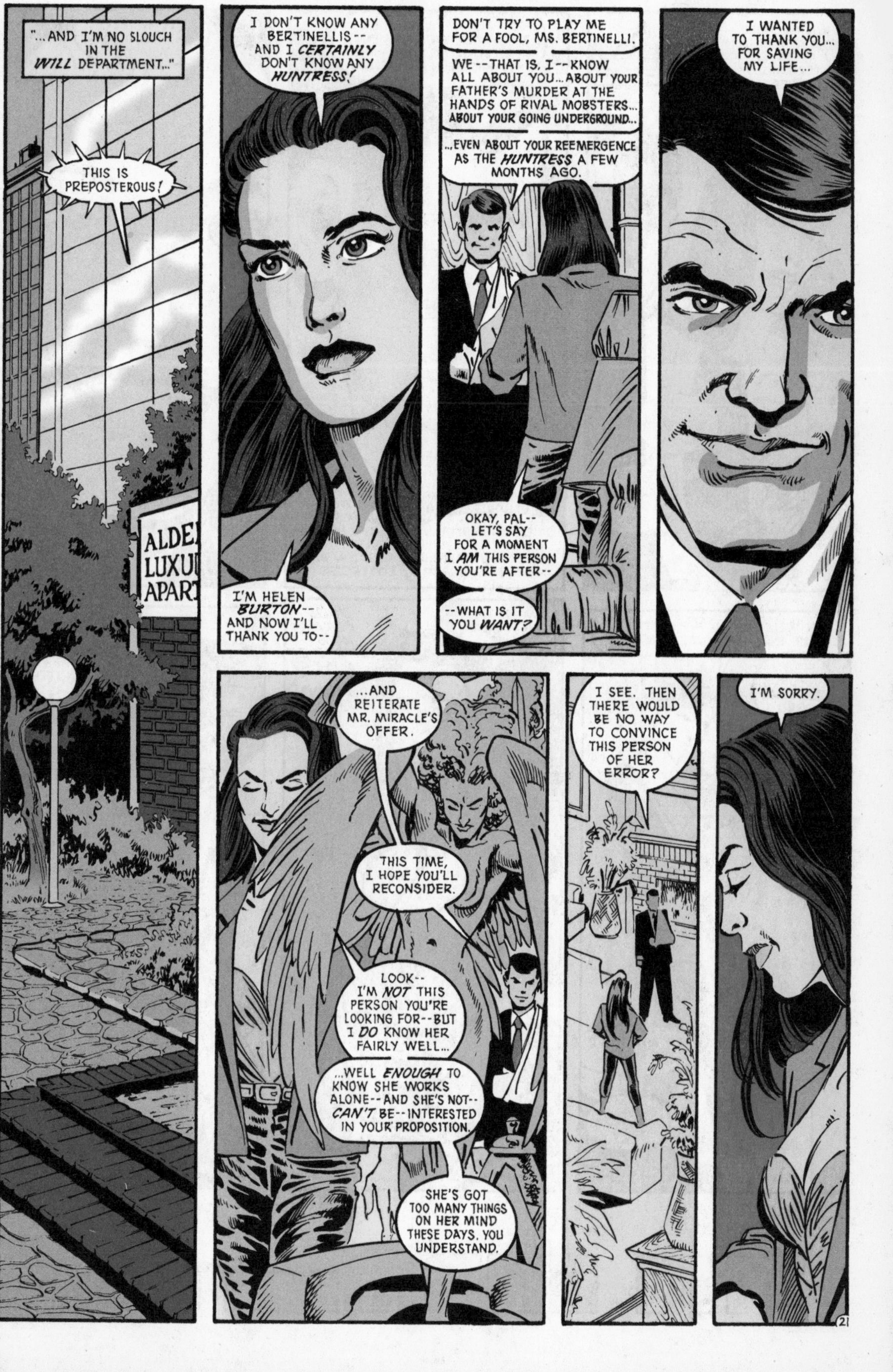
"...AND I'M NO SLOUCH IN THE WILL DEPARTMENT..."
THIS IS PREPOSTEROUS!
ALDE LUXU APART
I DON'T KNOW ANY BERTINELLIS-- AND I CERTAINLY DON'T KNOW ANY HUNTRESS!
I'M HELEN BURTON-- AND NOW I'LL THANK YOU TO--
DON'T TRY TO PLAY ME FOR A FOOL, MS. BERTINELLI.
WE--THAT IS, I--KNOW ALL ABOUT YOU...ABOUT YOUR FATHER'S MURDER AT THE HANDS OF RIVAL MOBSTERS... ABOUT YOUR GOING UNDERGROUND...
...EVEN ABOUT YOUR REEMERGENCE AS THE HUNTRESS A FEW MONTHS AGO.
OKAY, PAL-- LET'S SAY FOR A MOMENT I AM THIS PERSON YOU'RE AFTER--
--WHAT IS IT YOU WANT?
I WANTED TO THANK YOU... FOR SAVING MY LIFE...
...AND REITERATE MR. MIRACLE'S OFFER.
THIS TIME, I HOPE YOU'LL RECONSIDER.
LOOK-- I'M NOT THIS PERSON YOU'RE LOOKING FOR--BUT I DO KNOW HER FAIRLY WELL...
...WELL ENOUGH TO KNOW SHE WORKS ALONE--AND SHE'S NOT-- CAN'T BE--INTERESTED IN YOUR PROPOSITION.
SHE'S GOT TOO MANY THINGS ON HER MIND THESE DAYS, YOU UNDERSTAND.
I SEE. THEN THERE WOULD BE NO WAY TO CONVINCE THIS PERSON OF HER ERROR?
I'M SORRY.
21

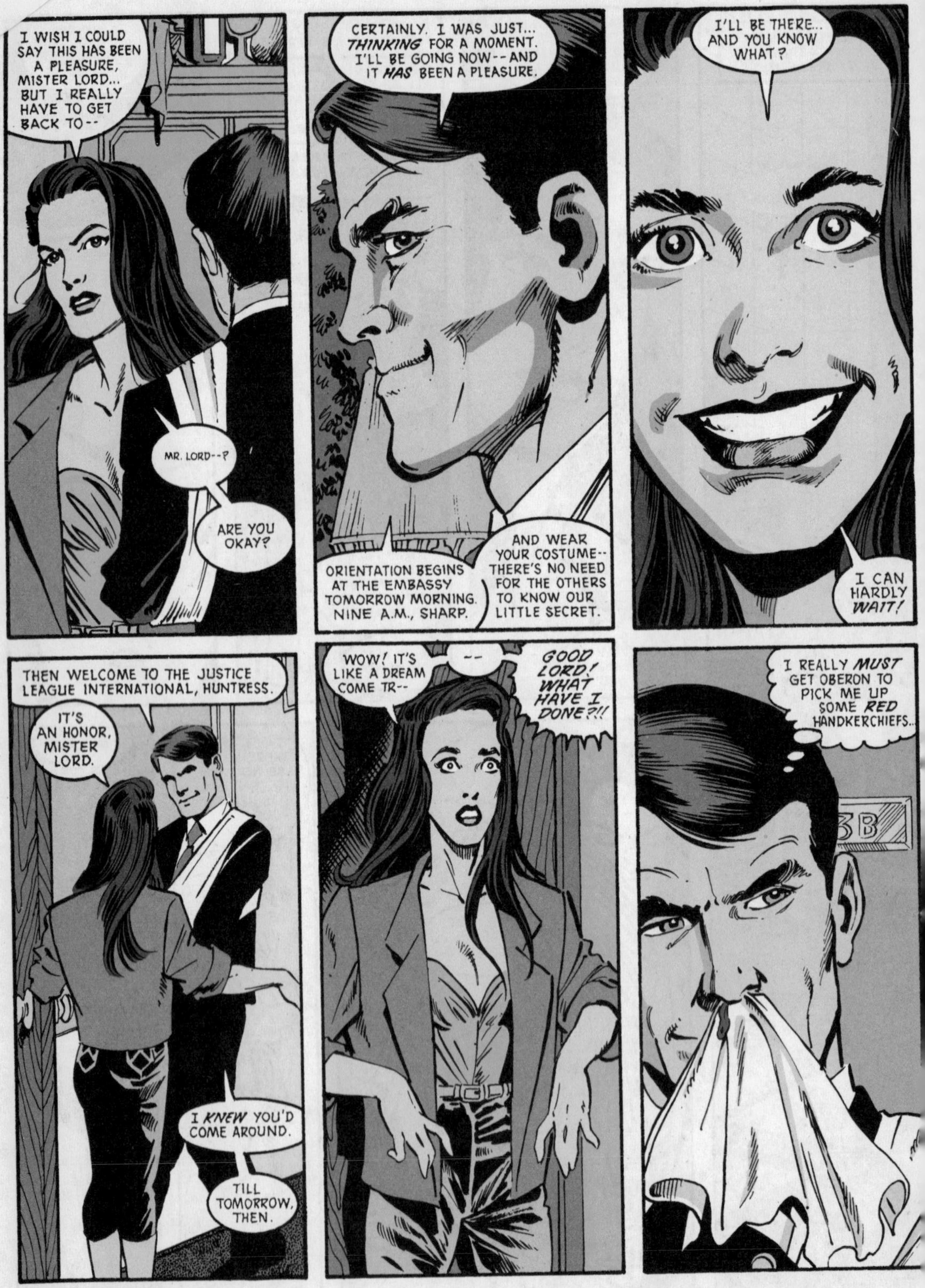
I WISH I COULD SAY THIS HAS BEEN A PLEASURE, MISTER LORD... BUT I REALLY HAVE TO GET BACK TO--
MR. LORD--?
ARE YOU OKAY?
CERTAINLY. I WAS JUST... THINKING FOR A MOMENT. I'LL BE GOING NOW--AND IT HAS BEEN A PLEASURE.
ORIENTATION BEGINS AT THE EMBASSY TOMORROW MORNING. NINE A.M., SHARP.
AND WEAR YOUR COSTUME--THERE'S NO NEED FOR THE OTHERS TO KNOW OUR LITTLE SECRET.
I'LL BE THERE... AND YOU KNOW WHAT?
I CAN HARDLY WAIT!
THEN WELCOME TO THE JUSTICE LEAGUE INTERNATIONAL, HUNTRESS.
IT'S AN HONOR, MISTER LORD.
I KNEW YOU'D COME AROUND.
TILL TOMORROW, THEN.
WOW! IT'S LIKE A DREAM COME TR--
--
GOOD LORD! WHAT HAVE I DONE?!!
I REALLY MUST GET OBERON TO PICK ME UP SOME RED HANDKERCHIEFS...
3B

THE END...FOR NOW!